ULTIMATE ARIZONA

ULTIMATE ARIZONA

David Stratton   *Richard Harris*
Carolyn Scarborough   *Mary Ann Reese*

RAY RIEGERT
Executive Editor

LESLIE HENRIQUES
Editorial Director

JOANNA PEARLMAN
Editor

GLENN KIM
Illustrator

ULYSSES PRESS

Published by: Ulysses Press
3286 Adeline Street, Suite 1
Berkeley, CA 94703

Library of Congress Catalog Card Number 93-60067
ISBN 0-915233-83-5

Printed in the U.S.A. by the George Banta Company

10 9 8 7 6 5 4 3 2 1

Managing Editor: Claire Chun
Editorial Associates: William Kiester, Lee Micheaux, Per Casey
Maps: Lee Micheaux, Wendy Ann Logsdon, Phil Gardner
Cover Designer: Bonnie Smetts
Paste up: Karen Marquardt
Indexer: Sayre Van Young
Cover Photography: Front cover by Gala/Superstock; back cover by
    Woody Woodworth/Superstock, Prim and Ray Manley/Superstock

Distributed in the United States by Publishers Group West, in Canada by Raincoast Books, and in Great Britain and Europe by World Leisure Marketing

Printed on recycled paper

Contents

ONE

The Grand Canyon State

If your image of Arizona is all cowboys, ranches and hitching posts, it's time for another look. For while the flavor of the Old West is certainly still in evidence throughout the state, the trappings of the 20th century are everywhere—indeed, flourishing and growing apace. Head to the major cities—including Phoenix, Scottsdale, Tempe and Tucson—and you'll find all the culture and amenities of any cosmopolitan metropolis: vibrant arts communities, professional sports galore, shopping centers and trendy stores as far as the eye can see, fine college campuses and museums, intriguing art galleries and architecture, as well as enough golf, tennis and other activities to satisfy anyone and everyone. But if you're hankering for a taste of the great outdoors or a glimpse of the frontier life, well, they're here, too: miles of open desert, rivers to swim and sail, trails to roam and towns set more in the past than the present. So saddle up, friend, because Arizona has it all. For each cowboy, you'll find a city slicker; for each country music bar, there's a rhythm-and-blues joint; for each thirsty desert view, add a snowcapped mountain; and for each rough 'n tough dude ranch, imagine a decadently luxurious resort.

Arizona covers a 114,000-square-mile chunk of land on the southwestern corner of the United States and is bordered by Mexico on the south, California and Nevada on the west, Utah to the north and New Mexico to the east. Although it is the sixth largest state in the nation, Arizona has fewer than 4,000,000 residents. Some have called it the most geographically diverse state in the United States, a point that's hard to argue. In the north are high mountains and the Grand Canyon, as well as the Mogollon Rim, a 1500-foot-high wall of land stretching

It may sound incredible, but London Bridge is the second-most popular tourist attraction in Arizona, surpassed only by the Grand Canyon.

for hundreds of miles. Indian reservations cover the northeast corner, a high plateau dotted with spectacular mesas and buttes and wide open spaces known for their stark beauty. On the western border, the Colorado River is a cool, blue waterway cutting through a hot, semi-barren landscape. The Sonoran Desert, characterized by giant saguaro cacti with their wildly splayed arms and accordion pleats, spreads from Mexico to central Arizona. To the east lie the White Mountains, covered with pine trees and dotted with lakes. From low desert to snowcapped mountains to wide rivers, Arizona is proud to show off its natural jewels.

Plan to spend some time in Arizona; its greatest attractions are not seen in a blur speeding down the highway. Venture off main roads and get to know the people and land. See which of those western myths you've seen in the movies are true, and which belong only to vivid imaginations.

But most of all, relax. The pace here is slow, the mood casual. Soak up the sun, leave your watch at home and simply enjoy. You're in Arizona.

Where to Go

This book covers everything you need to know about visiting Arizona—where to sleep, shop, dine, dance, be entertained and explore the outdoors. It is divided into ten chapters. This first chapter offers practical details for planning your trip. Chapter Two explores Arizona's natural landscape, while Chapter Three delves into the region's history, including Native American and Spanish influences. Chapter Four focuses solely on the Grand Canyon, which is worthy of a book in itself. Chapter Five heads to the northeast corner of the state and Indian Country, including the Painted Desert and Petrified Forest. Sedona, Jerome, Flagstaff and Prescott all are covered in Chapter Six, while Chapter Seven travels down the state's western edge from Kingman to Lake Havasu City and the London Bridge. Chapter Eight describes the Phoenix/Scottsdale area, while Chapter Nine ventures east into the mountains and scenic areas from Globe to Pinetop-Lakeside and the Coronado Trail. Chapter Ten moves farther south to Tucson, Tombstone and the Mexican border.

Many visitors begin a visit to Arizona by heading for the **Grand Canyon**, the largest single geological feature in the Southwest, which splits the region between north and south. The "village" on the South Rim of the Grand Canyon, just an hour's drive from interstate Route 40, is developed on a grand scale, complete with an airport. The North Rim, farther by road from major cities and main routes and closed during the winter months, is more relaxed and secluded, though still busy enough to make advance lodging or camping reservations essential.

Northeastern Arizona, also known as Indian Country, includes the vast, sprawling Navajo Reservation, larger than some East Coast states, as well as the remote, ancient mesa-top pueblos of the Hopi Reservation, a fiercely traditional and independent region although— or perhaps because—it's completely surrounded by Navajo land. The

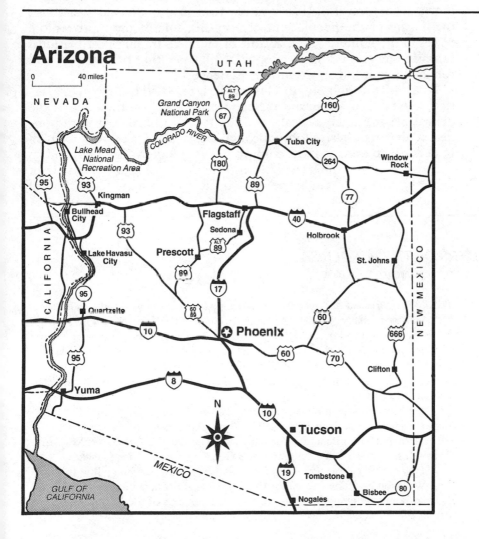

center of the Navajo world according to legend, Canyon de Chelly is still inhabited by people who herd sheep and live without electricity. Visitors can view the hogans (traditional Navajo log homes) and pastures from high up on the canyon rim, but can only enter the labyrinth accompanied by a Navajo guide. Another national park service unit operated by the tribe, Navajo National Monument protects some of the best Anasazi ruins in the Four Corners area—the region where Arizona, Utah, Colorado and New Mexico converge. The monument's biggest Indian ruin is only accessible on horseback. The third major park on the reservation is Monument Valley Tribal Park, a landscape so familiar from the many films, television shows and advertisements filmed here that visitors may feel like they're driving through a movie as they travel the backcountry road around the valley and visit the hogans of the people who live in this, one of the most remote places in the United States. A tour of Hubbell Trading Post National Historic Site and perhaps a stop at a still-operating trading post will round out your Indian Country experience.

Route 40 through **North Central Arizona** will bring you to Flagstaff, a winter ski resort and college town, sitting on the edge of the dramatic San Francisco Peaks at 7000 feet and blanketed with ponderosa pine trees. Drive south through spectacular Oak Creek Canyon to Sedona, an upscale artist community with a New Age bent and an abundance of shopping. This is also the heart of scenic Red Rock Country, where red sandstone has eroded into dramatic formations of

---

RIDERS OF THE PURPLE SAGE

The allure of Arizona has not gone unnoticed by the publishing and film industry. Zane Grey based many of his western novels on north central Arizona, and his books include Riders of the Purple Sage *and* West of the Pecos. *Tony Hillerman's contemporary murder mysteries are often set in the Navajo Reservation and Four Corners area and include* Thief of Time, The Blessing Way *and* Listening Woman. Laughing Boy *by Oliver LaFarge is a Pulitzer prize-winning novel that describes Navajo life.*

There have also been a number of films made in Arizona. Those filmed at Old Tucson Studios include John Wayne's Rio Lobo, Rio Bravo *and* El Dorado; *Paul Newman's* The Life and Times of Judge Roy Bean; *Clint Eastwood's* The Outlaw Josey Wales; *and* Gunfight at the O.K. Corral *with Kirk Douglas.*

Monument Valley was the setting for a number of films, including How the West Was Won *and* The Legend of the Lone Ranger. Oklahoma *and* Red Badge of Courage *were filmed in Patagonia. The* Riders of the Purple Sage *was filmed in the Sedona/Oak Creek Canyon area.*

It's amazing that a city of a million people could survive at all in such a sunbaked desert valley, but a complex system of dams and aqueducts has allowed Phoenix to become the ninth-largest city in the United States.

incomparable beauty. Jerome, scenically perched in the Mingus Mountains, is a former mining town that's now home to a small community of artists. Just down the road is Prescott, the original territorial capital of Arizona, which draws visitors with its numerous museums and low-key charm.

Never mind that **Western Arizona** is surrounded by parched desert. The 340-mile-long stretch of the Colorado River that establishes the state's "west coast" border has created an aquatic playground spilling over with unparalleled scenic and recreational opportunities. Kingman serves as a northern gateway to a succession of lakes, resorts and riverfront coves, as well as to the historic gold and silver mining ghost towns of Oatman and Chloride. The Lake Mead National Recreational Area extends to include Lake Mohave, where you'll find Bullhead City, the fastest growing city in Arizona. Farther south is Lake Havasu City, home to the authentic London Bridge, which was brought over from England and reassembled here. Continue down State Route 95 and you'll come to Quartzsite, which attracts more than half a million visitors every February for its annual rock and mineral extravaganza.

Phoenix, the state capital and the largest city in the Southwest, is the focus of **South Central Arizona**. At first, this rectilinear sprawl of suburbs and shopping malls, giant retirement communities, towering office buildings, industrial parks and farmlands full of year-round citrus and cotton crops may seem to offer few charms for the vacationer. But those who take time to explore Phoenix and beyond will soon discover that this city where it is often better to spend daytime hours indoors has more than its share of fine museums. The winter months are the time for outdoor adventuring in the Phoenix area, and hiking, horseback riding, boating and fishing opportunities abound. Nearby Scottsdale blends the architecture of the Old West with exclusive shops, galleries, restaurants and night clubs, while other towns within easy day-trip distance of Phoenix, such as Wickenburg, recall grittier and more authentic memories of the rough-and-rowdy mining boomtown era of turn-of-the-century Arizona.

Towering mountain peaks, sparkling streams and lakes, and dense pine forests surprise many travelers to the high country of **Eastern Arizona**. This forest primeval encompasses the mountain hamlets of Show Low, Pine Top and Lakeside, summer resorts famous for their hiking and fishing, and popular with those trying to escape the scorching temperatures on the desert floor. During winter, skiers flock to the downhill runs and cross-country trails at nearby Sunrise ski resort on the White Mountain Apache Reservation. The forests deepen as you travel east to Alpine, a mountain village just a few miles from the New Mexico border. At the heart of the "Arizona Alps," Alpine is a mecca for nature buffs, who love the profusion of outdoor activities—hiking, camping, hunting and fishing. Alpine is also a northern guidepost along the Coronado Trail, which snakes south through some of the most spectacular scenery in the Southwest to the historic mining town of Clifton. Built along the banks of the San Francisco River, Clifton and its historic Chase Creek Street give a glimpse of what Arizona was like at the turn of the century. Traveling south from Clifton, juniper foothills give way to rolling grasslands and the fertile Gila River Valley, where cotton is king and the town of Safford marks Arizona's eastern anchor of the Old West Highway. This strip of Arizona, stretching 203 miles from Apache Junction to the New Mexico state line, is rich in the frontier history of the Old West. Tracing a course first charted by Coronado, Geronimo, the Dutchman, Billy the Kid, Johnny Ringo and pioneers looking for a place to call their own, you'll pass through cactus-studded valleys, pine-topped mountains, rugged and craggy canyons, lost treasure and historic copper mines. Along the way you can sample the area's history in Globe's plantation-style mansions and antique shops and its pre-history at the Besh-Ba-Gowah archaeological site.

Southern Arizona in the springtime, when the desert flowers bloom, is as close as most of us will find to paradise on earth. The secret is well-kept because during the summer tourist season, when most visitors come to the Southwest, Tucson is considerably hotter than paradise—or just about anyplace else. Those who visit at any time other than summer will discover the pleasure of wandering through the stands of giant saguaro cactus that cover the foothills at the edge of town, perhaps learning more about the region by visiting the wonderful Arizona-Sonora Desert Museum and seeing the radiant 18th-century Spanish Mission San Xavier del Bac. For more desert beauty, drive west through the cactus forest of the Tohono O'Odham (Papago) Reservation to Organ Pipe Cactus National Monument on the Mexican border. Many people consider the monument to be the most beautiful part of the southwestern desert. Another great side trip from the Tucson area is Cochise County to the east. National monuments in the rugged, empty mountains preserve the strongholds of Apache warlords and tne cavalrymen who fought to subdue them. Old Bisbee, until recently the headquarters for one of the nation's largest open-pit copper mining operations, has been reincarnated as a picturesque, far-from-everything tourist town. Tombstone, meanwhile, enjoys its reputation as the site of a famous gunfight that occurred more than a century ago, and remains one of the most authentically preserved historic towns of the Old West.

Umbrellas are considered an oddity in these parts. When it rains, the approved means of keeping water from running down the back of your neck is a cowboy hat.

Climate

Many people imagine the Arizona to be a scorching hot place. Part of it—Tucson, Phoenix, southern and western Arizona—lives up to expectations with daytime high temperatures averaging well above the 100-degree mark through the summer months. Even in January, thermometers in this area generally reach the high 60s in the afternoon and rarely fall to freezing at night. The clement winter weather and practically perpetual sunshine have made the Arizona desert a haven for retired persons and seasonal residents seeking refuge from colder winters.

Yet less than 200 miles away, the North Rim of the Grand Canyon is closed in the winter because heavy snows make the road impassable. Northern Arizona has cold, dry winters with temperatures usually rising above freezing during the day, but often dropping close to zero at night. The high mountains remain snowcapped all winter and boast several popular ski areas. At lower elevations, lighter snowfalls and plenty of sunshine keep roads clear most of the time.

Where rugged mountains collide with the Sonoran Desert, small changes in elevation can mean big variations in climate. As a rule, climbing 1000 feet in elevation alters the temperature as much as going 300 miles north. For instance, the bottom of the Grand Canyon is always about 20 degrees warmer than the top rim. In Tucson, some people bask by swimming pools during the winter, while others ski on the slopes of nearby Mount Lemmon.

Springtime is a mixed blessing. Flooding rivers, chilly winds and sandstorms sometimes await visitors in March and early April, but those who take a chance are more likely to experience mild weather and spectacular displays of desert wildflowers. Leaves do not appear on the trees until late April at moderate elevations, late May in the higher mountains.

Throughout Arizona, June is the hottest month. In the southern and western parts of the state, the thermometer can, and often does, climb above a sweltering 100 degrees. Lizards are the most active form of life outside air-conditioned houses and buildings. People have even been known to fry eggs on the sidewalks and let popcorn pop inside closed automobiles. That's when desert dwellers vacation in northern states, or head to higher elevations, where temperatures average in the low 80s in summer.

"Snowbirds" are seasonal residents who come from colder climes to bask in the southern Arizona sun. When summer's 100-plus temperatures arrive, the snowbirds return home and southern Arizonans head for cooler parts of the state.

Much of the year's rain is dumped in what locals call the monsoon season—July, August and early September. Try to plan outdoor activities in the morning hours because during the afternoons or early evenings, winds gust and dark cumulus clouds roll in, emptying their store of water before moving on. While these thunderstorms usually cool things down on hot afternoons, the storms don't last long and the skies quickly clear. But when the rains do come, be alert to the dangers of flash floods. Water can quickly run off rocky desert surfaces and into canyons and gullies, sweeping away boulders, cars, people—anything in its path.

Autumn is the nicest time of year. Locals used to keep this fact to themselves, and until recently tourists in October were about as rare as snowflakes in Phoenix. Nowadays the secret is out, and record numbers of people are visiting during the fall "shoulder season" to experience autumn colors and bright Indian summer days.

Calendar

JANUARY

Northeastern Arizona   Relive a tradition of the frontier West on the **Hashknife Sheriff Posse's Pony Express Ride** from Holbrook to Scottsdale.

Western Arizona   Lake Havasu City's **Dixieland Jazz Festival** includes a parade, music aboard a riverboat, dancing and a banjorama.

South Central Arizona   Crowds gather in Scottsdale to watch some of the PGA Tour's best golfers at the **Phoenix Open**, one of Arizona's largest spectator events. The **Barrett-Jackson Auction** is a huge classic and collectible car auction in Scottsdale, with some 900 vehicles ranging in price from several thousand to millions of dollars.

Eastern Arizona   **Sled Dog Races** in Alpine attract entrants from as far away as the Yukon. Rock hounds and gem collectors will like the **Gila County Gem and Mineral Show** in Globe.

FEBRUARY

North Central Arizona   At the **Flagstaff Winter Festival**, events include star gazing, sled-dog races, snow games, a snow softball tournament, skiing, concerts and winetasting.

Western Arizona   The **Quartzsite Gemboree** attracts several hundred thousand rock hounds and gem collectors from around the world for its ten-day flea market and festival.

South Central Arizona   **Gold Rush Days** in Wickenburg features a parade, rodeo, arts-and-crafts show, melodrama, gold mucking and drilling competitions and a beard-growing contest. More than 400 artists display their wares amidst entertainment, hot-air balloons and sky divers at the **Great Fair** in Fountain Hills. Casa Grande is the site of **O'Odham Tash—Casa Grande Indian Days**, which includes Native American rituals and arts and crafts.

Eastern Arizona   Explore turn-of-the-century buildings on Globe's **Historic Home & Building Tour & Antique Show**. The **Arizona Renaissance Festival** in Apache Junction near Phoenix has music, theater, crafts, games and tournaments. **Lost Dutchman Days** in Apache Junction is another community celebration full of traditional small-town events—like a Fourth of July in February.

Southern Arizona   The **Tucson Gem and Mineral Show** draws jewelers and collectors from around the world. At Tucson's **La Fiesta de los Vaqueros**, events include bareback riding, steer wrestling, barrel racing, bull riding and the world's longest non-motorized parade. One of the oldest arts and crafts shows in Arizona, the **Tubac Festival** features artists from all over the country, as well as entertainment.

MARCH

South Central Arizona   The **Scottsdale Arts Festival** features dance and music performances and crafts exhibitions. The unusual **Chandler Ostrich Festival** has ostrich racing for a highlight, in addition to music, a parade, art exhibits, carnival rides and an automobile show. The huge **Old Town Tempe Spring Festival** features more than 450 national artists, as well as adult and children's entertainment.

Southern Arizona   The **Tucson Festival of the Arts** presents a three-day program of orchestral, choral and ensemble music, modern and interpretive dance and theater performances in the city parks, along with one of the Southwest's largest arts and crafts shows. The high point of **Tombstone Territorial Days** is a re-enactment of the events leading up to the gunfight at the O.K. Corral.

APRIL

Western Arizona   Anglers troll the waters of Lake Mohave for 40-pound stripers during the **U.S. Striper Bass Fishing Tournament** in Bullhead City/Laughlin. The **Route 66 Fun Run Weekend** in Seligman/Topock is a fundraiser that helps preserve the historic Route 66 between Chicago and Los Angeles. A street dance, car show, pageant and barbecue are all part of the festivities.

Southern Arizona   The **Tucson Festival**, which runs for three weekends, incorporates **Pioneer Days** and the **San Xavier Pageant and Fiesta**, both living-history re-enactments with Spanish priests, conquistadors, mountain men and the cavalry, as well as mariachi music, bonfires, fireworks, Native American foods and traditional Tohono O'Odham Indian dances. The festival also includes the lively, Mexican-style **Fiesta de la Placita**.

MAY

North Central Arizona   **Bill Williams Rendezvous Days**, held on Memorial Day weekend in Williams, re-creates the days of the mountain men with barn dances, black-powder shoots, a pioneer costume contest and evening "whooplas."

Western Arizona   You won't find the Nelson Riddle Orchestra, but you can get your kicks at the **Route 66 Classic Car Rally & Show** in Kingman.

Eastern Arizona   The state's toughest cowboys compete in the **Arizona High School Rodeo Association Rodeo** in St. Johns.

Southern Arizona   Tombstone's **Wyatt Earp Days** celebration fills the Memorial Day weekend with Old West costumes, staged shootouts in the streets, and arts and crafts.

JUNE

Northeastern Arizona   Holbrook's **Old West Day/Bucket of Blood Races** features an arts and crafts show, barbecue, Native American song and dance, a car and truck show and races.

North Central Arizona   The **Festival of Native American Arts** opens at the Museum of Northern Arizona in Flagstaff, with extensive exhibits and craft demonstrations continuing through early August.

Western Arizona   You might find the perfect piece of pressed glass at the **Downtown Antique Fair** in Kingman. Townsfolk dress up in frontier clothing to celebrate **Old Miner's Day** in Chloride. You won't need a seatbelt for **Parker's Inner Tube Races** down a seven-mile stretch of the Colorado River.

South Central Arizona   An **Oldtime Country Music and Bluegrass Festival** is held at the rodeo grounds in Payson.

JULY

North Central Arizona   **Frontier Days and World's Oldest Rodeo** in Prescott draws cowboys from all over the country and also has fireworks, a parade and a cowboy golf tournament.The **Hopi Craftsman Exhibit** is presented at the Museum of Northern Arizona in Flagstaff in early July in connection with the Festival of Native American Arts. The **Navajo Craftsman Exhibition** opens there later in the month.

Western Arizona   Beat the summer heat during **Laughlin's River Days**, which include a golf tournament, fireworks display and rubber duck races along the Colorado River.

South Central Arizona   The **Phoenix Parks Department Summer Show** is one of the Southwest's largest arts and crafts fairs. The rodeo grounds in Payson are the setting for the **Loggers Sawdust Festival**, a weekend of chopping, pole climbing and log burling contests.

Eastern Arizona   Enjoying Alpine's **Loggers Jamboree** is as easy as falling off of one.

AUGUST

North Central Arizona   Enjoy the evergreens of northern Arizona during the **Flagstaff Festival in the Pines**, which features more than 250 artisans, live entertainment and children's activities.

Eastern Arizona   The Southwest's best equestrians are represented at the **St. Johns Horse Trials**. Tighten your bow string and loosen your vocal chords for the **Archery Tournament and Elk Bugling Competition** in Alpine.

SEPTEMBER

Grand Canyon   The world's largest amphitheater is the setting for world-class music during the **Grand Canyon Chamber Music Festival**.

Northeastern Arizona   The **Navajo Nation Fair** in Window Rock has carnival rides, a rodeo, horse races, dance competitions, a pretty-baby contest, the Miss Navajo pageant and a wonderful arts and crafts pavilion.

North Central Arizona   The **Call of the Canyon Festival of the Arts**, held in Sedona, draws artisans from all over the West to participate in one of the region's major arts and crafts fairs.

Western Arizona   Kingman's favorite native son is remembered during **Andy Devine Days and P.R.C.A. Rodeo**.

South Central Arizona   Payson hosts the **Old-Time Fiddlers Contest and Festival** at the rodeo grounds.

Southern Arizona   **Wild West Days**, one of several practically identical town festivals held in Tombstone throughout the year, features a parade, rodeo, melodrama and quick-draw contest. Nogales joins its twin city across the border in celebrating **Mexican Independence Day** with food, live music and street dancing.

OCTOBER

Western Arizona   The **IJSBA World Jet Ski Finals** in Lake Havasu City offers high-speed races and a bathing suit competition, while **London Bridge Days** commemorates the relocation of the bridge to this improbable site with a parade, live entertainment, costume contests and lots of Olde English fun.

South Central Arizona   The **Arizona State Fair**, held in Phoenix, runs until early November.

Eastern Arizona   Traditional dances, folk art and food are featured during **Apache Days** in Globe.

Southern Arizona   The **Bisbee Copper Queen Fling** celebrates the town's flamboyant boom days with tours of the now-defunct Copper Queen open-pit mine and revelry all over Old Bisbee. **Rex Allen Days** in Willcox honors cowboy movie star Rex Allen with a golf tournament, parade, country fair, rodeo, art show and cowboy dances. Tombstone celebrates **Heldorado Days** with music, arts and crafts and gunfight re-enactments.

NOVEMBER

Western Arizona Radio-controlled model planes fill the skies during the **London Bridge Seaplane Classic** in Lake Havasu City.

South Central Arizona   The **Four Corner States Bluegrass Festival** in Wickenburg presents three days of music as bands compete for thousands of dollars in prize money. The **Thunderbird Balloon Classic and Airshow** in Glendale has more than 150 balloons, a balloon show and street dance.

Southern Arizona   The largest perimeter bicycling event in the U.S., **El Tour de Tucson** is a colorful spectator sport and a charity fundraiser. The **Papago All-Indian Fair** at Sells, west of Tucson on the Indian reservation, features outstanding pottery, rug and jewelry exhibits, as well as a rodeo.

DECEMBER

Western Arizona   Christmas lights sparkle during Lake Mead Marina's **Harbor Parade of Lights**.

South Central Arizona   The **Sunkist Fiesta Bowl Parade** in Phoenix has marching bands, equestrian units and floats. Tempe's **New Year's Eve Block Party** welcomes the two Fiesta Bowl teams with food, rides, music, fireworks and live entertainment.

Visitor Information

For free visitor information packets including maps and current details on special events, accommodations and camping, contact the **Arizona Office of Tourism** (1100 West Washington Street, Phoenix, AZ 85007; 602–542–3687). In addition, most towns have a chamber of commerce or visitor information center. As a general rule, these tourist information centers are not open on weekends.

Packing

Arizonans are casual in their dress and expect the same of visitors. Restaurants with dress codes are few and far between. Even if you attend a fancy $100-a-plate fundraiser or go out for a night at the opera, you'll find that a coat and tie or evening gown and heels instantly brand you as a tourist. Chic apparel in these parts is more likely to mean a western-cut suit, ostrich-hide boots and a bolo tie with a flashy turquoise-and-silver slide, or, for women, a fiesta dress with a concho belt, long-fringed moccasins and a squash blossom necklace—all fairly expensive items that you may never have occasion to wear back home. Relax. Sporty, comfortable clothing will pass practically anywhere.

When packing clothes, plan to dress in layers. Temperatures can turn hot or cold in a flash at any time of year. During the course of a

---

ONE-OF-A-KIND BOOKSTORES

If you like unusual bookstores, you'll find no lack of them in Arizona. Stop by the **Singing Wind Bookshop** *(Ocotillo Road, two-and-a-quarter miles north of Route 10, Benson; 602-586-2425) for a bookstore where the location, more than the contents, are what's different. It sits out in the country on a ranch, past cattle gates, with nothing but a name on the mailbox to announce it. The* **One Book Bookstore** *(38 Main Street; 602-432-5512) in Bisbee offers just that—a selection of one book. The* **Footprints of a Gigantic Hound** *(16 Broadway Village, Tucson; 602-326-8533) is a mystery bookstore where a giant Irish wolfhound takes up residence. And* **Those Were the Days!** *(516 South Mill Avenue, Tempe; 602-967-4729) has one of the largest selections of books on antiques and collecting in the Southwest with more than 3500 new titles, as well as used, out-of-print and rare titles on antiques. As an added bonus, you can buy antiques here and folk music constantly plays in the background.*

single vacation day, you can often expect to start by wearing a heavy jacket, a sweater or flannel shirt and a pair of slacks or jeans, peeling down to a T-shirt and shorts as the day warms up, then putting the extra layers back on soon after the sun goes down.

Other essentials to pack or buy along the way include a good sunscreen and high-quality sunglasses. Bear in mind that in many areas off the beaten path, you'll be unlikely to find a store selling anything more substantial than curios and beef jerky. If you are planning to camp in the mountains during the summer, you'll be glad you brought mosquito repellant.

For outdoor activities, tough-soled hiking boots are more comfortable than running shoes on rocky terrain. Even RV travelers and those who prefer to spend most nights in motels may want to take along a backpacking tent and sleeping bag for irresistible urges to stay out under star-spangled skies. A canteen, first-aid kit, flashlight and other routine camping gear are also likely to come in handy. Cycling enthusiasts should bring their own bikes. Especially when it comes to mountain biking, there are a lot more great places to ride than there are towns where you can find bicycles for rent. The same goes for boating, golf and other activities that call for special equipment.

A camera is essential for capturing your travel experience; of equal importance is a good pair of binoculars, which let you explore distant landscapes from scenic overlooks. And don't, for heaven's sake, forget your copy of *Ultimate Arizona*.

Driving in Arizona

The canyons, mountains and deserts of Arizona are clearly the major sightseeing attractions for many visitors. This is a rugged area and there are some important things to remember when driving on the side roads throughout the region. First and foremost, believe it if you see a sign indicating four-wheel drive only. These roads can be very dangerous in a car without high ground clearance and the extra traction afforded by a four-wheel drive—and there may be no safe place to turn around if you get stuck. During rainy periods, dirt roads may become impassable muck. And in winter, heavy snows often necessitate the use of snow tires or chains on main roads, while side roads may or may not be maintained at all.

Some side roads will take you far from civilization, so be sure to have a full radiator and tank of gas. Carry spare fuel, water and food. In winter, it is always wise to travel with a shovel and blankets in your car. Should you become stuck, local people are usually quite helpful about offering assistance to stranded vehicles, but in case no one else is around, for extended backcountry driving, a CB radio or a car phone would not be a bad idea.

Lodging

In Arizona, lodgings run the gamut from tiny one-room mountain cabins to luxurious hotels that blend Indian pueblo architecture with contemporary elegance. Bed and breakfasts can be found not only in chic destinations like Sedona but also in such unlikely locales as former ghost towns and the outskirts of Indian reservations. They come in all types, sizes and price ranges. Typical of the genre are lovingly restored old mansions comfortably furnished with period decor, usually with fewer than a dozen rooms. Some bed and breakfasts, however, are guest cottages or rooms in nice suburban homes, while others are larger establishments, approaching hotel size, of the type sometimes referred to as country inns.

Both rims of the Grand Canyon have classic, rustic-elegant lodges built during the early years of the 20th century. Though considerably more expensive than budget motel rooms, the national park lodges are moderate in price and well worth it in terms of ambience and location. Reservations should be made far in advance.

The abundance of motels in towns along all major highway routes presents a range of choices, from name-brand motor inns to traditional mom-and-pop establishments that have endured for the half-century since motels were invented. Older motels along main truck routes, especially interstate Route 40, offer some of the lowest room rates in the United States today.

At the other end of the price spectrum, the height of self-indulgent vacationing is to be found at upscale resorts in destinations such as Tucson and Sedona. These resorts offer riding stables, golf courses, tennis courts, fine dining, live entertainment nightly and exclusive shops right on the premises so that guests can spend their entire holidays without leaving the grounds—a boon for celebrities seeking a few days' rest and relaxation away from the public eye, but a way to miss out on the real Arizona.

CALLING ALL CITY SLICKERS

Fueled by romantic images of western heroes and desert sunsets, and hoping to escape to a simpler time, more people than ever are indulging in the fantasy and hanging their saddles at a dude ranch. Guest ranches in southern Arizona range from resorts where you're more likely to overheat in the jacuzzi than the saddle to working ranches where wranglers round 'em up and beans and burgers are the likely fare. Whichever you choose, most offer horseback riding and a range of outdoor activities in a secluded setting. Some close during the hot summer months, so be sure to call ahead.

Other lodgings throughout the state offer a different kind of personality. Many towns—preserved historic districts like Tombstone, as well as larger communities like Flagstaff—have historic hotels dating back before the turn of the century. Some of them have been lavishly restored to far surpass their original Victorian elegance. Others may lack the polished antique decor and sophisticated ambience, but make up for it in their authentic feel. These places give visitors a chance to spice up their vacation experience by spending the night at a place where they can look out their window onto a Main Street that has changed surprisingly little since the days of the Old West.

Whatever your preference and budget, you can find something in this book to suit your taste. Remember, rooms can be scarce and prices may rise during the peak season, which is summer throughout most of the region and winter in low-lying desert communities such as Phoenix, Scottsdale and Tucson. Travelers planning to visit a place in peak season should either make advance reservations or arrive early in the day, before the "No Vacancy" signs start lighting up. Those who plan to stay in Sedona or Grand Canyon National Park at any time of year are wise to make lodging reservations well ahead of time.

Accommodations in this book are organized by region and classified according to price. Rates referred to are high-season rates, so if you are looking for off-season bargains, it's good to inquire. *Budget* lodgings generally run less than $50 per night for two people and are satisfactory and clean, but modest. *Moderate* hotels range from $50 to $90; what they have to offer in the way of luxury will depend on where they are located, but they generally offer larger rooms and more attractive surroundings. At a *deluxe* hotel or resort you can expect to spend between $90 and $130 for a double; you'll generally find spacious rooms, a fashionable lobby, a restaurant and often a group of shops. *Ultra-deluxe* facilities, priced above $130, are a region's finest, offering all the amenities of a deluxe hotel plus plenty of extras.

ARIZONA CUISINE

While the specialty cuisine throughout most of Arizona consists of variations on Mexican and Native American food, you'll find many restaurants catering to customers whose tastes don't include hot chili peppers. You'll also find a growing number of restaurants offering "New Southwestern" menus that feature offbeat dishes using local ingredients. Green-chili tempura? Snow-crab enchiladas? If a newly invented dish sounds tempting, by all means give it a try!

Room rates vary as much with locale as with quality. Some of the trendier destinations have no rooms at all in the budget price range. In other communities—especially those along interstate highways where rates are set with truck drivers in mind—every motel falls into the budget category, even though accommodations may range from $19.95 at run-down, spartan places to $45 or so at the classiest motor inn in town. The price categories listed in this book are relative, designed to show you where to get the most out of your travel budget, however large or small it may be.

Restaurants

Within a particular chapter, restaurants are categorized by region, with each restaurant entry describing the establishment according to price. Dinner entrées at *budget* restaurants usually cost $8 or less. The ambience is informal, service usually speedy and the crowd often a local one. *Moderately* priced restaurants range between $8 and $16 at dinner; surroundings are casual but pleasant, the menu offers more variety and the pace is usually slower. *Deluxe* establishments tab their entrées from $16 to $24; the cuisine may be simple or sophisticated, depending on the location, but the decor is more plush and the service more personalized. *Ultra-deluxe* dining rooms, where entrées begin at $24, are often the gourmet places; here, cooking has become a fine art and the service should be impeccable.

Some restaurants change hands often and are occasionally closed in low seasons. Efforts have been made in this book to include places with established reputations for good eating. Breakfast and lunch menus vary less in price from restaurant to restaurant than do dinner offerings.

Camping

RV or tent camping is a great way to tour Arizona. Besides saving substantial sums of money, campers enjoy the freedom of watching sunsets from beautiful places, spending nights under spectacularly starry skies and waking up in lovely surroundings that few hotels can match.

Most towns have commercial RV parks of some sort, and long-term mobile-home parks often rent spaces to RVs by the night. But unless you absolutely need cable television, none of these places can compete with the wide array of public campgrounds available in national and state parks, monuments and forests. Federal campground sites are typically less developed and only the biggest ones have electrical hookups. National forest campgrounds don't have hookups, while state park campgrounds just about always do. The largest public campgrounds offer tent camping loops separate from RV loops, while backcountry camping areas offer the option of spending the night far from the crowds.

With the exception of both rims of the Grand Canyon, where campsite reservations are booked through **Ticketron** (Reservation Office, P.O. Box 617516, Chicago, IL 60661; 800-452-1111—credit cards only), you won't find much in the way of sophisticated reservation systems. The general rule in public campgrounds is still first-come, first-served, even though they fill up practically every night in peak season. For campers, this means traveling in the morning and reaching your intended campground by early afternoon. In many areas, campers may find it more convenient to keep a single location for as much as a week and explore surrounding areas on day trips.

For listings of state parks with camping facilities and reservation information, contact **Arizona State Parks** (800 West Washington Street, Phoenix, AZ 85007; 602-542-4174). Information on camping in the national forests in Arizona is available from **National Forest Service—Southwestern Region** (Public Affairs Office, 517 Gold Avenue Southwest, Albuquerque, NM 87102; 505-842-3292). Camping and reservation information for national parks and monuments is available from **National Park Service—Southwest Regional Office** (1100 Old Santa Fe Trail, Santa Fe, NM 87501; 505-988-6340) or from the individual parks and monuments listed in this book.

Many Indian lands have public campgrounds, which usually do not appear in campground directories. For information, contact the **Navajo Cultural Resources Department** (P.O. Box 308, Window Rock, AZ 86515; 602-871-4941); **Hopi Tribal Headquarters** (P.O. Box 123, Kykotsmovi, AZ 86039; 602-734-2415); **Havasupai Tourist Enterprise** (Supai, AZ 86435; 602-448-2121); and the **White Mountain Apache Game and Fish Department** (P.O. Box 220, Whiteriver, AZ 85941; 602-338-4385).

Wilderness Permits

Tent camping is allowed in the backcountry of all national forests here except in the few areas where signs are posted prohibiting it. You no longer need a permit to hike or camp in national forest wilderness areas, but plan to stop at a ranger station anyway for trail maps and advice on current conditions and fire regulations. In dry seasons, emergency rules may prohibit campfires and sometimes ban cigarette smoking, with stiff enforcement penalties.

For backcountry hiking in national parks and monuments, you must first obtain a permit from the ranger at the front desk in the visitor center. The permit procedure is simple and free. It helps park administrators measure the impact on sensitive ecosystems and distribute use evenly among major trails to prevent overcrowding.

Boating

Most of the large desert lakes along the Colorado and other major rivers are administered as National Recreation Areas and supervised by the U.S. Army Corps of Engineers. Federal boating safety regulations that apply to these lakes may vary slightly from state regulations. Indian reservations have separate rules for boating on tribal lakes. More significant than any differences between federal, state and tribal regulations are the local rules in force for any particular lake.

Ask for applicable boating regulations at a local marina or fishing supply store or use the addresses and phone numbers listed in "Parks" or other sections of each chapter in this book to contact the headquarters for lakes you plan to visit.

Boats, from small power boats to houseboats, can be rented for 24 hours or longer at marinas on several of the larger lakes. At most marinas, you can get a boat on short notice if you arrive on a weekday, since much of their business comes from local weekend recreation.

River rafting is a very popular sport and the ultimate whitewater rafting experience, of course, is a trip through the Grand Canyon. Independent rafters are welcome, but because of the bulky equipment and specialized knowledge of river hazards involved, most adventurous souls stick with group trips offered by any of the many rafting companies located in Flagstaff, Page and towns farther upriver. Rafters, as well as people using canoes, kayaks, windsurfers or inner tubes, are required by state and federal regulations to wear life jackets.

Fish and Fishing

As a state with no shortage of deserts, many Arizona residents seem to have an irresistible fascination with water. During the warm months, lakeshores and readily accessible portions of streams are often packed with anglers, especially on weekends. Vacationers can beat the crowds to some extent by planning their fishing days during the week.

Fish hatcheries keep busy stocking streams with trout, particularly rainbows, the most popular game fish throughout the region. Catch-and-release fly fishing is the rule in some popular areas, allowing more anglers a chance at bigger fish. Be sure to inquire locally about eating the fish you catch, since some seemingly remote streams and rivers have contamination problems from old mines and mills.

The larger reservoirs offer an assortment of sport fish, including crappie, carp, white bass, smallmouth bass, largemouth bass and walleye pike. Striped bass, an ocean import, can run as large as 40 pounds, while catfish in the depths of dammed desert canyons sometimes attain mammoth proportions.

For copies of state fishing regulations, inquire at a local fishing supply store or marina, or contact the **Arizona Game and Fish Commission** (2222 West Washington Street, Suite 415, Phoenix, AZ 85007; 602-542-4174). State fishing licenses are required for fishing in national parks and national recreation areas, but not on Indian reservations, where daily permits are sold by the tribal governments. For more information about fishing on Indian lands, contact the tribal agencies listed in "Camping" above.

Family Travelers

Any place that has cowboys and Indians, rocks to climb and limitless room to run is bound to be a hit with youngsters. Plenty of family adventures are available during a stay in Arizona, from man-made attractions to wilderness experiences. A few guidelines will help make travel with children a pleasure.

Book reservations in advance, making sure that the places you stay accept children. Many bed and breakfasts do not. If you need a crib or extra cot, arrange for it ahead of time. A travel agent can be of help here, as well as with most other travel plans.

If you are traveling by air, try to reserve bulkhead seats where there is plenty of room. Take along extras you may need, such as diapers, changes of clothing, snacks and toys or small games. When traveling by car, be sure to take along the extras, too. Make sure you have plenty of water and juices to drink; dehydration can be a subtle but serious problem. Most towns, as well as some national parks, have stores that carry diapers, baby food, snacks and other essentials, though they usually close early. Larger towns often have all-night grocery or convenience stores.

A first-aid kit is a must for any trip. Along with adhesive bandages, antiseptic cream and something to stop itching, include any medicines your pediatrician might recommend to treat allergies, colds, diarrhea or any chronic problems your child may have.

Arizona sunshine is intense. Take extra care for the first few days. Children's skin is usually more tender than adult skin and severe sunburn can happen before you realize it. A hat is a good idea, along with a reliable sunblock.

Many national parks and monuments offer special activities designed just for children. Visitor-center film presentations and rangers' campfire slide shows can help teach children about the natural history of Arizona and head off some questions. However, kids tend to find a lot more things to wonder about than adults have answers for. To be as prepared as possible, seize every opportunity to learn more—particularly about Native American history and culture, a constant curiosity for young minds.

Disabled Travelers

Arizona is striving to make public areas fully accessible to disabled persons. Parking spaces and restroom facilities for the handicapped are provided according to both state law and national park regulations.

THE CACTUS LEAGUE

Each year, eight major league baseball teams migrate to the sunny Arizona deserts from February to late March for their Cactus League spring training schedule, and the fans aren't far behind. It's become an increasingly popular way to spend a vacation as more and more fans take the opportunity to enjoy a little welcome sunshine, root for their favorite teams, and get a close-up look at some of professional baseball's super stars, all at the same time. Adding to the excitement is the intimacy and informality of the small-town ballparks, where stadium bleachers are much closer to the action, and ticket prices are substantially less than regular season prices, although tickets to some games—like the Chicago Cubs'—can be surprisingly hard to come by.

If you can't wait for the first ball of the regular season to be thrown out in April, catch the pre-season action with the following teams at their practice fields: San Francisco Giants (Scottsdale Stadium, 7408 East Osborn Road, Scottsdale; 602-994-5123); Chicago Cubs (Hohokam Park, 1238 Center Street, Mesa; 602-964-4467); Cleveland Indians (Hi Corbett Field in Reid Park, 22nd Street and Randolph Way, Tucson; 602-293-1008); Milwaukee Brewers (Compadre Stadium, 1425 West Ocotillo Road, Chandler; 602-821-2200); Oakland A's (Phoenix Municipal Stadium, 5999 East Van Buren Boulevard, Phoenix; 602-678-2222); San Diego Padres (Desert Sun Stadium, 1440 Desert Hills Drive, Yuma; 602-782-2567); Seattle Mariners (Diablo Stadium, 2200 West Alameda Street, Tempe; 602-731-8381); and the California Angels (Gene Autry Park, 4125 East McKellips Avenue, Mesa; 602-438-9300).

National parks and monuments also post signs that tell which trails are wheelchair accessible.

Information sources for disabled travelers include: the **Society for the Advancement of Travel for the Handicapped** (347 5th Avenue, Suite 610, New York, NY 10016; 212-447-7284); the **Travel Information Center** (Moss Rehabilitation Hospital, 12th Street and Tabor Road, Philadelphia, PA 19141; 215-329-5715); and **Mobility International USA** (P.O. Box 3551, Eugene, OR 97403; 503-343-1284). For general travel advice, contact **Travelin' Talk** (P.O. Box 3534, Clarksville, TN 37043; 615-552-6670), a networking organization.

Senior Travelers

Arizona is a hospitable place for older vacationers, many of whom turn into part-time or full-time residents thanks to the dry, pleasant climate and the friendly senior-citizen communities that have developed in southern Arizona and, on a smaller scale, in other parts of the state. The large number of national parks and monuments in the region means that persons age 62 and older can save considerable money with a Golden Age Passport, which allows free admission. Apply for one in person at any national park unit that charges an entrance fee. Many private sightseeing attractions also offer significant discounts for seniors.

The **American Association of Retired Persons** (AARP) (3200 East Carson Street, Lakewood, CA 90712; 213-496-2277) offers membership to anyone over 50. AARP's benefits include travel discounts with a number of firms. Escorted tours and cruises are available through AARP Travel Service (P.O. Box 5850, Norcross, GA 30091; 800-927-0111).

Elderhostel (75 Federal Street, Boston, MA 02110; 617-426-7788) offers educational courses as part of all-inclusive packages at colleges and universities. In Arizona, Elderhostel courses are available in numerous locations including Flagstaff, Nogales, Phoenix, Prescott and Tucson.

Be extra careful about health matters. In Arizona's changeable climate, seniors are more at risk of suffering hypothermia. High altitudes may present a risk to persons with heart or respiratory conditions; ask your physician for advice when planning your trip. Many tourist destinations in the state are a long way from any hospital or other health care facility.

In addition to the medications you ordinarily use, it's a good idea to bring along written prescriptions from your doctor for obtaining more if needed. Consider carrying a medical record with you, including your history and current medical status, as well as your doctor's name, phone number and address. Make sure that your insurance covers you while you are away from home.

Foreign Travelers

PASSPORTS AND VISAS   Most foreign visitors need a passport and tourist visa to enter the United States. Contact your nearest United States Embassy or Consulate well in advance to obtain a visa and to check on any other entry requirements.

CUSTOMS REQUIREMENTS   Foreign travelers are allowed to carry in the following: 200 cigarettes (or 100 cigars), $400 worth of duty-free gifts, including one liter of alcohol (you must be 21 years of age to bring in the alcohol). You may bring in any amount of currency but must fill out a form if you bring in over $10,000 (U.S.). Carry any prescription drugs in clearly marked containers. You may have to produce a written prescription or doctor's statement for the customs officer. Meat or meat products, seeds, plants, fruits and narcotics are not allowed to be brought into the United States. Contact the United States Custom Service (1301 Constitution Avenue Northwest, Washington, DC 20229; 202-566-8195) for further information.

DRIVING   If you plan to rent a car, an international driver's license should be obtained before arriving in the United States. Some car rental agencies require both a foreign license and an international driver's license. Many also require a lessee to be at least 25 years of age; all require a major credit card.

CURRENCY   United States money is based on the dollar. Bills generally come in denominations of $1, $5, $10, $20, $50 and $100. Every dollar is divided into 100 cents. Coins are the penny (1 cent), nickel (5 cents), dime (10 cents) and quarter (25 cents). Half-dollar and dollar coins are rarely used. You may not use foreign currency to purchase goods and services in the United States. Consider buying traveler's checks in dollar amounts. You may also use credit cards affiliated with an American company such as Interbank, Visa, Barclay Card and American Express.

ELECTRICITY   Electric outlets use currents of 110 volts, 60 cycles. For appliances made for other electrical systems, you need a transformer or other adapter.

WEIGHTS AND MEASURES   The United States uses the English system of weights and measures. American units and their metric equivalents are: 1 inch = 2.5 centimeters; 1 foot (12 inches) = 0.3 meter; 1 yard (3 feet) = 0.9 meter; 1 mile (5280 feet) = 1.6 kilometers; 1 ounce = 28 grams; 1 pound (16 ounces) = 0.45 kilogram; 1 quart (liquid) = 0.9 liter.

TWO

The Arizona Landscape

Geology

Arizona's geology can be summed up in one word—diverse. Its treasures include everything from spectacular canyons to high mountain peaks, from arid deserts to lush forests, from sparse volcanic fields to abundant alpine meadows.

Arizona's riches lie not only in grand overviews, but also in a myriad of unique details. Dinosaur tracks. Petrified wood. Pure white gypsum sand dunes. Huge underground caverns. Salt domes, arches, natural bridges, hoodoos and goblins fancifully shaped by water and weather.

Some of the state's greatest assets are its mountains, creatively dubbed "sky islands" by biologists. Humphrey's Peak, part of the San Francisco Peaks north of Flagstaff, soars up 12,670 feet to make it the highest point in Arizona. Other high mountain ranges are the White Mountains in the east, and the Santa Catalina and Santa Rita mountains around Tucson.

While the grandeur of Arizona's mountains are hard to miss, its desert beauty is much more subtle. It's a rugged, prickly area that welcomes with wide open vistas, cactus blooms and a profusion of texture and color.

Four deserts sprawl across Arizona. The grandaddy of them all is the Sonoran Desert, which gets more rain than any other desert in North America. Residents of Phoenix and Tucson call it home, as do more than 300 species of birds. The Chihuahuan Desert occupies just a fraction of land in southeastern Arizona, but offers some unusual geological features. One is Texas Canyon, a mountain range made of giant boulders. Another is the Willcox Playa, where what at first appears to be a lake proves instead to be a mirage—an empty, 50-mile-wide basin of glimmering sand. The Mohave Desert in northwestern Arizona is a dry, stark region of sand dunes, but man-made Lake Havasu lends some refreshing contrast. Finally, there's the Great Basin Desert in the Colorado Plateau, a majestic land of mesas, buttes, spires, cliffs and canyons.

Of course, Arizona's most famous geological formation is the Grand Canyon, sculpted by nature over the last five million years. Geological shifting slowly lifted the plateau up to higher elevations as the rushing waters of the Colorado River sliced it in half. The dark rocks at river level, which contain no fossils, are some of the oldest matter on the face of the earth. The different layers of color and texture seen in the cliffs attest to times when the area was sea floor, forest and swamp. Tiny fossilized sea creatures from the Paleozoic era, long before dinosaurs, trace the development of some of the first life on the planet up through strata of shale, limestone and sandstone.

A lesser known, miniature version of the Grand Canyon also inspires awe—Salt River Canyon in eastern Arizona. Spectacular views await at every corner as you drive down Route 60 between Show Low and Globe. At the Salt Banks, where a series of salt springs deposited travertine formations, visitors find colorful minerals and algae, as well as petroglyphs dating from the 13th century.

You can also trace the past with a visit to the Petrified Forest National Park, which includes the Painted Desert. The barren hills here contain a fossil record of life as far back as 225 million years ago, including fish, reptiles and amphibians. The petrified trees were created over time as minerals replaced the wood cells. The surrounding hills, mainly devoid of vegetation, have been called the Painted Desert because the sun reflects the iron, manganese and other minerals contained in the rocks, tinting them with shades of red, gray, white and orange.

South of the Petrified Forest, you'll come eventually to the Mogollon Rim, which slices across east-central Arizona like a sheer wall 200 miles long and up to 1500 feet high, dividing eastern Arizona into two halves—the mesalands to the north and the southern deserts.

Yet another unique feature of the Arizona landscape is Sunset Crater, a national monument in the San Francisco Volcanic Fields outside Flagstaff. The highlight here is a 1000-foot-tall volcanic cone that sprayed molten rock and ash when it first erupted in the winter of 1064–65. You can see the cinder and lava fields and climb nearby O'Leary Crater for a closer view. The fields of pumice gravel prevent vegetation from growing, but make hiking easy at the foot of these picture-perfect volcanic cones.

The geological features of Arizona are so spectacular that it is certainly possible to appreciate the various landscapes for their beauty

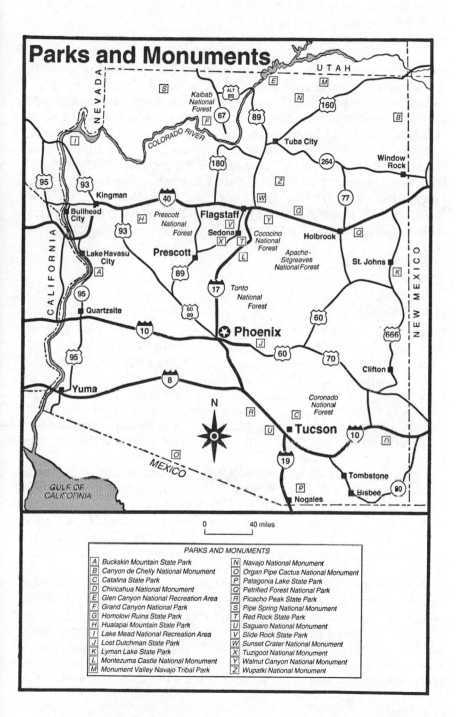

Parks and Monuments

PARKS AND MONUMENTS

A	Buckskin Mountain State Park	N	Navajo National Monument
B	Canyon de Chelly National Monument	O	Organ Pipe Cactus National Monument
C	Catalina State Park	P	Patagonia Lake State Park
D	Chiricahua National Monument	Q	Petrified Forest National Park
E	Glen Canyon National Recreation Area	R	Picacho Peak State Park
F	Grand Canyon National Park	S	Pipe Spring National Monument
G	Homolovi Ruins State Park	T	Red Rock State Park
H	Hualapai Mountain State Park	U	Saguaro National Monument
I	Lake Mead National Recreation Area	V	Slide Rock State Park
J	Lost Dutchman State Park	W	Sunset Crater National Monument
K	Lyman Lake State Park	X	Tuzigoot National Monument
L	Montezuma Castle National Monument	Y	Walnut Canyon National Monument
M	Monument Valley Navajo Tribal Park	Z	Wupatki National Monument

The cholla cactus prefers to grow in areas that were once stripped of vegetation, such as old Indian ruins.

without knowing how they were formed. But travelers who take a little time to learn about the region's geology by visiting the many natural history museums and park visitor centers along the way develop a different perspective. A closer look lets a visitor see how the many different colors and kinds of surface rock connect in a wonderfully complex formation hundreds of miles across. For example, Kaibab limestone (the 250,000,000-year-old, 300-foot-thick, grayish-white layer along the top rim of the Grand Canyon) is also visible at Lee's Ferry, a half-day's drive to the east. By stopping to explore the panorama in three dimensions, not just two, you'll gain a greater appreciation of the geological wonders that form the Arizona landscape.

Flora

Different kinds of plants thrive within Arizona's wide range of altitudes. Arid deserts below 4500 feet stretch over about a third of the state, including Phoenix and Tucson. This is home for saguaro, mesquite and paloverde trees, prickly pear, cholla and barrel cactus and creosote bushes. Climb from 4500 to 6500 feet, and tall grasses, agave plants, evergreen shrubs, oak, piñon and juniper trees will appear. This zone lies in central Arizona and a few other areas scattered throughout the state. In the fragrant ponderosa pine forests found at the 7000- to 9000-foot-level, mainly in northern Arizona and near Payson, pine trees grow up to 125 feet high.

And from the 7500- to 10,000-foot-level, Douglas and white fir and quaking aspen create thick forests. In some areas, accessible only by hiking trails, fir trees stand that are 100 feet tall and bigger around than a man's reach. This zone includes the Kaibab Plateau of the Grand Canyon North Rim, the San Francisco Peaks, the White Mountains and other high peaks. From desert cacti to mountaintop aspens, studying the flora of Arizona can be endlessly fascinating.

Built in the 1920s as an educational facility, **Boyce Thompson Southwestern Arboretum** (Route 60 near Superior; 602-689-2811; admission) with its large cactus gardens is a good place to study desert plants. A creek and pond area showcases plants that need more water, but the arboretum generally features drought-tolerant plants. Don't miss the boojum trees from Baja California with their thick trunks and sparse leaves, or a stop at the visitor center, a building on the National

Register of Historic Places. There are also potted plants for sale if you want to take a bit of Arizona with you.

One downright odd-looking plant is the elephant tree. Its massive, contorted papery trunk most closely resembles the roots of a tree turned upside down.

One of the oldest living things on earth makes its home in the Arizona desert—the creosote bush. These humble shrubs have been around for about 11,000 years, which makes the 500-year life span of the Joshua tree look like nothing. And then there's the organ pipe cactus and the saguaro. They may not live as long as the creosote, but they're so rare and interesting that whole monuments have been set up for them—the Organ Pipe Cactus National Monument and Saguaro National Monument.

The most famous of Arizona's plants is the saguaro, the giant, multi-armed cactus that poses for thousands of tourist snapshots and travels through the mail on slick postcards. The saguaro is found in the Sonoran Desert, the most diverse of Arizona's four deserts. In part, this is because the Sonoran averages seven-and-a-half to ten inches of rain annually, a lot of rain for the desert, and there is rarely a hard freeze. The saguaro reaches a ripe old age of 75 before even sprouting its arms. Most are pockmarked with holes. These are not decay; they're natural houses. The Gila woodpecker drills holes in mature saguaro trunks in order to nest in a cool, humid environment safe from predators. After they leave this "house," other species move in, anything from owls to purple martins. And the saguaro continues to give by providing nectar for bats via its white flowers.

There is a fascinating biological association between the yucca plant and the tiny yucca moth. Each is completely dependent on the other

---

HOW TREES TURN TO STONE

There are two explanations of how the trees in the Petrified Forest National Park turned to stone—one colorful, one scientific. The more riveting explanation is the Indian legend. They say that a goddess came into the area hungry and tired. She killed a rabbit and tried to make a fire to cook it, but the logs were wet and would not burn. Angrily, she put a curse on the area, turning the logs to stone.

The scientific explanation is that the forest was formed about 170 million years ago while part of a large valley. Over time, the valley filled with sediment, until large trees floated into the lowlands and were buried 3000 feet below the earth's surface. Before the trees could decay, water rich with silica, iron, manganese, copper and other minerals seeped into the trees, eventually turning them into "stone."

Once every seven years in the fall, piñon trees produce pine nuts, which many consider a delicacy.

to perpetuate its species. The female moths collect pollen from yucca flowers, fly to other yucca blossoms, then lay their eggs and deposit fertilizing pollen. Some of the plant's seeds become food for the moth larvae, while others mature and reproduce. The new larvae fall to the ground, burrow into it and remain there until spring when they become moths and repeat the cycle.

When spring rains come, which may be only once every few years, the desert bursts forth for a few weeks with a fantastic display of wildflowers. But there can be a downside to desert flora, as well. Many of the desert's plants have a special thorny sting for those who dare to touch them. In addition, it is against the law to destroy or even collect most desert plants and cacti. As one Phoenix man found out, it's not worth the trouble to harass a cactus—after he fired a gun at it, the saguaro cactus toppled and killed him.

Instead, it's better just to enjoy from a distance the beauty of the desert's botanical offerings, especially in spring when they're in bloom. Some of the more colorful you're likely to see are the yellow flowers of the brittlebush, the yellow to orange Mexican poppy, the blue desert lupines that dot roadsides and hills, and the brilliant orange blooms on the whiplike stems of the ocotillo. If you're lucky enough to arrive at the right time, you'll find this wildly colorful mix a truly memorable sight.

Fauna

Many animals of western legend still roam free in the forests and canyons of Arizona. Mountain lions, rarely seen because they inhabit remote areas and hunt in the dark, sometimes flash past late-night drivers' headlight beams. Black bears live deep in the mountains—in times of drought, when food is short, they may stray into towns to raid trash cans.

Coyotes, the most commonly seen southwestern predators, have been dubbed "urban coyotes" by wildlife management officials because of their adaptability to the urban landscape. They will eat almost anything, often feasting on rodents, rabbits, garbage can leftovers or, to the owner's dismay, household pets. Intelligence is another of their attributes; they'll look both ways before safely crossing busy highways. Even if you don't see them, it's not uncommon to hear their high-pitched yipping and howling on a desert night or at dawn.

Often found foraging in groups, the javelina is another common Arizona animal. It resembles a pig with its oversized head, short, muscular legs and canine teeth.

Some of the strangest animals are spadefoot toads, who spend most of their life alone in a sealed burrow three feet under the ground. When the ground shakes from thunder during summer storms, they come to the surface to feed and mate.

It's a stunning sight to watch bighorn sheep leaping and climbing on the rocky ranges that jut up from low desert plains. A ram usually weighs in at anywhere from 250 to 300 pounds, with a stocky body and massive, curved horns. They eat thistles, grasses and flowers, and even open barrel cacti with their horns to get to the succulent pulp.

One of the most distinctive regional birds is the magpie, an exotic-looking, long-tailed, iridescent, cousin of Asian mynah birds. Another is the roadrunner, with its bristle-tipped topknot and long tail. Named because of their penchant for sprinting along roadways, you'll see them out dodging cars while hunting for lizards.

Large birds often seen by motorists or hikers include turkey vultures, ravens and many different kinds of hawks. Both golden and bald eagles live throughout Arizona and are occasionally spotted soaring in the distance. Eagles and vultures are about the same size, and the easiest way to tell them apart is to remember that eagles glide with their wings horizontal, while vultures' wings sweep upward in a V-shape.

Dozens of hummingbird species fly from Mexico to southwestern Arizona for the summer, while Canadian geese and other northern waterfowl warm up for the winter on rivers and lakes in the desert area.

Many visitors come to Arizona with some trepidation about the area's less attractive species. Sharing the land with humans are 11 species of rattlesnakes, 30 species of scorpions, 30 kinds of tarantulas, as well as Gila monsters with their black and yellow bead-like skin. But these creatures would rather retreat than attack, and even people who live in Arizona rarely see them. Just remember to walk loudly and don't put your hand or foot where you can't see it—like most insects and mammals, these creatures would be just as happy without an introduction.

WHISKER CACTUS AND ORGAN PIPE FRUIT

The senita cactus is found only in Organ Pipe National Monument. Similar to the organ pipe cactus, the senita is called "whisker cactus" because of its long gray hair-like spines. Both it and the organ pipe cactus are night blooming, with flowers closing soon after sunrise. The fruit of the organ pipe cactus was harvested by the Papago Indians.

THREE

Arizona's History

Native Americans

At one time, nearly 25,000 Indians were the exclusive residents of what is now Arizona. The earliest were the Hohokam, who thrived from 30 A.D. until about 1450 A.D. Signs of their settlements remain intact to this day. Two other major tribal groups followed: the Anasazi (a Navajo word meaning ancient ones) in the state's northern plateau highlands, and the Mogollon People, in the northeastern and eastern mountain belt.

Their hunting/gathering lifestyle changed around 300 B.C., partly because of droughts that drove the antelope and mammoths away. People began cultivating food and shifting their focus to farming. Freed from having to constantly search for food, they developed complex societies and built large pueblos on mesas, in valleys and in the steep cliff walls of canyons.

By 200 A.D., the Anasazi began living in Canyon de Chelly, building spectacular cliff dwellings and living in harmony with nature. Remains of their works can be seen at Keet Seel and Betatakin at Navajo National Monument, and in ruins in Canyon de Chelly. These ruins reveal the dark, tiny, claustrophobic rooms that served as home, but afforded no luxuries. Possibly because of drought, the cliff dwellings were abandoned by 1300.

During this time, the Sinagua culture was developing northeast of what is now Flagstaff and farther south in the Verde River Valley. Settling in arid regions, they were named Sinagua, or "without water" in Spanish. Remnants of the Sinagua stone pueblos remain in Tuzigoot

The Hopi people have stayed on their remote desert mesa-tops a very long time. Some structures standing today have been used by the same families for 900 years.

and Wupatki national monuments, and their cliff dwellings are at Walnut Canyon and Montezuma Castle.

By 450 A.D., the Hohokam culture had begun to farm the Gila and Salt River valleys between Phoenix and Casa Grande. Eventually, they spread out across a third of the state and built an impressive 600-mile network of irrigation canals, planting corn, beans and squash. They vanished by 1450. Although few of the Hohokam dwellings remain, one prime example is the four-story-high pueblo at the Casa Grande Ruins National Monument about 20 miles east of Casa Grande.

The Pima, desert farmers who next occupied this region, were the ones who named their predecessors Hohokam, meaning "all used up." No one knows the real reason the Hohokam disappeared, but possible explanations have included a long drought, disease and the arrival of more aggressive tribes.

Some 600 years ago, during the century just before Columbus' ships reached American shores, a new group of people arrived in the region. They were Athabascans, nomads from the far north (from an area that is now Canada) who had gradually wandered down the front range of the Rocky Mountains in small groups. They were to become the Apache and Navajo, warlike hunters who eventually settled down as farmers—but only after another kind of stranger had come to change the character of the Southwest forever.

Spanish

In the mid-1500s, the Spaniards were the first Europeans to explore what is now Arizona. Lured by a Moorish legend about treasures in the Seven Cities of Cibola, the viceroy of New Spain sent explorers from Mexico City to search for the riches. Upon seeing pueblos glittering in the sun, the explorers returned home and reported their finding of a golden city. Francisco Vasquez de Coronado arrived a year later with great hopes, but discovered with disappointment that the "glitter" was only mica embedded in the adobe walls.

The conquistadors were looking not only for gold, but seeking souls to save. They found more souls than gold and in the process introduced the native peoples to cattle, horse raising and new farming methods, augmenting their crops of beans, squash and maize with new grains, fruits and vegetables. The Franciscans made forays into the area in the

1670s, founding missions among the Hopi and converting many of them to Christianity. In 1687, Jesuit priest Eusebio Francisco Kino began establishing missions in Arizona. He taught the Native Americans European farming techniques, planted fruit trees and gave them animals to raise. Kino visited the Pima village of Tumacacori in 1691, and in 1700 laid the foundation for the church at Mission of San Xavier del Bac.

Although the Spaniards brought some positive improvements, there was also a downside. The Spanish imported European diseases such as measles and smallpox and invaded Indian territory. As a result, the Native Americans staged several battles, including the violent revolt of

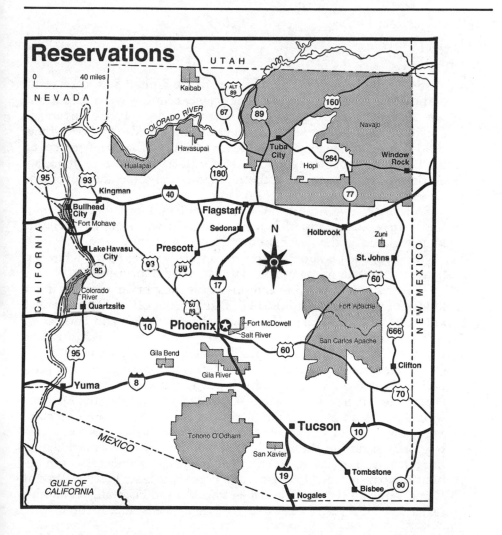

Coronado and his followers were the first Europeans to visit the Hopi mesas and the Grand Canyon.

1680. And in 1751, the normally peaceful Pima people rebelled, killing more than a hundred Spaniards, while the Apache continued their hit-and-run raids and ambushes on both the Spaniards and the Pima.

In response, the Spanish government built a presidio at Tubac. But after Mexico won its independence from Spain in 1821 and Spanish soldiers were withdrawn, the Indians again attacked. Settlers finally moved to the safety of walled cities such as Tucson.

Statehood

In 1848, most of Arizona became part of the United States as a result of the Mexican-American war. The only exceptions were Tucson and part of southern Arizona. This was soon to change. Having this area in Mexican hands became inconvenient during California's Forty-niner Gold Rush—the route to the gold went through what was Mexico. So the U.S. government negotiated the Gadsden Purchase in 1853, acquiring the remainder of southern Arizona and some additional land for a mere 10 million dollars.

Still, the Native Americans were a problem. Until about the mid-1860s, they accepted the few white miners, traders and farmers who came west, but as the number of settlers grew, friction arose and fighting resulted. The Navajo and Apache especially resented the white settlers. In the minds of many, a final solution had to be found.

The cavalry was called in and one of the most brutal chapters in the history of the Southwest followed. Black troops of the Tenth Cavalry, known as Buffalo Soldiers because of their dark skin and curly black hair, came in large numbers to protect settlers of the Arizona land where Geronimo, Cochise, Mangus, Alchise and other chieftains had dotted the terrain with the graves of thousands of emigrants and prospectors. Numerous sites still exist throughout the state that bring those days of conflict into vivid focus—Cochise Stronghold in the Dragoon Mountains south of Willcox, hideout of the notorious Apache chief; Fort Bowie National Historic Site, an adobe ruin that was a key military outpost during the Indian wars, and nearby Fort Huachuca, an important territorial outpost that's still in operation today as a communications base for the U.S. Army; and Fort Verde State Historic Park, in Camp Verde on Route 17 between Phoenix and Flagstaff, yet another military base that played a key role in subduing the Apache in the 1870s.

In 1864, under the leadership of Colonel Kit Carson, the Navajo were forced to surrender and were shipped to an internment camp in New Mexico. Although they returned to Arizona within five years, the Navajo were required to live on reservations. The longest and most violent army campaign against the Native Americans was the Apache Wars. Though never numerous, the Apache were so fierce and elusive that the wars lasted for 19 bloody years. The Apache fell when leader Cochise died in the Chiricahua Mountains and Geronimo was forced to surrender in 1886. Only then could settlers from the United States establish the first towns in Arizona.

During the 1860s and 1870s, the Arizona Territory was symbolic of the Wild West. Saloons did a bang-up business, literally, as shootouts and boisterous behavior were common events. Outlaws who were caught and tried were sent to Yuma, known for its strict Territorial Prison.

Soon the territorial sources of income began to shift toward grazing, farming and mining. Cattlemen established herds in the high desert grasslands of southeastern Arizona and the meadows of north central Arizona. But they created a modern environmental disaster. In 1870, about 5000 cattle grazed in Arizona; by 1891, this number had jumped to 1.5 million. The land simply could not support them. About 50 to 75 percent of the cattle died in the drought of 1892 and 1893. By the time the rains returned, thousands of square miles had been destroyed by hungry cows. The grasslands disappeared forever, replaced by raw desert.

Around this time, Mormons came to colonize farmlands, convert Indians and find refuges isolated enough to discourage the government from harassing the polygamists among them. They settled along the Little Colorado River and in Mesa, leaving behind a legacy of fertile farmland and top public schools.

BIRTH OF THE NAVAJO NATION

The Pueblo Revolt created the Navajo nation. To persuade their Athabascan neighbors to help chase away the Spanish, the Pueblo leaders agreed that the Athabascans could keep the livestock driven off from ranches they attacked. In that way, the tribe came to own sheep and horses, which would profoundly change their culture. When the Spanish colonists returned, many Pueblo people who had participated in the revolt fled to avoid retaliation and went to live with the nomads, bringing with them such advanced technologies as weaving cloth and growing corn. The Athabascan descendants who herded sheep and farmed became known as the Navajo people, while those who held to the old way of life came to be called Apache.

In 1857, a short-lived gold rush began, followed by silver. The most famous lode was discovered in 1877 by Ed Schieffelin, who found silver ore and named the first stake Tombstone. But in 1886, the mines flooded and Tombstone collapsed. The copper boom followed, transforming the territory from a frontier to a real cash economy. Since large investments were needed, much of the boom was financed by corporations back east. They brought with them their style of architecture; as a result, the boom towns of Jerome, Clifton, Globe and Bisbee still have picturesque Victorian homes perched on their hillsides. But it was the gold prospector who eventually became the very symbol of the Old West—an old man with a white beard, alone with his trusted burro, looking to strike it rich. You only have to go 30 miles east of Phoenix into the Superstition Mountains to find the lore and the legend and the lure of gold still very much alive today.

When the Civil War broke out, Arizona sided with the Confederacy. One reason was that citizens were mad at Congress for not making theirs a separate territory. In 1863, the area was declared the Arizona Territory. Over the following years, the capital jumped from the Prescott area to Tucson, and then finally Phoenix. On Valentine's Day in 1912, Arizona became the 48th state.

Modern Times

Arizona didn't boom in the years immediately after statehood and the reason was obvious—a lack of water. Providing water to the desert was quite a task. All that changed in 1911 when the Theodore Roosevelt Dam was completed on the Salt River. Not only did it curb the occasional river flooding, but it also provided irrigation water to Phoenix and the surrounding area. In 1936, the Hoover Dam was completed, forming Lake Mead, the largest man-made lake in North America. Once the water became plentiful, large-scale industry and agriculture followed.

THE LEGACY OF THE HOHOKAM

Inadvertently, it was the Native American's handiwork that led to the birth of Phoenix and lured more white men to the area. Upon discovering the Hohokam canals in 1867, a prospector named Jack Swilling realized that people could successfully farm the desert. He began dredging the prehistoric ditches, homesteading farmers arrived, and before long what is now the largest city in the state was flourishing.

The first English-speaking settlers in the region were Mormons, who chose to live free from persecution in the empty desert. Beginning in the 1840s, they established settlements throughout northern Arizona, often in places that are still remote today.

The economy was based on the three C's: cattle, cotton and copper. Copper mining boomed in the 1920s and 1930s and copper was really sought during WWII when it was used for military munitions. Towns that rose with the copper boom and died after the war include Jerome and Bisbee, which have had renaissances as artist communities.

During the postwar years, Arizona moved away from its agricultural economic base; today, electronics, aerospace engineering and other high-tech industries are large employers. In addition, the tourism industry is an important part of the Arizona economy, with people arriving daily to explore the natural and man-made attractions in the state. It has been a winter retreat for the wealthy since the 1920s with its warm climate and healthy, dry air that helped people suffering from allergies. Unfortunately, this is no longer the case. Today, imported plants irritate those with allergies and levels of smog during parts of the year have grown to alarmingly high levels.

As for the Native Americans, today there are 23 reservations in Arizona, more than any other state, with an estimated 50,000 people from 17 different tribes living in sad testimony to the white settlers' land grabs. The tribes speak 18 languages, and are spread across 31,000 square miles—about a quarter of Arizona. Some 150 miles east of Phoenix in the White Mountain region of eastern Arizona is the Fort Apache Reservation with a million and a half acres of land. Bordering it, with another two million acres, is the San Carlos Apache Reservation. The largest reservation in North America, Navajoland, home to 150,000 Navajo, begins 76 miles north of Flagstaff and extends into northwestern New Mexico and southeastern Utah. Located almost in the center of the Navajo Reservation is the Hopi Reservation, 6500 members strong, who have lived on the same site without interruption for more than 1000 years, retaining more of their ancient traditions and cultures than any other indigenous group.

The Spanish-Mexican influence is still strongly evident throughout the area. About 18 percent of the state's population is Hispanic, and that number is growing daily. The Hispanic culture permeates much of Arizona. Mexican restaurants are in almost every neighborhood, boasting thick enchiladas and mouthwatering burritos. Some are frequented by strolling mariachi bands, whose music goes back to a ribald Spanish song and dance form of the 18th century. Boisterous celebrations such as Cinco de Mayo liven up the cultural climate, and Hispanic artwork hangs in museums across the state. All this is just part of that unique cultural mix that is Arizona today.

GLENN KIM '92

The Grand Canyon

Awesome. Magnificent. Breathtaking. It's easy to slip into hyperbole
when trying to describe the Grand Canyon, but it's understandable.
No matter how many spectacular landscapes you've seen in your life-
time, none can compare with this mighty chasm stretching across the
northwest corner of Arizona.

The Grand Canyon comes as a surprise. Whether you approach the
South Rim or the North Rim, the landscape gives no hint that the
canyon is there until suddenly you find yourself on the rim looking
into the chasm ten miles wide from rim to rim and a mile down to the
Colorado River, winding silver through the canyon's inner depths.
From anywhere along the rim, you can feel the vast, silent emptiness
of the canyon and wonder at the sheer mass of the walls, striated into
layer upon colorful layer of sandstone, limestone and shale.

More than five million years ago, the Colorado River began carving
out this canyon that offers a panoramic look at the geologic history of
the Southwest. Sweeping away sandstones and sediments, limestones
and fossils, the river cut its way through Paleozoic and Precambrian
formations. By the time mankind arrived, the canyon extended nearly
all the way down to schist, a basement formation.

The Grand Canyon is aptly named—being, perhaps, the grandest
geological marvel of them all. It is as long as any mountain range in the
Rockies and as deep as the highest of the Rocky Mountains are tall.
For centuries, it posed the most formidable of all natural barriers to
travel in the West, and to this day no road has ever penetrated the
wilderness below the rim. No matter how many photographs you take,
paintings you make or postcards you buy, the view from anywhere

---

Ninety percent of the Grand Canyon's visitors make the South Rim their destination.

---

along the Grand Canyon rim can never be truly captured in two dimensions. Nor can the mind fully comprehend it; no matter how many times you have visited the Grand Canyon before, the view will always inspire the same awe as it did the first time you stood and gazed in wonder at the canyon's immensity and the silent grandeur of its massive cliffs.

The Grand Canyon extends east to west for some 277 miles, from the western boundary of the Navajo Indian Reservation to the vicinity of Lake Mead and the Nevada border. Only the highest section of each rim of the Grand Canyon is accessible by motor vehicle. Most of Grand Canyon National Park, both above and below the rim, is a designated wilderness area that can only be explored on foot or by river raft.

The South Rim and the North Rim of the Grand Canyon are essentially separate destinations, more than 200 miles apart by road. This chapter covers the developed national park areas on both rims. For the adventuresome, we've also included hiking possibilities in the canyon, as well as two lesser-known areas of the Grand Canyon that are challenging to reach—Toroweap Point in the Arizona Strip on the North Rim and the scenic area below the Indian village of Supai on the South Rim.

With more than four million visitors a year, the Grand Canyon is one of the most popular national parks in the United States. While many come to enjoy the panoramic vistas, others come to tackle the most challenging hiking trails in the country or to explore the narrow canyons and gorges by pack mule. Whatever reason you choose to visit the Grand Canyon, it will be worth it.

The South Rim

The **South Rim** of the Grand Canyon is the busy part of the park. From **Grand Canyon Village**, the large concession complex where the hotels, restaurants and stores are located on the rim near the south entrance, two paved rim drives run in opposite directions. The **East Rim Drive** goes 25 miles east to the national park's east entrance, which is the entrance you will use if you are driving in from the North Rim, Lake Powell or the Navajo Reservation. The first point of interest you come to after entering the park on East Rim Drive is the **Desert View Watchtower**, built in the 1930s as a replica of an an-

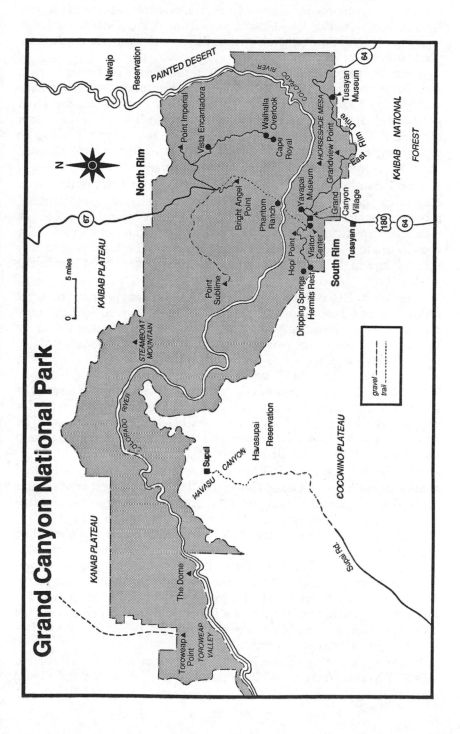

Grand Canyon National Park

cient Hopi watchtower. It offers the first panoramic view of the Grand Canyon. As you proceed along East Rim Drive toward Grand Canyon Village, other **overlooks**—Lipan Point, Zuni Point, Grandview Point, Yaki Point—will beckon, each with a different perspective on the canyon's immensity.

There are two interesting museums along East Rim Drive to visit. The **Tusayan Museum** (602-638-2305), 23 miles east of Grand Canyon Village near the park's east entrance, has exhibits on the Hopi people and their Anasazi ancestors who used to live along the rim of the Grand Canyon. In the Hopi belief system, the canyon is said to be the *sipapu*, the hole through which the earth's first people climbed from the mountaintop of their previous world into our present one.

The **Yavapai Museum** (602-638-7890), about half a mile east of the visitor center, offers detailed information on the canyon's geology, showing the ages and compositions of the many colorful layers of rock that make up its walls. You'll also find explanations of how and why the Colorado River could have formed the canyon by slicing its way through the highest plateau in the area instead of simply meandering around it.

The **West Rim Drive**, which follows the canyon rim for eight miles west of Grand Canyon Village, is closed to private vehicles during the summer months. Visitors see it by free park shuttle bus or by bicycle. The drive runs past the **Powell Memorial** honoring Major John Wesley Powell, the one-armed adventurer who first surveyed the Grand Canyon for the U.S. government in 1869—in a wooden boat. The road clings to the rim of the canyon as it takes you to a series of overlooks, each more spectacular than the last. **Pima Point**, in particular, offers what is probably the best of all Grand Canyon views. The drive ends at a place called **Hermit's Rest**, a former tourist camp where you'll find a snack bar and a hikers' trailhead.

The **Grand Canyon Visitor Center** (602-638-7888) is located about one mile east of Grand Canyon Village. We suggest leaving your car in the village and walking to the visitor center on the paved, magnificently scenic Rim Trail (or, if you're not spending the night at park lodgings, parking at the visitor center and walking to the village). The most interesting exhibit in the visitor center is the display in the outdoor central plaza of boats that have been used to explore the Grand Canyon by river. A burned fragment is all that remains of one of the original wooden boats used by Major Powell in 1869. Other wooden boats are of more recent vintage. There is also one of the original inflatable river rafts used by the woman who in 1955 invented whitewater rafting as we know it today.

Just outside the park's south entrance, the town of Tusayan has an **IMAX Theatre** (602-638-2203) that shows films about the Grand

Canyon on a seven-story, 82-foot-wide wraparound screen with six-track Dolby sound. **The Over the Edge Theatre** (Grand Canyon Village; 602-526-4575) also features Grand Canyon films. Why one should wish to watch a movie when the real thing is just a few minutes away is not immediately apparent, but in fact these two theaters add an extra dimension to the Grand Canyon experience by presenting river-rafting footage, aerial photography and close-up looks at places in the canyon that are hard to get to.

For the more intrepid adventurer, an intriguing Grand Canyon experience that is only accessible by foot is found far downriver near the west end of the canyon. The **Havasu Canyon Trail** (16 miles), entirely within the Havasupai Indian Reservation, is reached by leaving the interstate at Seligman (westbound) or Kingman (eastbound) and driving to the Supai turnoff near Peach Springs. From there, the Supai Road goes for 62 miles before the pavement ends. In another 11 miles, the road dead-ends and a foot trail descends 2000 feet in eight miles to the Indian village of **Supai** where about 500 people live. All hikers must check in at tribal headquarters. From there, the main trail continues for about four more miles into Havasu Canyon, a side canyon from the Grand Canyon, which includes a series of three high waterfalls— 75-foot Navajo Falls, 100-foot Havasu Falls and 200-foot Mooney Falls— with large pools that are ideal for swimming. There is a campground near Mooney Falls, and from there the trail continues down to the Colorado River in the bottom of the Grand Canyon, while another trail forks over to Beaver Canyon, where there is another waterfall. Whether you plan to stay in the campground or the modern lodge at Supai, advance reservations are essential. For camping, write Havasupai Tourist Enterprise, Supai, AZ 86435 or call 602-448-2121. For lodging, see "South Rim Lodging" below.

RIDE THE CANYON BALL EXPRESS

*You can take a nostalgic trip into yesteryear on the **Grand Canyon Railway** (Route 40, Williams; 800-843-8724). A turn-of-the-century steam train leaves Williams in the morning for a two-and-a-half-hour trip through Coconino National Forest, tracing the route that brought early tourists to the national park, and arriving around noon at the historic 1908 Santa Fe Railroad depot in Grand Canyon Village. The return trip departs for Williams in the late afternoon. Trains run daily from June through September, with a more limited schedule the rest of the year.*

Accommodations in the Grand Canyon are in great demand, so if you're planning to stay, be sure to make reservations way in advance.

SOUTH RIM LODGING

When visiting the South Rim, you'll find a variety of lodging choices. The phone number for all South Rim accommodations is 602-638-2631. Reservations at any of them can be made up to 23 months in advance by writing **Grand Canyon National Park Lodges** (P.O. Box 699, Grand Canyon, AZ 86023; 602-638-2401).

Top of the line is the deluxe-priced **El Tovar Hotel**. Designed after European hunting lodges, El Tovar was built by the Fred Harvey Co., a subsidiary of the Santa Fe Railroad, in 1905, and some staff members still wear the traditional black-and-white uniforms of the famous "Harvey Girls" of that era. Sitting just 20 feet from the edge of the Grand Canyon's south rim, the hotel is the epitome of rough-hewn elegance, constructed from native boulders and fir logs. The lobby retains its original backwoods elegance, with a big fireplace, copper chandeliers, massive wood ceiling beams and dark-stained pine decor throughout. The rooms were renovated in the 1980s. All have full baths, color television and telephones. Some have direct views of the canyon, as does the "great hall" dining room, designed by architect Charles Whittlesey.

More affordable historic lodging is available nearby at the **Bright Angel Lodge**. The main log-and-stone lodge was built in 1935 on the site of Bright Angel Camp, the first tourist facility in the park. Its lobby features Indian motifs and a huge fireplace. Rooms are clean but modest; most have televisions and phones. Besides rooms in the main building, the lodge also rents several historic cabins on the canyon rim, some with fireplaces. Budget to moderate.

Also in Grand Canyon Village, on the rim between El Tovar and Bright Angel Lodge, are the modern twin stone lodges, **Thunderbird Lodge** and **Kachina Lodge**. Located on the rim trail, these caravansaries are within easy walking distance of the restaurants at the older lodges. Rooms are moderate. All have televisions and phones.

The largest lodging facility in the park, **Yavapai Lodge** is situated in a wooded setting about a half-mile from the canyon rim, near the park store, across the road from the visitor center and about a mile from Grand Canyon Village. Rates are moderate and the contemporary rooms are equivalent in quality to what you would expect for the same price at a national chain motor inn.

The newest option is **Maswik Lodge**, set away from the canyon rim at the southwest end of Grand Canyon Village. Maswik Lodge presents a variety of motel-style room choices as well as cabins, with budget-to-moderate rates. About half the rooms have televisions.

An elegant modern-rustic building with the look of a ski lodge and a lobby with multistory picture windows, **Moqui Lodge** is managed as part of the national park lodge system although it is located in Kaibab National Forest just outside the park entrance. Moderate.

Just outside the South Rim entrance gate, the community of Tusayan has several motels and motor inns that are not affiliated with the national park. Rates are in the moderate range at all of them. If you cannot get reservations at one of the national park lodges, try one of the typical chain motels such as the **Red Feather Lodge** (602-638-2414); the **Grand Canyon Squire Inn** (602-638-2681); or the **Quality Inn Grand Canyon** (602-638-2673).

Located in a remote red rock canyon on the Supai Reservation, the 24 carpeted motel-style units at **Havasupai Lodge** (Supai; 602-448-2111) is a hidden destination. There's a café next door, swimming in the nearby creek and a convenient barbecue pit. Just two miles away are Navajo, Havasu and Mooney falls. You can also enjoy Native American-led horseback and hiking tours of this scenic region.

SOUTH RIM RESTAURANTS

The South Rim offers a number of restaurant options. The most elegant is **El Tovar Dining Room** (602-638-6292). Entrées such as filet mignon with crab legs béarnaise are served on fine china by candlelight. Prices are in the deluxe range, the ambience is classy, but casual dress is perfectly acceptable.

More informal surroundings and moderate prices are to be found at the **Bright Angel Restaurant** in the Bright Angel Lodge. Menu selections include chicken piccata, grilled rainbow trout and fajitas. Cocktails and wine are available. Adjoining the Bright Angel Lodge, the **Arizona Steakhouse** specializes in steaks and seafood and has a good, large salad bar. The open kitchen lets you watch the chefs cook while you eat. Moderate. The phone number for these and all other South Rim Grand Canyon restaurants is 602-638-2631.

In the Yavapai Lodge, across the highway from the visitor center, the **Yavapai Grill** serves fast food—burgers and fries, hot dogs, chicken nuggets—while the **Yavapai Cafeteria** offers a changing selection of breakfast, lunch and dinner items. Both are in the budget range. Nearby in the general store, **Babbitt's Delicatessen** features sandwiches, salads and fried chicken box lunches to go or eat on the premises.

There are two other cafeterias in the park—the **Maswik Cafeteria** at Maswik Lodge, at the west end of Grand Canyon Village, and the **Desert View Trading Post Cafeteria**, 23 miles east of the village along the East Rim Drive. Both serve a changing selection of hot meals. Ice cream, hot dogs and soft drinks are available at the **Hermit's Rest Snack Bar** at the end of the West Rim Drive, as well as at the **Bright Angel Fountain** near the trailhead for the Bright Angel Trail. All are budget.

Outside the park entrance, the town of Tusayan has a dozen eating establishments ranging from McDonald's to the beautiful, moderately priced **Moqui Lodge Dining Room** (602-638-2424), which specializes in Mexican food. One of the best dining bets in the area is the **Moqui Lodge Cowboy Cookout** (same phone), where a chuckwagon-style barbecue beef dinner is followed by a western music show nightly in the summer season.

SOUTH RIM SHOPPING

Of several national park concession tourist stores on the South Rim of the Grand Canyon, the best are **Hopi House** (602-638-2631), the large Indian pueblo replica across from El Tovar Hotel, and the adjacent **Verkamp's Curios** (602-638-2242). Both have been in continuous operation for almost a century and specialize in authentic Native American handicrafts, with high standards of quality and some genuinely old pieces.

Other Grand Canyon shops, at least as interesting for their historic architecture as their wares, include the old **Kolb Studio**, originally a 1904 photographic studio and now a bookstore, and the **Lookout Studio**, which has rock specimens and conventional curios. Both are in Grand Canyon Village. Other souvenir shops are the **Hermit's Rest Gift Shop** (at the end of West Rim Drive) and the **Desert View Watchtower** (East Rim Drive).

SOUTH RIM NIGHTLIFE

There is dancing nightly at the **Yavapai Lounge**, and **El Tovar Lounge** has a piano bar. In general, though, Grand Canyon National Park does not have much in the way of hot nightlife. We suggest taking in one of the ranger-produced slide shows presented in the amphitheater on either the South Rim or the North Rim, or simply sitting in the dark along the canyon rim and listening to the vast, deep silence.

The North Rim, snowed-in during the winter months, is only open mid-May through October, while the South Rim is open year-round.

The North Rim

The **North Rim** of the Grand Canyon receives only about one-tenth of the number of visitors the South Rim gets, partly because it is snowbound during the winter. The North Rim is 1200 feet higher in elevation than the South Rim. Because of its high elevation—up to 9300 feet in some areas—the North Rim is surrounded by an amply watered landscape of forests and meadows. White-barked aspen, ponderosa pine, blue spruce and Douglas fir create a diversity of habitats that makes the North Rim unique. So unique, in fact, that the Kaibab squirrel lives only in North Rim forests. On your walks, keep a sharp eye for this friendly creature with its charcoal gray body, white plume tail and kangaroo's face.

The North Rim does not have the long, heavily traveled scenic drives that the South Rim has. Perhaps this is why its visitors tend to stay longer and delve deeper into the park's environment: nearly double the number of North Rim visitors attend the park's interpretive programs than do South Rim visitors.

The main road into the park dead-ends at the **Grand Canyon Lodge: North Rim**, 12 miles from the park's boundary. With its forest-green roof, sandstone walls and ponderosa beams, the lodge blends readily with its surroundings, and makes a good starting point for exploring the area. An easy quarter-mile paved path begins at the lodge and leads to one of the most popular overlooks, **Bright Angel Point**. For more adventuresome hikers, the Widforss Trail winds for five miles along the lip of the plateau through scrubby oak, piñon pine, ponderosa pine and juniper to **Widforss Point**, where you can gaze at the thousands of vertical feet of red and iron-stained rock strata.

The only other paved road is **Cape Royal Road**, a 23-mile scenic drive through stately ponderosa pine forests that takes you to several of the national park's most beautiful **viewpoints**—Point Imperial, Vista Encantadora, Cape Royal and Walhalla Overlook, which was once the summer residence of the Anasazi people, believed to be the ancestors of the Hopi. Another road, unpaved and only passable in a high-clearance vehicle, runs 17 miles to Point Sublime. Other viewpoints on the North Rim are reached by foot trails. (Information on these can be found in the "Hiking" section at the end of the chapter.)

Extremely adventuresome motorists can visit a separate area along the North Rim of the Grand Canyon, **Toroweap Point**, by leaving

Correspondence mailed from Phantom Ranch is postmarked: "Mailed by Mule from the Bottom of the Canyon."

Route 89A at Fredonia, about 75 miles north of the North Rim entrance. Don't forget to fill up the gas tank in Fredonia, because you won't see another gas station for nearly 200 miles. Next, proceed west for 15 miles on Route 389 to **Pipe Spring National Monument** (602-643-7105). Take time to see the monument. The remote, fortress-like old Mormon ranching outpost, which had the only telegraph station in the Arizona Territory north of the Grand Canyon, was home to the Winsor family and their employees, thus its historical nickname, Winsor Castle. The ranch buildings and equipment are well-preserved, and the duck pond provides a cool oasis. Volunteers costumed in period dress re-create the pioneer lifestyle during the summer months.

From Pipe Spring, backtrack six miles to where an unpaved road turns off to the south. It goes 67 miles to the most remote point that can be reached by motor vehicle on the Grand Canyon rim. The road is wide and well-maintained, easily passable by passenger car, but very isolated. You will not find a telephone or any other sign of habitation anywhere along the way. In fact, you may not see another car all day. Several other dirt roads branch off along the way, but if you keep to the road that goes straight ahead and looks well-used, following the "Toroweap" and "Grand Canyon National Monument" signs whenever you see them, it's hard to get lost. Have fun experiencing this wide-open countryside that's still as empty as all of Arizona used to be long ago.

There is a small, primitive campground at Toroweap Point, but no water. As likely as not, you may find that you have the place all to yourself. The elevation is 2000 feet lower than at the main North Rim visitor area, so instead of pine forest, the vegetation around Toroweap Point is desert scrub. Being closer to the river, which is still some 3000 feet below, you can watch the parade of river rafts drifting past and even eavesdrop on passengers' conversations.

NORTH RIM LODGING

On the North Rim, the only lodging within the park is the **Grand Canyon Lodge: North Rim** (TW Recreational Services, P.O. Box 400, Cedar City, Utah 84721; 801-586-7686; 602-638-2611). The beautiful 1930s-vintage main lodge building overlooking the canyon uses native sandstone and ponderosa logs to blend with its rocky forested setting. The original structure burned down in 1928 and was rebuilt eight years later. The motel-style rooms are moderately priced.

There are also a number of cabins—some rustic, others modern, a few with canyon views. Clean and homelike, both rooms and cabins have an old-fashioned feel. About half the units have television sets, and a few have fireplaces. Rates vary from budget to moderate. North Rim accommodations are in very high demand, so reservations should be made far ahead. They are accepted up to 23 months in advance.

Aside from the national park lodge, the closest accommodations to the North Rim are 44 miles away at **Jacob Lake Lodge** (602-643-7232). This small, rustic resort complex surrounded by national forest offers both motel rooms and cabins, including some two-bedroom units, all priced in the budget range. Again, reservations should be made well in advance.

NORTH RIM RESTAURANTS

At the North Rim, the **Grand Canyon Lodge Dining Room** (602-638-2611) offers moderately priced breakfast, lunch and dinner selections. The food is good, conventional meat-and-potatoes fare and the atmosphere—a spacious, rustic log-beamed dining room with huge picture windows overlooking the canyon—is simply incomparable. Reservations are required for lunch and dinner. The lodge also operates a cafeteria serving budget-priced meals for breakfast, lunch and dinner in plain, simple surroundings.

PHANTOM RANCH

No survey of lodgings at the Grand Canyon would be complete without mentioning ***Phantom Ranch***. *Located at the bottom of the canyon, this 1922 lodge with cabins is at the lower end of the North Kaibab Trail from the North Rim and the Bright Angel and South Kaibab trails from the South Rim. It can only be reached by foot, mule or river raft. Cabins are normally reserved for guests on overnight mule trips, but hikers with plenty of advance notice can also arrange lodging. Prices, included in overnight mule trips, are in the moderate range. Bunk beds are available by reservation only in four budget-rate ten-person dormitories for hikers. There is no television at the ranch, and only one pay phone. There is outgoing mail service, however. Meals are served in a central dining hall, which becomes a beer hall after dinner. Do not arrive at Phantom Ranch without reservations! You can reserve space up to a year in advance by calling 602-638-2401 or by writing Grand Canyon National Park Lodges at the address listed under South Rim Lodging.*

The layers of rock exposed on the walls of the Grand Canyon by erosion range from 250 million to more than two billion years in age, the oldest exposed rock on earth.

NORTH RIM PARKS

The 1,500,000-acre **Kaibab National Forest** (602-635-2681), an expanse of pine, fir, spruce and aspen forest, includes both sides of the Grand Canyon outside the park boundaries. Most recreational facilities are near the North Rim, where they supplement the park's limited camping facilities. Wildlife in the forest includes mule deer, wild turkeys and even a few bison. The national forest visitor center is at Jacob Lake, located on Routes 89A at the Route 67 turnoff.

A nice spot for picnics and camping is at **Lee's Ferry, Glen Canyon National Recreation Area** (602-645-2471) halfway along the most direct route between the North Rim and South Rim. This beach area on the river below Glen Canyon Dam is situated at the confluence of the Colorado and Paria rivers, which often have distinctly different colors, giving the water a strange two-toned appearance. Historically, Lee's Ferry was the first crossing point on the Colorado River, established by John D. Lee in 1871. Lee, a Mormon, was a fugitive at the time, wanted by federal authorities for organizing the massacre of a non-Mormon wagon train from Arkansas. He lived here with one of his 17 wives for several years before federal marshals found and killed him. Today, Lee's Ferry is the departure point for raft trips into the Grand Canyon. It's located in Marble Canyon about two miles off Route 89A, 85 miles from the North Rim entrance and 104 miles from the east entrance to the South Rim.

Sporting Life

RIVER RAFTING

One Grand Canyon adventure that has become quite popular is river rafting. Raft trips operate from May through October. Most start at Lee's Ferry, northeast of the national park boundary near Page, Arizona, and just below Glen Canyon Dam. Rafting the full length of the canyon, 280 miles from Lee's Ferry to Lake Mead, takes eight days. Many rafting companies also offer shorter trips that involve being picked up or dropped off by helicopter part way through the canyon. Among the leading raft tour companies are **Grand Canyon Expeditions** (P.O. Box O, Kanab, Utah 84741; 801-644-2691); **Adventures West, Inc.**

(P.O. Box 9429, Phoenix, AZ 85068; 602-493-1558); **Arizona Raft Adventures** (4050 East Huntington Drive, Flagstaff, AZ 86004; 800-786-7237); **Wilderness River Adventures** (P.O. Box 717, Page, AZ; 800-992-8022); and **Arizona River Runners** (P.O. Box 47788, Phoenix, AZ 85068; 602-867-4866). A complete list of river trip outfitters is available from the South Rim visitor center (602-638-7888).

HORSEBACK RIDING

At the Grand Canyon, the **Moqui Lodge stable** (602-638-2891) in Tusayan, near the park's south entrance, offers a selection of guided rides to remote points along the South Rim. Most popular is the four-hour East Rim ride, which winds through Long Jim Canyon to a viewpoint overlooking the Grand Canyon. One- and two-hour rides are also available. Horseback rides do not go below the canyon rim, but for information on burro trips into the canyon, see "Tours" in the Transportation section at the end of this chapter.

BICYCLING

At the South Rim of the Grand Canyon, the **West Rim Drive** is closed to private motor vehicles during the summer months, but is open to bicycles. This fairly level route, 16 miles round-trip, makes for a spectacular cycling tour.

Although trails within the national park are closed to bicycles, **Kaibab National Forest** surrounding the Grand Canyon on both the North Rim and the South Rim offers a wealth of mountain biking possibilities. The forest areas adjoining the park are laced with old logging roads and the relatively flat terrain makes for low stress riding. One ride the National Forest Service recommends in the vicinity of the South Rim is the **Coconino Rim Trail**, which starts near Grandview Point and continues for more than ten miles north through ponderosa woods.

For other suggestions, stop in at the Tusayan Ranger Station just outside the South Rim entrance or the National Forest Information Booth at Jacob Lake or contact Kaibab National Forest Headquarter (800 South 6th Street, Williams, AZ 86046; 602-635-2681).

Toward the west end of the Grand Canyon on its North Rim, visitors to **Toroweap Point** will find endless mountain biking opportunities along the hundreds of miles of remote, unpaved roads in the Arizona Strip.

HIKING

The ultimate hiking experience in Grand Canyon National Park is an expedition from either rim to the bottom of the canyon and back. With an elevation change of 4800 feet from the South Rim to the river, or 5800 feet from the North Rim, the hike is as ambitious as scaling a Rocky Mountain Peak. Plan at least two, preferably three, days for the trip. An overnight wilderness permit is available free of charge at the visitor centers.

For an easy hike on the South Rim, the paved, handicapped-accessible **Rim Trail** (1.5 miles) goes between the Kolb Studio at the west side of Grand Canyon Village and the Yavapai Museum. A one-third-mile spur links the Rim Trail with the visitor center. At each end of the designated Rim Trail, the pavement ends but unofficial trails continue for several more miles, ending at Hopi Point near the Powell Memorial on West Rim Drive and at Yaki Point, the trailhead for the South Kaibab Trail, on East Rim Drive.

On the South Rim, **Bright Angel Trail** (7.8 miles to the river or 9.3 miles to Phantom Ranch) starts at Grand Canyon Village, near the mule corral. The most popular trail in the canyon (daily mule rides take this route), it has the most developed facilities, including resthouses, ranger station, emergency phones, water and a campground midway down at Indian Garden, where the Havasupai Indians used to grow crops. The shortest and steepest trail into the canyon is the **South Kaibab Trail** (6.4 miles to Phantom Ranch), which starts from the trailhead on East Rim Drive, four-and-a-half miles from Grand Canyon Village.

Several less-used trails descend from the South Rim, intersecting the **Tonto Trail** (92 miles), which runs along the edge of the inner gorge about 1300 feet above river level for the length of the Grand Canyon. The **Grandview Trail** (3 miles), an old mine access route that starts at Grandview Point on East Rim Drive, goes down to Horseshoe Mesa, where it joins a loop of the Tonto Trail that circles the mesa, passing ruins of an old copper mine. There is a primitive campground on the mesa. The **Hermit Trail** (8.5 miles) begins at Hermit's Rest at the end of West Rim Drive and descends to join the Tonto Trail. Branching off from the Dripping Springs Trail, which also starts at Hermit's Rest, the **Boucher Trail** (11 miles) also goes down to join the Tonto Trail and is considered one of the most difficult hiking trails in the park. Ask for details at the rangers' counter in the South Rim visitor center.

The main trail into the canyon from the North Rim is the **North Kaibab Trail** (14.2 miles), which starts two miles north of Grand Canyon Lodge and descends abruptly down Roaring Springs Canyon for almost five miles to Bright Angel Creek, where you'll find several swimming holes. The trail follows the creek all the way to Phantom Ranch at the bottom of the canyon. Allow a full day for the hike from the rim to the ranch, and two days back to the rim, stopping overnight at Cottonwood Camp, the midway point. Because of heavy snows on the rim, the trail is open only from mid-May through mid-October.

Without descending below the canyon rim, hikers can choose a variety of trails ranging from short scenic walks to all-day hikes. On the North Rim, the easy, paved, handicapped-accessible **Transept Trail** (2 miles) runs between the campground and the lodge, then continues gradually downward to Bright Angel Point. The **Uncle Jim Trail** (2.5 miles) starts at the same trailhead as the Roaring Springs Canyon fork of the Bright Angel Trail, two miles north of the lodge. The **Ken Patrick Trail** (10 miles) forks off the Uncle Jim Trail, continuing straight as the shorter trail turns south, and eventually reaches a remote point on the rim where it descends to follow Bright Angel Creek and eventually joins the Bright Angel Trail.

Visitors to remote Toroweap Point on the North Rim may wish to try the **Lava Falls Trail** (2 miles), which begins as a jeep road midway between the old ranger station and the point. Although the trail is not long, it is rocky, edgy and very steep, descending 2500 feet to the Colorado River and the "falls"—actually a furious stretch of white water formed when lava spilled into the river. Allow all day for the round-trip hike and do not attempt it during the hot months.

Transportation

BY CAR

The Grand Canyon's North Rim is at the end of **Route 67**, which forks off of **Route 89A** at the resort village of Jacob Lake. It is more than 150 miles from the nearest interstate highway—**Route 15**, taking exit 15 north of St. George, Utah—but is within an easy morning's drive of either Zion National Park or Bryce Canyon National Park or Lake Powell. The North Rim is about 250 miles east of Las Vegas and 320 miles north of Phoenix. The drive from the North Rim to the more populated South Rim is 215 miles around the east side of the canyon. Take Route 67, Route 89A, Route 89 and Route 64, crossing the Colorado River at Navajo Bridge. The only other alternative for driving from rim to rim is to go by way of Las Vegas—a trip of more than 500 miles.

From Route 40, eastbound motorists can reach Grand Canyon Village on the South Rim by exiting at Williams and driving 57 miles

For a breathtaking bird's-eye view of the Grand Canyon, take a helicopter or air-plane ride offered by any of the more than two dozen scenic-flight companies.

north on **Route 64** and **Route 180**. Westbound travelers, leaving the interstate at Flagstaff, have a choice between the more direct way to Grand Canyon Village, 79 mile via Route 180, or the longer way, 105 miles via Route 89 and Route 64, which parallels the canyon rim for 25 miles. These routes combine perfectly into a spectacular loop trip from Flagstaff.

BY AIR

Flights can be booked from most major cities to **Grand Canyon Airport**, which is located in Tusayan just outside the south entrance to the national park. America West, Air Nevada, Air Vegas, National Executive Airlines and Western Airlines service the area. A shuttle service runs hourly between the airport and Grand Canyon Village.

BY BUS

Nava-Hopi Tours (114 West Santa Fe Avenue, Flagstaff; 602-774-5003) provides bus service from Flagstaff to the Grand Canyon South Rim, as well as Sedona, Williams and Phoenix. **Trans Canyon Shuttle** (Grand Canyon; 602-638-2820) operates a daily shuttle bus service between the two rims.

CAR RENTALS

Rental cars available at the Grand Canyon Airport are **Budget Car Rental** (602-638-9360) and **Dollar Rent A Car** (602-638-2625).

TOURS

There are many ways to see the Grand Canyon, but the classic tour is by **mule train**. Trips range from one-day excursions as far as Plateau Point to two- and three-day trips to the bottom of the canyon, which cost several hundred dollars a person including meals and accommodations at Phantom Ranch. Mule trips depart from both the North Rim and the South Rim. Reservations must be made well ahead of time—as much as a year in advance for weekends, holidays and summer months. For South Rim departures, contact **Grand Canyon National Park**

Lodges (P.O. Box 699, Grand Canyon, AZ; 86023; 602-638-2631). For North Rim departures, contact **Grand Canyon Trail Rides** (P.O. Box 128, Tropic, UT 84776; in summer, 602-638-2292; the rest of the year, 602-679-8665).

Many **"flightseeing"** tours offer spectacular eagle's-eye views of the Grand Canyon. Air tour companies with flights from Las Vegas' McCarran Airport include **Adventure Airlines** (702-736-7511), **Las Vegas Airlines** (702-647-3056) and **Western Airlines** (702-891-0041). Tour flights from the Grand Canyon Airport near Tusayan are offered by **Grand Canyon Airlines** (P.O. Box 3038, Grand Canyon, AZ 86023; 602-638-2407), **Air Grand Canyon** (P.O. Box 3399, Grand Canyon, AZ 86023; 602-638-2686) and **Windrock Aviation** (P.O. Box 3125, Grand Canyon, AZ 86023; 602-638-9591).

Even more thrilling are the Grand Canyon helicopter tours offered by **Papillon Grand Canyon Helicopters** (P.O. Box 455, Grand Canyon, AZ 86023; 602-638-2419), **Kenai Helicopters** (P.O. Box 1429, Grand Canyon, AZ 86023; 602-638-2412) and **AirStar Helicopters** (Grand Canyon Airport; 602-638-2622).

FIVE

Northeastern Arizona

East of the Grand Canyon stretches a land of sandstone monuments   **59**
and steep-walled canyons that turns vermillion by dawn or dusk, a land
of foreign languages and ancient traditions, of sculptured mesas and
broad rocky plateaus, of pine forests and high deserts. This northeast
corner of Arizona is the heart of the Southwest's Indian Country.

This region is home to the Navajo, the biggest American Indian
tribe, and the Hopi, one of the most traditional. To them belongs the
top northeastern third of Arizona, 150 miles in length and 200 miles
across the state. Here, by horseback or jeep, on foot or in cars, visitors
can explore the stark beauty of the land, delve into its centuries of
history, then dine on mutton stew and crispy blue-corn *piki* bread. You
can watch dances little changed in generations or shop for a stunning
array of crafts in Native American homes, galleries and trading posts
dating back to the end of the Civil War. And here, in the pit houses,
pueblos and cliff dwellings of people who have occupied this land for
12,000 years, you'll find more remnants of prehistoric Native American life than anywhere else in the United States.

Five generations of archaeologists have sifted through ruins left by
the region's dominant prehistoric culture, the Anasazi—Navajo for
"ancient ones." None are more beautiful or haunting than Betatakin
and Keet Seel at Navajo National Monument, 45 miles due north of
today's Hopi mesas.

Hopi traditions today offer many insights into life in those ancient
cities. Traditional and independent, most villages are run by their religious
chiefs. Each maintains an ancient, complex, year-long dance cycle tied
to the renewal and fertility of the land they regard with reverence. As

After California and Oklahoma, Arizona has the third-largest Native American population among the states.

one Hopi leader put it, the land is "the Hopi's social security." Their multistoried architecture, much of it set within the protection of caves, has influenced many 20th-century architects.

Surrounding the Hopi is Navajoland, the largest Indian reservation in the United States. At 26,000 square miles, it is twice the size of Israel. Unlike the village-dwelling Hopi, most of the 150,000 Navajo still live in far-flung family compounds—a house, a hogan, a trailer or two, near their corrals and fields. Some clans still follow their livestock to suitable grazing lands as seasons change.

This is both an arid, sun-baked desert and verdant forested land, all of it situated on the southeastern quarter of the Colorado Plateau. At elevations of 4500 to 8000 feet above sea level, summer temperatures average in the 80s. July through September is monsoon season, when clear skies suddenly fill with clouds that turn a thunderous lightning-streaked black. These localized, brief, intense summer rains bearing wondrous smells have been courted by Hopi rituals for centuries and are crucial to the survival of their farms.

The Colorado Plateau is famous for its rainbow-colored canyons and monuments cut by rivers and eroded by weather. Erosion's jewels are Monument Valley on the Arizona-Utah border, a stunning pocket of towering red spires, bluffs and sand dunes, and Canyon de Chelly, a trio of red-rock canyons at the heart of Navajo country.

At Navajoland's southernmost boundary, the world's densest, most colorful petrified logs dot Petrified Forest National Park. They're located amid bare hills that look like they were spray painted by a giant artist and are aptly named the Painted Desert.

This mesmerizing geography serves as a backdrop to the region's riveting history. The Navajo probably began arriving from the north in small groups as nomadic hunters rode in from the south in the 1540s a century or two before the Spaniards. The conquistadors brought horses, sheep, peaches, melons, guns and silversmithing—all of which would dramatically change the lives of the indigenous Indians.

Cultural anthropologists now believe the turning point in Navajo history followed the Pueblo Indian Revolt of 1680 when all the village-dwelling Indians of the Southwest united to push the oppresive Spanish out of what is now New Mexico. When the Spaniards returned a dozen years later, heavily armed and promising slavery for unyielding villagers, many Pueblo people from the Rio Grande fled west to the canyons of Navajo country, intermarrying and living as neighbors for three-quarters of a century.

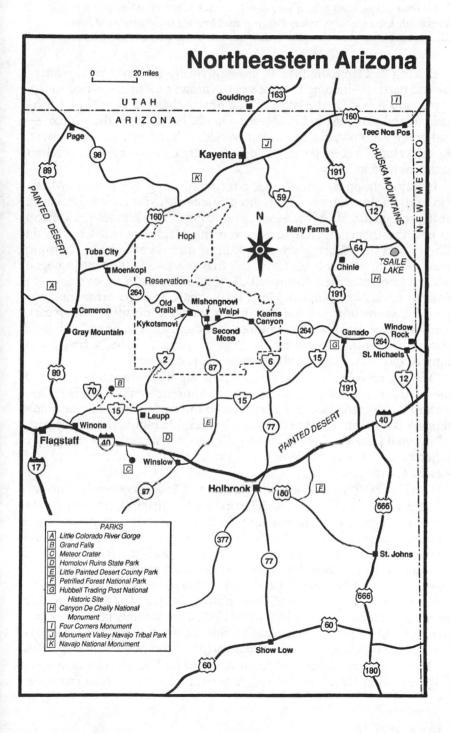

Northeastern Arizona

0   20 miles

UTAH
ARIZONA

Gouldings 163

160

I

Teec Nos Pos

Page
98

89

PAINTED DESERT

J

Kayenta

CHUSKA MOUNTAINS

NEW MEXICO

K

191

59

160

Hopi

N

Many Farms

191

Tuba City

12

Moenkopi

64

Chinle

TSAILE LAKE

Reservation

H

264

Old Oraibi

Mishongnovi

Walpi

Keams Canyon

191

Cameron

A

Kykotsmovi

Second Mesa

Ganado

Window Rock

Gray Mountain

264

264

G

St. Michaels

2

87

6

15

89

12

70

B

15

Leupp

191

E

15

Winona

77

PAINTED DESERT

40

Flagstaff
40

D

17

Winslow
C

Holbrook 180

F

666

87

377

77

St. Johns

666

60

60

Show Low

180

PARKS

A Little Colorado River Gorge
B Grand Falls
C Meteor Crater
D Homolovi Ruins State Park
E Little Painted Desert County Park
F Petrified Forest National Park
G Hubbell Trading Post National
    Historic Site
H Canyon De Chelly National
    Monument
I Four Corners Monument
J Monument Valley Navajo Tribal Park
K Navajo National Monument

Fall is the most pleasant time of year to visit Indian Country, when you'll find it uncrowded, less expensive, sunny but crisp and touched with splashes of color.

During that time the Navajo grew in wealth due to their legendary raiding parties—helping themselves to Indian or Anglo-owned sheep, horses and slaves. By the late 1700s, a much-changed race of part Athabascan and part Pueblo blood—the Dineh, Navajo for "the people"—had emerged. Powerful horsemen, wealthy sheepherders and farmers, they developed a complex mythology and surpassed their Pueblo teachers at the craft of weaving.

Navajo "shopping spree" raids continued along the Spanish, Mexican and Anglo frontier. The United States army built Fort Defiance, near present-day Window Rock, and dispatched Colonel Kit Carson to end the incursions. Carson starved the Navajo out of Canyon de Chelly and neighboring areas by killing their livestock and burning their fields. On March 14, 1864, the first of some 8000 Navajo began what is known as their "long walk"—300 miles at 15 miles a day—to Fort Sumner, New Mexico. Here, a 40-square-mile government compound became home to the Navajo for four of their most bitter years. They were plagued by crop failures, hunger, sickness, death and gross government mismanagement. Finally, on June 1, 1868, a treaty was signed, and some 7000 survivors moved back home.

Trading posts became the Indians' new supply source and conduit to the white man's world. While modern shopping centers, crafts galleries and convenience stores have replaced most of them, a few originals remain. The most famous is the rural, creekside Hubbell Trading Post, a National Historic Site at Ganado. Others worth seeking out include Oljeto near Monument Valley and posts at Cameron, Tuba City and Keams Canyon.

During the 20th century, the Navajo and Hopi have moved from a subsistence to a cash economy. The Indian Reorganization Act of 1934 ended overt repressive government policies toward Native Americans and launched an era of increased self-government. Since 1961, when oil and coal reserves were found on reservation lands, both tribes have parlayed millions of the resulting dollars into paved roads, schools, hospitals, civic centers, low-cost housing, expanded electrical services and running water for more homes. Three mines, three power plants, a 60,000-acre farming project, forest industries and scattered electronic assembly plants are gradually providing jobs for the Navajo. But the most widespread employment is in cottage industries—the creation of their own arts and crafts.

Today, in every village and town you will find the rich and wonderfully evolving legacy of Native American arts and crafts. From the

Navajo—weavings respected worldwide, sandpaintings and silver and turquoise jewelry. From the Hopi—some of the finest pottery in the Southwest, superb carvings of wooden kachinas, woven basketry and plaques and masterful incised silver jewelry. You can hear Native American languages and see rich spiritual traditions carried on by new generations. You can experience the history of this region with its blend of Native American, Spanish and Anglo cultures, all in a setting of striking geography.

Southern Navajo Country

Indian Country is a concept that barely does justice to the astonishing diversity of the southern Navajo realm. There is so much to see and do in this region, which also embraces the pastel realm of the Painted Desert, that you may be tempted to extend your stay. Ancient Anasazi ruins and colorful badlands are just a few of the highlights.

On the southwest corner of the Navajo Indian Reservation, during spring runoff—usually March and April—a detour off Route 40 brings you to the thundering, muddy **Grand Falls** of the Little Colorado River—plummeting 185 feet into the canyon below. A lava flow from Merriam Crater ten miles to the southwest created the falls about 100,000 years ago. Some years the flow is only a trickle, and even during the best years they dry up by May, resuming again briefly during abundant summer monsoons. It's a good idea to inquire in Winslow or Flagstaff about the level of the Little Colorado River before making the trip. To get to the falls, turn off Route 40 either at Winona, 17 miles east of Flagstaff, or at the Leupp Junction (Route 99), ten miles west of Winslow to Route 15. Either way, ask at the turnoff for exact directions. The Winona route is the shortest from the highway—about 20 miles, the last eight unpaved.

The scattered broken pottery, rock drawings and crumbling walls speak with quiet eloquence of an ancient past at **Homolovi Ruins State Park** (Route 87; 602-289-4106) three miles east of Winslow. The park contains six major 14th-century pueblos of 40 to 1000 rooms and more than 300 identified archaeological sites, as well as a visitor center and museum where interpretive programs are presented. Nine miles of paved roads and a mile of hiking trails lead to the ruins of the two largest villages, inhabited between 1150 and 1450 A.D. The park also includes petroglyphs and a pit-house village dating from 600 to 900 A.D. The Hopi believe this was home to their ancestors just before they migrated north to today's mesas. They still consider the ruins—located on both sides of the Little Colorado River—sacred and leave *pahos* (prayer feathers) for the spirits. The park's visitor center is located one mile north of Route 40 on Route 87.

Winslow, the hub of northeastern Arizona, is a railroad town that was an early trade center. Its current history goes back to Mormon pioneers who arrived in 1876 and built a small rock fort known as Brigham City along with a few other small settlements. The town grew, and soon a water system, stores and an opera house appeared, along with a school, saloons and, that harbinger of all frontier civilizations, sidewalks. The Aztec Land and Cattle Company purchased a million acres of land from the railroad in the late 1800s and thousands of head of cattle were brought in to be handled by local cowboys. The town was incorporated in 1900. For information, contact **Winslow Chamber of Commerce** (300 West North Road; 602-289-2434).

The **Old Trail Museum** (212 Kinsley Avenue; 602-289-5861) houses changing exhibits related to Winslow's history, including Native American and pioneering artifacts.

To the east of Winslow on Route 40, you'll come to **Holbrook**. Headquarters for the Apache-Sitgreaves National Forest, Holbrook was named for H. R. Holbrook, first engineer of the Atlantic and Pacific Railroad, forerunner of the Santa Fe Line. Built along the Little Colorado River and set at the edge of the Navajo Indian Reservation, Holbrook consists of a string of motels and restaurants, along with a half-dozen good souvenir shops specializing in petrified wood and other rocks and gems, as well as Native American arts, crafts and jewelry.

Founded in the 1880s as a railroad station and ranching center, Holbrook today is the gateway to the Petrified Forest. Once among the largest cattle ranches in the country with its 60,000 head of cattle, Holbrook was one of Arizona's toughest cowboy towns—ranch hands from the Aztec Ranch were a rough-and-tumble bunch who often shot up everything and earned the nickname the "Hashknife Posse." There are probably more people still wearing ten-gallon hats and cowboy boots here than in any other small town in the West.

The area's past is chronicled in the **Old West Courthouse Museum and Chamber of Commerce** (100 East Arizona Street; 602-524-6558), a yellow brick building that served as the original courthouse from 1898 until 1976. The chamber's counter dispenses maps and brochures, as well as an historic downtown tour map. The museum is more like a musty attic, stuffed with old photos, pioneer utensils and tortoise-shell combs, and even features an old parlor. There's a turn-of-the-century apothecary complete with snake oil and other wonder tonics, and an 1898 one-piece basement jail.

The signs advertising sale of "gems" and "petrified wood" on every other block in Holbrook offer a good clue that **Petrified Forest National Park** (602-524-6228) can't be far away. Entrances at the north-

Each January, members of the present-day Hashknife Posse carry the mail Pony Express-style from Holbrook to Scottsdale—the only mail run on horseback authorized by the U.S. Postal Service.

ern and southern gateways to this park are located 18 miles east of Holbrook—the northern entrance on Route 40, the southern one on Route 180. Either one launches you on the park's 28-mile scenic drive.

Eons ago, trees fell into an ancient swamp and were converted over time to rainbow-colored rock—much of it still in massive logs. These colorful rare stone trees lie scattered throughout the 100,000-acre park, which may be the largest forest of petrified wood in the world. There are also many other types of fossils, both plant and animal, as well as evidence of the Native Americans who once lived here.

The national monument was established in 1906, mainly in response to the large number of logs and fossils that were being poached. It became a national park in 1962. Despite the barren desert environment, the park is dotted with prickly pear, cholla cacti and other natural vegetation. Look closely and you may find evening primrose, Indian paintbrush, mariposa lily and other plants.

The most frequently visited area of the park is the southern section, which holds the greatest concentration of petrified wood. Here, you'll find a wide variety of specimens—giant logs, agatized stumps (some complete with root systems) and innumerable chunks. Farther north are prehistoric Indian sites and the petroglyphs left behind by the Anasazi, Sinagua and Mogollon tribes. Scientists have discovered petroglyphs here that were used as solar calendars. The northern end of the park penetrates the Painted Desert, an eerie landscape of colorful, heavily eroded mudstone and siltstone that resembles the moon's surface, except for the brightly hued formations.

The best way to tour the park is by taking the 28-mile scenic tour. Visitor centers at the north and south entrances provide maps, brochures, books and posters, as well as exhibits of the park's geology and history.

From the park's southern entrance, you can begin your tour by stopping at the **Rainbow Forest Museum and Visitor Center** (602-524-6822), which contains the skeleton of a crocodile-like dinosaur and other exhibits of the creatures that roamed the swamps here 200 million years ago. There are also artifacts of the ancient people who once made the area their home. Outside, a half-mile trail takes you through dozens of giant logs that look like huge crystallized jelly rolls. Many of the longest petrified logs (up to 170 feet) are found across the road at the **Long Logs** spur. A side trail leads to **Agate House**, a small seven-room pueblo-style structure built nearly 900 years ago entirely from chunks of petrified wood. Two of the rooms have been partially restored.

A trail at Crystal Forest leads you close to dense pockets of logs, many over 100-feet long. In 1886, on a $10 bet, a daring cowboy rode his steed across a treacherous divide spanned by a petrified long log, now shored up with cement.

Some of the oldest ruins in the park are found at the **Flattops**, a wilderness area named for its massive, mesa-like sandstone hills. The small village of about 25 round and oval shaped "pit houses" is believed to have been occupied from 300 to 600 A.D.

The **Crystal Forest** has a large concentration of petrified wood, mostly chunks scattered about like the remains of an ancient woodpile. Look closely at the logs and you'll see hollows and cracks where early souvenir hunters and gem collectors chipped away clear quartz and amethyst crystals. In fact, fossil destruction and poaching in this area prompted the Arizona Territory to petition Congress to preserve the petrified wood sites.

Photographers love the view from the **Jasper Forest Overlook**, which provides a panorama of the area and includes barren hills sprinkled with petrified logs. Notice how the softer clay-like soil has eroded from around the heavier petrified wood, creating a mosaic on the desert floor.

Blue Mesa is another favorite of photographers because of its blue, gray and white cone-shaped hills with chunks of agatized wood scattered about. The eroded sandstone formations suggest a mini Grand Canyon. This is also one of the best overlooks of the Painted Desert, whose strange multicolored buttes seem to glow in the distance.

Although named **The Tepees**, these giant cone-shaped mounds look more like ant hills, wrinkled through erosion and colored blue and gray by iron, manganese and other mineral deposits. Nearby, **Newspaper Rock**, a huge sandstone block, is covered with a fine collection of petroglyphs. You'll need binoculars to get a good look, or you can use the coin-operated telescopes.

The remnants of a Puerco Indian pueblo, as well as more petroglyphs, are at the **Puerco Indian Ruin**. Built of stone and masonry walls, the pueblo was home to about 75 people from 1100–1300 A.D. The ruin has been partially excavated and restored.

The overlooks at the north end of the park—**Lacey Point Overlook and Whipple Point Overlook**—provide good views of the Painted Desert. Here, you'll see bands of red, white and pink—the effect of the sun reflecting on mudstone and siltstone stained by iron, manganese and other minerals. Colors are the most intense at sunrise and sunset or on cloudy days. At the **Nishoni Point Overlook**, the hills below appear to sparkle with crystals. The minerals are actually selenite gypsum. If you're ready for a rest stop, there's sheltered tables, water and restrooms at the **Chinde Point Picnic Area**.

The **Painted Desert Visitor Center** (602-524-6228) at the north entrance of the park has a 17-minute film on the mysteries of the aricarixylon pine forest petrification (silica crystals replaced wood cells in the cone-bearing trees). The visitor center also offers a cafeteria and gift shop.

The **Painted Desert Inn Museum** (three miles north of the visitor center at Kachina Point on the scenic drive; 602-524-2550) is a 1930s pueblo-style building, once a Fred Harvey inn that serviced weary travelers along old Route 66 during the 1920s. The National Park Service now owns and operates it as a museum concession. The detailed, hand-carved wood and tin furnishings were made by the Civilian Conservation Corps. Murals painted by the late Hopi artist Fred Kabotie depict scenes of Hopi life: a January buffalo dance to ensure return of the buffalo each spring; the journey of two Hopi to Zuni lands to gather salt.

SOUTHERN NAVAJO COUNTRY LODGING

The top two hotels in Winslow are both Best Westerns. The two-story **Adobe Inn** (1701 North Park Drive; 602-289-4638) has 72 rooms, each decorated in contemporary fashion. You'll find a café and an indoor pool on the premises. **Town House Lodge** (West Route 66; 602-289-4611) has 68 rooms with modern furnishings and a guest laundry. Both are moderate.

Most of Holbrook's 23 motels are clustered on West Hopi Drive (Route 180 from the west) and East Navajo Boulevard (Route 77 from the east), which meet in downtown Holbrook.

CHECK INTO A WIGWAM FOR THE NIGHT

*If you enter Holbrook on Route 180, you won't miss the **Wigwam Motel** (811 West Hopi Drive; 602-524-3048), with its 15 dazzling white stucco wigwams, the sort of kitsch that old Route 66 was famous for. Built in 1950 by Chester Lewis (six other cities had wigwam motels of similar design; only one other survives), his children and grandchildren restored these and still operate them. Inside each, matching red-plaid curtains and bedspreads adorn original handmade hickory furniture. Scenes from Tony Hillerman's* Dark Wind *were filmed here in 1990. There's no extra charge for the lulling vibrations as trains rumble by in the night. Budget.*

The **Arizonian Inn** (2508 East Navajo Boulevard, Holbrook; 602-524-2611) is a well-groomed Best Western motel accented with red-brick veneer and wood-shake roof. The 70 guest rooms feature traditional dark-wood country English furniture and overstuffed love seats and wing chairs. The inn also has a pool and Denny's restaurant on premises. Prices are moderate.

Another Best Western motel is the **Adobe Inn** (615 West Hopi Drive, Holbrook; 602-524-3948), a two-story, 54-room Best Western that has modern furnishings and a pool. Budget.

With 39 rooms, the **Rainbow Inn** (2211 East Navajo Boulevard, Holbrook; 602-524-2654) falls into the small, no-frills category. But most of the modern, well-maintained rooms have refrigerators and Southwest paintings on the walls. Budget.

SOUTHERN NAVAJO COUNTRY RESTAURANTS

Dining out in the Southern Navajo Reservation area is not a very exciting experience. You can take a counter seat on one of the swivel stools or settle into a booth at **Falcon Restaurant** (1113 East 3rd Street, Winslow; 602-289-2342) where the menu includes steaks, chicken, roast turkey and seafood. This brown stucco establishment also features the only Greek mural we found in Navajo country. Moderate.

Celebrated in newspapers ranging from New York to San Francisco, the **Casa Blanca Café** (1201 East 2nd Street, Winslow; 602-289-4191) is known for its tacos, chimichangas, cheese crisps and burgers. Choose between booth and table seating at this ceramic-tiled establishment where cactus baskets grace the walls. The dining room is cooled by Casablanca-style fans but, alas, there's no trace of Bogie. Moderate.

At **Gabrielle's Pancake and Steak House** (918 East 2nd Street, Winslow; 602-289-2508), photos of the Painted Desert and a quartet of pancake-shaped clocks add a decorative touch. Inside this shake-shingle coffee shop you can enjoy booth or counter seating and dine on steaks, seafood and homemade pies. Moderate.

In Holbrook, the best spot for Mexican cuisine is **Romo's Café** (121 West Hopi Drive; 602-524-2153), which has been serving tasty South-of-the-Border dishes since the 1960s. The decor isn't fancy in this storefront café, but the rear dining room with its used-brick walls and hanging plants is a more private setting than the bustling area out front for enjoying green-chile chimichangas, fajitas or traditional enchilada dinners. In your world travels, don't be surprised to see a Romo sweatshirt—they've turned up as far away as Munich, Germany. Budget.

For a taste of the Old West, saddle up and head for the **Butterfield Stage Company Restaurant** (609 West Hopi Drive, Holbrook; 602-524-3447). The specialty here is sizzling porterhouse steak served with all the fixin's, as well as barbecue beef and prime rib. In addition to the cowboy tack and memorabilia on the walls, there's a stagecoach on display. Moderate.

For huge portions of Mexican and American specialties, come to **Aguilera's Restaurant** (200 Navajo Boulevard, Holbrook; 602-524-3806), which features a carpeted dining room decorated with pictures of roaming buffalo and bulls. This adobe-colored eatery is cooled by ceiling fans. Moderate.

Rock walls add an earthy note to **The Plainsman** (1001 West Hopi Drive, Holbrook; 602-524-3345). For casual dining, try the coffee shop where there's booth seating. Enjoy meals such as liver and onions, veal cutlet and turkey sandwiches. The dining room is popular with the local Chamber of Commerce, which meets here monthly. Popular items include châteaubriand, prime rib, frogs' legs and grilled trout. Moderate.

The **Roadrunner Café** (1501 East Navajo Boulevard; 602-524-2787) offers everything from grilled cheese sandwiches to pot roast and steaks. The carpeted dining room has both table and booth seating. Plants and wildflower photos bring the Southwest indoors. Budget to moderate.

SOUTHERN NAVAJO COUNTRY SHOPPING

Founded in 1903, **Bruchman's Gallery** (113 West 2nd Street, Winslow; 602-289-3831) features Indian art and handicrafts—fetishes, Hopi kachina dolls, Navajo jewelry, drums, baskets, wallhangings, saddle blankets and rare pottery.

Most of the souvenir and gift shops in Holbrook specialize in Native American handiwork, rocks, gems and petrified wood. One of the best is **Julien's Roadrunner** (109 West Hopi Drive; 602-524-2388) on Old Route 66. The well-stocked shop sells everything from precious stones and hand-etched Hopi silver jewelry to Indian kachinas and sand paintings. The proprietor, Ted Julien, is a long-time resident of Holbrook and a veritable expert on the area's history and attractions. Feel free to ask him anything (even about his competition), but be prepared for thorough and unabbreviated answers.

Linda's Indian Arts and Crafts (405 Navajo Boulevard; 602-524-2500) is a small shop, but offers a good selection of Native American jewelry and crafts.

For the largest selection of top-quality Native American arts and crafts, **McGee's Beyond Native Tradition** (2114 East Navajo Boulevard; 602-524-1977) sells everything from Hopi jewelry to Navajo blankets and drums. The spacious, split-level shop features an upstairs gallery filled with Native American art and other collectibles.

In business since the 1960s, **Nakai Indian Cultural Trade Center** (357 Navajo Boulevard; 602-524-2329) features top-quality Indian products, as well as jewelry made on the premises.

More Native American jewelry, kachinas, baskets and crafts can be found at **Tribal Treasure** (1601 Navajo Boulevard; 602-524-2847), in business over 20 years.

Painted Desert Visitor Center Gift Shop (Route 40 entrance to the Petrified Forest National Park; 602-524-6228) sells polished and natural petrified wood, from tiny pieces to great slabs, plus other gems and Southwest Indian crafts and curios.

You can find much of the same at **Fred Harvey Curios and Fountain** (Route 180 entrance to the Petrified Forest National Park; 602-524-6822), along with Native American jewelry, books and postcards.

In the basement of the restored pink 1930s lodge, the **Painted Desert Inn Shop** (602-524-2550) has a bookstore and gift shop selling a good selection of books on the Southwest, plus a variety of Indian crafts and curios.

Behind general merchandise and video displays at **R. B. Burnham & Co. Trading Post** (Route 666, at Route 40 in Sanders; 602-688-2777) is one room lined with naturally dyed yarns. Behind that room is a shrine to Hopi and Navajo crafts. Assembled with much care, and for sale, are gallery-quality Navajo rugs, carved furniture upholstered in Navajo weavings, plus the whole array of Indian arts and crafts. It's worth a stop just to look!

PETRIFIED FOREST TRADING POST

*While it's illegal to gather souvenir pieces of petrified wood within Petrified Forest National Park, just outside the southern entrance off Route 180 is a 6500-acre privately owned area where visitors, for a modest fee, can legally collect their own specimens of the multicolored fossilized wood. Check in at **Petrified Forest Trading Post** (602-524-3470) for a map to locate areas where the wood abounds. You can also rent a hammer, chisel and carrying bags. Popular with commercial petrified wood and gem buffs, some 200,000 pounds are collected here annually. The trading post also sells a variety of natural and polished petrified wood, from small $2 chunks to massive coffee-table slabs priced in the thousands of dollars.*

SOUTHERN NAVAJO COUNTRY NIGHTLIFE

It's pretty quiet out this way. For nightlife, the choices are limited.

The **Tumbleweed Lounge** (1400 East 3rd Street; 602-289-5213) is among the newest nightspots in Winslow and draws the biggest crowds, with guitars and country-and-western poetry put to music—Who's going to mend my broken heart?

In Holbrook, most of the action happens at **Young's Corral Bar** (865 East Navajo Boulevard; 602-524-1875), where weekends are filled with the sounds of live country-and-western music.

For more subdued atmosphere, you can have a drink in the **Holiday Cocktail Lounge** at the Western Holiday Motel (720 Navajo Boulevard, Holbrook; 602-524-6216).

If you're tired of reading, you can see a first-run movie at the **Roxy Theater** (153 West Hopi Drive, Holbrook; 602-524-2060), a tiny but quaint one-screen movie house reminiscent of *The Last Picture Show*.

SOUTHERN NAVAJO COUNTRY PARKS

One of the nicest, most colorful chunks of the 40-mile-long Painted Desert is concentrated in the 900-acre **Little Painted Desert County Park** (602-524-6161). Large 300- to 400-foot-tall fragile mounds of mud slate—shaded in grays, reds, purples and yellows—tend to change in color intensity throughout the day. Colors are most vivid at dawn and dusk. A strenuous, one-mile hiking trail descends some 500 feet into the mounds, from which you can explore on your own. Located 15 miles north of Winslow on Route 87 near the southern boundary of the Navajo Reservation.

McHood Park Clear Creek Reservoir (602-289-3082) was once an important water source for Winslow, but now the deep canyon five miles from town is a favorite boating, swimming and picnic area. Some camping is available.

Cholla Lake Park (602-288-3717), adjacent to a power station, is one of the larger bodies of water in northeastern Arizona. This man-made lake offers swimming, boating, fishing and picnicking, as well as camping. To get there, take Route 40 east from Winslow for about 20 miles to Exit 274, then follow the power plant road to the park.

Petrified Forest National Park (602-524-6228), abutting the southern boundary of the Navajo Reservation, is a 28-mile-long park featuring the rolling badlands of the Painted Desert—mainly red-hued hills—north of Route 40. South of Route 40 and extending to Route 180 is the densest concentration of petrified prehistoric fossils in the world. Each section has a wilderness area. A 28-mile road leads visitors past nine Painted Desert vistas and 13 Petrified Forest stops.

Western Navajo Country

The Western Navajo Reservation, bordering such wonders as the Grand Canyon National Park and Lake Powell National Recreation Area, is a land of great beauty and ancient sights. President William McKinley signed an order January 8, 1900, deeding these one-and-a-half-million acres of land to the Navajo who had migrated westward 32 years earlier after outgrowing their original reserve. Where Routes 89 and 64 meet, the Navajo operate **Cameron Visitor Center** (602-679-2303), offering advice and brochures on tribal attractions.

Follow Route 64 west ten miles to an unpaved spur road and walk a few hundred feet to a dramatic overlook. At the bottom of hundreds of feet of sheer canyon walls is the muddy ribbon of the Little Colorado River. Upper limestone cliffs, layered like flapjack stacks, contrast with massive sandstone slabs below, evidence of a shallow sea 250 million years ago. This **Grand Canyon of the Little Colorado Gorge Tribal Park** is owned by the Navajo. From Memorial Day through Labor Day, a festive air reigns as Indians set up their flag- and banner-bedecked crafts booths in the parking area.

A mile north of the visitor center is **Cameron Trading Post, Motel and Restaurant** (Route 89; 602-679-2231), a stone pueblo-style complex built in 1916 by the Hopi and Navajo, and recently restored. Long known as an oasis of hospitality, it's located by Tanner's Crossing, the last place wagons could cross the Little Colorado before the river enters gorges too deep to navigate. Quicksand pockets made this crossing especially treacherous.

Today, this mini-city is a great place to people-watch: old Navajo women in traditional velvet blouses, men in tall, black reservation hats and turquoise jewelry accompanied by youngsters in mod T-shirts and tennies. Inside the post, packed with curios and quality crafts, you'll often see a weaver at work. Next door, don't miss **Cameron Collector's Gallery** offering antique Indian crafts and outstanding works of

---

FOOTSTEPS FROM THE PAST

At **Dinosaur Tracks** (the turnoff is five miles west of Tuba City on Route 160, then north one-eighth mile along a dirt road), jewelry shacks mark the spot where scientists believe a 20-foot-long carnivorous Dilophosaurus left tracks. For a small tip, locals will escort you to the several impressions—three-toed footprints twice as big as adult hands. (Look for the reconstructed skeleton of this dinosaur in Window Rock at the Navajo Tribal Museum.)

The Painted Desert draws its name from the undulating mounds of purple, red and blue-gray sediments that grace the strange landscape.

---

contemporary Native American art—rare chief's blankets, pottery, dolls, weaponry and ceremonial garb. Behind the gallery, **Mrs. Richardson's Terraced Garden**, recently revived, is a garden spot of vegetables and flowers.

North of Cameron, continuing on Route 89 to The Gap, lies the northernmost extension of the **Painted Desert**, a multihued ancient land of silt and volcanic ash hills barren of vegetation. Red sphinx shapes astride crumbling pyramids of eroded solidified sand, these badlands are red and white along some miles; gray and white along others. They're part of the Chinle Formation beloved by geologists for its dinosaur-era fossils.

Worth a stop in Tuba City, named for a 19th-century Hopi leader, is the hogan-shaped, two-story native stone **Tuba City Trading Post** (Main Street and Moenave Avenue; 602-283-5441). Built in 1905 during a tourism boom, its door faces east to the rising sun; crafts, groceries and sundries are for sale. Next door, you can enter a built-for-tourists hogan replica. Now an administrative and trade center for western Navajo, Tuba City was founded by Mormons in 1877.

WESTERN NAVAJO COUNTRY LODGING

Lodging in Navajo and Hopi country can be summed up in one word: scarce. In an area about the size of Massachusetts, barely 600 rooms are available, so it's no wonder reservation motels claim 100 percent occupancy most nights from Memorial Day through Labor Day. If you get stuck, reservation border towns (Holbrook, Winslow and Flagstaff) usually have vacancies, though they too can sell out, especially on weekends of special events.

Padded headboards and blue bedspreads and drapes cozy up the 100 simple, cement-block rooms in the **Anasazi Inn** (Route 89; 602-679-2214) in Gray Mountain. It boasts the Western Navajo Reservation's only swimming pool. Budget.

Cameron Trading Post and Motel (Route 89, 30 miles east of the Grand Canyon's east entrance and 50 miles north of Flagstaff; 602-679-2231) in Cameron is a favorite overnight stop in Indian Country. This tiny, self-contained, 112-acre, privately owned outpost sits on a bluff overlooking the eastern prelude to the Grand Canyon of the Colorado. From 6 a.m. until 10 p.m. or later, the trading post is a beehive of tourists and Navajo mingling to shop, dine or pick up everything from

---

Many locals contend the most colorful and dramatic concentration of Painted Desert hills is at Little Painted Desert County Park.

---

mail and tack to baled hay. It's mainly the tourists who stay overnight in 45 rooms priced budget to moderate. Built in 1916, the motel rooms are two story and of native stone and wood architecture (variously called Pueblo-style or Victorian territorial), as is the rest of the compound. The rooms tend to be funkier than elsewhere on the reservation.

Adjacent to the historic octagonal-shaped Tuba City Trading Post is the pleasant, lawn-studded **Tuba City Motel** (Main Street; 602-283-4545), furnished with tan rugs and hand-carved southwestern furniture. It has 80 rooms. Moderate.

Students at Tuba City's Greyhills High School are learning the hotel management business by operating the 32-room **Greyhills Inn** (60 Warrior Drive, northeast of Bashas on Route 160; 602-283-6271) as an American Youth Hostel, open year-round to all ages. Rooms are comfy and carpeted, with hand-me-down Hyatt furniture. Guests share bathrooms, a television lounge and room with pool table, and for a modest fee can share meals with Navajo students in their cafeteria. For security reasons, doors lock at 12 a.m., so guests should inform the inn if they plan to be out past midnight. Budget.

WESTERN NAVAJO COUNTRY RESTAURANTS

Assuming you're not on a cholesterol-free diet, you'll find Indian Country food, as with everything else here, an adventure. Fry bread appears at lunch and dinner with taco trimmings as an Indian taco, or as bread for a sandwich, or as dessert dripping with honey. Other Indian Country favorites include mutton stew, usually served with parched corn, chili, Mexican food, burgers, steaks and, for breakfast, biscuits with gravy.

Gray Mountain Restaurant (Route 89, Gray Mountain; 602-679-2214) fills its walls with Southwest kitsch including a turquoise-covered cow skeleton. Entrées (baked ham, chicken-fried steak, broiled halibut, pepper steak) come with soup or salad, hot rolls, baked potato, cowboy beans or french fries and salsa. Budget to moderate.

A nice surprise is the **Cameron Trading Post Restaurant** (Route 89, Cameron; 602-679-2231). After walking through the typically low, open-beam ceiling trading post, you enter a lofty room lined with windows looking out onto the Little Colorado River. Tables and chairs are of carved oak and the ceiling glimmers silver from its patterned pressed-tin squares. Forty-one breakfast choices include Navajo taco with egg, *huevos rancheros* and hot cakes; for dinner, try the deep-fried fish and chicken or steak entrées. Budget to moderate.

Poncho's Family Restaurant (Main Street, Tuba City; 602-283-5260) amid open-beam and wood decor, offers dinners of steak and shrimp, Virginia baked ham, breaded veal with gravy, plus the inevitable Navajo taco, and a variety of Mexican entrées. Look for the large historic photos of Charles H. Algert, pioneer Indian trader and founder of Tuba Trading Post, shown on horseback in 1898, and an 1872 photo of the Hopi leader Tuba, standing with arms folded. Moderate.

WESTERN NAVAJO COUNTRY SHOPPING

In business for more than half a century, **Sacred Mountain Trading Post** (23 miles north of Flagstaff on Route 89; 602-679-2255), is often a good outlet for museum-quality Navajo pitch-glazed pottery; also available are glass beads and bead-making materials, Hopi pottery, kachinas and Navajo baskets.

The 1916 stone **Cameron Trading Post** (Route 89, Cameron; 602-679-2231) is like a department store of Native American crafts, crammed with a good selection of nearly everything—lots of Navajo rugs, cases of jewelry from all southwestern tribes, kachinas, sandpaintings, baskets and pottery. Cameron Gallery (adjoining) offers the most expensive crafts, including antique Native American weavings, Apache baskets, Plains beadwork, weaponry and ceremonial garb.

Tuba City Trading Post (Main Street and Moenave Avenue, Tuba City; 602-283-5441) emphasizes Navajo rugs, usually including large pictorials. Also for sale are kachinas, jewelry and the Pendleton blankets Native Americans like to give one another for births, graduations and other celebrations.

THE FINE ART OF SHOPPING

While shopping for arts and crafts in Indian Country, we've been invited into Hopi homes to eat corn fresh from the field, have discussed tribal politics with college-educated shopkeepers and met traditional basketmakers who spoke no English. At the same time, we've longingly admired contemporary Native American-crafted jewelry that would dazzle New York's Fifth Avenue crowd. Shopping opportunities can pop up anywhere in Indian Country. Once we bought sandpaintings from the trunk of an Native American artist's car while camping in the Chuskas. But Indian Country's main shopping avenue is Route 264 from Tuba City to Window Rock, where you'll find two fine old trading posts—Tuba City Trading Post (Main Street and Moenave Avenue; 602-283-5441) in Tuba City and Hubbell Trading Post (602-755-3254) near the town of Ganado.

Hopi Indian Country

Three sand-colored mesas stacked and surrounded by a dozen ancient villages form the core of the Hopi Reservation. Completely surrounded by the Navajo Reservation, the villages are strung along 90 miles of Route 264. Home for several centuries to the Hopi, this fascinating high-desert place (at about the 4000-foot elevation) looks stark and poor one minute, then ancient and noble the next.

For an inside look at Native American culture, be sure to browse the Hopi craftmakers' shops and attend a traditional tribal dance. **Hopi Indian Dances,** nearly all of them involving prayers for rain for their dry-farm plots, occur year-round. Dates are rarely announced more than two weeks in advance. Whether or not you can attend will vary with the dance and the village. To ask, call the **Hopi Tribal Council Office of Public Relations** (602-734-2441) or **Second Mesa Cultural Center** (602-734-2401). Don't miss a chance to attend one. Instructions for visitors will be posted outside most villages. In all cases, leave cameras, tape recorders and sketching pads in the car. Photography is not permitted in the villages or along Hopi roads.

Two miles southeast of Tuba City is **Moenkopi** ("the place of running water"), a village founded in the 1870s by a Hopi chief from Oraibi. Here, note the rich assortment of farm plots. This is the only Hopi village that irrigates its farmland—water comes from a nearby spring. Elsewhere, farmers tend small plots in several locations, enhancing their chance of catching random summer thundershowers. It's also the only one of 12 Hopi villages not situated on or just below one of the three mesas.

It's some 40 miles to the next two villages. **Bacavi,** comprised mostly of prefab homes, was built in 1909 following a political upheaval at Old Oraibi. **Hotevilla,** also a relatively new (built in 1906) village, with its mix of adobe and cinderblock homes at the edge of a mesa, is nonetheless a traditional village known for its dances and crafts. A few miles down the road, on the edge of Third Mesa, **Old Oraibi** is one of the oldest continuously inhabited villages in the United States. The Hopi lived here as early as 1150. Try the ten-minute walk from the south edge of the village to the ruins of a church built in 1901 by H. R. Voth, a Mennonite minister. It was destroyed by lightning. At Kykotsmovi, "mound of ruined houses," two miles east, then south one mile on Route 2, the Hopi Tribal Council Office of Public Relations (602-734-2441) provides visitor information.

Continue east on Route 264 a half-dozen miles to **Shungopovi,** Second Mesa's largest village, built at a cliff's edge. It's two more miles to the **Hopi Cultural Center** at Second Mesa (on Route 264; 602-734-2401), the biggest social center for Indians and visitors. Hopi staffers of this white, pueblo-style museum-restaurant-motel-gift shop complex always know when and where dances are scheduled; ask at the motel desk. Tribally owned, it includes the Hopi Museum, exhibiting murals, pottery and historic photos of each mesa. Shop spaces usually house galleries of Hopi-made arts and crafts. Just 100 feet west of the complex at the **Hopi Arts and Crafts Cooperative Guild** (602-734-2463) are silversmiths at work amid the biggest assortment of Hopi-made crafts on the reservation.

East of the cultural center, the two weathered villages of **Shipaulovi** and **Mishognovi** (a steep climb north to both up an unnamed road from Route 264) are strikingly placed above the desert floor on Second Mesa, many of their dwellings carved from stone. Founded in the 1680s, both are known for their dances and are worth a visit for the views.

If you have time to make only one stop, visit the trio of villages on First Mesa—**Hano, Sichomovi** and **Walpi** (six miles east of the Secakuku Trading Post). Perched atop the flat oblong mesa, its sides dropping precipitously 1000 feet to the desert below, the village locations help you understand why the Hopi believe they live at the center of the universe. Accessible only by a thrilling curvy drive up a narrow road with no guardrails (signs off Route 264 point the way), all three villages seem to grow out of the mesa's beige-colored stone. Vistas are uninterrupted for miles amid an eerie stillness.

Most awesome is Walpi. Built some 300 years ago on a promontory with panoramas in all directions, Walpi's houses stack atop one another like children's blocks, connected with wooden ladders. From the parking lot (no cars are permitted in Walpi), the village resembles a great stone ship suspended on a sea of blue sky. Leaders keep the village traditional so that neither electricity nor running water are permitted. Shy schoolgirls lead **tours of Walpi** daily in summer. Sign up at Ponsi

---

HOPI CEREMONIAL DANCES

Although some Hopi dances are held in plazas and are open to the public, others are held privately in underground kivas. Many of their dances are appeals for rain or to improve harmony with nature. Starting times are determined by Hopi elders according to the position of the moon, sun and vibrations. The Powamu Ceremony or Bean Dance in late February is a fertility ritual to help enhance the summer harvest, while The Snake Dance is usually done near the end of August. Live rattlesnakes are used during the ceremony as a form of communication with the Underworld.

If you attend a ceremony, remember to respect the proceedings and not take pictures or use tape recorders.

Nampeyo, a First Mesa woman inspired by ancient pottery shards, started the re-vival of yellow-to-orange pottery a century ago. First Mesa remains a major producer of pottery decorated with black, thin-curved-line motifs.

Hall (602-737-2262) or the Community Development Office (602-737-2670) in Sichomovi.

Here, as in the other villages, kivas, or ceremonial chambers dug into the earth, serve as they have since Anasazi days, as a refuge where clan dancers fast and observe rituals for days prior to dances. Then on dance days, no longer farmers in denims, the Hopi slowly emerge through ladders on kiva roofs to the hypnotic rhythm of drums and rattles. Transformed by masks, feathers, bells and pine boughs, they appear as sacred beings.

Everyday activities include women baking bread out of doors in beehive ovens or tending clay firings. These are excellent pottery villages. Crude signs in windows invite you into homes of kachina and pottery makers, a wonderful chance to get acquainted with these hospitable people.

Hano resembles its neighboring Hopi villages, but in language and custom it remains a Tewa settlement of Pueblo Indians who fled Spanish oppression in the Rio Grande region in the late 1690s.

Continuing east on Route 264, Hopi Indian Country ends at Keams Canyon, the federal government administrative center, with tourist facilities (restaurant, motel, grocery) clustered around **Keams Canyon Trading Post**. Well-chosen crafts are for sale; the finest art is in a side room.

Follow the canyon northeast into the woods. About two miles in on the left, near a ramada and a small dam, you'll find **Inscription Rock** where Kit Carson signed his name on the tall sandstone wall about the time he was trying to end Navajo raiding parties.

HOPI INDIAN COUNTRY LODGING

Designed by Arizona's award-winning architect Benny Gonzales, Second Mesa offers the only Hopi-owned tourist complex. Here are the 33 moderately priced rooms of the **Hopi Cultural Center Motel** (Route 264; 602-734-2401) with their white walls, blonde furniture, television, desk, vanity, dusty rose rug and Indian-print wall decor.

Old trailer-home modules make up the **Keams Canyon Motel** (Route 264; 602-738-2297). The 20 units are a little depressing (with sagging curtains and scratches on wood walls and stains on the carpets), but clean; at budget rates, they are often sold out during summer.

HOPI INDIAN COUNTRY RESTAURANTS

The primary meeting place for the Hopi, the **Hopi Cultural Center Restaurant** (Route 264 at Second Mesa; 602-734-2401) with open-beam ceiling and sturdy, wood-carved furniture, offers Hopi options at all meals. Breakfasts include blue-corn pancakes, blue-corn cornflakes with milk and fry bread. For lunch or dinner, there's Nok Qui Vi—traditional stew with corn and lamb, served with fresh-baked green chilies and fry bread—along with steak, chicken and shrimp entrées to round out the menu. For dessert, there's strawberry shortcake. Budget to moderate.

Second Mesa Nova-Ki (602-737-2525) next to the pueblo-style Secakuku Supermarket serves up burgers, grilled pork chops and Mexican plates amid mauve walls, blue tablecloths and Native American paintings. Budget.

Murals depicting Hopi mesa life decorate the exterior at **Keams Canyon Café** (Route 264 in Keams Canyon; 602-738-2296). This simple eatery has such dinner entrées as filet mignon, T-bone steak, roast beef and barbecued ribs, all served on formica tables. Meals fall in the moderate price range.

HOPI INDIAN COUNTRY SHOPPING

The number of roadside Hopi galleries and shops have doubled in recent years. Owned by individual families, groups of artists or by craftsmakers with national reputations, all these Hopi crafts enterprises are on or near Route 264.

Third Mesa's **Monongya Arts and Crafts** has large rooms filled with Hopi jewelry, some pottery and kachina doll sculptures.

Driving east a half-mile, follow the Old Oraibi signs south to **Old Oraibi Crafts** specializing in Hopi *dawas*—wall plaques made of yarn. This tiny shop with a beam ceiling also sells stuffed Hopi clown dolls.

KACHINAS

The Hopi believe that kachinas are ancestral spirits who periodically visit the pueblo. Elaborately costumed dancers dressed up as kachinas perform during important ceremonies. Kachina dolls are often carved in traditional Hopi dancers' poses, then painted or dressed in cloth, feathers and bright acrylics. The newer trends feature stylized, intricately detailed figures carved from one piece of cottonwood root, then stained. The Navajo are now making kachinas, too, to the irritation of Hopi carvers.

Eastbound on 264, **Calnimpetwa's Gallery** looks like a house. Spacious, white-walled rooms are lined with gallery-quality baskets, pots and jewelry made primarily by Hopi, Navajo and Santa Domingo people. Many of the crafts have a sleek contemporary look.

Continue east, then south a half-mile on the Kykotsmovi road to **Hopi Kiva Indian Arts and Crafts** (602-734-6667), specializing in Hopi overlay jewelry, kachinas, cradle dolls and gourd earrings.

The family-owned **Dawa-ki House of the Sun** (one-fourth mile west of the Hopi Cultural Center, Second Mesa; 602-734-9288) sells Hopi overlay silver work, kachina dolls, pottery and wicker baskets. Often you can see jewelers at work.

In Second Mesa, by the Hopi Cultural Center, the pueblo-style **Hopi Arts and Crafts Cooperative Guild Shop** (602-734-2463) sells work by more than 350 Hopi craftsmakers, often introducing new artists. You'll see fine, reasonably priced samples of all Hopi crafts— coil baskets, wicker plaques, kachina dolls—from traditional to the contemporary baroque and even the older-style flat dolls, plus silver jewelry, woven sashes and gourd rattles. Prices are good. Staff members are knowledgeable about the best craftsmakers in any specialty and where to find them. In the shop, you'll also see Hopi silversmiths at work.

East of the Hopi Cultural Center one-and-a-half miles on the left, stop at an unassuming-looking **Tsakurshovi** (602-734-2478) to find the funkiest shop en route, the only place you can buy sweetgrass, bundled sage, cottonwood root, fox skins, elk toes, warrior paint, dance fans and the oldest-style kachina dolls, amid a delightful hodgepodge of crafts and trade items adored by Hopi dancers. (Owners invented the "Don't Worry, Be Hopi" T-shirts.)

Phil Sekaquaptewa's Gallery (one mile east of the Hopi Cultural Center, next to Secakuku Supermarket, Second Mesa; 602-737-2211), has eight Hopi artists who share space devoted to contemporary jew-

---

HOPI CRAFTS

Hopi wedding and other ceremonial baskets are still woven by Hopi women. Third Mesa villages are also known for their wicker plaques of colorfully dyed sumac and rabbit brush, while coiled yucca plaques are preferred at Second Mesa. Trays of plaited yucca over a willow ring serve as sifters and are made at First and Second Mesa villages. The favorite Hopi jewelry form is overlay—designs are cut from silver sheets, then soldered onto a second silver piece. Finally, cut-out areas are oxidized black.

Among the Hopi, it's the men who do the weaving—mostly ceremonial belts and some rugs.

elry baskets, kachinas, Zuni fetishes and even edible paper-thin blue-corn Hopi *piki* bread.

Honani Crafts Gallery (five-and-a-half miles east of the Hopi Cultural Center; 602-737-2238), with its stained-glass windows of Hopi dancer designs, sells jewelry by 16 silversmiths from all three mesas plus kachinas, books and concho belts.

It's seven more miles to First Mesa, the most picturesque Hopi village, where Walpi residents proudly display their pottery and kachinas.

Twenty miles east, visit **McGee's Indian Art Gallery** (602-738-2295) at Keams Canyon Trading Post, distinctive for its Hopi village murals. For sale are a tasteful variety of Hopi and Navajo crafts—concho belts, silver jewelry, wicker plaques, kachinas, sandpaintings, moccasins and rugs. Be sure to look in the room that houses their finest award-winning crafts.

Central Navajo Country

This is the heart, soul and capital of Navajoland—a strikingly beautiful land of canyons, red rocks, forests and mountains where the Navajo have recorded their proudest victories and most bitter defeats. The longer you stay and explore, the more you'll appreciate the ever-evolving culture that is The Navajo Way.

The ruins of ancient cities you'll see in this region serve as reminders that long before the Navajo arrived, this, too, was homeland to the ancestors of the Hopi—the Anasazi.

Forty miles east of Keams Canyon on Route 264, near the small village of Ganado, follow a shaded road a half-mile west along a creek to **Hubbell Trading Post National Historic Site** (602-755-3254), which still operates as it did when Lorenzo Hubbell, dean of Navajo traders, set up shop here last century. Now run by the National Park Service, Hubbell's remains one of the few trading posts with the traditional "bullpen" design—shoppers stand outside a wooden arena asking for canned goods, yards of velvet, tack and such. Built in the 1870s, part museum and part gallery, these single-story stone rooms smell and look their age—the floors uneven from years of wear. Walls are jammed to their open-beam ceilings with baskets, books, rugs, historical photos, jewelry and postcards. Tack and tools still dangle from the rafters.

Self-guiding tours of the 160-acre complex and exhibits in the **Visitor Center** (602-755-3254) explain how trading posts once linked the Navajo with the outside world, and how Hubbell was not just a trader but a valued friend of the Indian community until his death in 1930. The Hubbell family continued to operate the post until it was given to the National Park Service in 1967. Also in the Visitor Center is a good selection of Indian-related books. And for a tip, Navajo weavers and silversmiths demonstrating their crafts will pose for photos. Hour-long tours of the **Hubbell House**, which displays Lorenzo Hubbell's excellent collection of crafts, give further insights into frontier life and the remarkable trader who lies buried on a knoll nearby.

Navajo-owned ponderosa pine forest lands comprise part of the 30-mile drive to Window Rock, eastward along Route 264. Picnickers may wish to stop awhile at **Summit Campground** 20 miles east of Ganado, where the elevation reaches 7750 feet.

Seven miles east of Summit Campground, before entering Window Rock, stop in St. Michaels, at trailers labeled **Industrial & Tourism Department** (602-871-6436) for Central Navajo Country maps and tourism information.

Here, you'll find **St. Michaels Historical Museum** (next to the post office; 602-871-4171) in the white, hand-hewn native stone building. In the late 1890s, it was the four-bedroom living quarters and chapel for Franciscan friars from Cincinnati. (Sleeping must have been tough on such thin mattresses atop box crates!) Other displays

---

JOHN LORENZO HUBBELL

To Native Americans at the turn of the century, John Lorenzo Hubbell was all but a hero. He operated a trading post at Ganado, giving the Indians important contact with the outside world. Here, they traded silver work, wool, sheep and rugs for essentials such as flour, coffee, sugar, tobacco and clothing. To smooth the trading process, Hubbell was fluent in four languages—English, Spanish, Navajo and Hopi.

Hubbell was born in New Mexico in 1853, but lived in the town he named for 54 years. He homesteaded the land before it became part of the Navajo Reservation. In addition to his work with the trading post, Hubbell was also a sheriff and a member of the territorial legislature.

Hubbell tried improving the lot of Native Americans by bringing in a silversmith from Mexico to teach them silver working. But he really gained their respect during a smallpox epidemic. Having had smallpox when he was younger, he had developed an immunity to it. So during the epidemic, he was able to treat the Navajo without getting the disease himself.

Note that prohibition is still observed throughout the Hopi and Navajo country. It is illegal to bring or drink alcoholic beverages here.

---

include everything from uncomfortable-looking wooden saddles to vintage typewriters to old photographs that depict their work and life. You'll see pages of the first phonetic systems they made to help create the written Navajo language. Outside, towering cottonwoods and a friar's three-quarter-acre flower garden create a park-like oasis.

Three miles east on Route 264, a rare Indian Country traffic light (at Route 12) marks "downtown" **Window Rock**, a growing, modern Navajo Nation capital. West of the Navajo Nation Inn, the **Navajo Tribal Museum** (east of Route 12 on Route 264; 602-871-6673 or 602-871-6675) and **Navajo Arts & Crafts Enterprise** share space. The former, with sophisticated exhibits, leads visitors through an overview of historic and contemporary Navajo life and traditions. Mannequins were created via plaster casts from real Navajo. One room is devoted to changing exhibits by noted and emerging Navajo artists. The crafts guild encourages innovation among its members and guarantees the quality of everything it sells.

A short distance east on Route 264 is the **Navajo Nation Zoological Park** (602-871-6573). In this natural setting roam domestic and wild animals that figure in Navajo culture and folk lore—everything from coyote, wolves, cougars, bears, deer, elk, bobcats, rattlesnakes and prairie dogs to goats. In all, 53 species live in the park. Look for the churro sheep, brought by the Spanish. Herds are being increased because of their proven resistance to disease and the excellent weaving quality of their wool. Displays include fork-stick and crib-log examples of hogan architecture. A modest botanical garden here labels some typical high-desert plants: Indian rice grass, Navajo tea, lupine, asters and junipers.

A row of towering red sandstone pinnacles that resemble the **Haystacks**, for which they are named, forms the zoo's eastern boundary. The zoo and pinnacles are part of **Tse Bonito Tribal Park**, a primitive campground and shaded picnic area where the Navajo camped in 1864 on their "Long Walk" from their homeland.

When you arrive at the street light at the town of Window Rock, follow Route 12 north past Window Rock's shopping center, then drive right a mile to **Tseghahodzani**—"the rock with the hole in it." Here, you'll find a sweeping wall, several stories tall, of vermilion-colored sandstone. Nearly dead center is an almost perfectly circular "window" 130 feet in diameter eroded in it, offering views to the mountains beyond. John Collier, Commissioner of Indian Affairs in the 1930s, was so stirred by it, he declared it the site for the Navajo administrative center. Visitors can picnic and walk here.

Nearby, visit the octagonal stone **Council Chambers**, designed as a great ceremonial hogan. Murals painted by the late Gerald Nailor depict tribal history. This is where the 88-member Tribal Council meets four times a year to set policy. You'll hear Navajo and English spoken at all proceedings.

The prettiest route in Indian Country is **Route 12** from Route 40 through Window Rock and continuing north another 65 miles. The road hugs red rock bluffs while skirting pine forests, lakes, Navajo homes and hogans surrounded by pasture, orchards and cornfields.

Follow signs to the pine-clad Navajo Community College's **Tsaile Campus** (Route 12, about 60 miles north of Window Rock) and its tall glass hogan-shaped Ned Hatathli Cultural Center, with two floors devoted to the **Hatathli Museum and Gallery** (602-724-3311). From prehistoric times to the present—dioramas, murals, photographs, pottery, weaponry and other artifacts fill the grounds of this two-year college and expose many traditions of Native American culture. Wonderfully detailed murals tell the Navajo story of Creation, but you'll need to find someone to interpret it for you as there's little text. Books and crafts are sold in the adjacent gallery. Visitors are also welcome in the college's library and dining hall.

Route 64, west of Route 12, leads to a favorite and often mispronounced tourist destination, **Canyon de Chelly National Monument** ("Chelly" is actually pronounced "shay"). Access is also available off Route 191, six miles west of Ganado. By the time the Spanish arrived in the 1540s, the Navajo already occupied this trio of slick, towering red-walled canyons that converge in a Y. Navajo families still tend

---

NAVAJO CEREMONIAL DANCES

Three popular Navajo dances, which you may be lucky enough to see, are the Fire or Corral Dance, the Yeibichai Ceremony or Night-Way Dance, and the Enemy-Way Dance.

*The **Corral Dance** seeks divine help to avoid dangerous lightning and snake-bites; it's so named because part of the ceremony takes place within a corral of branches around a bonfire. The nine-day-long **Night-Way Dance** supposedly helps people suffering from nervousness or insanity. And the **Enemy-Way Dance** during the summer is a purifying ceremony to help people suffering from nightmares and other "enemies of the mind." Activities are held in a different place for each of the three nights of the ceremony and, at the conclusion, a sheep is slaughtered for breakfast.*

sheep and raise horses in the rugged terrain. Water near the surface sustains corn, squash and melon crops, apple and peach orchards.

It's hard to decide if Canyon de Chelly is most impressive from the rim drives, with their bird's-eye views of the hogan-dotted rural scenes, or astride a horse or an open-air jeep, sloshing (during spring runoff) through Chinle Wash. The best introduction for any adventure is the **Visitor Center** (along the main road through Chinle; 602-674-5436). Chinle, the shopping and administrative center for this part of the reservation, is as plain as its famed canyons are spectacular.

Be sure to stop at the visitor center museum where exhibits on 2000 years of canyon history, plus cultural demonstrations, local artists' exhibits and a ranger-staffed information desk will enlighten you about the area. Next door is a typical Navajo hogan; bring your cup and join rangers for coffee and questions most mornings. The center is also the place to hire Navajo guides—required if you hike, camp, or drive your own four-wheel-drive vehicle into the canyons.

Proud tales of the most daring Navajo victories are retold daily by guides who also point out bullet holes in the walls from brutal massacres. Thousands of much older ruins leave haunting clues to a people who lived here from about 200 A.D. until the late 1300s, when prolonged drought throughout the Four Corners region probably forced them to move to the Rio Grande and other regions of Arizona and New Mexico. Each bend in the canyon reveals ever-taller canyon walls, more pictographs and petroglyphs (historic and prehistoric art drawn on the rock). Each turn showcases vivid red walls and the yellow-green of leafy cottonwoods thriving along the canyon floor.

North and South Rim drives, each 21 miles one-way, take about two hours each to see. (It's a good idea to bring along brochures that point out geological, botanical and historical sites at each overlook.) **South Rim Drive** follows the Canyon de Chelly, which gives the monument its name. Highlights include: **White House Overlook** (located at 6.4 miles; the only nonguided hike into the canyon begins here), with a view of the remains of a multistory masonry village where about 100 persons lived about 800 years ago; **Old Hogan and Sliding Rock Overlook** (at 11 miles), where you will see ruins of a hogan; and shallow basins eroded out of sandstone (at 12.9 miles). The Navajo still sometimes gather fresh water from these basins. On a narrow ledge across the canyon, ancients built retaining walls to keep their homes from sliding off the sloping floor into the canyon.

Spider Rock Overlook (at 21.8 miles) is a vista of the steepest canyon walls, which are about a 1000-foot vertical drop. Look right to see Monument Canyon; left to see Canyon de Chelly. The 800-foot-tall spire at their junction is **Spider Rock**, where Spider Woman is said to carry naughty Navajo boys and girls. Those white specks at the top of her rock, Navajo parents say, are the bleached bones of boys and girls who did not listen to their parents. Legend has it she also taught the Navajo to weave.

North Rim Drive explores the **Canyon del Muerto**—"Canyon of the Dead"—named in 1882 by Smithsonian Institution expedition leader James Stevenson after finding remains of prehistoric Indian burials below Mummy Cave. Highlights include:

Antelope House Overlook (at 10.2 miles), which is named for paintings of antelope, probably made in the 1830s, on the canyon wall to the left of this four-story, 91-room ruin. Prehistoric residents contributed hand outlines and figures in white paint. Viewers from the overlook will see circular structures (kivas, or ceremonial chambers) and rectangular ones (storage or living quarters). Across the wash in an alcove 50 feet above the canyon floor is where, in the 1920s, archaeologists found the well-preserved body of an old man wrapped in a blanket of golden eagle feathers; under it was a white-cotton blanket in such good shape it appeared brand-new. It's believed he was a neighborhood weaver. Also here, at Navajo Fortress Viewpoint, the isolated high redstone butte across the canyon was once an important Navajo hideout from the Spanish and Americans, and perhaps from other Indian raiders.

Mummy Cave Overlook (at 19 miles), is the site of the largest, most beautiful ruins in Canyon del Muerto. The 1880s discovery of two mummies in cists found in the talus slope below the caves inspired this canyon's name.

Massacre Cave Overlook (at 21 miles) is site of the first documented Spanish contact with Canyon de Chelly Navajo. In the winter of 1805, a bloody battle is believed to have occurred at the rock-strewn ledge to the left, under a canyon rim overhang. Hoping to end persistent Navajo raiding on Spanish and Pueblo Indian villages, Antonio de Narbona led an expedition here and claimed his forces killed up to 115 Navajo, with another 33 taken captive.

CENTRAL NAVAJO COUNTRY LODGING

The Navajo Nation's only tribally owned motel, **Navajo Nation Inn** (at Window Rock's intersection of Routes 264 and 12; 602-871-4108) bustles with a mix of Navajo politicians and business people in suits and cowboys in black "reservation hats." The 56 rooms are pleasantly decorated with turquoise carpet, southwestern-style wood furniture, matching bedspreads and curtains with traditional Navajo rural scenes. Moderate.

A park-like scene is the setting for the historic stone and pueblo-style **Thunderbird Lodge** (a quarter-mile southeast of Canyon de Chelly National Monument Visitor Center, Chinle; 602-674-5841).

All 90 adobe-style rooms handsomely blend Navajo and Southwest architectural traditions. Each features Native American prints and is an easy walk to the canyon entrance. There's a gift shop and cafeteria on the premises.

Canyon de Chelly Motel (a block east of Route 191 on Route 7, Chinle; 602-674-5875) makes up for its sterile architecture by providing Chinle's only swimming pool (indoor, for guests only); 68 rooms, some for nonsmokers. Moderate.

CENTRAL NAVAJO COUNTRY RESTAURANTS

Café Sage (turn right a half-mile east of Hubbell's on Route 264), located in a two-story, brown stucco building, once the former Presbyterian College campus, welcomes tourists to dine in the Navajo Nation Health Foundation cafeteria where daily dinner specials might include tortellini and chicken with vegetables and garlic toast. Budget.

A trailer wide enough for two rows of sky-blue booths makes up **Tuller Café** (on the south side of Route 264 in St. Michaels; 602-871-4687). Here, they dish up meat loaf, pork chops, fish and chips, Navajo sandwiches, Navajo stew and Homer's goulash (macaroni, meat, green pepper, tomatoes) with garlic toast; budget.

Navajo Nation Inn Dining Room (at Window Rock's intersection of Routes 264 and 12; 602-871-4108), set in a modern, spacious room, is the Navajo capital's biggest restaurant. Seating 250 and decorated with Navajo art, the menu includes a taco platter, chicken, steak, Navajo sandwich, Navajoburger, beef stew, vegetable stew and sometimes a mutton buffet for moderate prices. Lunch is always busy when the restaurant fills up with politicians from the nearby tribal headquarters offices.

Junction Restaurant (adjacent to Canyon de Chelly Motel—a block east of Route 191 on Navajo Route 7; 602-674-8443) is one of

---

BED AND BREAKFAST NAVAJO-STYLE

The only enterprise on the entire Navajo reservation letting you experience life with a rural Navajo extended family is Tsosie's Bed and Breakfast (near Tsaile; 602-724-3383). Prices are moderate, accommodations primitive. Guests sleep in an authentic dirt-floor log hogan and use old-fashioned outhouses. Scholars, artists and folks eager for a change from more predictable conveniences have found the Coyote Clan hospitality a refuge. Special tours to favorite backcountry haunts can be arranged.

only two sit-down (non-buffet) restaurants in Chinle. A mix of peach-and-blue booths and blonde-wood tables and chairs set the mood for patrons dining on everything from *huevos rancheros* or biscuits and gravy for breakfast to a crab Louis or hot sandwiches for lunch to Mexican specialties for dinner. Budget to moderate.

Located in the original 1902 trading post built by Samuel Day, **Thunderbird Restaurant** (part of Thunderbird Lodge, near Canyon de Chelly National Monument in Chinle; 602-674-5841) serves up half a dozen entrées cafeteria-style for each meal. The menu offers a good variety, and changes some each day. You sit in a choice of booths or tables surrounded by walls decorated with top-quality, for-sale Navajo crafts. Moderate.

CENTRAL NAVAJO COUNTRY SHOPPING

Be sure to stop at the **Hubbell Trading Post** (Ganado; 602-755-3254), whose low stone walls, little changed in 90 years, contain the best Navajo rug selection en route, plus several rooms crammed with jewelry, dolls, books, baskets and historic postcards.

Navajo Arts and Crafts Enterprise (sharing a building with the Navajo Nation Museum, Window Rock; 602-871-4095) sells the work of some 500 Navajo craftsmakers. Selection is excellent and quantity is large including rugs of all styles, Navajo jewelry of all kinds and stuffed Navajo-style dolls.

Thunderbird Lodge Gift Shop (Chinle; 602-674-5841) provides a good selection of rugs, many of them made in the Chinle area, plus kachinas, jewelry, baskets and souvenirs. Some of the fine-quality crafts decorating the neighboring cafeteria walls are also for sale.

NAVAJO CRAFTS

The most popular basket style of the Navajo is the coiled wedding basket, with its bold red zigzag design. Other baskets found in Navajo trading posts are likely to be made by Paiutes, who also live in the area. Since the 1860s, the Navajo have engaged in the art of silversmithing, shaping silver to fit turquoise stones. Popular items are stoneless silver rings, bolos, earrings and necklaces— especially the squash blossom—made by handwrought or sand-cast methods. Rugs are still being woven on the reservation by thousands of Navajo women and a few dozen Navajo men, but only a small percentage of them are considered master-weavers, commanding the highest prices. Still, even a saddle blanket can be a treasured memento.

CENTRAL NAVAJO COUNTRY PARKS

Prior to their historic "Long Walk" to Fort Sumner, New Mexico, in 1864, the Navajo camped among the prominent red-sandstone hills called "Haystacks" in what is now **Tse Bonito Tribal Park**. The park encompasses the Navajo Nation Zoological Park, which houses 53 native and domestic species of animals, birds and other wildlife culturally important to the Navajo. The park is in Window Rock on Route 264.

Lake Asaayi Bowl Canyon Recreation Area is one of the prettiest of the Navajo fishing lakes, located in the Chuska Mountains known as the "Navajo Alps." Lake Asaayi is popular for fishing, picnicking and primitive camping. The 36-acre lake and creek are fishable year-round. From Window Rock, take Route 12 to Route 134. Drive northeast about four miles then south seven miles on a graded dirt road to the lake.

Canyon de Chelly National Monument, a 130-acre land of piñon and juniper forests cut by a trio of red-walled sandstone canyons, is the most famous and popular Navajo Reservation attraction. Extending eastward from Chinle to Tsaile, the canyon's rim elevations range from 5500 to 7000 feet, while the canyon bottoms drop from 30 feet nearest Chinle to 1000-feet deep farther east. Cottonwood trees and other vegetation shade farms connected by miles of sandy wash along the canyon bottom. Two major gorges, 27 and 34 miles long, dramatically unveil walls of 250-million-year-old solidified sand dunes in a strata geologists call the Defiance Plateau.

Northern Navajo Country

There's something both silly and irresistible about driving to **Four Corners** to stick each foot in a different state (Colorado and Utah) and each hand in still two others (Arizona and New Mexico) while someone takes your picture from a scaffolding. But then, this is the only place in the United States where you can simultaneously "be" in four different states. The inevitable Navajo crafts booths offer up jewelry, T-shirts, paintings, sandpaintings, fry bread and lemonade—a splendid way to make something festive out of two intersecting lines on a map.

To get there from the south, you'll have to pass by **Teec Nos Pos Arts and Crafts Center** (Routes 160 and 64), the usual roadside gallery of southwestern Indian crafts, with an emphasis on area sandpaintings.

Heading west on Route 160, even before travelers reach Kayenta, amazing eroded shapes emerge on the horizon—like the cathedral-sized and shaped Church Rock. Kayenta, originally a small town that grew up around John Wetherill's trading post at the 5564-foot elevation, today is both Arizona's gateway to Monument Valley and a coal-mining center.

The 24 miles north to Monument Valley on Route 163 is a prelude to the main event, huge red-rock pillars. Half Dome and Owl Rock on your left form the eastern edge of the broad Tyende Mesa. On your right rise **Burnt Foot Butte** and **El Capitan**, also called Agathla Peak—roots of ancient volcanoes whose dark rock contrasts with pale-yellow sandstone formations.

A half-mile north of the Utah state line on Route 163 is a cross-roads; left two miles to Gouldings Trading Post and Lodge, or right six miles to **Monument Valley Navajo Tribal Park Headquarters** (P.O. Box 93, Monument Valley, UT 84536; 801-727-3287) and Monument Valley Visitor Center. Inside the park headquarters are excellent views from a glass-walled observatory. This was the first Navajo Tribal Park, set aside in 1958. Within the park itself, you'll see more than 40 named and dozens more unnamed red and orange monolithic sandstone buttes and rock skyscrapers jutting hundreds of feet. It's here that you can arrange for Navajo-owned jeep tours into the monument.

For a small fee, you can explore the **17-mile Loop Drive** over a dirt road, badly rutted in places, to view a number of famous landmarks with names that describe their shapes, such as **Rain God Mesa, Three Sisters** and **Totem Pole**. At **John Ford's Point**, an Indian on horseback often poses for photographs, then rides out to chat and collect a tip. A 15-minute round-trip walk from **North Window** rewards you with panoramic views.

The Navajo and this land seem to belong together. A dozen Navajo families still live in the park, and several open their hogans to guided tours. For a small fee, they'll pose for your pictures. A number of today's residents are descendants of Navajo who arrived here in the mid-1860s with Headman Hoskinini, fleeing Kit Carson and his round-up of Navajo in the Canyon de Chelly area. Hoskinini lived here until his death in 1909.

NATIVE AMERICAN ARCHITECTURE

The first talented architects of Arizona were the Native Americans, with their handiwork ranging from cliff dwellings to pit houses. The Anasazi specialized in pueblos on cliff walls in northern Arizona. They mortared together cut stones for walls, while using logs and earth for the ceiling. Considering that rooms were small and without windows, they spent much time on their flat roofs, a perfect surface for chores. The Anasazi also built pit houses, flat-roofed stone houses partially dug into the ground. The Sinagua built pueblos similar to the Anasazi, but they preferred hills rather than canyons. And the Navajo people favored six-sided hogans made of logs and earth.

The ultimate cowboy-Indian western landscape, Monument Valley has been the setting for many movies—*How the West Was Won, Stagecoach, Billy the Kid, She Wore a Yellow Ribbon, The Trial of Billy Jack* to name just a few. In all, seven John Ford westerns were filmed here between 1938 and 1963.

Gouldings Trading Post, Lodge and Museum (two miles west of Route 163; 801-727-3231), a sleek, watermelon-colored complex on a hillside, blends in with enormous sandstone boulders stacked above it. The original Goulding two-story stone home and trading post, now a museum, includes a room devoted to movies made here. Daily showings can be seen in a small adjacent theater.

From Gouldings, it's nearly eight miles northwest on paved Oljeto Road to the single-story stone **Oljeto Trading Post**, its Depression-era gas pumps and scabby turquoise door are visible reminders of its age. Inside, ask to see a dusty museum room filled with Native American crafts hidden behind the turquoise bullpen-style mercantile. Often you can buy a fine used Navajo wedding basket for a good price.

Returning to Kayenta and Route 160, it's a scenic 18-mile drive northwest to the turnoff for the **Navajo National Monument**, which encompasses some of the Southwest's finest Anasazi ruins. This stunning region showcases the architectural genius of the area's early inhabitants.

To gain an overview of the Navajo National Monument, stop by the **Visitor Center and Museum** (nine miles north of Route 160 on Route 564, Black Mesa; 602-672-2366) featuring films and exhibits of the treasures tucked away beneath the sandstone cliffs. You'll be impressed by pottery, jewelry and tools created by the Kayenta Anasazi who lived in these exquisite canyons. There's also a craft gallery selling Zuni, Navajo and Hopi artwork.

From the visitor center, you can hike an undemanding forest trail to Betatakin Point Overlook, where you'll get an overview of Tsegi Canyon. One of the ruins here, **Inscription House**, is closed to protect it for posterity. However, it is possible to make the strenuous but rewarding hike to **Betatakin Ruin**, located in a dramatic alcove 500 feet above Tsegi Canyon. On this trip back in time, you'll see a 135-room ledge house that rivals the best of Mesa Verde. Also well worth a visit is remote **Keet Seel**. Even some of the roofs remain intact at this 160-room, five-kiva ruin. You can only reach this gem with a permit obtained at the visitor center. For more information on the ranger-led walks to these two well-preserved ruins see the "Hiking" section at the end of the chapter.

Back to Route 160, it's about 28 miles southwest to **Elephant Feet**, roadside geological formations that resemble the legs and feet of a gigantic sandstone elephant.

NORTHERN NAVAJO COUNTRY LODGING

Wetherill Inn (Route 163, a mile north of Route 160; 602-697-3231) in Kayenta has 54 spacious rooms sporting dark-brown furniture, upholstered chairs, black-and-brown spreads and matching curtains in Southwest style. Moderate.

Tour buses full of French, German, Italian and Japanese guests frequent the 160-room **Holiday Inn Kayenta** (Route 160 just west of Route 163; 602-697-3221). All rooms in the two-story adobe brick buildings offer floral carpets in hallways, cherry-wood furniture, upholstered chairs and spacious bathrooms. There's also a pool. Deluxe.

Sliding glass doors lead to balconies for each of 62 rooms at **Gouldings Lodge** (six miles east of the tribal park, Monument Valley, UT; 801-727-3231), so guests can enjoy the eroded Mitten Buttes. The only lodging right at Monument Valley, open since the 1920s, it takes brilliant advantage of the views. Deluxe.

Anasazi Inn at Tsegi Canyon (ten miles west of Kayenta on Route 160; 602-697-3793), with 52 rooms and a view of the canyon, is the closest lodging to Navajo National Monument; moderate.

NORTHERN NAVAJO COUNTRY RESTAURANTS

A hogan-style doorway sets the Indian theme at Kayenta's **Holiday Inn Restaurant** (Route 160 just west of Route 163; 602-697-3221), complete with Anasazi-style walls and sandpainting room dividers. Tables and matching chairs are of rattan. There's a continental breakfast buffet for diners in a hurry; a salad bar and burgers, sandwiches, Navajo tacos for lunch or dinner; meat and fish entrées for dinner only. Moderate.

Navajo owned and staffed **El Capitan Café** (Route 160, just east of Route 163; 602-697-8560) is popular with the locals, including the Navajo police. Folks come for Indian tacos and mutton stew. Budget.

Old West saloon architecture signals Kayenta's **Golden Sands Café** (Route 163, adjacent to the Wetherill Inn, a mile north of Route 160; 602-697-3684). Inside, wagon-wheel lamps, miniature stagecoaches and

---

THE HEALING ART OF SANDPAINTING

Medicine men will perform curing ceremonies while their assistants create elaborate pictures on the ground using sand and crushed minerals in an astonishing assortment of colors. These sandpaintings are destroyed at the ceremony's end, but similar designs glued onto wood are available for sale in shops and galleries throughout the region.

Navajo ceramics are simple, unadorned brown pieces glazed with hot pitch. The pieces look wonderful when made by a master.

---

other Old West memorabilia continue the theme. Breakfast specials include waffles with strawberries or blueberry pancakes; dinner features rib steak, barbecued chicken, veal cutlets, liver and onions; budget.

Lively, crowded and cheery, **La Fiesta Café** (on the east side of Route 163, a mile north of Route 160; 602-697-8513) serves very respectable Mexican entrées amid blue-and-white tablecloths. Moderate.

Three levels of dining stairstep a bluff in the **Stage Coach Dining Room** (at Gouldings Lodge near Monument Valley; 801-727-8231) where patrons can enjoy the panoramas of Monument Valley while eating. Part of a late 1980s major expansion and remodel, this former cafeteria now offers sit-down service. The peach-and-burnt umber booths and tables compliment the stunning sandstone bluffs and views outside. A dinner favorite is the roast leg of lamb. Desserts worth a splurge include pecan pie or a fudge brownie with ice cream. There's a salad bar, and nonalcoholic wine and beer are offered. Moderate.

An all-American menu at **Canyon Inn Café** (on Route 160, ten miles west of Kayenta; 602-697-3793) offers burgers, steak and chicken at moderate prices.

NORTHERN NAVAJO COUNTRY SHOPPING

Lee's Trading Post (next to Bashas grocery store in Kayenta at the Tee h'indeeh Shopping Center; 602-697-8439) sells beads, dolls, raw craft materials, Pendleton blankets, sandpaintings, corn necklaces, kachinas and a great choice of jewelry.

Ask to see the crafts room at the 1921 **Oljeto Trading Post** (801-727-3210), ten miles northwest of Gouldings near Monument Valley, and you'll be led into a dusty museum-like space. The room is crammed with antiques, as well as recently made crafts, some for sale, some for admiring. Best buys here are Navajo wedding baskets popular with today's local brides and grooms. Simple, brown-pitch Navajo pottery made in this area is also sold along with cedar cradleboards, popular on the "res" as a baby's safety seat.

Yellow Ribbon Gift Shop (part of the Gouldings complex at Monument Valley; 801-727-3231) provides southwestern tribal crafts and souvenirs for all budgets; closed in winter.

NORTHERN NAVAJO COUNTRY PARKS

Monument Valley Navajo Tribal Park (801-727-3287), straddling the Arizona-Utah border, is the jewel of tribally run Navajo Nation parks. With its 29,816 acres of monoliths, spires, buttes, mesas, canyons and sand dunes—all masterpieces of red rock erosion—it is a stunning destination. With dozens of families still living here, it is also a sort of Williamsburg of Navajoland. There's a visitor center with museum and shops, tribal food booths (mainly summer months) and arts and crafts. The park is located on Route 163, 24 miles northeast of Kayenta. The visitor center is east another four miles.

Three of the Southwest's most beautiful Anasazi pueblo ruins are protected in the canyons of **Navajo National Monument** (602-671-2366), a 360-acre park at the 6000-foot elevation swathed in piñon and juniper forests. Inscription House Ruin is so fragile it is closed. Betatakin Ruin, handsomely set in a cave high up a canyon wall, is visible from an overlook. But close looks at Betatakin and the largest site, Keet Seel, require fairly strenuous hikes permitted between Memorial Day and Labor Day. There is a visitor center, museum and gift shop. To get there, take Route 160 west of Kayenta, turn right at Route 564 and continue nine miles.

The Sporting Life

FISHING

Fishing is permitted year-round with a one-day to one-year Navajo tribal license required at all lakes, streams and rivers in the Navajo Nation. Exceptions are **Whiskey Lake** and **Long Lake**, known for their trophy-size trout, located in the Chuska Mountains, a dozen miles south of Route 134 via logging routes 8000 and 8090. Their season is May 1 through November 30.

Popular all-year lakes stocked with rainbow trout each spring include **Wheatfields Lake** (44 miles north of Window Rock on Route 12) and **Tsaile Lake** (a half-mile south of Navajo Community College in Tsaile). Tsaile Lake is also popular for bass and catfish.

No fishing tackle or boats are for rent on the reservation. Boats are permitted on many of the lakes; most require electric motors only. Get fishing license and boating permits from the following locations: **Red Barn Trading Post** (Sanders; 602-688-2762); **CSWTA Inc. Environmental Consultant** (Tuba City; 602-283-4323); **Cow Springs Trading Post** (Tonalea; 602-283-5377); **Navajo Fish & Wildlife** (Window Rock; 602-871-6451); **Kayenta Trading Post** (Kayenta; 602-

697-3541); **Lakeside Store Wheatfields** (Wheatfields Lake; 602-724-3262); or **Tsaile Trading Post** (Tsaile; 602-724-3397). Most of them also sell fishing gear.

GOLF

In Holbrook, you can tee up at **Hidden Cover Golf Course** (Exit 283 two miles west of Route 40; 602-524-3097), an 18-hole course carved out of the high desert grasslands and surrounded by scenic mountains and hillsides.

JOGGING

Navajo and Hopi, who pride themselves on their long-distance running traditions that date back to first contact with whites in the 1540s, host races at every tribal fair. Races are open to non-Indians, as well. And it is common to see Native American joggers daily along virtually any route, so bring your togs and run too.

At Canyon de Chelly, try the White House Ruins trail or either of the rim trails; also the four-mile road leading into Monument Valley or roads to Oljeto and around Gouldings Lodge.

HORSEBACK RIDING

A horse is a great way to connect with a Navajo guide while seeing awesome country through his eyes. Most offer one-hour to overnight or longer options; there's flexibility on where you go and how long you stay.

In Canyon de Chelly, **Justin Tso's Tsegi Stables** (602 674-5678) offers tours to White House Ruins and elsewhere in and beyond the canyon. **Twin Trails Tours** (602-674-3466) depart from the North Rim of Canyon de Chelly, just past Antelope House turnoff.

In Monument Valley, **Ed Black's Horse Riding Tours** (located via a dirt road north from the visitor center a quarter-mile; 801-739-4285) can be an hour around The Mittens, or all day or longer into the valley. **Bigman's Horseback Riding** (along the four-mile park entrance road; 602-677-3219), offers an hour-and-a-half ride to overnight rides into the monument's buttes, mesas and canyons.

Arrange for horse rides to Keet Seel Ruin in Navajo National Monument through the **National Park Service** (602-671-2366).

BICYCLING

Bicycling is permitted on any paved roads throughout Navajo Country, but only on the main paved highways on the Hopi Reservation.

While you'll find no designated bike paths or trails within either reservation, bicycles are well suited to both rim roads at Canyon de Chelly and along the paved, pine-clad nine miles of Route 564 into Navajo National Monument Visitor Center. Mountain bikes are particularly suited to the 17-mile rutted dirt loop open to visitors in Monument Valley. Cyclists from around the world are attracted to the uphill challenges of the Chuska Mountain Routes 134 (paved), 68 and 13 (partially paved). Petrified Forest National Park routes will often be too hot for daytime summer riding, but offer a splendid way to sightsee in cooler spring and fall seasons.

HIKING

Because most of the land covered in this chapter is tribally owned or in national parks and monuments, hiking trail options are limited. Hopi backcountry is not open to visitors; the backcountry is, however, on the Navajo Indian Reservation. For the mountains, ask for suggestions from area trading posts, or hire an Indian guide by the hour or overnight or longer. Guides know the way and can share stories about the area; they're available through the **Navajo Tourism Office** (602-755-3254) near Window Rock; **Canyon de Chelly National Monument Visitor Center** (602-674-5436); or at the **Monument Valley Visitor Center** (801-727-3287).

SOUTHERN NAVAJO RESERVATION TRAILS **Little Painted Desert County Park** has a strenuous one-mile hiking trail descending 500 feet into some of the most colorful hills in all the Painted Desert. Colors are most intense early and late in the day.

NAVAJO RODEO

The Navajo love ropin' and bronco ridin'. Their statisticians claim the Navajo host more rodeos per year than all other United States tribes combined. Rarely does a summer weekend pass without Navajo cowboys and cowgirls of all ages gathering somewhere on the reservation. To find one when you visit, call The Navajo Nation Today Free Press, a weekly, in Window Rock (602-871-4289); the Navajo Tourism Office (602-871-6659); or Navajo Radio Station KTNN (602-871-2666).

Horses have been an important part of Navajo culture since the Spanish first introduced them in the mid-16th century.

Homolovi Ruins State Park offers a one-mile hiking trail leading past two of the largest Anasazi Indian village ruins; at each you'll see skeletal walls outlining living quarters and kivas (ceremonial chambers) from villages thought to have belonged to the ancestors of today's Hopi Indians before they moved to their current mesas.

Petrified Forest National Park's summertime temperatures often soar into the 90s and 100s, so hiking is best done early or late in the day. During the winter, daytime temperatures seldom reach 50 degrees, so dress warmly. Water is available only at the visitor centers at the north and south end of the park, so you're wise to carry extra with you.

The Petrified Forest National Park's scenic loop, **Crystal Forest Interpretive Trail** (.5 mile), leads past the most concentrated petrified wood stands in the park. You can see how tall these ancient trees were, and the great variety of colors that formed after crystal replaced the wood cells.

An introduction to the Chinle Formation, **Blue Mesa Hike** (1 mile) is a loop interpretive trail that leads past a wonderland of blue, gray and white layered hills. Signs en route explain how the hills formed and are now eroding.

The Flattops (unlimited miles) trailhead descends off sandstone-relic mesas several hundred feet into Puerco Ridge and other areas of the 10,000-acre Rainbow Forest Wilderness at the park's southeastern end. A quarter-mile trail leads into the area, and then you're on your own, exploring a vast gray-and-brown mudstone and siltstone badlands with wide vistas around every hill. The backcountry permits required to visit this remote portion of the park are free from the visitor center; you can stay up to 14 days.

Painted Desert Wilderness Area (unlimited miles) trailhead begins at Kachina Point at the park's north end. A brief trail descends some 400 feet, then leaves you on your own to explore cross-country some 35,000 acres of red-and-white-banded badlands of mudstone and siltstone, bald of vegetation. The going is sticky when wet. Get free backcountry permits at either visitor center.

CENTRAL NAVAJO COUNTRY TRAILS   **Canyon de Chelly**'s only hike open to visitors without a guide is **White House Ruin Trail** (1.25 miles), beginning at the 6.4-mile marker on the South Rim Drive. The trail switchback is down red sandstone swirls, then crosses a sandy wash (rainy seasons you will do some wading in Chinle Creek; bring dry socks) to a cottonwood-shaded masonry village with 60 rooms surviving at ground level, and an additional ten rooms perched in a cliff's alcove above.

From 9 a.m. to noon, free ranger-led hikes of varying lengths elsewhere in the canyon begin most mornings at the visitor center. Navajo guides can be hired at the visitor center to take you on short or overnight hikes into the canyon.

Hiking is not permitted in **Monument Valley** without a Navajo guide. Hire one at the visitor center (801-727-3287) for an hour, overnight or longer. Fred Cly (801-727-3283, or ask at the visitor center) is a knowledgeable guide who's especially good at recommending photo angles and best times of day.

Navajo National Monument trails include **Sandal Trail** (.5 mile), a fairly level self-guided trail to Betatakin Ruin overlook; bring binoculars.

The ranger-led hike to **Betatakin Ruin**, or "ledge house" in Navajo (2.5 miles), is strenuous, requiring a return climb up 700 steps. But it's worth the effort for the walk through the floor of Tsegi Canyon. National Park Service guides lead three tours limited to 24 hikers each day, May through September. Tokens are awarded on a first-come, first-served basis at the visitor center beginning daily at 8 a.m.

The hike to **Keet Seel** (8 miles), the biggest Anasazi ruin in Arizona (160 rooms dating from 950 to 1300 A.D.) is open to hikers for long weekends, May through October. Much of the trail is sandy, making the trek fairly tiresome. You can stay only one night; 20 people a day may hike in. Reservations are made 60 days in advance, call 602-671-2366. Or take your chances and ask for cancellations when you get there.

Transportation

BY CAR

This is a land of wide-open spaces, but don't despair. Roads have vastly improved in the last decade, easing the way for travelers. Bounded on the south by **Route 40**, two parallel routes farther north lead east and west through Indian Country: the southern Route 264 travels alongside the three Hopi mesas and Window Rock; the northern Route 160, en route to Colorado, is gateway to all the northern reservation attractions. **Route 89**, the main north-to-south artery, connects Flagstaff with Lake Powell, traversing the Western Reservation. Five other good, paved north-south routes connect Route 40 travelers with Indian Country. **Route 99/2** and **Route 87** connect the Winslow area with Hopi villages. **Route 191** leads to Ganado, Canyon de Chelly and Utah. **Route 12**, arguably the prettiest of all, connects Route 40 with Window Rock and the back side of Canyon de Chelly. This is desert driving; be sure to buy gas when it is available.

BY AIR

There is no regularly scheduled commuter air service to Hopi or Navajo lands. The nearest airports are Gallup, New Mexico; Flagstaff, Arizona; and Cortez, Colorado.

BY BUS

Navajo Transit System (based in Fort Defiance; 602-729-5449) offers weekday bus service between Fort Defiance and Window Rock in the east and Tuba City in the west. The system also heads north from Window Rock to Kayenta on weekdays, with stops including Navajo Community College at Tsaile.

BY TRAIN

Amtrak's (800-872-7245) daily "Southwest Chief" connecting Los Angeles with Chicago stops at three Indian Country gateway cities: Flagstaff, Winslow and Gallup. Nava-Hopi Tours (602-774-5003) out of Flagstaff offers people arriving on Amtrak bus tours of this area.

JEEP TOURS

Jeeps, either with tops down or with air conditioning on (not all jeeps have air conditioning, so ask operators before you pay money) are a popular way to see Navajo Reservation attractions noted for occasional sand bogs and even quicksand pockets. Navajo guides often live in the region and can share area lore and Native American humor.

At Canyon de Chelly, **Thunderbird Lodge Tours** (Thunderbird Lodge, Chinle; 602-674-5443) offer half- or all-day outings in large, noisy, converted all-terrain Army vehicles.

Monument Valley tour operators offer half-day and all-day tours of Monument and adjoining Mystery Valley. It's the only way visitors can see the stunning backcountry. Most tours include visits to an inhabited hogan. Some offer lunch or dinner. Licensed operators include **Gouldings Monument Valley Tours** (at Gouldings Lodge near Monument Valley; 801-727-3231); **Tom K. Bennett Tours** (801-727-3283); **Golden Sands Tours** (from the Golden Sands Café on Route 163, a mile north of Route 160 in Kayenta; 602-697-3684); **Bill Crawley Monument Valley Tours** (Kayenta; 602-697-3463); **Frank and Betty Jackson's Dineh Guided Tours** (Monument Valley Visitor Center; 801-727-3287); and **Navajo Guided Tour Service** (Monument Valley Visitor Center; 801-727-3287).

GLENN KIM

SIX

North Central Arizona

When it comes to north central Arizona, visitors soon discover that it's a region of vivid contrasts. The many unusual places to be found in this area vary dramatically in everything from altitude to attitude, from climate to culture. Here, you'll find communities that range from Old West to New Age, from college town to artist colony, along with lava cones and red rock spires, Native American ruins and vast pine forests, even a meteor crater, all just waiting to be explored.

Set at the edge of a huge volcano field, Flagstaff grew up as a railroad town in the midst of the world's largest ponderosa pine forest. The town was founded in 1881, less than a year before the first steam train clattered through, and thrived first on timber and later on tourism. Today, both freight and passenger trains still pass through Flagstaff. The largest community between Albuquerque and the greater Los Angeles area on Route 40, one of the nation's busiest truck routes, Flagstaff's huge restaurant and lodging industry prospers year-round. In fact, casual visitors detouring from the interstate to fill up the gas tank and buy burgers and fries along the commercial strip that is Flagstaff's Route 40 business loop can easily form the misimpression that the town is one long row of motels and fast-food joints. A closer look will reveal it as a lively college town with considerable historic charm. A short drive outside of town will take you to fascinating ancient Indian ruins as well as Arizona's highest mountains and strange volcanic landscapes.

Less than an hour's drive south of Flagstaff via magnificent Oak Creek Canyon, Sedona is a strange blend of spectacular scenery, chic resorts, western art in abundance and New Age notions. You can go jeeping or hiking in the incomparable Red Rock Country, play some

Flagstaff has been called "The City of Seven Wonders" because of its proximity to the Grand Canyon, Oak Creek Canyon, Walnut Canyon, Wupatki National Monument, Sunset Crater, Meteor Crater and the San Francisco Peaks.

of the country's most beautiful golf courses, shop for paintings until you run out of wall space or just sit by Oak Creek and feel the vibes. People either love Sedona or hate it. Often both.

You'll also have the chance to visit one of the state's best-preserved ghost towns. Jerome, a booming copper town a century ago, was abandoned in the 1950s and then repopulated in the 1960s by artists and hippies to become a tourist favorite today.

Prescott is a quiet little town with a healthy regard for its own history. Long before Phoenix, Flagstaff or Sedona came into existence, Prescott was the capital of the Arizona Territory. Today, it is a city of museums, stately 19th-century architecture and century-old saloons. Change seems to happen slowly and cautiously here. As you stroll the streets of town, you may feel that you've slipped back through time into the 1950s, into the sort of all-American community you don't often find any more.

Flagstaff Area

Visitors who view Flagstaff from the mountain heights to the north will see this community's most striking characteristic: It is an island in an ocean of ponderosa pine forest stretching as far as the eye can see. At an elevation of 7000 feet, Flagstaff has the coolest climate of any city in Arizona. Because of its proximity to slopes in the San Francisco Peaks, Flagstaff is the state's leading ski resort town in the winter. It is also a lively college town, with students accounting for nearly 20 percent of the population.

A good place to start exploring the Flagstaff area is downtown, toward the west end of Santa Fe Avenue (the business loop of Route 40). The downtown commercial zone retains its turn-of-the-century frontier architecture. Neither run-down nor yuppified, this historic district specializes in shops that cater to students from Northern Arizona University, on the other side of the interstate and railroad tracks. A building-by-building historic downtown **walking tour brochure** is distributed by the Arizona Historical Society—Pioneer Museum (2340 North Fort Valley Road; 602-774-6272); the Main Street Foundation (114 North San Francisco Street; 602-774-1330); and the Flagstaff Visitor Center (101 West Santa Fe Avenue; 602-774-9541). Take time to stroll through the old residential area just north of the downtown business district. Attractive Victorian houses, many of them handmade from volcanic lava rock, give the neighborhood its unique character.

On a hilltop just a mile west of downtown is the renowned **Lowell Observatory** (1400 West Mars Hill; 602-774-3358; recorded schedule information, 602-774-2096; admission). Another sightseeing highlight in the university area is **Riordan Mansion State Historic Park** (1300 Riordan Ranch Road; 602-779-4395; admission), a block off Milton Road north of the intersection of Route 40 and Route 17. The biggest early-day mansion in Flagstaff, it was built in 1904 by two brothers who were the region's leading timber barons. Constructed duplex-style with 40 rooms and 13,000 square feet of living space, the mansion blends rustic log-slab and volcanic rock construction with turn-of-the-century opulence and plenty of creativity and imagination. Tour

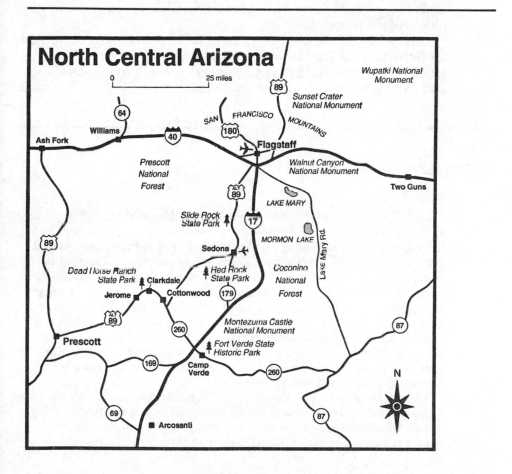

guides escort visitors through the mansion to see its original furnishings and family mementos.

Just north of town on Route 180, the **Museum of Northern Arizona** (301 North Fort Valley Road; 602-774-5211; admission) is known worldwide for its exhibits of Indian artifacts, geology, biology and Southwest art. During the summer months, the museum hosts separate exhibitions of Navajo, Hopi and Zuni artists.

Nearby, the **Coconino Center for the Arts** (2300 North Fort Valley Road; 602-779-6921) provides space for fine-arts exhibits, musical performances, workshops and a folk-arts program. In summer, coinciding with the Museum of Northern Arizona's Indian artists exhibitions, the Center for the Arts presents a two-month Festival of Native American Arts.

In the same vicinity, the **Arizona Historical Society—Pioneer Museum** (2340 North Fort Valley Road; 602-774-6272; admission) exhibits memorabilia and oddities from Flagstaff's past, including a stuffed bear, Percival Lowell's 1912 mechanical computer and early-day photos of the Grand Canyon.

Not far beyond the Museum of Arizona on Route 180 is the turnoff for **Schultz Pass Road**. This unpaved scenic drive offers a close-up look at the spectacular San Francisco Peaks, which tower above Flagstaff. About 14 miles long, the road comes out on Route 89 a short

---

STARGAZING FLAGSTAFF-STYLE

Lowell Observatory (on Mars Hill one mile west of downtown Flagstaff on Santa Fe Avenue; admission) was built by wealthy astronomer Percival Lowell in 1894 to take advantage of the exceptional visibility created by Flagstaff's clean air and high altitude. His most famous achievement during the 22 years he spent here was the discovery of canals on the planet Mars, which he submitted to the scientific community as "proof" of extraterrestrial life. Building the observatory proved to be a great accomplishment in itself, though. The planet Pluto was discovered by astronomers at Lowell Observatory 14 years after Dr. Lowell's death, and the facility continues to be one of the most important centers for studying the solar system. Take a guided tour of the observatory and see Dr. Lowell's original Victorian-era telescope. On some summer evenings, astronomers hold star talks and help visitors stargaze through one of the center's smaller telescopes.

*Overshadowed by Lowell Observatory, the **Northern Arizona University Campus Observatory** (west side of San Francisco Street on campus; 602-523-7170) actually offers visitors a better chance to look through a larger telescope. Public viewing sessions are held every Thursday night when the sky is clear.*

Flagstaff got its name when a local pine tree was used as a flagstaff for the 1876 Fourth of July festivities. The flagstaff later became a landmark for passing wagon trains.

distance north of the turnoff to **Sunset Crater National Monument** (602-527-7024). Sunset Crater, a brightly colored 1000-foot-tall volcanic cone in the San Francisco Volcano Field, is of recent origin. It first erupted in the winter of 1064–65 and kept spraying out molten rock and ash until 1250. A one-mile self-guided nature trail leads from the visitor center through cinder and lava fields. The ice cave along the trail has been closed because of unstable conditions since a 1984 cave-in. Hiking is no longer permitted on the slopes of Sunset Crater, either, since footprints create streaks visible from a great distance and mar the beauty of the perfect cone, but rangers guide trips up nearby O'Leary Crater, outside the monument boundary in the national forest. Several other volcanic craters in the national forest are also open to hikers and off-road vehicles.

Near Sunset Crater National Monument, **Wupatki National Monument** (602-527-7040) preserves numerous pueblo ruins on the fringes of the volcano field. They were inhabited in the 12th and 13th centuries, at the same time the volcanic activity was at its peak. Repeatedly, fiery eruptions would drive the Native Americans out of the area and volcanic ash would fertilize the land and lure them back. As a result, Wupatki's communities were small, architecturally dissimilar, often designed for defense as different groups competed for use of the rich farmland. A paved 36-mile loop road takes motorists through Sunset Crater and Wupatki national monuments, rejoining Route 89 about 15 miles from its starting point.

Sinagua Indians (the name is Spanish for "without water," referring to their farming methods) lived from the Grand Canyon southward throughout central Arizona and are thought to be the ancestors of the Hopi people. One of the most interesting Sinagua sites is at **Walnut Canyon National Monument** (602-526-3367). Take exit 204 from Route 40 just east of Flagstaff. Here, the Indians built more than 300 cliff dwellings in the walls of a 400-foot-deep gorge. A paved trail takes visitors around an "island in the sky" for a close-up look at the largest concentration of cliff dwellings, while a second trail follows the rim of this beautiful canyon.

Another fascinating bit of this region's flamboyant geology can be found at **Meteor Crater** (602-289-2362; admission), located off Route 40 some 30 miles east of Flagstaff. This giant hole in the ground is the result of a shooting star 80 feet in diameter that collided with the earth at an unimaginable speed long ago.

Movie stars such as Humphrey Bogart, Cornell Wilde and Walter Brennan used to stay at Flagstaff's Monte Vista in its glory days. Some rooms bear plaques naming a famous person who slept in them.

FLAGSTAFF AREA LODGING

Flagstaff offers a good selection of bed-and-breakfast accommodations. Among the antique-furnished vintage lodgings available in the downtown area is **The Inn at Four Ten** (410 North Leroux Street; 602-774-0088), a beautifully restored 1907 home with three guest suites featuring period decor. Rates are moderate in the summer, budget off-season. Other bed and breakfasts in the historic district include the homelike, moderately priced **Birch Tree Inn** (824 West Birch Street; 602-774-1042) and the budget-priced **Dierker House** (423 West Cherry Street; 602-774-3249), where the three guest rooms have king-sized beds with down comforters and share a common sitting room.

A large, rather elegant modern hotel in the moderate price range is the **Woodlands Plaza Hotel** (1175 West Route 66; 602-773-8888). Rooms are spacious and modern, with pastel color schemes and king-size beds. Facilities include whirlpool spas, a steam room, sauna, fitness center and heated swimming pool. Room service, valet service and complimentary limousine service are also among the hotel's amenities.

The **Monte Vista Hotel** (100 North San Francisco Street; 602-779-6971), a 1927 hotel now listed on the National Register of Historic Places, has spacious rooms that feature oak furniture, king-size brass beds, velvet wall coverings and gold-tone bathroom fittings—a touch of old-time elegance priced in the budget range.

The other downtown historic hotel, the **Weatherford Hotel** (23 North Leroux Street; 602-774-2731) operates as a youth hostel and also offers a few very plain private rooms in the budget price range. Flagstaff has two other hostels as well—the **Downtowner Independent Youth Hostel** (19 South San Francisco Street; 602-774-8461) and the **Du Beau Motel International Hostel** (19 West Phoenix Avenue; 602-774-6731). Especially in the summer months, all three host backpack travelers of all ages from all parts of the world, and solitary travelers are sure to make instant friends here.

In the pines just five minutes out of town, the **Arizona Mountain Inn** (685 Lake Mary Road; 602-774-8959) offers bed-and-breakfast rooms in the main inn at the low end of the moderate price range and one- to five-bedroom cottages with fireplaces and cooking facilities at the high end. Amenities include baseball, volleyball, horseshoe and basketball areas, as well as hiking and cross-country skiing trails.

FLAGSTAFF AREA RESTAURANTS

For fine dining in Flagstaff, one good bet is the small, homey-feeling **Cottage Place Restaurant** (126 West Cottage Avenue; 602-774-8431). Specialties include châteaubriand and roast duck à l'orange, as well as a vegetarian pasta con pesto. Prices fall in the moderate range; reservations recommended.

Another good place for a romantic dinner is the **Woodlands Café** (1175 West Route 66; 602-773-9118). There's booth and table seating at this southwestern-style dining room with atrium windows and forest views. Navajo white walls are decorated with Navajo rugs and baskets; the chandelier is crafted from deer racks. You can select from such entrées as Atlantic salmon with béarnaise sauce and chicken breast with smoked gouda cream sauce. Prices are moderate; reservations are recommended.

Yet another of Flagstaff's finest restaurants is **Chez Marc** (503 Humphreys Street; 602-774-1343), a small, intimate restaurant in a house listed on the National Register of Historic Places. A typical dinner might consist of duck pâté with pistachio hors d'oeuvre, salad niçoise and roast Arizona squab atop green cabbage and wild mushrooms. Prices start in the moderate range.

The **Main Street Bar and Grill** (4 South San Francisco Street; 602-774-1519) is a student favorite serving an array of budget-to-moderate-priced dishes such as fajitas, Philly cheesesteaks, quiche Lorraine and barbecued ribs. Other great little contemporary restaurants in the downtown area, featuring menu selections that emphasize healthy gourmet food, include **Charly's** (23 North Leroux Street; 602-779-1919) on the ground floor of the Weatherford Hotel youth hostel and **Café Espress** (16 North San Francisco Street; 602-774-0541), both in the budget-price range.

As a university town, Flagstaff has a plethora of budget-priced pizzerias—18 of them at last count. We recommend **NiMarco Pizza** (101 South Beaver Street; 602-779-2691). Besides the largest pizza-by-the-slice selection, NiMarco also has Italian-style baked stuffed sandwiches including exceptional stromboli.

For an unusual dining environment, head out of town to the **Mormon Lake Lodge Steak House & Saloon** (Mormon Lake Road; 602-354-2227), which has been in operation since 1924 and is reputed to be one of the West's finest steak houses. The restaurant also features ribs, chicken and trout, all cooked over a bed of mountain oak embers. The authentic brands from ranches all across Arizona, which have been seared into the wood paneling of the restaurant's walls, are said to be the result of one of the wildest branding parties ever. Prices are moderate.

FLAGSTAFF AREA SHOPPING

The **Art Barn** (2320 North Fort Valley Road; 602-774-0822) next to Coconino Center for the Arts offers works of local and reservation artists for sale. A nonprofit, member-supported organization, the Art Barn provides artist facilities including classes, exhibition space and a bronze foundry.

Flagstaff also boasts quite a few regional arts and crafts galleries, most of them featuring traditional and contemporary Navajo and Hopi work. One of the largest is **Four Winds Traders** (118 West Santa Fe Avenue; 602-774-1067). Wander around the downtown area and you will find a number of others. East of downtown, **Jay's Indian Arts** (2227 East 7th Avenue; 602-526-2439) is a branch of Tucson's famous Native American arts and crafts "supermarket." In operation since 1953, Jay's keeps mobile units on the road throughout the Southwest buying rugs, jewelry, pottery, kachinas and the like direct from artists on the Navajo, Hopi, Papago, Apache and Pueblo reservations.

FLAGSTAFF AREA NIGHTLIFE

Because of the university, Flagstaff boasts both a busy cultural events calendar and a lively nightclub scene. On the cultural side, the performing arts roster includes the **Flagstaff Symphony Orchestra** (602-774-

---

METEOR CRATER

Be glad that you weren't anywhere near Flagstaff 49,000 years ago. That's when a huge nickel-iron ball, weighing several million tons and traveling 133,000 miles per hour, hit the earth and exploded. All life within a 100-mile radius was destroyed. The crater it left is nearly 600 feet deep and about a mile across. Later, prehistoric people took advantage of the crater and settled here.

The large hole remained a mystery for many years. Geologist Daniel Barringer theorized a century ago that this was a meteor impact crater. Experts scoffed at the idea, especially since volcanic craters, so common east of Flagstaff, suggested a more rational explanation for the phenomenon. He staked a mining claim to search for the huge, valuable mass of iron and nickel which he was convinced lay buried beneath the crater. An ambitious drilling operation did not strike a mother lode from outer space but did come up with fragments proving the theory, and the geologist's family has been operating the claim as a tourist attraction ever since. The visit to Meteor Crater (about 30 miles east of Flagstaff, five miles off Route 40 at exit 233; 602-289-2362; admission) is worth the fairly steep admission fee if you take time to hike out along the spectacular three-mile trail that goes all the way around the rim.

The Apollo astronauts trained at Meteor Crater before their moon landings in the late 1960s.

5107), **Coconino Chamber Ensemble** (602-523-3879), Flagstaff Master Chorale (602-523-2642), **Flagstaff Oratorio Chorus** (602-523-4760) and **NAU Opera Theatre** (602-523-3731). Most performances are held at the **Coconino Center for the Arts** (2300 North Fort Valley Road; 602-779-6921) or at the **Northern Arizona University School of Performing Arts** (602-523-3731).

The **Theatrikos Community Theatre Group** performs at the Flagstaff Playhouse (11 West Cherry Street; 602-774-1662). For current performance information, inquire at the Flagstaff Visitor Center (101 West Santa Fe Avenue; 602-774-9541) or tune to the university's National Public Radio station, KNAU, at 88.7 on your FM dial.

As for nightclubs, the most popular university hangout is **Fiddlestix** (702 South Milton Road; 602-774-6623), featuring live rock and Top-40 dance music. Another hot spot is **The Monsoons** (22 East Santa Fe Avenue; 602-773-9923), a rock-and-roll club attached to a barbecue restaurant. **Charly's** (23 North Leroux Street; 602-779-1919), on the ground floor of the Weatherford Hotel youth hostel, features jazz and blues.

For a more intimate atmosphere, check out **Granny's Closet** (218 South Sitgreaves Street; 602-774-8331) or the **Mad Italian** (101 South San Francisco Street; 602-779-1820), known locally as the "Mad I."

The sometimes rowdy **Museum Club** (3404 East Santa Fe Avenue; 602-526-9434), better known among the locals as the "Zoo Club," is one of the best examples in the West of an authentic cowboy club. The huge log-cabin-style building began as a trading post and taxidermy shop in 1918 and has operated as a nightclub since 1936. The decor includes an ornate 1880 mahogany back bar and an astonishing collection of big-game trophies. Legendary country-and-western artists who have performed here include Willie Nelson, Bob Wills and the Texas Playboys, Commander Cody and the Lost Planet Airmen and many others.

FLAGSTAFF AREA PARKS

Lake Mary (602-556-7474) is actually two long reservoirs. Upper and Lower Lake Mary provide the primary water supply for Flagstaff. They were created by damming Walnut Creek, cutting off the water flow through Walnut Canyon National Monument. The National Forest Service operates picnic areas on the wooded lakeshore and the small Lakeview Campground overlooks the upper lake. Both are popular

The elevation drop from Flagstaff to Sedona is 2500 feet, and the temperature is often 20 degrees higher in Sedona than in Flagstaff.

places to fish for northern pike, walleye pike and catfish. The upper lake is also used for power boating and waterskiing. You'll find the park eight miles south of Flagstaff on Lake Mary Road. From Route 40, take exit 195-B and follow the signs.

Mormon Lake (602-556-7474) is the largest natural lake in Arizona, covering over 2000 acres when full. But the lake is very shallow, averaging only ten feet in depth, and often shrinks to practically nothing during spells of dry weather. Because the shoreline keeps changing, there is no boat ramp and anglers must carry their boats to the water by hand. Still, it is a good place to catch pike and catfish. Several hiking trails run along the lakeshore and into the surrounding forest. There's also a lodge and restaurant. The lake is located 20 miles southeast of Flagstaff via Lake Mary Road.

Sedona Area

Sedona. The creative and mystical have always been intrigued by the place. Indians once came here to worship, New Agers to feel the "vibrations," artists to capture the beauty. But no matter the number of its devotees, no one knows exactly why this place has such appeal. Its essence remains elusive. Perhaps part of the seduction are the colors— red rock mountains that rise from the earth to nestle in brilliant blue sky. The landscape is a dreamy mix of fancifully shaped hoodoos, buttes and spires rising above green piñon and juniper trees, low shrubs and stark patches of reddish rock. Adjacent to Sedona is the spectacular Oak Creek Canyon, named after the creek that formed it by carving into the southern edge of the Colorado Plateau. All of these natural elements are highlighted by an intense sunlight that brings out contrast and color.

Sedona is located about halfway between Phoenix and the Grand Canyon. The first to discover this special spot were the Indians. About 800 years ago, the Southern Sinagua Indians settled here, leaving behind a 200-room cliff dwelling ruin called Honaki, which is now on the National Register of Historic Places. If you're out hiking, it's worth a side trip to discover these ruins. They're located on an alcove on the west side of Loy Butte next to Lincoln Canyon.

More settlers came at the turn of the century. At the time, the economic base of the economy was ranching and farming, and apple orchards dotted the area. Writer Zane Grey was also charmed by the area, drawing attention to it in the book *Call of the Canyon* in the 1920s and publicizing it even more in the film version, which was shot on location.

With all this attention, it was only a matter of time before tourism became the main attraction. Today about 2.5 million people visit the town annually. They come to shop at the numerous art galleries, to nurture their spirits, and to relax amidst a red rock fantasy.

One of the most scenic ways to enter Sedona is via Route 89A from Flagstaff. Route 89A runs the length of **Oak Creek Canyon**, the most accessible of several magnificent canyons that plunge from the high forests of northern Arizona down toward the low deserts of southern Arizona. Route 89A makes for a wonderful, though often crowded, scenic drive. After a long, thrilling descent from Flagstaff to the bottom of the canyon, where the creek banks are lined with lush riparian vegetation, the highway passes a number of picnicking, camping and fishing areas. Midway down the canyon is one of Arizona's most popular state parks, **Slide Rock State Park** (see "Sedona Area Parks" below). At the lower end of the canyon, travelers emerge into the spectacular Red Rock Country, the labyrinth of sandstone buttes and mesas and verdant side canyons surrounding Sedona.

THE VORTICES

The "Vortices" idea was "channeled" through members of Sedona's highly visible New Age community several years ago and keeps evolving. Believers expound at length on various theories underlying the Vortices' existence, from their being focal points in the earth's "natural energy grid" to their coming from energy seeping out of fissures in the earth, and explain them in terms of electrical and magnetic forces, yin/yang energy, ancient Indian beliefs and so on. It is commonly claimed that psychic powers, emotions and talents are stronger there and that UFOs frequently visit them.

*While some local visionaries claim to have identified as many as 13 Vortices, only four are generally recognized. The **Airport Mesa Vortex** is a little more than a mile south of Route 89A on the way to the airport. The **Boynton Canyon Vortex**, one of the area's most popular hiking areas, is several miles north of West Sedona via Dry Creek Road and Boynton Pass Road. The **Cathedral Rock Vortex** is by a lovely picnic area alongside Oak Creek, reached from Route 89A in West Sedona via Red Rock Loop Road and Chavez Ranch Road; the rock itself is one of the most photographed places in the area. The **Bell Rock Vortex**, a popular spot for UFO watchers, is just off Route 179 south of Sedona near the Village of Oak Creek.*

Sedona is a town for shopping, outdoor recreation and luxuriating in spectacular surroundings. It is not the kind of place where you will find tourist attractions in the usual sense. Other than Oak Creek Canyon, Sedona's most popular tourist spots are spiritual in nature. The **Chapel of the Holy Cross**, south of town on Route 179, is a Catholic "sculpture church" built between two towering red sandstone rock formations. It is open to visitors daily. The **Shrine of the Red Rocks**, on Table Top Mesa two miles off Route 89A on Airport Road, features a large wooden cross and a great view of the Red Rock Country.

A half-hour's drive south of Sedona via Route 179 and Route 17, **Montezuma Castle National Monument** (Camp Verde; 602-567-3322; admission) protects 800-year-old cliff dwellings built by the Sinagua people, ancestors of the Hopi. The ruins got their name from early explorers' mistaken belief that the Aztec fled here and built the structures after the Spanish conquest of Mexico. Though there is no truth to the old theory, archaeologists now know that several centuries before the Spanish arrived, Toltec traders used to visit the region, bringing with them architectural methods from central Mexico. The main "castle" is a five-story residential structure set high on the cliff. Although visitors cannot climb up to the ruin, the view from the nature trail below will captivate the imagination. The visitor center displays artifacts of the Sinagua and Hohokam cultures.

SEDONA SIGHTSEEING TOURS

For Sedona visitors wishing to explore the surrounding Red Rock Country, the town has an extraordinary number of sightseeing tour services. **Pink Jeep Tours** *(204 North Route 89A; 602-282-5000);* **Sedona Adventures** *(Uptown Mall; 602-282-3500);* **Time Expeditions** *(276 North Route 89A; 602-282-2137); and* **Sedona Red Rock Jeep Tours** *(270 North Route 89A; 602-282-6826) all offer four-wheel-drive backcountry trips ranging from one hour to all day and will pick you up at any Sedona lodging. While each of these tour companies offers trips to Sedona's highly touted "sacred places," two other companies promote explicitly New Age trips to the area's "Vortices," along with guides who will share secrets of the Medicine Wheel, magic plants, crystal energy and such. They are* **Sacred Earth Tours** *(260 North Route 89A; 602-282-6826, with a second location at 251 Route 179; 602-282-2026) and* **Earth Wisdom Tours** *(293 North Route 89A; 602-282-4717).*

For the most spectacular guided tour going, see the Red Rock Country from the sky with **Red Rock Balloon Adventure** *(3230 Valley Vista Drive; 602-284-0040) or* **Northern Light Balloon Expeditions** *(P.O. Box 1695, Sedona, AZ 86336; 602-282-2274).*

Adjoining the national monument, the **Yavapai-Apache Visitor Activity Center** (602-567-5276) offers museum exhibits of the culture and crafts of the Native Americans who have occupied the area during historic times. Eleven miles north of the main unit of the national monument is a second, smaller unit called Montezuma's Well, a pool of water in a limestone sinkhole surrounded by small pueblo ruins.

South of Montezuma's Castle via Route 17, in the small town of Camp Verde, portions of an old cavalry fort from the Apache Wars in the 1870s and early 1880s are preserved as **Fort Verde State Historic Park** (Lane Street; 602-567-3275; admission). Visitors can walk through the former hospital and officers' quarters, and there is a museum of Native American, pioneer and military artifacts. The fort formed the end of the General Crook Trail, the major patrol and supply route during the Apache Wars, which followed the Mogollon Rim west for more than 100 miles from Fort Apache. The trail is drivable today, as a mostly unpaved road, from Camp Verde through Coconino and Apache-Sitgreaves national forests.

Near the little town of Cottonwood, on Route 89A en route from Sedona to Prescott, is **Tuzigoot National Monument** (602-634-5564), an uncharacteristically large Sinagua Indian pueblo ruin. Once home to about 250 people, the limestone pueblo stood two stories high and had 92 rooms. Today, its white walls still stand on the hilltop and command an expansive view of the valley. Although the vista is marred by slag fields from a refinery that used to process copper ore, the museum at the national monument offers a good look at the prehistoric culture of the Sinagua people.

One of the most beautiful canyons in the area is **Sycamore Canyon**, which parallels Oak Creek Canyon. Turn off at Tuzigoot National Monument and follow the well-maintained dirt road past the golf course for about 12 miles to the trailhead at the end of the road. Sycamore Canyon is a designated wilderness area, meaning that no wheeled or motorized vehicles are allowed. The Parsons Trail takes you up the wild, lushly wooded canyon for most of its 21-mile length, passing numerous small cliff dwellings resting high above.

SEDONA AREA LODGING

As you drive down Oak Creek Canyon from Flagstaff to Sedona, you will notice several privately owned lodges and cabin complexes in the midst of this spectacular national forest area. You can reserve accommodations at these places and enjoy the canyon in the cool of the evening and early morning, avoiding the midday throngs and traffic of peak season and weekends. Several places are located just below Slide Rock State Park.

Top of the line, **Junipine Resort** (Oak Creek Canyon; 602-282-3375) offers modern suites and two-bedroom "creekhouses" with rates in the ultra-deluxe range. These individually decorated one- and two-story units are all crafted from wood and stone. Offering mountain and forest views, each 1300- to 1500-square-foot unit comes with a kitchen and redwood deck overlooking the canyon.

Slide Rock Cabins (Oak Creek Canyon; 602-282-6900) offers one old-fashioned log cabin and three chalets with loft bedrooms, all in the deluxe-price range, within walking distance of swimming holes, fishing spots and hiking trails. In the same part of the canyon are the more modest accommodations at **Don Hoel's Cabins** (Oak Creek Canyon; 602-282-3560), where rates range from budget to moderate. Moderate-priced cabins, some with fireplaces, are available at **Forest Houses** (Oak Creek Canyon; 602-282-2999).

Farther down the canyon, **Oak Creek Terrace** (Oak Creek Canyon; 602-282-3562) offers resort accommodations ranging from moderately priced motel-style rooms with king-sized beds, color television and fireplaces to ultra-deluxe two-bedroom suites with heart-shaped jacuzzis.

Sedona specializes in upscale resorts. Among the poshest accommodations in town is **Los Abrigados** (160 Portal Lane; 602-282-1777). Situated next to the atmospheric Tlaquepaque shopping area, Los Abrigados features fanciful Mexican-inspired modern architecture throughout and stylishly elegant suites with kitchens, fireplaces and patios or balconies. Guest facilities include tennis courts, swimming pool, weight room, golf parcourse and spa. Ultra-deluxe.

Another top-of-the-line Sedona accommodation is **L'Auberge de Sedona** (301 L'Auberge Lane; 602-282-1661). Individually designed guest rooms and cottages are decorated with furnishings imported from Provence, France, to re-create the atmosphere of a French country inn on ten acres of creekside grounds within walking distance of uptown Sedona. Deluxe to ultra-deluxe.

Although it's a good-sized hotel, **Poco Diablo Resort** (Route 179, Sedona; 602-282-7333 or 800-528-4275) manages to maintain an intimate, friendly atmosphere. A library off the lobby is full of books. Walking trails circle the 9-hole golf course landscaped with willow trees and a pond. Many of the 150 rooms have freestanding fireplaces, refrigerators, wet bars, double sinks, coffee makers and some even have an elevated whirlpool in the room. There's also a restaurant, tennis courts, swimming pools and outdoor hot tubs. Deluxe to ultra-deluxe.

Views. Views. Views. Sedona resorts have great views, but those at **Enchantment Resort** (525 Boynton Canyon Road, Sedona; 602-282-2900 or 800-826-4180) outdo them all. Set on Native American worshiping grounds in Boynton Canyon amidst soaring buttes and jagged cliffs, staying here is like camping out—luxuriously. The 56 adobe-style casitas have sliding glass doors leading out to private balconies, beehive fireplaces and beamed ceilings. A newspaper and fresh-squeezed juice are delivered to your door in the morning. Other than hiking—a must out here—other activities include tennis, swimming and golfing. There's also a restaurant, lounge, gift shop and children's programs. Deluxe to ultra-deluxe.

Charming, more affordable lodging in Sedona can be found at the **Rose Tree Inn** (376 Cedar Street; 602-282-2065), which strives for an "English garden environment" and has patios and a jacuzzi. Rates are in the moderate range for units in this small bed-and-breakfast inn close to uptown.

A Touch of Sedona Bed and Breakfast (595 Jordan Road; 602-282-6462), uphill from uptown, offers four individually decorated theme rooms with corresponding motifs—the "Hummingbird," "Contemporary Eagle," "Kachina" and "Roadrunner"—all moderate to deluxe.

It may not be historic, but the sleek, contemporary **Canyon Villa** (125 Canyon Circle Drive, Sedona; 602-284-1226 or 800-453-1166) bed-and-breakfast inn has other charms. A cozy library. Rooms with themes ranging from Victorian to Santa Fe-style. French doors leading to balconies. And, of course, views of the red rocks. Deluxe.

Another inn is **The Graham Bed & Breakfast Inn** (150 Canyon Circle Drive, Sedona; 602-284-1425), where each room has views of Sedona's famous red rocks. Features found in some of the five deluxe rooms are king-sized brass beds, marble showers, private balconies, fireplaces and jacuzzis. Breakfast is included.

Greyfire Farm (1240 Jacks Canyon Road; 602-284-2340) is one of the area's more unusual bed and breakfasts. Nestled among the pines in a rural valley between the Red Rock Country and Wild Horse Mesa, near hiking and horseback riding trails in the national forest, the "farm" can accommodate two guest horses. It provides bed and breakfast for human guests, as well. Rooms are bright and contemporary; moderate in price.

For basic motel rooms in Sedona, the **White House Inn** (2986 West Highway 89A; 602-282-6680) in West Sedona at the Dry Creek Road turnoff provides lodging with phone and cable television in the budget-price range. Near uptown Sedona, the **Star Motel** (295 Jordan Road; 602-282-3641) also offers standard rooms in the budget to moderate range.

Visitors seeking to change their lives in Sedona might want to consider staying at the **Healing Center of Arizona** (25 Wilson Canyon Road; 602-282-7710). Rates for accommodations in this dome complex are in the moderate range and budget-priced gourmet vegetarian meals are served. Amenities, offered for reasonable fees, include a sauna, a spa and a flotation tank. Holistic therapies available to guests at the center include acupressure treatments, herbology, rebirthing, crystal healing, psychic channeling and more.

SEDONA AREA RESTAURANTS

A favorite Sedona restaurant since 1958, the **Oak Creek Owl** (561 Route 179; 602-282-3532) serves Continental and New Southwest cuisine at deluxe prices. Specialties include Southwest shrimp (sautéed with chilis, cilantro, garlic, tomato and sherry), chicken Sedona (layered with prosciutto, spinach and Parmesan cheese) and roasted quail stuffed with piñon nuts.

L'Auberge de Sedona (301 L'Auberge Lane; 602-282-1661) has an outstanding French restaurant with a view of Oak Creek and memorable prix fixe dinners. The six-course menu, which changes nightly, typically features pâté, soup, a small baby green salad and entrées such as poached salmon, grilled lamb or chicken. Prices can reach into the ultra-deluxe range.

Another outstanding Continental restaurant in the deluxe-price range is **Rene at Tlaquepaque** (Tlaquepaque; 602-282-9225), also specializing in French fare. The most elaborate neo-Spanish-colonial decor in the Southwest makes this restaurant extra special. Open-air patio dining is available.

A good, moderately priced Mexican restaurant is **Oaxaca** (231 Route 89A; 602-282-4179), which has an outdoor deck for dining with a view of uptown Sedona.

And for a synthesis of ethnic cuisines—European, Mediterranean and Oriental cooking techniques used to create highly original, healthy dishes such as red cabbage with goat cheese, hazelnuts and apples or Cajun fish with raspberry glazed cucumbers—head for the **Heartline Café** (1610 West Route 89A, Sedona; 602-282-0785). Moderate.

Amidst Aegean blue walls and plastic tablecloths topped with fresh flowers, diners enjoy Greek and Continental food at **Fournos Restaurant** (3000 West Route 89A, Sedona; 602-282-3331). Watch the chef cook in the open kitchen, whipping up such specialties as Flaming Shrimp Santorini flambéed in ouzo and baked with feta cheese and Santorini sauce, or fish baked in a sauce of yogurt, steamed onions and butter. Moderate.

The food may be hot, but the atmosphere is cool and soothing at **Thai Spices** (2986 West Route 89A, Sedona; 602-282-0599). Soft music floats out from speakers amidst pink walls, mint-green seat cushions, plants and indirect lighting from chandeliers. The food spices things up. Try the appetizer of *larb gai*—ground chicken mixed with lime juice, mint leaves and green onion. Or red curry—a blend of red chili and vegetables in coconut milk. For a really, really hot dish, taste the stir-fried mint leaves and chili. Budget.

A choice of 101 omelettes is the main attraction at the **Coffee Pot Restaurant** (2050 West Route 89A, Sedona; 602-282-6626), a local dining spot since the 1950s. Although the brass rails and sautillo tile floors add charm, the brown plastic booths give away the casual atmosphere. On the wall hangs artwork by White Bear, a former Hopi Indian chief who's now in his 80s. A nice touch is the outdoor patio, where light music is played in the mornings. Budget.

The outdoor patio with a red rock view is the main reason to eat at **The Hideaway** (Highway 179, Sedona; 602-282-4202), a modest establishment with pasta, pizza, salads and sandwiches. Budget.

The view is also the draw at **La Mediterranee** (771 Route 179, Sedona; 602-282-7006) with its second-story, floor-to-ceiling windows facing the mountains and an outdoor patio. The moderately priced Mediterranean entrées are a bit high given the portions served, but the atmosphere makes up for it.

More views and an elegant setting await diners at the **Yavapai Dining Room** at Enchantment Resort (525 Boynton Canyon Road, Sedona; 602-282-2900). Typical of the deluxe Southwest cuisine served here is the rack of Colorado lamb roasted with an herb and pistachio nut crust along with sage and sun-dried tomatoes. And don't miss the Sunday jazz champagne brunch.

Rattan furniture covers the long, narrow balcony where diners can enjoy seafood and steak at the **Willows Restaurant** at the Poco Diablo Resort (Route 179, Sedona; 602-282-7333 or 800-528-4275). The moderately priced cuisine has a hint of Southwest flavor and ingredients. A pianist performs at Sunday brunch.

For just plain good, just-like-mom's food at budget to moderate prices in Sedona, the place to go is **Irene's Restaurant** (Castle Rock Plaza; 602-284-2240) at the corner of Route 179 and Verde Valley School Road. Irene's is famous for home-cooked desserts, including deep-dish apple pie, peach cobbler and giant cinnamon rolls.

Another good budget place is **Phil and Eddie's Diner** (1655 West Route 89A; 602-282-6070), offering all-day breakfasts, burgers, blue-plate specials and soda fountain suggestions with a 1950s ambience.

SEDONA AREA SHOPPING

Sedona's shopping district is one of the three or four best in Arizona. Many of the galleries, boutiques and specialty shops are labors of love, the personal creations of people who spent years past daydreaming about opening a cute little store in Sedona. The town has more than 60 art galleries, most of them specializing in traditional and contem-

Sedona was named after the wife of the town's first postmaster, Sedona Schnebly.

porary Native American art, "cowboy" art and landscape paintings. Quality is relatively high in this very competitive market. You can easily spend a whole day shopping your way up and down the main streets of town, leaving your feet sore and your credit cards limp.

Most galleries and boutiques, as well as tourist-oriented shops, are in "uptown" Sedona, on Route 89A above the "Y" (the junction where Route 89A curves right toward West Sedona while the road continuing straight becomes Route 179). Virtually all supermarkets, shopping malls and places where practical things can be purchased are in West Sedona.

Sedona's most relaxing and enjoyable place to browse is **Tlaquepaque**, a large, eye-catching two-story complex of specialty shops and restaurants below the "Y" on Route 179. Built in Spanish colonial style with old-looking stone walls, courtyards, tile roofs and flowers in profusion, Tlaquepaque looks more like Old Mexico than the real thing. Representative of the range of stores here are several that deal in animal motifs: **Aguajito del Sol** (602-282-5258) exhibits animal sculptures; **Mother Nature's Trading Company** (602-282-5932) carries games, playthings and educational toys having to do with endangered species; the **Cuddly Coyote** (602-282-4480) presents a wide selection of stuffed toy animals; and **Geoffrey Roth Ltd.** (602-282-7756) has taxidermy and painted birds.

Across the highway from Tlaquepaque, you'll find the **Crystal Castle** (313 Route 179; 602-282-5910), one of the larger New Age stores in this town which, according to many, is the New Age capital of the known cosmos. It carries unusual books, incense, runes, visionary art and, of course, crystals. In front of the store, a "networking" bulletin board lets you scan the array of alternative professional services in town— channelers, psychic surgeons, clairvoyants, kinesiologists, numerologists and many more. Other stores in the same vein include **Crystal Magic** (2978 West Route 89A; 602-282-1622), **Angels, Art & Crystals** (3006 West Route 89A; 602-282-7089), the **Golden Word Book Centre** (3150 Route 89A; 602-282-2688) and the **Crystal Pyramid** (6446 Route 179; 602-284-1737). Can't get enough? The **Center for the New Age** offers Vortex information, networking for New Age activities, psychic readings daily and a "Psychic Faire" every Saturday.

Garland's Navajo Rugs (411 Route 179, Sedona; 602-282-4070) has one of the largest collections of Navajo rugs in the world with a selection of more than 5000. They hang on rafters, grouped according to subjects ranging from people to storm patterns. There are also about 500 kachina dolls in stock.

There are a variety of specialty shops and galleries at **Hozho** shopping center (431 Route 179, Sedona) including **Design Imports** (602-282-1328) with clothing, jewelry and art from around the world. Here, you'll find colorful, intricately woven Coogi sweaters from Australia that are designed on computers. **Acrey's Fine Art Photography** (602-282-2983) features photography by Jack Acrey. The **Lanning Gallery** (602-282-6865) has contemporary artwork made by people from Arizona, Colorado, New Mexico and California, including ceramic Native American folklore characters by Susan Wagoda-Bergquist.

The **Hillside Courtyard & Marketplace** (671 Route 179) is a two-level center with about 25 shops, galleries and restaurants set amidst waterfalls and sculptures. **Agnisiuh** (602-282-5622), a sanskrit word meaning the Creative Fires of Mankind, carries works by mainly local artists in a variety of mediums, as well as the Greg Rich/Gibson collection of art instruments—guitars and banjos, selling from $10,000 to $250,000, that are hand decorated with pearl, abalone, brass, copper and gold. Next door at the **Soderberg/Stenson Sculpture Galleries** (602-282-3818) are life-size and monumental bronze sculptures, as well as works in other mediums. **Points West Collections** (602-282-5889) has contemporary, innovative lighting such as lamps made of sand, along with furniture and interior design accessories. And **The Clay Pigeon** (602-282-2862) specializes in hand-crafted southwestern crafts such as the whimsical rabbit sculptures of Jeanne Stevens-Sollman and handmade musical instruments.

The **Sedona Arts Center** (Route 89A at Art Barn Road, Sedona; 602-282-3809) features artwork by local and regional artists; in addition, plays and musical performances are also held here.

Our favorite art gallery in Sedona is **Elaine Horowitz Galleries** (Schnebly Hill Road at Route 179; 602-282-6290). The late Ms. Horowitz endowed this and her other galleries in Scottsdale and Santa Fe with an eye for quality in contemporary art and a rare sense of humor.

Shopping enthusiasts will also want to visit **Oak Creek Factory Stores** (Route 179, Oak Creek), a mall south of town. This is factory-direct outlet shopping with a difference. The factories represented include **Capezio** (602-284-1910), **Sarah Coventry** (602-284-1965), **Mikasa** (602-284-9505), **Izod/Gant** (602-284-9844) and **Anne Klein** (602-284-0407)—designer goods at discount prices.

SEDONA AREA NIGHTLIFE

Sedona has surprisingly little nightlife. Besides the lounges in the major resort hotels, your best bet is to call the **Sedona Arts Center** (Route 89A at Art Barn Road; 602-282-3809) for their current schedule of theatrical and concert performances.

SEDONA AREA PARKS

Slide Rock State Park (602-282-3034), popular with students from the University of Northern Arizona, is a swimming area midway between Flagstaff and Sedona in the heart of Oak Creek Canyon that is almost always packed during the warm months. It is like a natural water park, with placid pools, fast-moving chutes and a wide, flat shoreline of red sandstone for sunbathing. The state park also includes apple orchards and an abandoned homestead from the 1920s. Visitors are not allowed to pick the apples, but cider made from them is sold at a stand on the trail to the swim area.

Beautiful Oak Creek runs through the 286-acre **Red Rock State Park** (602-282-6907). Dotted with sycamore and cottonwood trees and situated in the heart of Red Rock Country, naturalists offer guided walks daily along the six-mile trail system. One route leads to a 1948 house that resembles an Indian pueblo and, sitting atop a hill, affords great views of the area. The visitor center has natural history exhibits and videos. Fishing is allowed on Oak Creek, with catches including warm-water catfish and sunfish. To get there, drive four miles southwest of Sedona on Route 89A, then turn south on Lower Red Rock Loop Road; the park appears in three miles.

Dead Horse Ranch State Park (602-634-5283) is a 325-acre park along the Verde River. The park has both desert and lush areas that can be enjoyed by walking the extensive hiking trails. Fishing is allowed in the Verde River and the four-acre lagoon, which is stocked with panfish, catfish, bass and trout. From Cottonwood, take Main Street to Fifth Street, then go south about a mile.

Jerome

Jerome is one of Arizona's most intriguing ghost towns. After having been completely abandoned in the 1950s, it was resettled by hippies in the late 1960s and now has a population of about 500 people—a mere shadow of the 15,000 population it had in the first decades of the 20th century, when it was a rich silver mining district and the fifth-largest city in Arizona. The history of Jerome's mining era is brought to life in three museums. The old Douglas Mansion in **Jerome State Historic Park** (602-634-5381; admission) at the lower end of town offers a glimpse into the lifestyle of a turn-of-the-century mining baron, from marble-paneled bathrooms and a large wine cellar to balconies from which you can see a hundred miles. For a look at mining tools, old photos, and other exhibits about old-time copper mining, enter the **Jerome Historical Society Mine Museum** (602-634-5477; admission) on Main Street. The **Gold King Mine Museum** (602-634-0053; admission) at the upper end of town has a re-created assay office, a replica mine shaft and a petting zoo.

The real pleasure of Jerome lies in strolling the streets that switchback up Cleopatra Hill, browsing in the shops along the way and admiring the carefully preserved turn-of-the-century architecture. Many of the town's buildings were constructed of massive blocks of quarried stone to withstand the blasts that frequently shook the ground from the nearby mine. The entire town has been declared a National Historic District.

JEROME LODGING

In Jerome, you can spend the night in Victorian style and comfort at a very affordable rate. The **Jerome Inn** (311 Main Street; 602-634-5094)—formerly the Miner's Roost, the oldest hotel in Jerome—offers comfortable, budget-priced rooms. In the same price range is the **Conner Hotel** (168 Main Street; 602-634-5792), which has the town's most popular saloon on the ground floor. It can be noisy.

Smaller and very homey is **Nancy Russel's Bed & Breakfast** (P.O. Box 791, Jerome, AZ 86331; 602-634-3270), in a turn-of-the-century miner's house with guest rooms decorated in the style of the period. Rates are moderate.

JEROME RESTAURANTS

In Jerome, the elegant place to dine, open for dinner on weekends only, is the **House of Joy** (Hull Street; 602-634-5339), a former house of ill repute whose past is recalled in the decor—red lights, red candles, red flowers, red placemats, red everything. The fairly limited menu features veal, lamb and poultry. Moderate to deluxe.

A TRAIN RIDE INTO THE PAST

*An historic railroad that carries sightseers through some of Arizona's most spectacular country is the **Verde River Canyon Excursion Train** (300 North Broadway Street, Clarkdale; 602-639-0010). Revived in November 1990, this train achieved instant popularity as a major tourist attraction. It takes passengers on a 40-mile round trip from Clarkdale, 26 miles west of Sedona and just below Jerome. On the way, the diesel-powered train winds along sheer cliffs of red limestone in curve after curve high above the Verde River, through a long, dark tunnel, over bridges, past gold mines and Indian Ruins, to the ghost town of Perkinsville and back.*

The **Jerome Palace** (Clark Street; 602-634-5262) specializes in moderately priced barbecue, served in an upstairs dining room with a spectacular view of the Verde Valley. For breakfast or lunch, try **Macy's European Coffeehouse & Bakery** (Main Street at Hull Avenue; 602-634-2733), serving croissants, scones and pastries along with gourmet coffees and teas in historic surroundings. Budget.

JEROME SHOPPING

With all the artists in town, it's no surprise that art is the main item for sale here. Most shops are along the town's switchback Main Street, but a few side streets have unusual shops, as well. You're likely to find pottery, jewelry, handmade clothing, stained glass and other wares.

You can watch jewelers create contemporary designs at **Aurum Jewelry** (355 Main Street, Jerome; 602-634-3330). About 20 or 30 local artists show their work here, which ranges from a sculptured iron spoon and fork to belt buckles, bolo ties, custom knives and jewelry.

Jewelry and large engraved copper pieces embellished with beads, some as old as 3000 B.C., represent the work at the **Lauren Renee Gallery** (Unit 2, Main Street, Jerome; 602-634-2008). A good place to hunt for a souvenir that recalls Jerome's mining origins is **The Copper Shop** (Main Street; 602-634-7754).

Rattan couches with fluffy pillows beckon people inside the two-story **Designs on You** (233 Main Street, Jerome; 602-634-7879) shop that sells natural fiber clothing, shoes and lingerie. Around the corner at the **Raku Gallery** (250 Hull Avenue; 602-639-0239), about 30 artists sell raku and contemporary artwork. It's worth stopping by just for the dramatic views from the glass wall facing the mountains.

In the last few years, the heart of the working art movement in town has been centered at the **Old Mingus High School** (Highway 89A, Jerome), which is now filled with studios and galleries carrying everything from paintings to blown glass. The biggest is the **Anderson/Mandette Art Studios** (602-634-3438). One of the largest private art studios in the country, it feels more like a museum as you walk through it. One level contains working studios and a 9' × 17' canvas titled "Arizona." Upstairs, paintings hang by Robin Anderson and Margo Mandette, while downstairs is a gallery with African and wearable art.

JEROME NIGHTLIFE

The Old West saloon tradition lives on in Jerome, where the town's most popular club is the **Spirit Room** (Main Street at Jerome Avenue; 602-634-5792) in the old Conner Hotel. There is live music on weekend afternoons and evenings and the atmosphere is as authentic as can be.

Prescott

Over the top of the hill from Jerome, in the next valley, sits the city of **Prescott**, the original territorial capital of Arizona from 1864 to 1867. President Abraham Lincoln decided to declare it the capital because the only other community of any size in the Arizona Territory, Tucson, was full of Confederate sympathizers. Today, Prescott is a low-key, all-American city with a certain quiet charm and few concessions to tourism. Incidentally, Prescott is located at the exact geographic center of the state of Arizona.

Built in 1916, the **Yavapai County Courthouse** sits at the heart of Prescott, surrounded by a green plaza where locals pass the time playing cards and chatting, and tourists rest awhile on park benches. Surrounding the plaza are many of the town's shops, in addition to historic Whiskey Row, where at one time some 20 saloons were open day and night.

The major sightseeing highlight in Prescott is the **Sharlot Hall Museum** (415 West Gurley Street; 602-445-3122), which contains a large collection of antiques from Arizona's territorial period, including several fully furnished houses and an excellent collection of stagecoaches and carriages. Sharlot Mabridth Hall was a well-known essayist, poet and traveler who explored the wild areas of the Arizona Territory around the turn of the century. In 1909, she became the territorial historian, a position she held until Arizona achieved statehood. Seeing that Arizona's historic and prehistoric artifacts were rapidly being taken from the state, Ms. Hall began a personal collection that grew quite large over the next three decades and became the nucleus of this large historical museum. The museum's collections are housed in several Territorial-era buildings brought from around the county, including two governors' mansions, in a large park in downtown Prescott.

Prescott also has some other noteworthy museums. The **Phippen Museum of Western Art** (Route 89; 602-778-1385), six miles north of town, honors cowboy artist George Phippen and presents changing exhibits of works by other cowboy artists. It is generally considered one of the best cowboy art museums in the country.

The **Smoki Museum** (100 North Arizona Street; 602-445-2000; admission) houses a large collection of Indian artifacts from throughout the Southwest, as well as some pseudo-Indian items. The Smoki "tribe" is a secret society of non-Indian Prescott residents that was formed in the 1920s and still performs spectacular ceremonials annually in August despite the objections of legitimate Native American tribes.

Probably the most unusual of Prescott's museums is the **Bead Museum** (140 South Montezuma Street; 602-445-2431), displaying a phenomenal collection of beads, jewelry and other adornments from around the world and explaining their uses as trade goods, currency, religious items and status symbols. Visitors to this one-of-a-kind nonprofit museum discover that there's more to beads than they ever suspected.

Thirty-four miles south of Prescott you'll find **Arcosanti** (Route 17, Exit 262 at Cordes Junction; 602-632-7135; admission), a planned community that will eventually be home to 5000 people. Arcosanti was designed by famed Italian designer Paolo Soleri as a synthesis of architecture and ecology. It is pedestrian-oriented, and its unusual buildings with domes, arches, portholes and protruding cubes, make maximum use of passive solar heat. Tours are offered daily. Continuing construction is financed in part by the sale of handmade souvenir items such as Cosanti wind bells.

PRESCOTT LODGING

Prescott has several historic downtown hotels. The most elegant of them is the **Hassayampa Inn** (122 East Gurley Street; 602-778-9434), a 1927 hotel listed on the National Register. The lobby and other common areas have been restored to their earlier glory and furnished with antiques. The rooms have been beautifully renovated and all have private baths, telephones and color televisions. Rates are moderate, with some suites in the deluxe range.

A smaller hotel on a side street is the **Hotel Vendome** (230 South Cortez Street; 602-776-0900). Rooms in this 1917 hotel have been nicely restored and decorated in tones of blue. Some have modern bathrooms, while others have restored Victorian-style baths. Moderate.

Sitting atop Nob Hill with a view of Courthouse Square is **The Marks House** (203 East Union Street; 602-778-4632), a yellow Queen

---

SHARLOT HALL

One of the most admired women in Arizona history was Sharlot Hall, who arrived in Prescott on horseback in 1882. At first she helped manage the family ranch east of Prescott, passing time writing poetry and panning for gold. But in 1909 she became the territorial historian and the first woman in Arizona to hold a political office.

In 1924, Hall was asked to go east and represent Arizona in the electoral college. Originally she turned down the offer, not having enough money for suitable clothes. But officials at the United Verde Mine at Jerome saved the day, buying her a blue silk dress with a fine copper mesh coat. This "copper dress" was a hit back east and gave a free shot of publicity to the Arizona copper industry.

After returning, Hall restored the territorial capitol building and lived there until her death in 1944. Today, you can learn all about her in the Sharlot Hall Museum.

Anne Victorian house that now opens its doors to overnight guests. Built in 1894, the house and its four moderately priced guest rooms are decorated with antiques such as an 1800s bathhouse-style copper tub. All rooms have feather beds and private baths. Mornings begin with a full family-style breakfast.

Another hilltop accommodation, although on a much larger scale, is the **Sheraton Resort and Conference Center** (1500 Highway 69, Prescott; 602-776-1666). The views are beautiful from the floor-to-ceiling windows in the lobby, and suites on the west end of the hotel have a view of the city and sunset. The pastel, Southwest-style rooms all have refrigerators, couches, a desk and a balcony. Lining corridors in the hotel is artwork by Yavapai County artists. The hotel also has a gift shop, health club, indoor racquetball courts, tennis courts, swimming pool, beauty salon, and a lounge with free hors d'oeuvres and live jazz music every night. Most of the 161 rooms are deluxe-priced.

More modest rooms, all with private baths, are available at budget prices at the **St. Michael Hotel** (104 South Montezuma Street; 602-776-1999). The location couldn't be better for those who wish to enjoy the Wild West nightlife of Whiskey Row, on the same block.

A posh bed and breakfast in a 1902 main house with four guest houses is the **Prescott Pines Inn** (901 White Spar Road; 602-445-7270). Its 13 Victorian-style guest rooms are beautifully decorated in subdued color schemes. Some have fireplaces and others have kitchens. Full breakfasts are served on rose patterned china. Reservations are recommended as much as a year in advance for peak season. Moderate.

Prescott also has more than its share of low-priced, basic lodging from which to explore the wild canyons and forests surrounding the city. The prices can't be beat at the once-charming, now somewhat run-down Mediterranean-style **American Motel** (1211 East Gurley Street; 602-778-0787), where rooms have telephones and wonderful old murals on the walls.

PRESCOTT RESTAURANTS

Prescott's finer restaurants include the **Peacock Room** (122 East Gurley Street; 602-778-9434) in the Hassayampa Inn. Here, you'll find a full menu of moderately priced Continental and American specialties in an elegant old-time atmosphere. An etched-glass peacock ornament graces the front door of the art deco dining room. Choose between seating at tables or semicircular booths. High ceilings and Tiffany-style lamps add to the quaint atmosphere.

A century-old general merchandise store that has been transformed into a popular restaurant, **Murphy's** (201 North Cortez Street; 602-445-4044) is a walk through history. A leaded-glass divider decorated with photos of Prescott's mining heyday separates the bar and restaurant sections. Mahogany bar booths and a burgundy carpet add to the charm of this establishment. You can also enjoy a drink in the lounge offering views of Thumb Butte. Specialties include mesquite-broiled seafood and prime rib, along with fresh home-baked bread.

With many plants and a creekside view, the **Prescott Mining Company** (155 Plaza Drive; 602-445-1991) is a large, modern restaurant with an entrance styled after a mine shaft. Its steak and seafood dishes are moderately priced.

For breakfast or lunch in Prescott, a very popular place downtown is **Greens and Things** (106 West Gurley Street; 602-445-3234), which serves homemade Belgian waffles, build-your-own omelettes and homemade soups. Also good is the **Prescott Pantry** (1201 Iron Springs Road; 602-778-4280) in the Iron Springs Plaza shopping center. This bakery-deli-wine shop has restaurant seating and offers ever-changing daily specials, hearty sandwiches, espresso and cappuccino and fresh-baked pastries. Prices are in the budget range at both places.

Some of the best low-budget home-style cooking in Prescott is to be found at the **Dinner Bell Café** (321 West Gurley Street; 602-445-9888). It may not look like much from the outside, but give it a try and you'll find out why this is one of the most popular restaurants in north central Arizona. For breakfast, try the hubcap-size pancakes or three-egg omelettes. Lunch specials include pork chops, chicken fried steak and chili. Be sure to sample the homemade salsa.

PRESCOTT SHOPPING

Because it is old as Arizona towns go, and perhaps because of Sharlot Hall's recognition that it was important to preserve the everyday objects of 19th-century Arizona, Prescott is a good place for antique shopping. As in most antique hunting areas, some items offered for sale do not come from the Prescott area but have been imported from other, less visited parts of the country. Most, however, are the real

---

YOUNG'S FARM

Elmer Young started farming 80 acres in 1947, and now visits to his dream, *Young's Farm (east of Prescott at the intersection of Routes 69 and 169, Dewey; 602-632-7272), are an Arizona tradition. People gather here year-round, but crowds are especially thick during seasonal festivals. Treats include pumpkins, turkeys, sweet corn, vegetables and meat, as well as more unusual pumpkin butter, Hopi Corn jelly and fruit cakes. There's also a restaurant and bakery.*

Most of the bars that line Prescott's Whiskey Row have been in operation since the late 19th century, when this was one of the most notorious sin strips in the West.

---

thing, and antique buffs will find lots of great shops within walking distance of one another in the downtown area, especially along the two-block strip of Cortez Street between Gurley and Sheldon streets.

Some of the best places to browse are the indoor mini-malls where select groups of dealers and collectors display, such as the **Merchandise Mart Mall** (205 North Cortez Street; 602-776-1728), **Prescott Antique & Craft Market** (115 North Cortez Street; 602-445-7156) and **Deja Vu Antique Mall** (134 North Cortez Street; 602-445-6732), which also features an old-fashioned soda fountain.

Beside the historic Hotel St. Michael are a group of shops called St. Michael's Alley (110 Montezuma Street). The dozen or so shops include **Puttin' on the Hats** (602-776-1150), which has everything from Greek Fisherman's hats to cowboy hats. **Lida** is a designer boutique that sells southwestern-style items made in their local factory. The **Desert Lights** gift shop offers candles, candy and other gifts.

Stuffed deer greet patrons at **The Cattleman's Shop** (124 Whiskey Row; 602-445-8222), where you'll find western wear ranging from frilly toddler cowgirl dresses to spurs. One of the best galleries in Prescott is **Sun West** (152 South Montezuma Street; 602-778-1204). Arizona and local artists sell sculpture, pottery, furniture, paintings and jewelry, and there are also rugs woven by the Zapotec Indians.

PRESCOTT NIGHTLIFE

If old-time saloons appeal to you, don't miss Prescott's **Whiskey Row**, downtown on the block of Montezuma Street directly across from the Yavapai County Courthouse. You'll find the saloons remain authentically Old Western, and so do most of the customers.

The fanciest of the bunch is the **Palace** (120 South Montezuma Street; 602-778-4227) in the center of the block. Others typical of the genre include the **Bird Cage Saloon** (148 South Montezuma Street) and the **Western Bar** (144 South Montezuma Street; 602-445-1244), which has live country-and-western music Thursday, Friday and Saturday.

For nondrinkers, there are the nonalcoholic hangouts **Hikkups** (116 South Montezuma Street; 602-776-8715) and the San Francisco-style coffee house in the **St. Michael Hotel** (104 South Montezuma Street; 602-776-1999) where, on weekend evenings, folk singers take you back to a different era.

PRESCOTT PARKS

Granite Dells, a labyrinth of granite rock formations along Route 89 just outside of Prescott, surrounds pretty little **Watson Lake** (602-778-4338), a man-made reservoir that is locally popular for boating and fishing. The area used to be a stronghold for Apache Indians. More recently, from the 1920s to the 1950s, there was a major resort at Granite Dells and some artifacts still remain from that era.

The Sporting Life

HORSEBACK RIDING

Areas offering interesting horseback outings including guided "Indian Sacred Ceremonial" rides in Sedona. Try **Hitchin Post Stables** (448 Lake Mary Road; 602-774-1719); **Fairfield Flagstaff Resort** (2380 North Oakmont Drive; 602-526-3232); **Ski Lift Lodge Stables** (Route 180 at Snow Bowl Road; 602-774-0729); **Perkins Wilderness Trail Rides** (Route 40 exit 171, Williams; 602-635-9349); **Kachina Stables** (Lower Red Rock Loop Road, Sedona; 602-282-7252); and **High Country Stables** (200 Stable Lane, Prescott; 602-776-4192).

CROSS-COUNTRY SKIING

For cross-country skiers, the **Flagstaff Nordic Center** (Route 180; 602-774-6216), 14 miles north of Flagstaff in Coconino National Forest, maintains an extensive system of trails from mid-October through mid-April. The center offers equipment rentals, guided tours and a ski school. Another great cross-country skiing facility is the **Mormon Lake Ski Touring Center** (Mormon Lake Village; 602-354-2240), 28 miles southeast of Flagstaff off Lake Mary Road.

GOLF

This area of Arizona is a golfer's paradise. Tee off at **Fairfield Flagstaff Resort** (2380 North Oakmont Drive, Flagstaff; 602-527-7997); **Sedona Golf Resort** (7256 Route 179, Sedona; 602-284-9355); **Village of Oak Creek Country Club** (690 Bell Rock Boulevard, Sedona; 602-284-1660); **Canyon Mesa Country Club** (500 Jacks Canyon Road, Sedona; 284-2176); **Poco Diablo Resort** (1752 Route 179, Sedona; 602-282-7333); and **Antelope Hills Golf Course** (19 Club House Drive, Prescott; 602-445-0583).

TENNIS

Public tennis courts in Flagstaff are located in **Thorpe Park** (Toltec Street) and **Bushmaster Park** (Lockett Road). Sedona has no public tennis courts. For a fee, courts are available to the public at the **Sedona Racquet Club** (West Route 89A; 602-282-4197) and **Poco Diablo Resort** (1752 Route 179; 602-282-7333). In Prescott, tennis courts are open to the public during the summer months at **Yavapai College** (1100 East Sheldon Street; 602-445-7300), **Prescott High School** (146 South Granite Street; 602-445-5400) and **Ken Lindley Field** (East Gurley Street at Arizona Street).

BICYCLING

Flagstaff has about eight miles of paved trails in its **Urban Trail System and Bikeways System**, linking the Northern Arizona University campus, the downtown area and Lowell Observatory. Maps and information on the trail system are available upon request from the **City Planning Office** (211 West Aspen Street; 602-779-7632).

Outside the city, a popular route for all-day bike touring is the 36-mile paved loop road through Sunset Crater and Wupatki national monuments, starting at the turnoff from Route 89 ten miles northeast of town.

For mountain bikers, several unpaved primitive roads lead deeper into the San Francisco Volcano Field in **Coconino National Forest**. Check out the forest road that leads to the base of Colton Crater and SP Crater. For complete information, contact the **Peaks Ranger Station** (5075 North Route 89; 602-526-0866).

The **Flagstaff Nordic Center** (Route 180; 602-774-6216), 14 miles north of Flagstaff in Coconino National Forest, opens its extensive trail system to mountain bikers from mid-May through September and offers mountain bike and helmet rentals.

The same network of unpaved back roads that makes the **Red Rock Country** around Sedona such a popular area for four-wheel-drive touring is also ideal for mountain biking. Get a map from one of the local bike shops and try the dirt roads leading from Soldier Pass Road to the Seven Sacred Pools or the Devil's Kitchen. Or follow the Broken Arrow Jeep Trail east from Route 179 to Submarine Rock. The Schnebly Hill Road climbs all the way north to Flagstaff, paralleling the Oak Creek Canyon Highway. The upper part of the road is steep, winding and very rough, but the lower part, through Bear Wallow Canyon, makes for a beautiful mountain biking excursion.

BIKE RENTALS   In Flagstaff, you can rent mountain bikes and get trail information at **Absolute Bikes** (18 North San Francisco Street; 602-779-5969); **Cosmic Cycles** (113 South San Francisco Street; 602-779-1092); or **Mountain Sports** (1800 South Milton Road; 602-

*Arizona's premier alpine ski area is **Fairfield Snowbowl** (Snowbowl Road; 602-779-1951; snow report, 602-779-4577) on the slopes of the San Francisco Peaks.*

779-5156). In Sedona, you'll find information and rentals at **Mountain Bike Heaven** (1449 West Route 89A; 602-282-1312) and **Canyon Country Mountain Bikes** (in Sedona Sports, 245 North Route 89A; 602-282-6985).

HIKING

FLAGSTAFF AREA TRAILS   Just north of Flagstaff rise the San Francisco Peaks, the highest in Arizona. Numerous trails start from Mount Elden and Schultz Pass roads, which branch off Route 180 to the right a short distance past the Museum of Northern Arizona. Other trailheads are located in Flagstaff at Buffalo Park on Cedar Avenue and near the Peaks Ranger Station on Route 89.

From the ranger station, the **Elden Lookout Trail** (1.5 miles) climbs by switchbacks up the east face of 9299-foot Mount Elden, with an elevation gain of 2400 feet and, waiting to reward you at the top, a spectacular view of the city and the volcano fields around Sunset Crater.

Fatman's Loop Trail (1 mile), branching off Elden Lookout Trail for a shorter hike with a 1600-foot elevation gain, also offers a good view of Flagstaff.

From the Buffalo Park trailhead, the **Oldham Trail** (3 miles) ascends the west face to the top of Mount Elden. The longest trail on the mountain, this is a gentler climb. The Oldham Trail intersects Mount Elden Road three times, making it possible to take a shorter hike on only the higher part of the trail. **Pipeline Trail** (1.5 miles) links the lower parts of the Oldham and Elden Lookout trails along the northern city limit of Flagstaff, allowing either a short hike on the edge of town or a long, all-day loop trip up one side of the mountain and down the other.

Perhaps the most unusual of many hiking options in the strange volcanic landscape around the base of the San Francisco Peaks is on **Red Mountain**, 33 miles north of Flagstaff off Route 180. A gap in the base of this thousand-foot-high volcanic cone lets you follow the **Red Mountain Trail** (1 mile) from the end of the national forest access road straight into the crater without climbing. Not often visited by tourists, this is a great place to explore with older children.

For maps and detailed hiking information on these and many other trails in Coconino National Forest, contact the **Peaks Ranger Station** (5075 North Route 89; 602-526-0866).

SEDONA/PRESCOTT AREA TRAILS   While every visitor to Flag-staff or Sedona drives through often-crowded Oak Creek Canyon, one of north central Arizona's "must-see" spots, few stop to explore the canyon's west fork, a narrow canyon with sheer walls hundreds of feet high in places, which is only accessible on foot.

The **West Fork Trail** (7 miles) starts at a chained-off road about ten miles north of Sedona. There is a small parking area nearby, often full. The first three miles of the fairly level trail, which pass through a protected "research natural area," are heavily used and easy to hike. Farther up, the trail becomes less distinct and requires fording the creek repeatedly.

A very popular hiking spot in the Red Rock Country is Boynton Canyon, one of Sedona's four recognized "Vortex" areas. According to Sedona's New Age community, Boynton Canyon is the most powerful of the Vortices, emanating an electromagnetic yin/yang psychic energy that can be felt for miles around. Whether you believe in such things or not, it is undeniably beautiful. From the trailhead on Boynton Pass Road—a continuation of Dry Creek Road, which leaves Route 89A in West Sedona—the nearly level **Boynton Canyon Trail** (1.5 miles) goes up the canyon through woods and among red rock formations. There are several small, ancient Sinagua Indian cliff dwellings in the canyon.

A right turn from Dry Creek Road on the way to Boynton Pass will put you on unpaved Sterling Canyon Road, which is rough enough in spots that drivers of low-clearance vehicles may want to think twice before proceeding. From this road, the **Devil's Bridge Trail** (1 mile) climbs gradually through piñon and juniper country to a long red sandstone arch with a magnificent view of the surrounding canyon-lands. You can walk to the top of the arch. Three miles farther, at the end of Dry Creek Road, is the trailhead for the **Vultee Arch Trail** (2 miles), which follows Sterling Canyon to another natural bridge.

There are many hiking trails in the national forest around Prescott. One of the most popular is the **Thumb Butte Trail** (1.7 miles), a loop trip that goes up a saddle west of town, through oak and piñon woods, offering good views of Prescott and Granite Dells. The trail starts from Thumb Butte Park. To get there, go west on Thumb Butte Road, an extension of Gurley Street.

More ambitious hikers may wish to explore the **Granite Mountain Wilderness**. Of its several trails, the one that goes to the summit of the 7125-foot mountain is **Granite Mountain Trail** (3.7 miles), a beautiful all-day hike with an elevation gain of 1500 feet. For information on this and other trails in the area, contact the Prescott National Forest—Bradshaw District ranger station just east of Prescott (2230 East Route 69; 602-445-7253).

Transportation

BY CAR

One hundred and thirty eight miles north of Phoenix via Route 17, Flagstaff is located on Route 40, the main east-west route across northern Arizona. Grand Canyon-bound travelers leaving the interstate at Flagstaff have a choice between the more direct way to Grand Canyon Village, 79 miles via Route 180, or the longer way, 105 miles via Route 89 and Route 64, which parallels the canyon rim for 25 miles. These routes combine perfectly into a spectacular loop trip from Flagstaff.

Another scenic loop trip from Flagstaff goes south on Route 89A, descending through Oak Creek Canyon to the trendy town of Sedona in the magnificent Red Rock Country, a distance of 26 slow miles. From Sedona, Route 89A continues for 58 more miles through the historic mining town of Jerome, with a steep climb over Cleopatra Hill, to Prescott, the old territorial capital. From there, a 51-mile drive on Route 89 returns travelers to interstate Route 40 at Ash Fork, about 55 miles west of Flagstaff.

BY AIR

Flagstaff Pulliam Airport is served by Skywest-Delta and Mesa-America West airlines.

Air Sedona provides commuter service between the **Sedona Airport** and Phoenix.

BY BUS

Nava-Hopi Tours (114 West Santa Fe Avenue, Flagstaff; 602-774-5003) provides bus service to the Grand Canyon South Rim, as well as Flagstaff, Sedona, Williams and Phoenix.

Greyhound Bus Lines stops at the bus terminals in Flagstaff (399 South Malpais Lane; 602-774-4573) and Prescott (820 East Sheldon Street; 602-445-54770).

BY TRAIN

Amtrak (1 East Santa Fe Avenue, Flagstaff; 800-872-7245) serves Flagstaff daily on its "Southwest Chief" route between Chicago and Los Angeles. The westbound passenger train stops in Flagstaff late in the evening, so arriving passengers will want to make hotel reservations in advance with a deposit to hold the room late. Amtrak offers a complimentary shuttle bus service to the Grand Canyon for its Flag-staff passengers.

CAR RENTALS

Flagstaff has about a dozen car-rental agencies, most of them located at the Flagstaff Municipal Airport. Among the airport concessions are **Avis Rent A Car** (602-774-8421), **Budget Car Rental** (602-779-0306) and **Hertz Rent A Car** (602-774-4452). Downtown at the corner of Humphreys (Route 180 North) and Aspen streets, more convenient for those arriving by train or bus, are **Sears Rent A Car** (602-774-1879) and a second **Budget Car Rental** (602-774-2763). **Admiral Car Rental** (602-774-7394), located in the lobby of the University Inn, will accept a cash deposit in lieu of a credit card. Also in Flagstaff is an office of **Cruise America** (824 West Route 66; 602-774-4797), a nationwide motorhome rental agency.

At the Sedona Airport, rentals are available from **Budget Car Rental** (602-282-4602).

Prescott Municipal Airport's car-rental agencies include **Hertz Rent A Car** (602-776-1399), **Sears Rent A Car** (602-778-4282) and **Toyota Rent A Car** (602-778-3806). Jeeps and vans can be rented by the day or week at **York Motors** (602-445-4970).

TAXIS

Flagstaff has more than its share of taxi companies because many public transportation travelers stop there en route to the Grand Canyon. These cabs will take you anywhere in central Arizona at any time of day or night. Sedona? Phoenix? No problem. Call **City Taxi & Tours** (602-779-2867); **Northland Taxi** (602-526-2338); **Alpine Taxi Cab Co.** (602-526-4123); **B&D Taxi Service** (602-779-2867), **Flagstaff Taxi & Limousine** (602-774-1374); or **Dream Taxi** (602-774-2934). Shop and compare—rates vary.

Sedona's local taxi service is **Twenty Eight Four A Cab** (602-282-7891). Prescott has two taxi companies—**Ace City Cab** (602-445-1616) and **Mile High Taxi** (602-778-7728); both offer discounted rates for senior citizens and physically challenged persons.

SEVEN

Western Arizona

Heading west, the mighty Colorado River pours out of the Grand   **135**
Canyon, spreads itself into Lake Mead, proceeds through a succession
of scenic lakes, resorts and riverfront coves, then rolls south until it reaches
the Gulf of California. In its wake, visitors to the region will discover a
number of unusual points of interest and unparalleled recreational opportunities—each one surrounded by a distinctive landscape, each one
quite different from the others. Here, you'll find broad expanses of
sparkling water, summer breezes whipping up whitecaps, waterskiers
cutting crystal wakes, colorful sails curled above catamarans, and miles of
sandy beaches—all along the Colorado River on Arizona's "West Coast".

Kingman is a good starting point for exploring Arizona's western
edge. Set at the crossroads of Routes 93 and 40, the town is strategi-
cally placed for excursions to Lake Mead and Hoover Dam, Bullhead
City/Laughlin and Lake Mohave, Lake Havasu and its London Bridge,
and the Parker Strip and Quartzsite. Along the way, you can explore
gold and silver mining ghost towns such as Oatman and Chloride,
which cling to a tenuous existence amid scenic surroundings. From
Kingman, there's also a steep road that leads to the alpine greenery of
Hualapai Mountain State Park, where you can picnic and camp.

About 80 miles north of Kingman, on Route 93, is man-made Lake
Mead, which is shared by Arizona and Nevada. Created in the 1930s
when the Colorado River was backed up by Hoover Dam, Lake Mead
is a popular recreation area.

In the forbidding, rocky hills of western Arizona's Mohave Desert,
real estate promoters used to sell lots in planned communities sight
unseen to gullible people in the East. Most of these would-be towns

In Arizona, the Colorado River runs for 688 miles and forms almost the entire western boundary of the state.

never even came close to reality, but two "cities" set in the middle of nowhere along desolate stretches of the Colorado River have become the twin hubs of a genuine phenomenon.

Bullhead City, the fastest-growing city in Arizona, is an isolated resort and retirement community of about 25,000 people. Founded as the construction camp for Davis Dam, Bullhead City has no visible reason for its existence except daily sunshine, warm weather year-round, boating and fishing access to the Colorado River—and a booming casino strip across the river in Laughlin, at the extreme southern tip of Nevada.

Even more improbable than Bullhead City is Lake Havasu City, which the *Los Angeles Times* has called "the most successful freestanding new town in the United States." Though it enjoys a great wintertime climate and a fine location on the shore of a 45-mile-long desert lake, there is really no logical explanation for Lake Havasu City—except that, in the 1960s, chainsaw tycoon Bob McCulloch and partner C. V. Wood Jr., planner and first general manager of Disneyland, decided to build it. Since their planned community had no economic base, they concluded that what it needed was a tourist attraction. They came up with a doozie—the London Bridge. Yes, the *real* London Bridge, bought at auction and moved block by massive granite block across the Atlantic, where it was reassembled over a channel to connect to an island in Lake Havasu. The unprecedented, seemingly absurd plan actually worked, and you can see the result for yourself today. The London Bridge is the second-most popular tourist attraction in Arizona, surpassed only by the Grand Canyon.

In addition to the bridge, Lake Havasu City has an "English Village" to compliment it. Nearby, the two sections of Lake Havasu State Park are well-developed recreational areas that take advantage of the lake's 45 miles of shoreline. The Windsor Beach Unit on the upper level of the lake has boat ramps, shaded picnic areas, campsites and more primitive camping areas accessible by boat. The Cattail Cove Unit has similar facilities, plus a marina, restaurant, store and boat rentals.

Near Parker Dam, which impounds Lake Havasu, Buckskin Mountain State Park attracts tube floaters, boaters and waterskiers. Hiking trails into the Buckskin Mountains lead to panoramic vista points, and, for some lucky hikers, sightings of desert bighorn sheep.

About halfway down the "coast," the Bill Williams River empties into the Colorado River just above Parker Dam. Upstream is Alamo

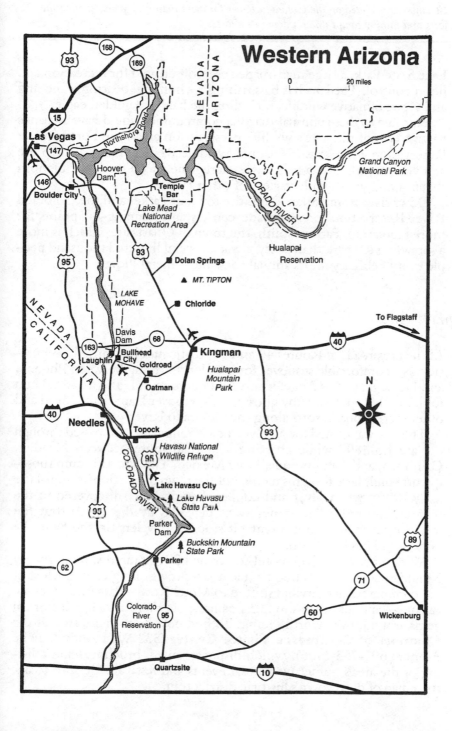

Western Arizona

0   20 miles

168
93
169
15
Las Vegas
147
Hoover
Dam
146
Boulder City
Northshore Road
NEVADA
ARIZONA
Temple
Bar
COLORADO RIVER
Grand Canyon
National Park
Lake Mead
National
Recreation Area
95
93
Dolan Springs
Hualapai
Reservation
▲ MT. TIPTON
LAKE
MOHAVE
Chloride
NEVADA
CALIFORNIA
Davis
Dam
68
163
Bullhead
City
Laughlin   Goldroad
Oatman
Kingman
Hualapai
Mountain
Park
To Flagstaff
40
N
40
Needles
Topock
Havasu National
95   Wildlife Refuge
93
CO-LORADO RIVER
95
Lake Havasu City
Lake Havasu
State Park
Parker
Dam
Buckskin Mountain
State Park
89
62
Parker
71
Colorado
River
Reservation
95
60
Wickenburg
Quartzsite
10

Steamboats operated on the Colorado River for more than fifty years, serving the forts and mining camps up and down its shores.

Lake State Park, a large man-made reservoir created for recreation and flood control. The lake has bass fishing, swimming, boating, canoeing and views of native wildlife, including the bald and golden eagle.

En route to these unusual Arizona communities, you'll have a chance to visit two of the state's wildlife preservation areas, the Fort Mohave Reservation and Havasu National Wildlife Refuge. Keep a sharp eye and you may glimpse a bald eagle, peregrine falcon or desert bighorn sheep, along with a wide variety of other fauna.

Downriver from Parker Dam, the town of Parker and the Colorado River Reservation serve as trade centers and jumping-off points for more recreation. Farther south, the town of Quartzsite, which is more a sprawling RV park than a city, attracts several hundred thousand people every February for its annual rock and mineral show.

Kingman Area

At the crossroads of Routes 40 and 93, **Kingman** has earned a reputation as a comfortable stopover for travelers hurrying between Phoenix and Las Vegas or Los Angeles and Albuquerque. It is also a natural hub for leisurely trips to nearby ghost towns, Hoover Dam, Lake Mead and other recreational resorts along the Colorado River.

The city was named for surveyor Lewis Kingman, who passed through the area in 1892 while charting a railroad route between Needles, California, and Albuquerque, New Mexico. The railroad camp subsequently built here took his name, but the town didn't flourish until the early 1900s, when silver and copper deposits were discovered in the surrounding hills. The mines were depleted by the 1940s, but the town survived as an important pit stop for travelers on the Santa Fe railway and old Route 66.

With more than 1700 motel rooms and 50 restaurants, modern-day Kingman continues its tradition as a key provisioning center. Most of the commercial activity has shifted to Motel Row—East Andy Devine Avenue—and suburban shopping centers, but there are a few historical gems around town worth seeing. To find out about them, stop at the **Chamber of Commerce Visitor Center** (333 West Andy Devine Avenue; 602-753-6106), which dispenses maps, brochures and a listing of the area's numerous annual events and festivals. Be sure to ask for a map of downtown's historic district tour.

An interesting stop is the **Mohave Museum of History and Arts** (400 West Beale Street; 602-753-3195), which gives visitors a glimpse of many of the unusual aspects of western Arizona. A mural and dioramas in the lobby depict the settlement of the region and show how camels used to be used as beasts of burden in these parts. Kingman is the source of much of the turquoise mined in the United States, and the museum has a fine collection of carved turquoise objects. Native American exhibits include portrayals of the traditional ways of the Hualapai and Mohave Indians. Other rooms contain a collection of paintings of U.S. Presidents and their first ladies by local artist Lawrence Williams, as well as memorabilia of the town's most famous native son, the late actor Andy Devine.

To see how Kingman's upper crust lived after the turn of the century, visit the **Bonelli House** (430 East Spring Street; 602-753-1413), an impressive two-story, balconied mansion constructed in 1915 of native tufa stone. The home was built by Swiss Mormons who made a fortune in the jewelry business. Inside, the rooms are decorated with furnishings and fixtures that reflect the elegance of the era—Victorian brass beds, ornately carved music boxes, antique wall clocks, and an unusual water-jacketed stove.

A TALE OF TWO GHOST TOWNS

Arizona has two types of ghost towns—those that have been abandoned to the ravages of time and those that have been brought back to life thanks to tourism. Good examples of each type can be found along the beat-up old segment of Route 66 that climbs and winds over the mountains between Kingman and Topock near the state's western boundary.

Goldroad was once a prosperous town whose residents dug $7 million worth of gold ore out of the desert hillsides between 1901 and 1931. Now all that remains are mine shafts, a few crumbling walls and stone foundations from the town's larger buildings.

Oatman, just nine miles away, was another gold-mining town of about the same size, founded and abandoned at about the same time. But many of its old buildings are still standing, used to house curio shops and snack bars, and tourists come from all over to see the sights.

Why the difference? The landowners of Goldroad destroyed their building on purpose to reduce their property taxes, while a small group of Oatman's residents stayed on through the lean years, surviving by selling refreshments to passersby. Eventually, Hollywood discovered Oatman, spruced up the old storefronts and used it as a set for several movies, including How the West Was Won. *Now the town has been declared a National Historic District.*

A drive through the older section of Kingman, away from the chain-store motels and generic coffee shops, reveals a turn-of-the-century downtown area on the brink of fading away. For the time being, you can still admire the architectural splendor the proud buildings once enjoyed, from Victorian mansions to simple adobe shacks. Some of the sights on the chamber's historic district tour include the Spanish colonial **Santa Fe Railroad Depot** at Andy Devine Avenue and Fourth Street; the mission revival-style **IOOF** building at Fifth and Beale streets; the classic Greek-style tufa-stone, glass-domed **Mohave County Courthouse** at Spring and Fourth streets; and, just east of the museum, **Locomotive Park**, a collection of early train locomotives, with a 1927 Baldwin steam engine and bright red caboose as the centerpiece.

To step even further into the area's past, drive to the old gold-mining town of **Oatman**, about 25 miles southwest of Kingman via Route 66. Founded in 1906 and mostly abandoned in 1942, Oatman is a funky collection of rickety, Old-West buildings—some look ready to collapse, while others are occupied by souvenir stores and yogurt shops. This is one of the better preserved of Arizona's ghost towns, thanks largely to the fact that it has been used several times as a movie set. A healthy tourist trade also keeps the town going. Weekends are lively with country music and staged shootouts in the streets. Besides the usual assortment of antique and curio shops, the **Oatman Hotel** features an upstairs museum of old movie posters, rusty mining equipment and pioneer clothing. In 1939, Carole Lombard and Clark Gable spent their wedding night here after getting married in Kingman. One of her dresses is displayed in the honeymoon suite.

A more pristine example of an Arizona ghost town is **Chloride**, located about 23 miles northwest of Kingman via Route 93. Named for the salt deposits in the surrounding hills, Chloride is a weathered gathering of wood-planked buildings, miner's shacks and processing mills. Although not as rehearsed as Oatman's, the townsfolk put on amateurish skits and shootouts on the weekend. Although the high melodrama would be better accompanied by a player piano, everyone seems to have a good time. The sights here include several galleries

---

OATMAN'S BEGGING BURROS

Tourism keeps dozens of wild burros, descendants of the work animals who once hauled gold ore out of the local mines, loitering in the streets of Oatman. They've learned that panhandling snacks from sightseers beats scrounging around for food in the Mohave Desert any day.

and antique shops, and a restored miner's shack next door to Shelp's General Store. If the salty atmosphere makes you thirsty, head to the **Old Tennessee Saloon**, part of the general store built in 1928. Just a couple of miles outside of town off Tennessee Avenue are giant color murals painted on rockfaces by Southwest artist Roy Purcell. Created in 1966 and 1975, the murals include surrealistic images of Native American folklife.

KINGMAN AREA LODGING

It seems nearly every motel chain is represented in Kingman. Most are located along East Andy Devine Avenue and West Beale Street, and provide dependable lodging at budget to moderate prices. Among the nicer ones, the **Quality Inn** (1400 East Andy Devine Avenue; 602-753-5531) features modern guest rooms, some equipped with kitchenettes and refrigerators. Fitness buffs will like its pool, sauna and workout room. In the downtown area, the **Rodeway Inn** (411 West Beale Street; 602-228-2000) is within walking distance from the historic downtown sights. Comfortable rooms are decorated with dark-wood furniture and cool pastels. Both motels are moderately priced, and offer budget rates during the off-season.

In the ghost town of Oatman, the old **Oatman Hotel** has reopened as a bed-and-breakfast establishment. The authentic two-story adobe with arched facade and corrugated iron walls and ceilings may induce you to take a room, as it did Clark Gable and Carole Lombard on their wedding night after a surprise ceremony in Kingman. Oatman was on the main highway—Route 66—to Hollywood back then, and a peek into the honeymoon "suite," with its bare hanging light bulb and crumbling walls, will give you an idea of how eager Clark and Carole must have been. Although the light bulb may have been changed, the rates remain in the budget range.

KINGMAN AREA RESTAURANTS

Dozens of chain restaurants and coffee shops line East Andy Devine Avenue in Kingman, but for some local flavor try **The Kingman Deli** (419 Beale Street; 602-753-4151), an adobe-style café with hardwood floors, knotty-pine walls and dark-wood furniture. The homemade chile is thick and spicy, and of the 36 different kinds of sandwiches, the most popular are the turkey salad and chopped chicken liver. Budget.

The **Route 66 Distillery** (1400 East Andy Devine Avenue; 602-753-6101) in the Quality Inn Motel has a massive collection of memorabilia from the 1950s and 1960s, including old signs, posters and vending machines. The kitchen turns out reliable renditions of roast beef, steaks, chicken and seafood dishes. Moderate.

The Hualapai Indians lived in the mountains south of Kingman until forced by the U.S. military in the 1870s to relocate. Their name translates to "Pine-tree folk."

KINGMAN AREA SHOPPING

Most of Kingman's commercial activity takes place along Beale Street and Andy Devine Avenue, parallel one-way streets that form a loop through the downtown area. The two merge at the eastern end, where there are a pair of regional shopping centers. There's not much in between, except a country store and gift shop that occupies the historic **Kayser House** (616 East Beale Street), a quaint 1920s bungalow that's part of the downtown tour. Here, you can purchase hand-made quilts and folk art, baskets, dried flower arrangements and the like.

KINGMAN AREA NIGHTLIFE

You won't find Kitty or Festus at the **Long Branch Saloon** (2255 Airway Avenue, Kingman; 602-757-8756), but you can kick up your heels to live or deejay country-and-western music nightly. Or you can catch a movie at **The Movies** (4055 Stockton Hill Road, Kingman; 602-757-7985).

KINGMAN AREA PARKS

An island of forested slopes in the middle of the Mohave Desert, **Hualapai Mountain State Park** (602-757-0915) is a popular retreat for hiking, camping and picnicking that's located about 14 miles east of Kingman on the paved Hualapai Mountain Park Road. These mountains were once the ancestral home of the Hualapai Indians, who now live farther north on a reservation at the west end of the Grand Canyon. Today, the forests are home to such wildlife as deer, elk, coyotes and occasional mountain lions. Facilities include picnic areas, cabins, softball diamonds, hiking trails and a winter snow play area. Overnight camping is allowed, and there are also 15 cabins—built in the 1930s for the Civilian Conservation Corps—that can be rented at budget prices, but you have to call ahead for reservations.

Lake Mead Area

Downriver from the Grand Canyon, the Colorado River becomes a series of man-made desert lakes formed by the dams of the Colorado River Project, which provides: electricity for South California, a steady supply of irrigation water for Imperial Valley agriculture, and flood control for all the communities along the once-raging river. With Nevada and California on the other side, the river and lakes form the Arizona state line.

The largest of the reservoirs is 115-mile-long **Lake Mead**, about 80 miles north of Kingman on Route 93, not far from Las Vegas. Created when the Colorado River was backed up by Hoover Dam from 1935 to 1938, Lake Mead is a popular destination for boating, fishing, windsurfing, waterskiing, lying on the beach or exploring hidden coves and inlets by houseboat. The sheer size of the lake—822 miles of shoreline and nine trillion gallons of water—and the surrounding jagged canyons and desert sand dunes are reason enough to visit the largest man-made lake in the United States.

The lake is especially popular with anglers, who take a run at large-mouth bass, rainbow, brown and cutthroat trout, catfish and black crappie. Striped bass, which can reach 50 pounds, are the most popular game fish in recent years.

The easiest way to access Lake Mead from the isolated Arizona shore is at **Temple Bar Marina** (602-767-3211), reached by a well-marked, paved 28-mile road that turns off Route 93 about 55 miles north of Kingman. Here you can rent a moderately priced room at the modern motel, or one of the older cabins with kitchenettes. You'll also find a café, cocktail lounge, campground, boat-launching ramp, fuel dock and store. This is the last outpost for supplies if you plan to boat north of Temple Bar.

Although more remote, **South Cove/Pearce Ferry** is recommended for its scenic vistas of the lake and craggy peaks of Iceberg Canyon,

---

ALAN BIBLE VISITOR CENTER

*A good way to learn about Lake Mead is to stop at the **Alan Bible Visitor Center** (Highway 93 and Lakeshore Road, Boulder City, NV; 702-293-8906). Located midway between Boulder City and Hoover Dam, the center's botanical garden, exhibits and short movie shown periodically throughout the day describe the area's history and attractions. There are also books for sale that can provide more in-depth information on the area's history, flora and fauna.*

about 46 miles east of Hoover Dam. Take Route 93 north from Kingman about 40 miles to the Dolan Springs turnoff and drive east. After
passing Dolan Springs, you'll enter a massive forest of Joshua trees and
the retirement resort of Meadview. Soon, you'll begin to catch glimpses
of Lake Mead, framed by the jagged peaks of Iceberg Canyon. South
Cove has only a boat ramp and toilets, but it offers a serene respite,
accented by the deep blue waters of Lake Mead and rough-hewn mountains that frame it. The final four-mile stretch of dirt road to Pearce Ferry
drops down through steep canyon walls and granite buttes. At the shoreline are camping facilities, boat ramps and plenty of peace and quiet. If
the rocky granite corridors remind you of the Grand Canyon, it's because the park's western boundary is just a mile east of here.

There's also a scenic drive that runs along the Nevada side of the
lake, where there are more marinas, a campground, a popular public
beach and a few small resorts. Take Route 166 from Boulder City through
the washes and canyons above the lake until you reach **Northshore
Road** (Routes 147 and 167). You can stay on the highway that follows
the shoreline all the way to the Valley of Fire State Park, or drop down
to the lake at Callville Bay, Echo Bay or Overton Beach. You'll find
food and facilities at all three resorts.

One of the best views of the lake is from the **Hoover Dam cruise
boat** (Lake Mead Tours, 702-293-6180), which leaves from the Lake
Mead Marina (322 Lakeshore Road, Boulder City, Nevada; 702-293-
3484) several times a day. **Lake Mead Cruises** (1646 Nevada Highway, Boulder City, NV; 702-293-6180) offers several cruises, the best
aboard a three-deck paddleboat, the *Desert Princess*. The 100-foot-long
sternwheeler is the largest vessel to ply the waters of the lake, and

---

HOOVER DAM

*Long before gambling became king, **Hoover Dam** was the number-one tourist attraction in Nevada. Completed in 1935, the dam was touted as the Eighth Wonder of
the World. And for good reason. The dam is one of the world's engineering marvels.*

*The horseshoe-shaped plug that holds back two-years' flow of the mighty
Colorado River is as tall as a 54-story building. The base is 600 feet thick and
contains enough concrete to build a two-lane highway from San Francisco to New
York. Inside, there's as much reinforced steel as in the Empire State Building.*

*The dam took five years to build, at a cost of $175 million. At the peak of
construction, 5000 workers labored night and day. An average of 50 injuries a day
and 94 deaths were recorded before the flood gates were closed and Lake Mead
began to fill.*

Lake Mead attracts more than 10 million visitors annually.

---

features a snack bar, two glass-enclosed decks, an open promenade deck, an 80-seat dining room, cocktail lounge and dancefloor. The late afternoon cruise features a sunset dinner and stunning views of illuminated Hoover Dam.

Today, **Hoover Dam** is one of the Southwest's top tourist attractions. About 56 miles north of Kingman via Route 93, the dam is open for tours every day of the year. Begin your visit at the **Exhibit Center** (Route 93, on the Nevada side of the dam; 702-293-8367). Notice the 30-foot-tall Art Nouveau figures outside—the Winged Figures of the Republic, cast in bronze by sculptor Oskar Hansen. Inside, you'll find further evidence of the 1930s architecture influenced by the WPA era: ornate railings and fixtures, floors and doors. The history of the Colorado River, the building of the dam and how it is used for electrical power, flood control and irrigation is told in scale models, movies and brochures.

The guided tour (admission), which takes about 35 minutes, begins with an elevator ride to the base of the dam. You'll feel the temperature drop as you descend—the the dam's interior averages between 55 and 60 degrees year-round. At the base you'll enter a monumental room housing the seven-story-high turbines that took three years to build and assemble, and which generate four billion kilowatt-hours of electricity.

The base of the dam is honey-combed with tunnels. One leads to a 30-foot diversion pipe; another to an outdoor observation deck where you can enjoy a fish-eye perspective of the dam and the rugged canyon it bridges. Returning to the top, you'll find a snack bar and souvenir shop. Keep in mind that Nevada time is one hour earlier than Arizona's.

LAKE MEAD AREA LODGING AND RESTAURANTS

The only lodging on the Arizona shore of Lake Mead is at **Temple Bar Marina** (602-767-3211), where you can rent a moderately priced room at the modern motel, or one of the older cabins with kitchenettes. There is also a café, cocktail lounge, campground, boat-launching ramp, fuel dock and store. This is the last outpost for supplies if you plan to boat north of Temple Bar.

There's a motel on the Nevada shore of the lake at **Echo Bay Resort and Marina** (702-394-4000). Along with a restaurant, coffee shop and lounge, the motel offers modern, budget-priced rooms, an RV village and an airstrip for light aircraft.

---

*In Nevada near Echo Bay is **Rogers Spring**, a warm-water oasis where prehistoric Indians once camped.*

About a mile north of the Boulder Beach, **Lake Mead Marina** (322 Lakeshore Road; 702-293-3484) has hundreds of boat slips and a popular floating restaurant, coffee shop and cocktail lounge. Farther north, the **Las Vegas Boat Harbor** (702-565-9111) has more boat slips, a picnic area and campground. You can also camp or park your RV at **Callville Bay Resort Marina** (Star Route 10, off Northshore Road; 702-565-8958), which also has a coffee shop and cocktail lounge.

LAKE MEAD AREA PARKS

Most of Lake Mead's shoreline consists of rocks and gravel, but you can spread a beach towel at **Boulder Beach**, just a few minutes north of the Alan Bible Visitor Center. The two miles of sandy beach and the clear water of Lake Mead attract year-round sunbathers. Picnic areas, campsites, a snack bar and convenience store are nearby. The clear water and warm temperatures attract divers, who can explore the ill-fated yacht, *Tortuga*, near the Boulder Islands, the *Cold Duck*, submerged in 35 feet of water, and the remains of Hoover Dam's asphalt factory and the old Mormon settlement of St. Thomas.

Bullhead City/Laughlin Area

Bullhead City, 35 miles west of Kingman via Route 68, may be Arizona's fastest-growing city, but it owes its prosperity to Laughlin, Nevada, on the far side of the river. The city of Laughlin is a shimmering riverfront resort that has blossomed into Nevada's third-largest gambling center. Because it has few residential and commercial areas of its own, most of the thousands of people who work there live, shop and send their kids to school in its Arizona sister, Bullhead City. The closest gambling zone to the greater Phoenix area, Laughlin is packed to overflowing every weekend. The rest of the week, the casinos, buffets, lounges and showrooms play host to motorhome nomads who appreciate the opportunity to avoid Las Vegas traffic and avail themselves of Laughlin's vast, free RV parking lots.

But gambling isn't the only attraction in the Bullhead City/Laughlin area. The Colorado River and nearby Lake Mohave are major draws, offering year-round water sports such as swimming, boating, fishing and waterskiing. Also within short driving distance are ghost towns, historic mines, and intriguing lost canyons waiting to be explored.

Commercial boat cruises are also a popular pastime. Before the bridge across the Colorado River was built in the mid 1980s, visitors used to park on the Arizona side of the river and ride passenger ferries across to the casinos on the Nevada shore. Now, on busy weekends when parking lots in Laughlin are full, the ferries still carry people across the river, making for a brief, fun, and, best of all, free cruise. Several companies also offer longer riverboat sightseeing tours down the river from casino docks. Among them are **Blue River Safaris** (702-298-0910), which operates the Colorado River King jet cruiser from the Riverside Casino dock, and **Laughlin River Tours** (702-298-1047), which runs the Little Belle paddlewheel steamer from the Edgewater Casino dock and even offers on-board weddings.

Bullhead City was incorporated in 1984, but it was founded in 1945 when it was the construction camp for Davis Dam, three miles upstream. The town, named for a rock formation now submerged by Lake Mohave, is a lowrise collection of housing tracts, shopping centers and mobile home parks. New housing developments and retirement communities along the Colorado River—Riviera, Fort Mohave and Golden Shores—have extended Bullhead City's outskirts as far south as Topock, at the junction of Route 40.

The best time to visit Bullhead City/Laughlin is during the winter and spring months, when the daytime temperatures range from 65 to 80 degrees. Temperatures in July and August can reach an astounding 120 degrees or more, making this area the hottest spot in the nation.

There's not much to see or do in Bullhead City, unless pre-fab homes and tilt-up shopping centers are your idea of excitement. So it's no surprise that the most-visited attraction in the area is the strip of ten casinos across the water on the river's western shore. Unlike their larger cousins on the famed Las Vegas Strip, the Laughlin hotel/casinos are close together and are easily accessible by a concrete strand that follows the river. The best is the **Colorado Belle** (2100 South Casino Drive, Laughlin; 702-298-4000), a 600-foot replica of a Mississippi steamboat, complete with three decks and four black smokestacks 21 stories tall. In the evening, the paddlewheel "turns" by strobe light. Inside, the decor is turn-of-the-century New Orleans, with lots of plush red carpeting, glass-globe lamps, brass railings and wrought-iron fixtures. The cluster of shops on the mezzanine level has several restaurants, an old-fashioned candy store, and wandering clowns to keep your spirits up. For a bit of Dodge City by the river try the **Pioneer Hotel** (2200 South Casino Drive, Laughlin; 702-298-2442) next door. The two-story hotel looks like a U-shaped fort, finished with weathered wood panels. The facade of the casino entrance suggests a Wild West boarding house. Swinging doors and a wooden porch lead into a hectic casino, decorated with dark-wood floors and distressed paneling. On the river side of the hotel is a waving neon cowboy—River Rick— Laughlin's version of Vegas Vic. The grounds facing the river include a lush flower garden, green grass and shade trees. There are also benches for relaxing and watching the ferry boats and jetskiers on the river.

Also worth visiting is the **Riverside Resort** (1650 South Casino Drive, Laughlin; 702-298-2535). Be sure to stop in at the antiques shop just off the casino. The small but interesting collection consists of slot machines, juke boxes, vintage radios and a variety of old neon signs. On display, but not for sale, are antique slots from Don Laughlin's personal collection, including a 1938 vest pocket slot machine and a 1931 slot that paid off in golf balls.

About three miles north of Bullhead City is the **Davis Dam and Powerplant** (602-754-3628), built in 1953 to produce hydroelectric power and regulate water delivery to Mexico. The powerplant, downstream from the dam embankment on the Arizona side of the river, is open daily for self-guided tours, which include recorded lectures, illustrated maps and close-up views of the plant's turbines.

Behind the dam lies **Lake Mohave**, which extends 67 miles upstream to Hoover Dam. The long, narrow lake (four miles across at its widest point) provides a multitude of recreational opportunities, including fishing, boating, waterskiing and windsurfing.

BULLHEAD CITY/LAUGHLIN AREA LODGING

Just a stone's throw from the Colorado River, the **Arizona Clearwater Resort Hotel** (1081 Route 95, Bullhead City; 602-754-2201; 800-654-7126) is a small but modern hostelry, with a combination Southwest and Seven Seas motif—nautical rigging and fish nets are accented by howling coyote statues. But the rooms, some with river

---

RIVER OF THE DAMMED

Davis Dam is one of three dams operating to control flooding and produce hydroelectric power along the Colorado River. Along with the other two—Hoover Dam to the north and Parker Dam, about 80 miles downstream—they form the Lower Colorado River Dams project. They also divert river water to form three lakes: Lake Mead, Lake Mohave and Lake Havasu. Another six large dams in Colorado, Utah and New Mexico also control the waters of the mighty Colorado.

views, are exceptionally large and tastefully decorated in muted pastels and light-wood furniture. Moderate.

There are also a score of motels in Bullhead City; most are clean and modern but unexceptional, and room rates tend to run higher than in the Laughlin hotels across the river. Besides the national chains, try the **Park Oasis Motel** (7th and Lee streets; 602-754-2829) and **Bullhead Riverlodge Motel** (455 Moser Street; 602-754-2250). Both are moderate-priced, all-suite motels, ideal for families; the Riverlodge has a boat and fishing dock available for guests' use at no charge.

Although there are 10,000 hotel rooms in Laughlin, busy weekends often attract up to 50,000 visitors. You don't need a calculator to figure the result: reservations are a must. Like their Vegas cousins, the hotels in Laughlin offer the basic amenities—casinos, bars, restaurants, inexpensive buffets, and lounge entertainment—and the guest rooms are comparable. Here are a few that offer unusual amenities. All rooms are moderately priced on weekends and budget priced during the week.

For gorgeous river views, check out the **Edgewater Hotel** (2020 South Casino Drive, Laughlin, NV; 702-298-2453, 800-257-0300), whose frosty-white, 26-story tower has the most rooms fronting the Colorado. All 1470 guest rooms are tastefully decorated with rattan club chairs and white-wood furniture, plush green carpets, and sand-colored walls accented by Southwest print spreads, drapes and ceiling runners. At the dock, you can take a free shuttleboat ride to the Arizona bank, or pay for a river cruise on the *Little Belle* paddleboat.

The covered terrace and pool area at **Sam's Town Gold River** (2700 South Casino Drive, Laughlin; 702-298-2242; 800-835-7903) with its palm trees, green lawns and river view is a great spot for lounging. Inside, the 1000 rooms are bright and airy with a touch of the Southwest—plush carpeting, smoked-glass tables, velour-upholstered chairs, and Southwest-print upholstery. Be sure to check out the casino with its high ceilings and neon mining signs hanging from the rafters.

Just around a bend in the river is **Harrah's Del Rio** (2900 South Casino Drive, Laughlin; 702-298-4600; 800-447-8700), which sits isolated in a mini-canyon at the south end of casino row. The cove fronting the hotel offers the only sandy beach on casino row. With a south-of-the-border theme, fiesta colors are splashed throughout the casino, four restaurants, three bars and the 1000 guest rooms.

The newest and largest hotel on the river is the **Flamingo Hilton** (1900 South Casino Drive, Laughlin; 702-298-5111; 800-445-8667), where ribbons of pink neon wrap through the casino and restaurants. The 2000 rooms in the shiny pink twin towers are typically Hilton—spacious and modern, and decorated in cool shades of blue and green. Hotel amenities include six restaurants, a production show and a beautifully landscaped garden overlooking the river.

For half the year, Bullhead City, AZ is one hour ahead of Laughlin, NV, which is in another time zone. The rest of the time Nevada switches to Daylight Savings and you won't need to adjust your watch each time you cross the Colorado River.

It's not the Reading, but you can ride the rails on a mini-passenger train at the **Ramada Express** (2121 South Casino Drive, Laughlin; 702-298-4200, 800-272-6232). The narrow-gauge railroad shuttles you on a ten-minute ride from the parking lot to the casino, decorated like a Victorian railroad station. Guest rooms in the 400-room tower behind the casino feature deep earth-tone colors, dark-wood furniture and brass lamps and fixtures.

BULLHEAD CITY/LAUGHLIN AREA RESTAURANTS

Beef eaters will love the **Rib Ranch** (135 Route 95, Bullhead City; 602-754-3349), a western-style steak house decorated with dark-wood walls, wrought-iron fixtures and a few well-worn leather equestrian accessories. From the mesquite broiler comes New York, porterhouse, T-bone, and a debilitating 16-ounce rib-eye steak. Locals consider the sweet, barbecued ribs the best in town. Moderate.

Along with a nice view of Lake Mohave, **Lake Mohave Resort Restaurant** (Katherine Landing just above Davis Dam; 602-754-3245) serves a tasty blackened catfish and other seafood dishes, plus steaks and chops, at moderate prices.

In Laughlin, the casinos are famous for their inexpensive all-you-can-eat buffets. Some of the better dining rooms include **Sutter's Lodge** (2700 South Casino Drive, Laughlin; 702-298-2242) at Sam's Town Gold River, fashioned after a 19th-century hunting lodge with a veranda and lots of open beams and wood paneling. The specialty on the moderately priced menu is baby back pork ribs. Also featured are steaks, chicken and seafood, and 100 brands of imported beer.

Country cooking is never out of reach at the **Boarding House Restaurant** (2200 South Casino Drive, Laughlin; 702-298-2442) at the Pioneer Hotel, where you can feast on a combination dinner of fried chicken and barbecued ribs at budget prices. Go easy on the cornbread and save room for homemade strawberry shortcake.

Also worth mentioning are Laughlin's **William Fisk's Steakhouse** (Harrah's Del Rio, 2900 South Casino Drive; 702-298-6832) for steaks, seafood and Continental cuisine in a Southwest setting overlooking the river; **Prime Rib Room** (Riverside Resort, 1650 South Casino Drive; 702-298-2535) where you can supervise the carving at your table; and the **Alta Villa** (Flamingo Hilton, 1900 South Casino Drive; 702-298-5111) for Italian specialties. All moderately priced.

BULLHEAD CITY/LAUGHLIN AREA NIGHTLIFE

Virtually all of the nightlife in the area happens in Laughlin, where free lounge acts are presented in most of the casinos, usually rock or country-and-western groups. The **River Boat Lounge** (2100 South Casino Drive; 702-298-4000) at the Colorado Belle also has a Dixieland band, singers and dancers in a Bourbon Street Revue each night, and a 12-piece orchestra playing Big Band music Sunday afternoons.

Most of the celebrity headliners appear at **Don's Celebrity Room** (1650 South Casino Drive; 702-298-2535) at the Riverside Resort, the only theater-sized showroom in Laughlin. Acts range from Roger Miller and Slappy White to Charley Pride and competition kick boxing. Cover. Also at the Riverside, the **Western Dance Hall** features dancing to country music (live or videotaped), and the **Starview Showroom** hosts a Sunday afternoon Big Band dance and radio show.

The town's only production show is staged at **Club Flamingo** (1900 South Casino Drive, Laughlin; 702-298-5111) in the Flamingo Hilton. Past acts have included top impersonators and a Broadway-style revue; Cover. **Concert Under the Stars** at the Flamingo's outdoor amphitheater usually features nostalgic rock bands. Cover.

For a dose of laughter, go to **Sandy Hackett's Comedy Club** (2700 South Casino Drive, Laughlin; 702-298-2242) at Sam's Town Gold River. The performers' names won't make you forget the Tonight Show, but their jokes will make you forget the slots, at least for a while. Cover.

BULLHEAD CITY/LAUGHLIN AREA PARKS

The Colorado River and Lake Mohave provide a multitude of recreational activities, including boating, fishing, waterskiing, scuba diving and windsurfing. Landlubbing hikers will love the desert and canyons surrounding Bullhead City/Laughlin. Lake Mohave above Davis Dam actually resembles the river below the dam—the lake stretches for 67 miles through jagged canyons and rocky mountains. At its widest point, it is only four miles from shore to shore.

The lake's closest public beach is at **Katherine Landing** (602-754-3272), three miles north of the dam. The landing also has a full-service marina, boat launching docks, campground, motel, restaurant and grocery store. You can rent boats, fishing tackle and waterskis here.

The only public beach on the Colorado River is at the **Davis Camp County Park** (602-754-4606), about a mile north of Laughlin on the Arizona side of the river. Here, you'll find a stretch of sandy beach where you can swim, fish or launch a jet ski. At the south end of the park is a marsh that's home to variety of birds and other small wildlife.

Willow Beach (602-767-3311), on Lake Mohave about 15 miles south of Hoover Dam, has a motel, trailer park, marina, restaurant, grocery store, gas station and picnic grounds. Nearby, you can tour the Willow Beach National Fish Hatchery that keeps both lakes stocked, and its small exhibit room where you can learn about the Colorado River's history.

Lake Havasu Area

About 20 miles upstream from Parker Dam, **Lake Havasu** may be the prettiest dammed lake along the Colorado River. Cool and bright blue in the heart of the desert, this 46-mile-long lake has become a very popular recreation area. Its main claim to fame, however, is **London Bridge** in **Lake Havasu City**, 68 miles southwest of Kingman via Routes 40 and 95. Except for the Grand Canyon, London Bridge is the most visited tourist attraction in Arizona.

The audacity and monumental pointlessness of the city fathers' decision to move the bridge here when the city of London decided to replace it draws curiosity seekers in droves. To believe it, you have to see it. The bridge is 35 feet wide and 952 feet long, and you can drive or walk across it. Every year, millions do. Is it worth seeing? Absolutely! It's a giant lesson in the fine line between madness and genius—and one of the strangest things in the entire Southwest.

To add more British atmosphere, the developers built an English-style village nearby. Here, you'll find a London cab, double-decker bus, bright-red wooden phone booth and a somewhat authentic Liverpool pub—the City of London Arms. In recent years, however, the "shoppes" in the English village have begun to look more like Coney Island than Picadilly Circus, with a slew of T-shirt and ash-tray souvenir stores, fast-food stands that dispense tasteless fish-and-chips, even a Wild West gift shop.

Nevertheless, the stately London Bridge is an impressive sight with its sweeping arches of chiseled granite. A great time to see it is at night, when it glows against the cobalt sky.

A BIT OF LONDON IN THE ARIZONA DESERT

Originally built in 1825 to replace a still older London Bridge that had lasted 625 years, this bridge was sold at auction in 1968. Lake Havasu City's promoters bought it for $2,460,000. The 10,000 tons of granite facing were then disassembled into blocks weighing from 1000 to 17,000 pounds each, shipped and trucked 10,000 miles to this site and reconstructed on the shore of Lake Havasu when the city was practically nonexistent. Then a canal was dug to let water flow under the bridge.

In Lake Havasu City, a number of boats offer sightseeing tours from London Bridge. They range from the first cruise boat on the lake, the cute little *Miss Havasupai* operated by **Lake Havasu Boat Tours** (602-855-7979), to the large Mississippi riverboat replica Dixie Belle (602-855-0888). **Bluewater Charters** (602-855-7171) runs daily jet boat excursions from London Bridge up to Topock Gorge and the Havasu-Topock National Wildlife Refuge.

LAKE HAVASU AREA LODGING

Lake Havasu City boasts many fine resort hotels. The best is the **Ramada London Bridge Resort** (1477 Queen's Bay Road; 602-855-0888), with its blend of Tudor and medieval castle-style architecture and beautiful contemporary guest rooms. It also has its own golf course, tennis courts, swimming pools, lovely green landscaped grounds and a waterfront location right next to London Bridge and Olde English Village. Don't miss the replica of Britain's gold coronation coach in the lobby. Moderate to deluxe.

Across the bridge on the island, the **Nautical Inn** (1000 McCulloch Boulevard; 602-855-2141) also has a golf course, as well as a private dock with waterskiing, sailing, boating, jetskiing and windsurfing equipment for guests. All the rooms are on the waterfront. Each carpeted unit comes with two double beds, a patio and direct access to the lawn and beach. The suites include refrigerators and kitchenettes. Deluxe.

Within a mile of the bridge, budget-priced standard motel rooms are available at the **Windsor Inn** (451 London Bridge Road; 602-855-4135) and the **Shakespeare Inn** (2190 McCulloch Boulevard; 602-855-4157).

If you need room to roam, spacious one-bedroom suites are available at the **Sands Vacation Resort** (2040 Mesquite Avenue; 602-855-1388). Pictures of the Southwest decorate the pastel walls of these courtyard units. Each carpeted suite includes a living room, dining area and kitchenette. Two-night minimum stay; budget to deluxe.

LAKE HAVASU AREA RESTAURANTS

Oddly, Lake Havasu City has virtually no high-priced haute cuisine, but it does have a selection of pleasant, affordable restaurants. A good moderate-priced place for salads and seafood is **Shugrue's** (1425 McCulloch Boulevard; 602-453-1400) in the Island Fashion Mall, which has an unbeatable view of London Bridge from the island side through tall wraparound windows. Fresh bakery goods are the specialty.

Also on the island, the **Captain's Table at the Nautical Inn** (1000 McCulloch Boulevard; 602-855-2141) serves a wide range of tradi-

---

*In Lake Havasu's Olde English Village, the only truly authentic English shop is
the **London Gift shop**, which sells high-quality English imports.*

---

tional American menu selections along with a lakeside view overlooking the resort's private dock. Moderate.

Away from the water, a local favorite in the moderate range is **Krystal's**
(460 El Camino Way; 602-453-2999), featuring seafood specialties
such as Alaskan king crab legs, lobster tails and mahi mahi. Another
long-time local favorite is **Nicolino's Italian Restaurant** (86 South
Smoketree Avenue; 602-855-3484), serving 30 varieties of pasta with
prices ranging from budget to moderate. In the English Village on the
mainland side of the bridge, you can make a quick refueling stop at the
usually busy **Mermaid Inn,** which serves budget-priced fish and chips.

LAKE HAVASU AREA SHOPPING

The most interesting shopping district in the area is the **Olde English
Village** on the mainland side of London Bridge in Lake Havasu City,
and the most remarkable thing about it, other than its vast expanse of
bright-green lawn in the heart of one of America's most desolate deserts, is that the land on which it was built is owned by the city of
London—making the bridge a symbolic link between London and
Lake Havasu City. The cute Olde English buildings housing the shops
and snack bars remind us that the city and the bridge were the brain-
child of the retired general manager of Disneyland. The Olde English
Village has about two dozen theme gift shops such as the Copper
Shoppe, the Gallerie of Glasse, and the Curiosity Shoppe, as well as
the London Bridge Candle Factory, which claims to be the world's
largest candle shoppe.

At the other end of the bridge, the **Fashion Mall** houses about a
dozen more traditional shops and boutiques selling men's and women's
fashions, sportswear and fine jewelry.

LAKE HAVASU AREA NIGHTLIFE

In addition to Lake Havasu City's hotel cocktail lounges, a nice spot
for an intimate encounter is **The City of London Arms,** a British-
style pub that looks transplanted from Walpole Street. Besides the used-
brick facade, curved glass windows, wrought-iron fence and stately
carriage lamps, the pub features a dark-wood bar accented by brass
fixtures, private leather-lined booths and an assortment of ales and
other imported potables.

LAKE HAVASU AREA PARKS

Lake Havasu State Park encompasses most of the lake's shoreline with several campgrounds, boat ramps and rocky swimming beaches in four developed units—Windsor Beach and Crystal Beach, both north of the center of town, and Cattail Cove, about 15 miles south of town. Cattail Cove has a state-run marina. Besides these four areas, the park includes the Aubrey Hills Natural Area, a wild shoreline inaccessible by road. Facilities include picnic areas, restrooms, showers, boat ramps, marinas, nature trails, restaurants, groceries and lodging in Lake Havasu City. Overnight camping is available at Windsor Beach and at Cattail Cove (full RV hookups). There are also primitive boat slips along the shore in the Aubrey Hills Natural Area north of Lake Havasu City. To get to Cattail Cove, take Route 95 south of Lake Havasu City; Windsor and Crystal beaches are access points in Lake Havasu City, with Pittsburg Point on the island across London Bridge from town.

Nature buffs will enjoy the **Havasu National Wildlife Refuge** (1406 Bailey Avenue, Needles, CA; 619-326-3853), which straddles the Colorado River from Topock, 20 miles north of Lake Havasu City, to Pittsburg Point, about two miles north of the city. Another section protects the lower 12 miles of the Bill Williams River where it empties into the Colorado, about 18 miles south of Lake Havasu City. Hikers through the marshy trails are often rewarded with views of a bald eagle, peregrine falcon, desert bighorn sheep or a number of winter visitors: snow and Canadian geese and other waterfowl. Camping, boating and fishing are permitted except where signs are posted.

Parker Dam Area

Downstream from Parker Dam, which impounds Lake Havasu, the Colorado River flows through the Colorado River Reservation to Parker, a nondescript trade center about 32 miles south of Lake Havasu City. Just two miles north of Parker, Headgate Rock Dam impedes the Colorado to form Lake Moovalya, an 11-mile stretch of water recreation better known as "The Parker Strip."

Parker was founded in the late 1800s, but remained nothing more than a postal stop until the railroad came through in 1908. Most of the town's development, however, occurred after the river was dammed and tourists began flocking to the lakes upstream. Recreation remains Parker's main reason for existing, along with a moderate climate that attracts several thousand snowbirds, mostly retirees, each winter.

The town itself has little to offer; many of its 3000 citizens live in wall-to-wall RV parks scattered across the scrub-brush hillsides, dotted with an occasional red–tile–roof home. Despite Parker's lackluster appeal, the area is besieged by visitors who enjoy year–round boating, waterskiing and inner–tubing (there's even an annual seven–mile inner–tube race) along the scenic Parker Strip.

The city's main attraction is the **Colorado River Indian Tribes Museum** (2nd Avenue and Mohave Road; 602-669-9211), a storehouse of prehistoric Native American artifacts from the Anasazi, Hohokam and other tribes, as well as dioramas of pueblos and other dwellings, crafts and folk art of the more modern Mohave, Chemehuevi, Navajo and Hopi Indians. Most interesting is the photo gallery of early reservation life and archival library of old manuscripts, books and other documents. Visit the gift shop before leaving; it has a good assortment of Native American publications, baskets, beadwork and other crafts.

About 15 miles upstream sits **Parker Dam**, a virtual twin to Davis Dam. One significant difference is you that can see only one-third of Parker Dam; the bedrock foundation is 235 feet below the riverbed. Like its upstream cousin, Parker Dam is open for self-guided tours. Be sure to step into the turbine room and watch the massive generator shaft spinning; you'll feel like you're in the Queen Mary's engine room.

If you'd like a change of pace, drive 34 miles south on Route 95 to **Quartzsite**, the site of one of the strangest reunions in Arizona, and possibly the world. Although the dusty scrub-brush town—if you can call it that—consists of just a few motels, restaurants, and RV parks, each winter its population swells from several hundred to several hundred thousand. The reason? The **Quartzsite Gemboree**, a sort of Bedouin bazaar for rock-swappers and gem collectors, who flock here in droves in early February for a ten-day metallurgical freakout. In addition to the 6000 booths, where you can buy everything from healing crystals to 5000-pound slabs of quartz, the festival features flea markets, antique and collectibles shows, a rodeo, camel and ostrich races, country and western music, an auto show—all choreographed in the tradition of Hunter Thompson. Started in 1964 by a rag-tag group of rock hounds, the annual event has grown to become Quartzsite's main reason for existence. For further details about the Quartzsite Gemboree, contact Howard Armstrong (P.O. Box 2801, Quartzsite, AZ 85346; 602-927-5213).

PARKER DAM AREA LODGING

You won't find a bellhop in this part of the country, but there are clean and budget-priced rooms at **El Rancho Motel** (709 California Avenue, Parker; 602-669-2231), along with a few kitchenettes, refrigerators, a pool and in-room coffee. Traveling families will like the **Stardust Motel** (700 California Avenue, Parker; 602-669-2278) because of its over-sized rooms and mini-suites, most with refrigerators and microwave ovens, all clean, well-maintained and budget-priced.

PARKER DAM AREA RESTAURANTS

One of the best places to eat in Parker is **El Palacio Restaurant** (1884 Route 95; 602-763-2494), a bustling Mexican restaurant with hand-painted pottery and other folk art on the walls. The food is spicy hot and delicious, especially the port tamales, menudo and chile relleno. Budget to moderate.

For home-cooked American dishes, try the **Paradise Café** (Route 95 at Casa del Rio Avenue, Parker; 602-667-2404), a formica-topped, family-run eatery that caters to regular locals who feast on the barbe-cued chicken, pork ribs, biscuits and gravy, and homemade pies. Prices are budget.

In Quartzsite, the main event is the **Main Event** (Route 10 at Route 95; 602-927-5974), a combination restaurant, truck stop, general store, curio shop and gas station. The ponderous dining area is of the neo-coffee-shop genre with vinyl booths and formica tables, but the simple American dishes such as chicken-fried steak, liver and onions, and grits and gravy are served in huge portions and at budget prices. After you've refueled, check out the gift shop, which has a strange collection of carved wooden animals.

PARKER DAM AREA PARKS

About eight miles north of Parker via Route 95, you can spread a beach towel or picnic blanket along the Colorado River at **La Paz County Park** (602-667-2069; admission), a grassy recreational area with tennis courts, swimming beach and boat ramp.

Near Parker Dam, **Buckskin Mountain State Park** (602-855-8017) caters to tube floaters, boaters and waterskiiers. But you can also hike the nature trails in the mountains that surround the eastern edge of the park. In addition to panoramic vistas of the Colorado River, hikers can sometimes catch a glimpse of desert bighorn sheep that roam the area. Facilities include a picnic ground, campsites, marina, boat launch, inner-tube rentals and snack bar.

Sporting Life

BOATING AND WATERSKIING

Along Arizona's West Coast, it's water, water everywhere. Starting at its northern tip, you can skip across Lake Mead in a power or ski boat, or simply relax under sail or on the deck of a houseboat. For rentals, try the **Callville Bay Resort Marina** (Star Route 10, off Northshore Road; 702-565-8958); **Lake Mead Marina** (322 Lakeshore Road; 702-293-3484); **Overton Beach Resort and Marina** (702-394-4040); and the **Echo Bay Resort and Marina** (702-394-4000).

In the Bullhead City/Laughlin area, waterskiing is permitted along the Colorado River from Davis Dam to Needles. The sparsely populated area just below Bullhead City is the best choice. You can also waterski on Lake Mohave north of Davis Dam. For boat rentals and equipment, check out **Lake Mohave Resort** (Katherine Landing; 602-754-3245).

The lower Colorado River and Lake Havasu are a mecca for watersport enthusiasts, and there are craft of all kinds available for rent. In Lake Havasu City, pontoon boats are available at **Island Boat Rentals** (1580 Dover Avenue; 602-453-3260) and **Rick's Pontoon Boat Rentals and Sales** (602-453-1922). Power boats for fishing and waterskiing are for rent at **Village Boat Rentals** (1600 West Acoma Street; 602-855-6668); **Rent A Boat** (London Bridge Resort; 602-453-9613); **Lake Havasu Marina** (1100 McCulloch Boulevard; 602-855-2159); and **Resort Boat Rentals** (English Village; 602-453-9613). Thirteen miles south of Lake Havasu City, **Sand Point Marina** (602-855-0549) rents fishing boats, pontoons and houseboats. Waterskiing lessons are offered by **Havasu Adventures Water Ski School** (1425 McCulloch Boulevard; 602-855-6274).

FISHING

It's open season on all fish year-round at **Lake Mead**, where you'll find an abundance of catfish, bluegill, trout, crappie and striped bass, often tipping the scales at 30 pounds. One of the best spots for bass is near the Las Vegas Boat Harbor because of the waste-water nutrients that dump from the Las Vegas Wash into this section of the lake. Anglers consider the Overton arm of Lake Mead one of the best areas for striped bass, whose threadfin shad schools often churn the water in their feeding frenzies. Also worth trying are Calico Basin, the Meadows, Stewarts Point and Meat Hole. For tips on other spots, ask any park ranger or try any of these marinas, which also sell licenses, bait and tackle: **Lake Mead Marina** (322 Lakeshore Road; 702-293-3484);

Las Vegas Boat Harbor (702-565-9111); **Callville Bay Resort Marina** (Star Route 10, off Northshore Road; 702-565-8958); **Echo Bay Resort and Marina** (702-394-4000); and **Temple Bar Marina** (602-767-3211).

Fishing is also excellent along the **Colorado River** near Laughlin/Bullhead City. Anglers can fill their creels with striped bass, rainbow trout, bass, catfish, bluegill and crappie. A good spot is the cold water below Davis Dam. There's also good fishing above the dam on **Lake Mohave**, noted for its rainbow trout and bass.

RIVER RAFTING

The 11-mile stretch of Colorado River from Hoover Dam to Willow Beach is open year-round to rafts, canoes and kayaks, but the best time is spring and fall. River running requires a permit from the **U.S. Bureau of Reclamation, Lower Colorado Region** (P.O. Box 299, Boulder City, NV 89005; 702-293-8356). For canoe and kayak rentals, try **Wilderness Outfitting** (205 Rainier Court, Boulder City, NV; 702-293-7526). It's not exactly white-knuckle rafting, but you can float down the Colorado River from Hoover Dam to Black Canyon and see waterfalls, hot springs and geological formations. For details, contact **Black Canyon, Inc.** (1417 Pueblo Drive, Boulder City, NV; 702-293-3776).

GOLF

Serving the Lake Mead and Hoover Dam area is the **Boulder City Municipal Golf Course** (1 Clubhouse Drive, Boulder City, NV; 702-293-9236).

In the Bullhead City/Laughlin area, tee off at the **Emerald River Golf Course** (1155 South Casino Drive, Laughlin; 702-298-0061); **Riverview Golf Course** (2000 East Ramar Road, Bullhead City, AZ; 602-763-1818); **Chaparral Country Club** (1260 East Mohave Drive, Bullhead City; 602-758-3939); and **Desert Lakes Golf Course** (5835 Desert Lakes Drive, Ft. Mohave, AZ; 602-768-1000), about ten miles south of the Laughlin/Bullhead City bridge off Route 95.

Golfers can choose from two excellent courses at the Lake Havasu resort: **Queen's Bay Golf Course** (1477 Queen's Bay Road; 602-855-4777), and **London Bridge Golf Club** (2400 Clubhouse Drive; 602-855-2719).

Kingman visitors won't be disappointed with **Valley Vista Country Club** (9686 Concho Drive; 602-757-8744) and **Kingman Municipal Golf Course** (1001 East Gates Road; 602-753-6593).

For more information on courses, contact the **Arizona Golf Association** (11801 North Tatum Boulevard, Suite 247, Phoenix, AZ 85028; 602-953-5990).

TENNIS

In the Bullhead City/Laughlin area you can hold court at the **Pioneer Hotel** (2200 South Casino Drive, Laughlin; 702-298-2442); **Flamingo Hilton Hotel** (1900 South Casino Drive, Laughlin; 702-298-5111); and the **Riverview RV Resort** (2000 East Ramar Road, Bullhead City; 602-763-5800).

HIKING

About 14 miles southeast of Kingman, Hualapai Mountain Park has an extensive network of hiking trails from a single trailhead through piñon, oak, aspen and ponderosa forest teeming with bird and animal life. Six interconnecting trails branch from the **Aspen Springs Trail** (1 mile) to let you custom-design your own hike, whether you want to take an easy walk to **Stonestep Lookout** (.5 mile) or a more ambitious hike to the summit of **Aspen Peak** (2.5 miles with a 3200-foot elevation gain) or **Hayden Peak** (2.75 miles with a 3400-foot climb). The Aspen Springs Trail can be combined with the **Potato Patch Loop** (2 miles) for a great five-mile loop trip.

In the Bullhead City/Laughlin area bring your hiking shoes and enthusiasm to **Grapevine Canyon**, about six miles west of Davis Dam, just off the Christmas Tree Pass road. Fed by a spring, the canyon is a desert oasis with an abundance of Canyon grape, Fremont cottonwood, cattails and rushes, and wildlife who come to feed or drink at the shallow stream. Hundreds of petroglyphs—symbolic rock art—are evidence that early Native Americans were also drawn to this area. To reach Grapevine Canyon, drive northwest on Route 163 to mile marker 13, about six miles from the dam. Turn right onto Christmas Tree Pass and follow the road for two miles until you reach a sign indicating parking to the left. A trail from the parking lot leads to the canyon entrance, where boulders on either side are carved with an array of petroglyphs.

The **Mohave Sunset Walking Trail** in Lake Havasu State Park winds for two miles between Windsor Beach and Crystal Beach through a variety of terrains from lowlands dense with salt cedar to ridgelines commanding beautiful views of the lake. Signs along the sometimes hilly trail identify common Mohave Desert plant life.

Transportation

BY CAR

On Arizona's "West Coast" along the lower Colorado River, the Bullhead City-Laughlin resort area is reached by exiting **Route 40** at Kingman and driving 26 miles on **Route 68** through the most starkly stunning scenery in the Mohave Desert, or by exiting Route 40 at Topock, 12 miles east of Needles, California, and driving 35 miles north on **Route 95**. The other major Colorado River resort, Lake Havasu City, is 21 miles south of Route 40 on Route 95. A fascinating back-road route connecting Route 95 with Route 40 at Kingman goes through the historic gold-mining town of Oatman on its steep climb over Sitgreaves Pass, a drive challenging enough to make it hard to believe that this numberless road used to be part of Old Route 66, the main highway across the Southwest to Los Angeles in the days before the interstate was built.

BY AIR

Mesa Airlines serves the **Laughlin/Bullhead Airport** in Bullhead City, **Mohave County Airport** in Kingman and the **Lake Havasu City Airport**. States-West Airlines also provides service to Bullhead City and Lake Havasu City. From Las Vegas' **McCarran International Airport**, Scenic Airlines (702-739-1900, 800-634-6801) has two flights daily to the **Laughlin/Bullhead Airport**.

BY BUS

Greyhound Bus Lines stops at the bus terminals in Kingman (303 Metcalf Road; 602-753-2522) and Bullhead City (1010 Route 95; 602-754-4655).

CAR RENTALS

Car rental agencies at the Laughlin/Bullhead Airport are **Avis Rent A Car** (602-754-4686), **Budget Rent A Car** (602-754-3361), **Hertz Rent A Car** (602-754-4111) and **Rebel Rent A Car** (602-754-5544).

EIGHT

South Central Arizona

Rising up out of the very center of the rugged south central Arizona
landscape is the biggest metropolis between southern Texas and California and the eighth largest in the country—you could say Phoenix is
a city taking flight. The population of Phoenix proper is 1,036,000,
which balloons to 2,100,000 when you include the 23 satellite towns
that blend seamlessly along the broad valley of the Salt River. A thousand families a month set up homes, as subdivisions and shopping centers continue to mushroom.

Metropolitan Phoenix, or the Valley of the Sun, originated in 1850
on the banks of the Salt River and became the capital of the Arizona
Territory in 1889. At one time, nearly 25,000 Indians were the exclusive inhabitants of the region. The earliest were the Hohokam, who
thrived from 30 A.D. until about 1450 A.D. Signs of their settlements
remain intact to this day.

Phoenix today is a far cry from the era of the Hohokam Indians.
The Hohokam, meaning "those who vanished," built a network of
irrigation ditches to obtain water from the Salt River, part of which is
still in use today. Then, as now, irrigation was vital to Phoenix. So
much water is piped in to soak fields, groves and little kids' toes that
the desert air is actually humid—uncomfortably so through much of
the summer. Lettuce, melons, alfalfa, cotton, vegetables, oranges, grapefruit, lemons and olives are grown in abundance in the irrigated fields
and groves, lending a touch of green to the otherwise brown landscape. Boating, waterskiing, swimming and even surfing—in a gigantic, mechanically activated pool—are splendid byproducts.

*Arizona's broad central band stretches across the state in what visiting English au-
thor J. B. Priestley once described as "geology by day and astronomy by night."*

Once hailed as the agricultural center of Arizona, Phoenix by 1920
was already highly urbanized. Its horse-drawn carriages represented
the state's first public transportation. Its population reached 29,053 and
the surrounding communities of Tempe, Mesa, Glendale, Chandler
and Scottsdale added 8636 to the count. As farmers and ranchers were
slowly being squeezed out, the early years of Phoenix's development saw a
rugged frontier town trying to emulate as best it could famous cities back
East. It had a Boston store, a New York store, three New England-style
tea parlors and a number of gourmet shops selling everything from
smoked herring to Delaware cream cheese. The region's dry desert air
also began to attract scores of "health-seekers." The advent of scheduled airline service and the proliferation of dude ranches, resorts and
other tourist attractions changed the character of the city still further.

Today, high-tech industry forms the economic core of Phoenix,
while tourism remains the state's number-one job producer. Not surprisingly, construction is the city's third major industry. But Phoenix
retains a strong community flavor. Its downtown area isn't saturated
with block after block of highrises and apartment houses. The city and
all its suburbs form an orderly, 800-square-mile pattern of streets and
avenues running north and south and east and west, with periphery
access gained by soaring Los Angeles-style freeways. Beyond are the
mountains and desert, which offer an escape from city living, with
camping, hiking and other recreational facilities.

If the desert isn't your scene, neighboring Scottsdale just might be.
Billing itself as "The West's Most Western Town," Scottsdale is about
as "western" as Beverly Hills.

Scottsdale's population of 134,000 appears to be made up primarily
of "snowbirds" who came to stay: rich retirees from other parts of the
United States who enjoy the sun, the golf courses, the swimming pools,
the mountains, the bolo ties and the almost endless selection of handi-
craft shops, boutiques and over 120 art galleries. Actually, retired persons
account for only 20 percent of this fast-growing city, whose median
adult age is 34. There are far more yuppies than grandmas.

Scottsdale was only desert in 1888 when U.S. Army Chaplain Win-
field Scott bought a parcel of land near the Arizona Canal at the base of
Camelback Mountain. Before long, much of the cactus and greasewood
trees had been replaced by 80 acres of barley, a 20-acre vineyard and 50
orange trees. Scottsdale remained a small agricultural and ranching
community until after World War II. Motorola opened a plant in

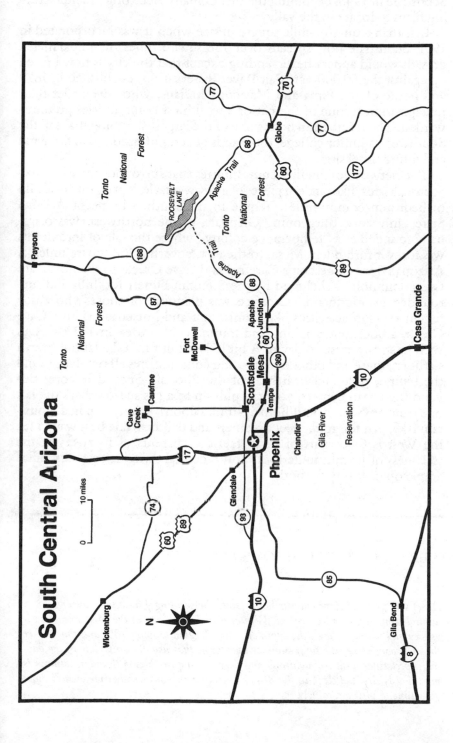

Scottsdale in 1945, becoming the first of many electronics manufacturing firms to locate in the valley.

Less than a quarter-mile square in size when it was incorporated in 1951, Scottsdale now spreads over 138 square miles. Its unparalleled growth would appear never-ending except that the city is now braced up against the 50,000-acre Salt River Reservation, established in 1879 and home of the Pima and Maricopa Indians, who haven't let their juxtaposition to one of the nation's wealthiest communities go unrewarded. The reservation boasts one of the largest shopping malls in the Southwest, a junior college, thousands of acres of productive farmland and future hotel sites.

The network of satellite communities that surrounds the Phoenix-Scottsdale area, like random pieces of a jigsaw puzzle, is primarily made up of bedroom communities. Tempe to the south is home of Arizona State University. Burgeoning Glendale, to the northwest, was originally founded as a "temperance colony" where the sale of intoxicants was forever forbidden. Mesa, to the east, covering 100 square miles, is Arizona's third-largest city. Carefree and Cave Creek, to the north, are two communities sheltered by the Sonoran Desert foothills and surrounded by mountains. Carefree was planned for those who enjoy fun-in-the-sun activities like tennis, golf and horseback riding. Cave Creek, a booming ranching and mining center back in 1873, thrives with its strong western flavor. A bit hokey, but fun. Like fallout from a starburst, these and other neighboring communities all revolve around the tempo, pace and heartbeat of the Phoenix-Scottsdale core. Beyond the urban centers, you can pull up to a gas station that's the last one from anywhere, visit honkey-tonk saloons, skinny-dip in a mountain lake, pan for gold, meet dreamers and drifters. The best way to see the West is to be part of it, to feel the currents of its rivers or the steepness of its hills underfoot. South central Arizona certainly offers ample opportunity for both.

WEATHER OR NOT? WHILE SOME LIKE IT HOT. . .

All of south central Arizona gets hot, despite the seemingly innocuous average annual temperature of 72 degrees. Winter is cool and clear, in the 60s; spring is breezy and warm, in the 90s; summer is torrid, often topping 100, and that's when the monsoons come, the swift summer rainstorms that usually arrive late in the day with spectacular flashes of lightning and deep, rolling rumbles of thunder; autumn is marvelously dry and clear, in the 80s. Depending on your weather preference, choose your time to visit accordingly.

It was the disappearance of the Hohokam Indians that led settlers to select the name "Phoenix," from the symbol of immortality of the ancient Egyptians, who believed the legendary bird set itself afire every six centuries, only to rise again from the ashes.

Phoenix

The history of south central Arizona unravels in smooth, easy chapters through Phoenix's museums and attractions, particularly highlighting its Indian heritage. But this is by no means all you'll find here. The city is also a bustling art mecca, evident from the moment visitors arrive at Sky Harbor Airport, with its array of contemporary and western artworks on display. The airport's program of changing art exhibits, in conjunction with the Phoenix Art Commission, is a model for similar programs at airports throughout the country.

While the city offers a wealth of sophistication and culture, the last of the rugged Marlboro men can still be seen in Phoenix astride handsome, well-groomed horses. But they're not riding off into the sunset, never to be seen again. Chances are they're heading into the vast expanse of desert land that still surrounds the city proper to recharge their motors. Long considered a scourge of man, arid and untamable, the desert with its raw awesome beauty is now seen by many as the last vestige of America's wilderness. Numerous tour operators offer guided jeep and horseback tours into the desert, but as any Arizonan will tell you, it is best appreciated alone. Southwest Indians have long known the secrets of the desert. Now, more-recent settlers come to turn their faces skyward into the pale desert sun.

But whether the city proper or its environs are your scene, trying to take in all the sights and sounds in one trip is a bit like counting the grains of sand in a desert. We suppose it can be done, but who on earth has the time? To help you on your quest, here are some of this city's highlights.

Southwest anthropology and primitive arts are featured at **The Heard Museum** (22 East Monte Vista Road; 602-252-8840; admission). The 18 exhibition galleries on three levels include a Hopi kachina collection, Cochi storyteller figures, pottery by Maria Martinez, silver and turquoise jewelry, basketry, blankets and other Native American crafts. Indian art demonstrations are frequently presented.

The **Phoenix Art Museum** (1625 North Central Avenue; 602-257-1222; admission), adjacent to the Phoenix Public Library, features exhibits on western, contemporary and decorative arts. This Frank Lloyd Wright-style, two-story stucco building has an outstanding collection of Arizona costumes, accessories and textiles, as well as an Asia

*Minerals and ores are displayed at the **Arizona Mining & Mineral Museum** (1502 West Washington Street; 602-255-3791), one of the finest of its kind in the Southwest.*

Gallery of Oriental paintings, ritual objects, porcelains and cloisonné. The research library includes more than 32,000 books, monographs and art periodicals. Kids won't want to miss the junior museum downstairs, where they can indulge their creativity in a variety of media.

Literally a museum piece of a museum, the state's first, **Phoenix Museum of History** (1002 West Van Buren Street; 602-253-2734) is housed in its original adobe building (circa 1927). Here, you'll find a marvelous collection of curios and antiquities covering 2000 years of Arizona history all jammed into the museum's tiny confines. Highlights include prehistoric Native American artifacts and a display on the evolution of Phoenix through the 1930s. Paintings by early Arizona artists, the state's oldest railroad locomotive, instruments from the Phoenix band and political memorabilia can also be found here. The gift shop has a good selection of Arizona history books.

Wander over to the **Arizona State Capitol Museum** (1700 West Washington Street; 602-542-4675), built in 1900 to serve as the Territorial Capitol. The building has been restored to the 1912 era when Arizona won statehood. Guided tours feature permanent exhibits in the Senate Chambers, the Governor's Suite and the Rotunda. A wax figure of the state's first Governor, George Hunt, is seated at his rolltop desk surrounded by period furnishings. Major artifacts include the original silver service taken from the *U.S.S. Arizona* before the battleship was sunk at Pearl Harbor and the roughrider flag carried up Cuba's San Juan Hill during the Spanish American War.

Over at the **Hall of Fame Museum** (1101 West Washington Street; 602-255-2110), you'll find exhibits dedicated to the women, territorial lawmen and cattle ranchers who made Arizona what it is today. Crammed with artifacts, each section offers insight on the colorful lives of pioneers who built this state. Among the highlights is Wyatt Earp's gun.

Painted in 35 colors, **The Mercado** (Van Buren Street between 5th and 7th streets; 602-256-6322) is composed of a half-dozen commercial buildings patterned on a traditional Mexican village. This two-block-long complex includes shops offering western wear, Native American jewelry and African American handicrafts. Beautiful courtyards add to the charm of this eclectic complex that features two restaurants.

A Mercado highlight, **Museo Chicano** (641 East Van Buren Street; 602-257-5536; admission) features changing displays ranging from local to international in focus. Hispanic culture, arts and history are exhib-

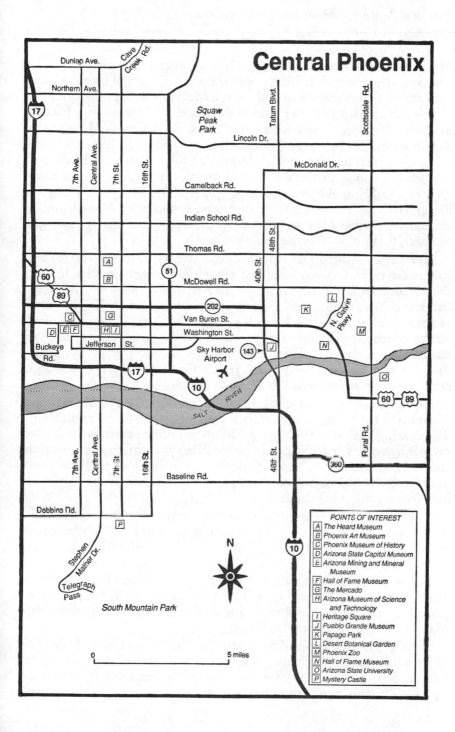

Central Phoenix

Dunlap Ave.

Cave Creek Rd.

Northern Ave.

17

Squaw Peak Park

Tatum Blvd.

Scottsdale Rd.

Lincoln Dr.

McDonald Dr.

7th Ave.

Central Ave.

7th St.

16th St.

Camelback Rd.

Indian School Rd.

48th St.

Thomas Rd.

A

60

B

51

40th St.

McDowell Rd.

89

202

L

K

N. Galvin Pkwy.

C

G

Van Buren St.

D

E F

H I

Washington St.

M

Buckeye Rd.

Jefferson St.

Sky Harbor Airport

143

J

N

17

O

10

60 — 89

SALT RIVER

Rural Rd.

7th Ave.

Central Ave.

7th St.

16th St.

48th St.

Baseline Rd.

360

Dobbins Rd.

P

10

Stephen Mather Dr.

N

Telegraph Pass

South Mountain Park

0   5 miles

POINTS OF INTEREST
A The Heard Museum
B Phoenix Art Museum
C Phoenix Museum of History
D Arizona State Capitol Museum
E Arizona Mining and Mineral
    Museum
F Hall of Fame Museum
G The Mercado
H Arizona Museum of Science
    and Technology
I Heritage Square
J Pueblo Grande Museum
K Papago Park
L Desert Botanical Garden
M Phoenix Zoo
N Hall of Flame Museum
O Arizona State University
P Mystery Castle

Phoenix is the most air-conditioned city in America.

---

ited, as well as the work of both well-known and emerging artists. In addition, the museum offers a popular series of cultural programs and performing arts events, such as the city's Mexican Ballet Folklorico.

It seems appropriate—a museum of science and technology located in a parking garage! That's where you'll find the **Arizona Museum of Science and Technology** (80 North 2nd Street; 602-256-9388; admission), which features energy, physics and life sciences exhibits, and a hands-on young people's discovery arcade, all located on the main level of the Hyatt Regency parking garage. The focus is on subjects like gravity, momentum, energy, nutrition and infinity. Also on display are star residents of the southwestern desert such as the iguana, gila monster, python, vine snake and tortoise.

Heritage Square (7th and Monroe streets; 602-262-5071) is a southwestern time warp featuring eight turn-of-the-century homes, the Arizona Doll and Toy Museum, an Artist's Cooperative, the Heart and Hand Tea Room and Jack and Jenny's Barn and Grill. The **Silva House**, a Victorian-style bungalow, has exhibits ranging from turn-of-the-century swimsuits to origami. At the **Rosson House**, an 1895 Eastlake Victorian, you'll see a beautiful collection of period furniture. Be sure to browse at the **Artist's Cooperative** for weavings, raku pottery, jewelry, wearable art and ceramics.

For a glimpse into the Hohokam tribe's past, visit the **Pueblo Grande Museum** (4619 East Washington Street; 602-495-0901; admission). The exhibits include a prehistoric Hohokam ruin, a permanent display on this legendary tribe and a changing gallery featuring southwestern Indian arts and crafts. Of special interest is an outdoor trail that leads visitors to the top of a Hohokam platform mound. There is also an interactive exhibit for children.

Not far from the central Phoenix museums is the **Desert Botanical Garden** (1201 North Galvin Parkway; 602-941-1225; admission) where more than 15,000 plants from desert lands of Africa, Australia, North and South America are displayed. You can see this beautiful garden via a self-guided nature walk or a group tour. New is a three-acre showcase of native Sonoran Desert plants, a saguaro forest, a mesquite thicket, a desert stream and an upland chaparral habitat, complete with historic Native American dwellings.

Nearby is the **Phoenix Zoo** (5810 East Van Buren Street; 602-273-1341; admission), which uses natural settings, including a four-acre African Savanna, to showcase more than 1300 mammals, birds and reptiles. Phoenix newcomers are frequently startled to find themselves driving along busy Van Buren alongside a family of trumpeting elephants. For a convenient zoo overview, take the Safari Train. Popular highlights are the World Herd of Arabian Oryx, a rare Sumatran tiger exhibit and the Baboon Kingdom. Children will especially enjoy the hands-on participatory exhibit called Wildlife Encounters-Mammals. Be sure to visit the one-acre tropical rainforest, the home of 15 bird and animal species adopted from around the world.

The largest firefighting museum in the nation is the **Hall of Flame Museum** (6101 East Van Buren Street; 602-275-3473; admission). On display are more than 90 restored hand-drawn, horse-drawn and motorized fire engines and hundreds of artifacts. Special games, exhibits and programs, all stressing fire safety, are offered for children.

Tucked away in the foothills of South Mountain Park, the **Mystery Castle** (800 East Mineral Road, end of South 7th Street; 602-268-1581; admission) is an 18-room extravaganza fashioned from native stone, sand, cement, water, goat's milk and Stutz Bearcat wire-rim wheels. Warmed by 13 fireplaces, the parapeted castle has a cantilevered stairway, chapel and dozens of nooks and crannies and is furnished with southwestern antiques. It's known as the "Mystery Castle" because the builder, Boyce Luther Gulley, thinking he was about to die from tuberculosis, ran away from his Seattle home in a Stutz Bearcat and devoted 15 years to the construction project. It was only after his death in 1945 that the missing builder's family learned of his whereabouts and inherited the castle.

The **Pioneer Arizona Living History Museum** (Pioneer Road, exit off Route 17; 602-993-0212; admission) re-creates an Old West town using original buildings—a church, schoolhouse, printing shop and blacksmith shop—and featuring costumed interpreters. Living-history exhibitions include cooking, gardening and sewing. At the opera house, you'll see melodramas, music and dance performances all themed to the territorial period, 1858 to 1912. Of special interest is one of our nation's last remaining herds of colonial Spanish horses. You can also enjoy weekend wagon rides, a picnic area and a restaurant specializing in barbecue.

PHOENIX LODGING

As a major resort and convention center, the Valley of the Sun features some of the most spectacular hotel resorts in the country. It has had the rare distinction of having more *Mobil Travel Guide* Five Star resorts (three of the 12 top-rated resorts nationwide) than any other city in the United States. Yet it's not without its share of budget- and moderate-priced hotels and motels, as well as a proliferation of bed and breakfasts.

An elegant scene of the past is mirrored in the glossy facade of the present with the rebirth of the **San Carlos Hotel** (202 North Central Avenue; 602-253-4121) in the heart of downtown. Built in 1927, the seven-story San Carlos was overhauled recently, but its charm was kept intact—a crystal chandelier and period furnishing in the lobby, original bathtubs, basins and furniture in the 120 guest rooms. Deep carpets line the hallways. There's even a London taxi (circa 1932) to pick guests up at the airport. Afternoon tea and light snacks are served in the Palm Room. The San Carlos is one of the largest hotels listed in the National Register of Historic Places. Moderate.

The 24-story **Hyatt Regency Phoenix** (2nd and Adams streets; 602-252-1234) is across from Civic Plaza downtown. With 711 rooms, it's the city's largest hotel. It has a heated swimming pool, exercise equipment, a café, lounges and revolving roof-top dining room. Rooms are smallish but tastefully furnished in a light, Southwest style. Deluxe.

For luxurious accommodations in the heart of the upscale Biltmore area, check out **Crown Sterling Suites** (2630 East Camelback Road, Phoenix; 602-955-3992). Walk through the doors and your first sight is a huge atrium complete with palm trees, tropical plants and waterways shimmering with goldfish. With the ultra-deluxe price tag comes a complimentary cooked-to-order breakfast and cocktails in the evening. The 233 modern two-room suites each offer a microwave oven, wet bar, refrigerator and dining area.

The Pointe Hilton Resort at Squaw Peak (7677 North 16th Street; 602-997-2626 or 800-876-4683) is an all-suite resort on 300 acres near the Phoenix Mountain Preserve. The architecture and ambiance are a cross between southwestern and Mediterranean. The 576 ultra-deluxe suites have French doors in the bedrooms that open to private balconies, as well as desks, marble bathroom countertops, fully stocked refrigerators and computerized safes. There are also 78 one- and two-bedroom villas. Amenities include an 18-hole golf course,

---

THE ARIZONA BILTMORE

Designed by Frank Lloyd Wright and Albert Chase McArthur, the newly refurbished **Arizona Biltmore** *(24th and Missouri streets, Phoenix; 602-955-6600) has maintained an aura of ease and luxury since its opening in 1929. From its palm-lined drive, elaborate high portico and immense lobby to its bright, handsomely furnished guest rooms, the 530-room Biltmore is as dramatic and visually exciting as it is comfortable. "Arizona's Grande Dame" provides a full range of activities: golf courses; tennis courts; pools; a health club; and nearby riding facilities. Ultra-deluxe.*

tennis courts, horse stables, a fitness center, swimming pools and the Coyote Camp for kids.

Another ultra-deluxe establishment in Phoenix is **The Phoenician** (6000 East Camelback Road; 602-941-8200), the most prestigious and talked-about resort in the Valley of the Sun. Sprawled over 130 acres along the sun-dappled flanks of Camelback Mountain, it's set within a tiered oasis of waterfalls and pools, the largest of which is tiled entirely with mother-of-pearl. Its 442 guest rooms are large and lavish with most situated in the main hotel, others in surrounding casitas. There are also 107 casita units with parlor suites that have hand-carved travertine fireplaces. If you really want to make a night of it, there are two presidential and 29 luxury suites. Recreational facilities run the gamut—a golf course, lighted tennis courts, tournament croquet and a health and fitness spa.

A find, price-wise, is the **Pyramid Inn** (3307 East Van Buren Street; 602-275-3691), an attractive two-story brick inn with 30 large, newly decorated rooms—mauve and green color themes predominating—and a swimming pool. Budget.

If you want to keep in shape while you're away from home, try the **City Square Hotel & Athletic Club** (100 West Clarendon Avenue; 602-279-9811), a full-service hotel with 171 rooms, restaurant and lounge along with a full-scale athletic club facility, including sauna, steamroom and swimming pool. Rooms are standard Southwest decor, but the workout's great. Moderate.

If you're on a budget, you've come to the right place. **Warren House East** (2911 East Indian School Road; 602-956-1345) is a motel with a restaurant, swimming pool and tennis courts. Its 89 rooms are furnished in contemporary styles, with light desert colors. Best yet, most have kitchen units and refrigerators. Budget.

Desert Sun Hotel (1325 Grand Avenue; 602-258-8971) offers 100 rooms with modern furnishings and various color themes. It has a 24-hour restaurant, lounge, swimming pool, and the price is right—budget.

The **Maricopa Manor** (15 West Pasadena Avenue; 602-274-6302) is a Spanish-style bed and breakfast situated in a garden-like setting of palm trees and flowers in the heart of north central Phoenix. Built in 1928, the inn has five individually decorated suites, all with private baths. Typical is the Library Suite with its canopied king-sized bed, private deck entrance, handsome collection of leather-bound books and an antique work desk. Guests may also use the inn's spacious Gathering Room, as well as the formal living, dining, music rooms, patio and gazebo spa. Moderate.

Set in a desert mountain preserve in a serene foothill setting in northwest Phoenix, **Westways** (P.O. Box 41624, Phoenix, AZ 85080; 602-582-3868) is a six-room bed-and-breakfast mini-resort with its own swimming pool and nearby country club privileges. The building is styled in a contemporary Spanish Mediterranean design with interior furnishings that include leather and oak in the sunken-fireplace living room, an antique Victorian dining room and rattan and oak in the large leisure room, all with vaulted ceilings. Each room is furnished with brass, wicker, oak, rattan, antiques and period Southwest pieces. Continental breakfasts are served in the summer, full American breakfasts during the rest of the year. Moderate.

PHOENIX RESTAURANTS

Looking for a quick snack? Go to the toney **Arizona Center** (Van Buren between 3rd and 5th streets; 602-271-4000) and take the elevator or stairs to the second floor and, viola! Here, you'll find an array of attractive fast-food restaurants sharing a mutual sit-down dining area— **Fajita Willy's, Hello Deli, Hot Dogs on a Stick, Scotto Pizza, Teriyaki Temple, Chinese Cake** and more, all budget-priced.

More traditional restaurants in Arizona Center include the **Copper Creek Steakhouse and Grille** (602-253-7100) for steaks, chicken and fish, and **Hooters** (602-257-0000), as in owls, an unrefined, delightfully tacky spot for shrimp, clams, oysters and seafood salads. Both moderate.

It's said breakfast is the most important meal of the day, which makes the **Cadillac Café** (4540 North 7th Street; 602-266-2922) an important place indeed—fresh-baked breads, muffins, biscuits, pastries, cinnamon rolls and Kona coffee from Hawaii highlight breakfast served in this pleasant little café filled with antiques and fresh-cut flowers. Lunch of the soup, salad and sandwich variety is also served. Budget.

If you're looking for a large, festive, family-oriented Mexican restaurant, **Carlos O' Briens** (1133 East Northern Avenue; 602-274-5881) fits the bill. Exposed ductwork, hanging plants and modern

---

WHO SAYS THE WEST IS WILD?

*The **Wigwam** (300 East Indian School Lane, Litchfield Park; 602-935-3811) west of Phoenix is an upper-upper-scale resort on 75 acres of what was originally virgin desert. The design is pueblo-style, with 331 desert-brown adobe casitas set in a lavish golf and country-club setting—towering palms, green lawns, cascading flowers and fragrant orange trees. Through the use of building materials native to the Southwest, architecture blends with nature. Slate, stone and wood surfaces are accented with Indian themes and desert colors. Championship courses, riding, tennis, swimming and other activities keep the body occupied while the mind relaxes. Ultra-deluxe.*

artwork supply the ambience for chowing down on fajitas, enchiladas and chimichangas at budget to moderate prices.

A colorful coffee house with a touch of bohemia is **Dos Estrellas Coffeehouse** (4745 North 20th Street; 602-957-2236) in the Town & Country Shopping Center. A red neon espresso sign in the window greets people; inside, red, yellow and turquoise colors add to the decor. Don't expect meals here—just good pastry and coffee. A bin of newspapers will keep you entertained, as will people-watching or the live folk music on weekends. There are also a handful of outdoor tables at this budget coffeehouse.

What it lacks in decor, **Ham's** (3302 North 24th Street; 602-954-8775) makes up for in great cooking and affordable prices. Specials change daily and include Yankee pot roast, fried chicken, liver and onions, barbecued beef and meatloaf, all served with heaps of mashed potatoes, veggies and biscuits. Budget to moderate.

A spot popular with the downtown office workers anxious for a touch of home cooking, **Mrs. White's Golden Rule Café** (808 East Jefferson Street; 602-262-9256) offers pork chops, chicken, cornbread and cobbler. Get there early for a table. Closed weekends. Moderate.

The chef at **Eddie's Grill** (4747 7th Street; 602-241-1188) has elevated cooking to an art form by blending culinary traits from America's diverse ethnic groups into a "New American" cuisine. Try the toasted seafood wontons with raspberry-jalepeño sauce or grilled chicken breast with ginger cream sauce. As multicultural as this restaurant may sound, it's truly American at heart, from the U.S.-produced meats and vegetables to the water. Don't ask for Evian. Moderate.

A popular neighborhood restaurant, **Lone Star Steaks** (6003 North 16th Street; 602-248-7827) really looks like it was transferred over from Dallas with its neon beer signs, glowing jukebox, antique wall memorabilia (old Texas license plates and the like) and chalkboard menus. Seating is in booths and formica-topped tables. Steaks come in a variety of sizes, from an eight-ounce fillet to an 18-ounce Lone Star, but the biggest sellers of all are the chicken-fried steaks served with heaps of mashed potatoes and buttermilk biscuits, just like in Texas. Moderate.

The Gold Room Bar & Grill (24th Street and Missouri Avenue; 602-954-2504) is the open, airy dining room at the Arizona Biltmore. Its traditional grille menu includes mesquite-grilled steaks, seafood, veal and poultry, as well as such bistro-style items as white bean casserole, garlic herb sausage with duck confit, and braised osso buco and potato gnocchi. Pastas are also available. Deluxe.

With a dozen aquariums scattered around the lobby and dining room, the **Golden Phoenix** (1534 West Camelback Road; 602-279-4447) appears to have the largest tropical fish population of any restaurant in Arizona. While the decor of this stucco-style establishment offers few Asian touches, the kitchen does wonders with Mandarin dishes like *kung pao* shrimp, hot sizzling beef and chicken. Moderate.

Christopher Gross, the chef-owner of **Christopher's** (2398 East Camelback Road; 602-957-3214), was recently named one of the ten top chefs in the country and now you can hardly get into the place. It's located in the Biltmore Financial Center, which is good; wait 'til you see the bill. Contemporary French food is served in a small (16 tables) candlelit dining room, all new and gleaming. The attentive waiters really know their wines, so helpful advice is available, if needed. Ultra-deluxe. Adjacent to Christopher's is **The Bistro**, same owner, same kitchen, different entrances, but far more casual, with a marble floor and open kitchen. Deluxe.

At **Sam's Café** (455 North Third Street; 602-252-3545), a large patio set amidst fountains is one draw; good southwestern cuisine is another. Start with poblano chicken chowder, then have chile-rubbed shrimp topped with lemon butter and pico de gallo, or cheese-filled tortellini with chorizo and black beans. If the weather is inclement (which it rarely is), indoor dining is also nice, with more fountains, terra-cotta colored walls and a turquoise floor. Moderate.

Ever try duck tamales? Mix Southwest and French cuisine, as they do at **Vincent Guerithault** (3930 East Camelback Road; 602-224-0225), and that's the result. You'll find a country French atmosphere, complete with floral seat cushions and dried floral table centerpieces, while diners enjoy chimichanga of lobster or grilled ahi tuna with papaya cilantro salsa. Top it off with crème brulée in, what else, a taco shell. Valet parking is available in this deluxe establishment.

Comfort is not a problem at **Richardson's** (1582 East Bethany Home Road; 602-265-5886), where lots of plump pillows adorn pink faux adobe booths. This New Mexico-style eatery is irreverent (political commentary often livens up the chalkboards), intimate and lively, with lots of music and talk competing at loud decibels. Favorites here include the cilantro fettuccine with shrimp and the Santa Fe chicken with jalapeño hollandaise. Moderate.

RoxSand (2594 East Camelback Road; 602-381-0444) located in the Biltmore Fashion Park offers "transcontinental food"—in other words, a little bit of everything, from Thai to European. Dine amidst a cool black-and-white interior dotted with modern art and suffused with jazz music; the menu features chicken wrapped in phyllo with eggplant and hummus, duck with plum sauce, and roast rack of lamb. Deluxe.

Known for its steaks and its bakery, **Oscar Taylor's** (2420 East Camelback Road; 602-956-5705) is a handsome oak-paneled restaurant appointed with leaded glass and historic photos of the windy city, Chicago. There's booth and table seating, as well as patio dining off the bakery and lounge. The menu features prime rib, barbecued spe-

With the construction of the first railroad in 1887, fast-paced expansion took hold as Phoenix drew settlers from all over the United States. In 1889, it was named the capital of the Arizona Territory, and statehood was declared in 1912.

cialties, pasta and veal. And then there's the excellent desserts and homemade breads. Moderate.

At **Ayako of Tokyo** (2564 East Camelback Road; 602-955-7009), teppan yaki chefs grill chicken, scallops, shrimp, filet mignon and lobster at your table. Each entrée comes with soup, salad, rice, vegetables and green tea. Rice-paper screens add a Japanese touch to the decor of this restaurant graced with Oriental paintings and panels. There are also sushi and tempura bars, as well as a lounge. Moderate to deluxe.

Havana Café (4225 East Camelback Road; 602-952-1991) offers the not-too-spicy cuisine of Spain and Cuba in an atmosphere that's more reminiscent of a small, cozy café than it is Hemingway's Havana. *Chicharitas*, an appetizer of fried green plantain chips, will get the juices flowing. There's saucy chicken with blends of herbs, spices, rice, tomatoes and olive oil, and paella(the house specialty), sausage, *sopa de ajo* (garlic soup), *escabeche*, *picadillo* and more. Moderate.

The moderately priced **Christo's** (6327 North 7th Street; 602-264-1784) specializes in Northern Italian cuisine, which means less pasta in favor of meatier fare—chicken *zingarella*, osso buco veal, rack of lamb—and fish dishes such as halibut topped with goat cheese, olive oil, garlic and sliced tomatoes. Sparkling stemware, crisp pink-and-white tablecloths and table flowers add a festive note.

With legions of regulars stopping by, **Chubb's** (6522 North 16th Street; 602-279-3459) is dimly lit and comfortable with fine decor (dark-wood paneling, columns, booths, tables and captain's chairs, ceiling fans and globed chandeliers). That sets the tone for hearty meals such as juicy prime rib, steak, pork chops and teriyaki chicken. Moderate.

If you thought diners went the way of the dinosaur, step into **Ed Debevic's Short Orders Deluxe** (2102 East Highland Drive; 602-956-2760), where you'll find yourself back in the 1950s, complete with tabletop jukeboxes, photos of Marilyn, blue-plate specials, burgers, shakes and fries. The budget prices are right out of the past, too.

PHOENIX SHOPPING

Western wear would seem a natural when hitting the Phoenix shopping scene—and you're right. There's a herd of places selling boots, shirts, buckles and whatever else you might want. If you're in the market for western clothes, either to look the part or to get ready for your next rodeo appearance, you might start with **Aztex Hats** (15044 North Cave Creek; 602-971-9090), which offers the largest selection of western hats in Arizona. **Frontier Boot Corral** (7th and Van Buren streets; 602-258-2830), with a complete line of western wear, has been in business for more than 40 years. **Saba's Western Store** (2901 West Bell Road; 602-993-5948), in business since 1927, includes Barry Goldwater among its clientele. Saba's also has stores in Mesa, Chandler and Scottsdale. **Sheplers** (9201 North 29th Avenue; 602-870-8085) is part of the world's largest western-wear chain.

If you like malls and shopping complexes, get ready. Phoenix has them in great abundance. One entertainment complex that has helped revitalize the downtown Phoenix area is **Arizona Center** (455 North Third Street; 602-271-4000), with about 45 restaurants, bars and shops on two levels. It attracts people for dining, meandering through the three-acre garden area, browsing amidst the shops, or listening to live entertainment in the evenings. Shops here include **Catherine's Rare Papers** (602-252-6960), where papers are imported from all over the world, including Nepal and Israel. You can find anything from antique Japanese paper to southwestern colored paper made in a local plant from desert plants. The **Arizona Highways Gift and Information Center** (602-257-0381) offers travel books and information about Arizona, while **Yippie-Ei-O** (602-495-1048) highlights western home accessories, clothing and gift items. At **Phases of the Moon** (602-254-7533), you'll find ethnic, exotic and mystical women's jewelry, accessories and apparel.

Town & Country Shopping Center (2021 East Camelback Road; 602-955-6850) showcases more than 70 shops, restaurants and services. Red brick sidewalks, fountains and soft music set the tone at this outdoor shopping center. Highlights include **Jutenhoops** (602-957-8006) with a whimsical, funky blend of gifts, cards and jewelry. **Bookstar** (602-957-2001) offers a huge selection of new books. Other draws at this shopping center are the **T. J. Maxx** (602-957-1122) department store and **Bellini Juvenile Designer Furniture** (602-956-6002) for pricey children's furnishings.

Located just blocks from the Town & Country Shopping Center, but infinitely more exclusive, is **Biltmore Fashion Park** (Camelback Road and 24th Street; 602-955-8400). Stroll along brick-paved walkways lined with green trees and shrubs, and peek into the expensive galleries, restaurants, jewelry stores and clothing stores. For women's clothing, names include **Adrienne Vittadini** (602-957-3212), **Ann Taylor** (602-468-3339), **Lillie Rubin** (602-553-8922) or **Capriccio** (602-955-5550) with international designer apparel. Larger stores featured here include **Saks Fifth Avenue** (602-955-8000) and **Broadway Southwest** (602-468-2100). On the cutting edge, **Stetter**

Every Wednesday afternoon, farmers from around the community sell their produce at low prices at **Heritage Square** *(Monroe and 7th streets, Phoenix; 602-262-5071).*

Gallery of the Senses (602-955-9636) offers new American artwork in their gallery and live performance art in the evenings.

Park Central Mall (Central Avenue and Earll Drive; 602-264-5575) is the city's best-known shopping center and the oldest. Fashionable **Dillard's** department store can be found here.

Metrocenter (9617 Metro Parkway West; 602-997-2641) is an enclosed double-deck mall that includes **Robinson's, Dillard's** and **Broadway**.

One of the newest additions to downtown Phoenix is **The Mercado** (Van Buren Street between 5th and 7th streets; 602-256-6322), a festive mall and Mexican cultural center adjacent to the Phoenix Civic Plaza, with colorful buildings, brick-lined streets and outdoor dining. Mexican shops and restaurants feature arts, crafts, fashions and good things to eat of the hot and spicy persuasion.

For designer merchandise at legendary low prices head for **Loehmann's** (3135 East Lincoln Drive).

Located in a 90-year-old Heritage Square home, **Craftsmen's Gallery** (614 East Adams Street; 602-253-7770) is an intriguing art cooperative. Here, 26 artists exhibit dolls, basket weaving, pottery, wearable art and wood-dried flowers.

Museum gift shops also offer unique finds for selective shoppers. For instance, the **Phoenix Art Museum** (1625 North Central Avenue; 602-257-1222) offers books, posters, catalogs and art-replica gifts. It also has a special section for children.

The **Desert Botanical Garden** (1201 North Galvin Parkway; 602-941-1225) has a gift shop offering foods, spices and jellies made from desert plants, as well as nature books and Southwest souvenirs and crafts; plants are sold in an adjoining greenhouse.

A small town south of Phoenix is the setting for the **Guadalupe Farmer's Market** (8808 South Avenida del Yaqui, Guadalupe) for fresh vegetables, exotic fruits and dried chili peppers.

Located a few blocks north of the Guadalupe Farmer's Market is the **Mercado Mexico** (8212 South Avenida del Yaqui, Guadalupe; 602-831-5925), where Mexican *dulces* (sweets) are sold—*ates* (jellied fruit candies), sugared pecans, lightly dusted chocolate balls, jars of cajeta, a caramel sauce made from goat's milk and other sticky delights. And when your sweet tooth is satisfied, you can check out the fine selection of handicrafts and souvenirs from Mexico.

American Park N Swap (3801 East Washington Street, Phoenix; 602-273-1258) is the largest open-air flea market in the Southwest.

PHOENIX NIGHTLIFE

Nightlife in Central Arizona is as diverse and far-reaching as the area itself, from the twanging guitars of country-and-western bands to symphony strings. There are Indian ceremonials and sophisticated jazz, as well. To find out what's happening, check the entertainment pages of the *Arizona Republic* and the *Phoenix Gazette.*

With its array of major resorts, much of the valley's nightlife centers around the hotel entertainment scene. If you feel more adventurous, you might try some of the following: **Graham Central Station** (40029 North 33rd Avenue; 602-279-4226) where traditional and country-and-western music can be heard nightly, with big-name acts, concerts and live bands. Friday's happy hour is one of the best in town.

From the sound of things, **America's Original Sports Bar** (455 North 5th Street; 602-252-2502), on the ground level of the Arizona Center, might seem to newcomers like a place for nightly brawls. No way. There are basketball hoops to shoot at, miniature golf, and even a volleyball court, all in the valley's trendiest new bar. Food is served, and, of course, plenty of drinks (with all that action you can work up a thirst). Cover. Also located here, upstairs, is the **Cheyenne Cattle Company** (455 North 5th Street; 602-253-6255), a glitzy country-and-western nightspot with live music, cowgirl waitresses and a goodly share of business-expense-account types (the Convention Center is nearby) among the loyal crowd of hooters and honkers. There's a cover on the weekend.

A valley institution for the two-step crowd, **Mr. Lucky's** (3660 West Grand Avenue; 602-246-0686) has live country-and-western music upstairs and recorded Top-40 rock-and-roll downstairs. There's a weekend cover.

"Home of the Nashville Stars," **Toolies Country** (4231 West Thomas Road; 602-272-3100) is a 600-seat frontier western cabaret with dinner and dancing nightly to the music of big-name country entertainers. Cover.

Acapulco Beach Club (3837 East Thomas Road; 602-273-6077) offers nightly live music, half Latin, half rock. With its south-of-the-border spirit and lively crowd, it's one of the most popular spots in town. Wednesday and weekend cover.

As the name suggests, everyone comes dressed in everything from Levi's to dinner jackets at **Denim and Diamonds** (3905 East Thomas

Road; 602-225-0182). Both recorded and live country sounds, special events and surprise free buffets are offered.

Timothy's (6335 North 16th Street; 602-234-2205) is a cross between a restaurant and a nightclub. The ivy-covered cottage oozes romance with live jazz music nightly in an intimate setting. Jazz festival posters cover the walls, and the paint-splattered beams add a bohemian twist. For that extra bit of class, valet parking is available.

The Rhythm Room (1019 East Indian School Road; 602-265-4842) is a sophisticated blues nightclub. Framed black-and-white photographs of blues greats hang on gray wood walls in this clean, uncluttered bar. Live bands play nightly, and a good-sized dancefloor in front of the stage invites audience participation.

Char's Has the Blues (4631 North 7th Avenue; 602-230-0205) has live rhythm-and-blues music nightly. Inside this old house, intimate burgundy curtains cover the windows and people dance on worn wooden floors. Wall sconces and tiny Christmas lights provide the soft lighting.

The name **Library Café** (208 West Indian School; 602-241-1469; admission) is misleading. It's really a bar with live acoustic and rock music nightly and, well, a library inside. Shelves lining every wall are filled with thousands of books, from self-help to surgery. Too bad the lights are too dim for reading.

Nightlife isn't restricted to the bar and two-step scene. A more refined look at the arts flourishes here, as well. **The Herberger Theater Center** (221 East Monroe Street; 602-252-8497) is an ultramodern theater complex housing two separate theaters, **Center Stage** and **Stage West**, where professional theater performances take place. The Center is also home to **Ballet Arizona**, the **Phoenix Little Theater**, the **Desert Dance Theater** and numerous traveling troupes. The 2500-seat **Phoenix Symphony Hall** (225 East Adams Street; 602-262-7272) is home to the Phoenix Symphony and stages entertain-

---

ONE MAN'S ART IS ANOTHER'S CHAMBER POT

Art is everywhere in Phoenix. Along Squaw Peak Freeway, a ten-mile stretch that connects downtown with the city's northern suburbs, you may think you're seeing things, and you are. The freeway is lined with 35 giant three- and four-foot sculptures—vases, cups, Indian-style pots and other utensils, all part of the city's public arts project "to make people feel more at home with the freeway." Not everyone in Phoenix loves the idea. Detractors have dubbed the freeway art project "Chamber Pots of the Gods."

The downtown area of Phoenix is in the midst of a billion-dollar redevelopment. Testimony to the effort are the glitzy Arizona Center, the Mexican-themed Mercado and the America West Arena.

---

ment ranging from opera and ballet to Broadway shows and name concert performers.

Performing in Phoenix for more than 25 years, the **Arizona Theatre Company** (222 East Monroe Street; 602-252-8497) does comedy, musicals and dramas at the Herberger Theater Center.

The nationally acclaimed **Arizona Opera Company** (4600 North 12th Street; 602-266-7464) presents four operas per season, with classics such as Verdi's *Don Carlo* and Puccini's *La Boheme*.

PHOENIX PARKS

With 15,000 acres, **South Mountain Park** (10919 South Central Avenue; 602-495-0222) is the largest metropolitan park in the United States, a vast rugged mountain range that was once Indian hunting ground. A spectacular view of Phoenix can be seen from Dobbins Lookout, 2300 feet above the desert floor. The park offers 40 miles of well-marked hiking and riding trails. Its steep canyons reveal evidence of ancient Indian artifacts and petroglyphs.

Papago Park is a neat blend of hilly desert terrain, quiet lagoons and glistening streams. The former Indian townsite now offers golf, picnic sites, ballfields and fishing. Also within its boundaries are the Phoenix Zoo, the Desert Botanical Garden and the Hall of Flame Museum. Located at 6000 East Van Buren Street.

With its craggy, easily identifiable pinnacle, **Squaw Peak Recreation Area** (2701 East Squaw Peak Drive; 602-495-0222) is one of Phoenix's most familiar landmarks. Squaw Peak is primarily known for its hiking trails. However, the rocky terrain has been moderately developed for other recreational pursuits, as well, and you can enjoy a picnic in the shade of a towering saguaro.

Estrella Mountain Regional Park (602-506-2930), with 19,200 acres, offers abundant vegetation and spectacular mountain views. Peaks within the Sierra Estrella Mountains reach 3650 feet. The park has excellent areas for hiking and riding, camping, a rodeo arena and golf course. Horse and hiking trails abound. The park is located 18 miles southwest of Phoenix via the access road two miles south from Route 85, on Bullard Avenue. Cross the Gila River and then turn right on West Vineyard Avenue for one-quarter mile.

Scottsdale

Like neighboring Phoenix, Scottsdale is proud of its frontier heritage, which can be traced at a number of locations in and near the town. In the Old Scottsdale section, where only 35 years ago Lulu Belle's and the Pink Pony were the only two watering holes for miles around, the buildings all have falsefronts, hand-crafted signs and hitching posts, and horses still have the right of way. Many restaurants feature waiters and waitresses in period dress. The women have teased hairdos, and the men are all called Slim, Ace, Tex, Shorty and Stretch.

But that's about as *western* as it gets. Otherwise, Scottsdale is chic, elegant and expensive. Despite its ties to the past, Scottsdale is a show-place of innovative architecture. The Frank Lloyd Wright Foundation is located here (at Taliesin West), as is the Cosanti Foundation, design headquarters for the controversial prototype town of Arcosanti.

Scottsdale is also the center of the Arizona art scene. Galleries flourish here. The **Southwestern Art and Cultural Adventures** (3533 North 70th Street, Suite 201/202; 602-946-8860) offers day and half-day visits to artists' studios, galleries, museums and architectural sites, with art experts leading the groups.

Housed in a building made of adobe blocks mixed with desert plants (for strength), the **Hoo-Hoogam Ki Museum** (10000 East Osborn Road; 602-941-7379; admission: free to Native Americans) is located on the Salt River Pima-Maricopa Reservation bordering the city. Here, you will find displays of baskets, artifacts, pottery and historical photographs. Basket-weaving demonstrations are presented daily.

Don't miss **Rawhide-Arizona's 1880 Western Town** (23023 North Scottsdale Road; 602-563-5111; some attractions have charges) with its colorful variety of rides and attractions, shops, a steakhouse and a saloon—all mostly located along a rickety Main Street where visitors dodge real sheep and goats. Western shootouts, fiddlers, a gypsy for-tuneteller, stunt shows, a full-size 1880s-style locomotive, a carriage exhibit, a covered-wagon circle and an Old West museum are all part of the fun.

McCormick Railroad Park (7301 Indian Bend Road; 602-994-2312) is a child's and adult's locomotive fantasy. Start by riding around the park on a miniature steam railroad, then take a whirl on the 1929 carousel. Afterward, tour the railroad museum located in a Pullman car that President Eisenhower used during his whistle-stop campaign in 1952. Finally, bring your kids for an eye-level view of trains whizzing along model railroad tracks through tiny villages.

Adams Arabians (12051 North 96th Street; 602-860-1218) is a world-renowned Arabian horse breeding and training ranch whose owners are receptive to occasional visitors checking out the scene and chatting with the trainers. As a private working ranch, it offers no organized programs or facilities, apart from a Coke machine in the tack room.

WestWorld (16601 North Pima Road, Scottsdale; 602-483-8800; admission) is a special events facility with a restaurant and large arena hosting the world's largest Arabian horse show, car auctions, polo matches, rodeos and musical entertainment.

Lots of green lawn, fountains and almost 20 sculptures lure families to the **Civic Center Mall** (bounded by Indian School Road, Brown Avenue, 2nd Street and Civic Center Boulevard). In addition, culture thrives here with the Center for the Arts and an outdoor amphitheater hosting live performances year-round. After the show, stop by one of the restaurants or shops lining the mall's periphery. For more information, contact the **Scottsdale Chamber of Commerce** (7343 East Scottsdale Mall; 602-945-8481).

Fleisher Museum (17207 North Perimeter Drive; 602-585-3108) has rotating shows and permanent exhibits devoted to "American Expressionism, California School," with lots of paintings of ladies from that stylish period between the turn of the century and the 1940s, plus misty, dreamlike landscapes, architectural and still-life paintings.

SCOTTSDALE LODGING

Holiday Inn-Scottsdale (5101 North Scottsdale Road; 602-945-4392) lifts itself out of the ordinary chain-motel category with a stunning landscape of desert palms and a mountain backdrop. It has 216 rooms and suites—lots of yellows and beige, with floral paintings on the walls and bright Southwest colors for the slipcovers—built around a large swimming pool, spa and patio. On-premise facilities include the Flamingo Dining Room, Versailles Lounge and a gift shop. Prices are moderate.

FRANK LLOYD WRIGHT'S HOME

Taliesin West/Frank Lloyd Wright Foundation (13201 North 108th Street, Scottsdale; 602-860-2700; admission), a National Historic Landmark owned by the Frank Lloyd Wright Foundation, was the architect's Arizona home and studio. Situated on 600 acres of rugged Sonoran Desert, this remarkable set of buildings still astounds architectural critics with its beauty and unusual forms. A variety of guided tours are offered. There's also a lecture series.

The **Buffalo Museum of America** *(10261 North Scottsdale Road, Scottsdale;
602-951-1022; admission) displays such items as Buffalo Bill's original hunting
rifle, buffalo props from motion pictures and photos of buffalos.*

Why go to a water park when the **Hyatt Regency Scottsdale**
(7500 East Doubletree Ranch Road; 602-991-3388) is around? Lounge
on the sand beach, take a dip in the jacuzzi beneath a Greek water
temple, or swim in the ten pools connected by a network of fountains,
waterfalls, and a three-story waterslide. The 493 ultra-deluxe-priced
rooms, suites and casitas are modern with pastel greens, pinks and
blues. Amenities here include a health spa, three restaurants, golfing,
tennis and horseback riding.

The revamped **Scottsdale Plaza Resort** (7200 North Scottsdale
Road; 602-948-5000) is a true find. Set within 40 acres, with 404
rooms and 180 suites, the resort features Spanish/Mediterranean-style
villas throughout, accented with courtyard swimming pools. The
rooms are large and styled with Southwest furnishing and art. Fountains, palm trees, earth-tone tiles, mauve carpeting, acres of fresh-cut
flowers and potted greens add cooling touches. There are swimming
pools, outdoor spas, tennis courts, indoor racquetball courts, a pro
shop, gym and, if you need more, croquet. Ultra-deluxe.

If you're looking for a gem of a mini-resort, try the 58-room
Papago Inn & Resort (7017 East McDowell Road; 602-947-7335).
This Best Western property has a heated pool, sauna and hot tub,
lounge and dining room. Guest rooms all overlook a tree- and flower-
filled interior courtyard with swimming pool. Moderate.

Camelview (701 East Indian Bend Road; 602-991-2400), a Radis-
son Resort located on 35 lushly landscaped acres in the heart of Scottsdale,
has 200 guest rooms (including 17 one- and two-bedroom suites). All
reflect the natural colors of the desert and are richly appointed with
Southwest and Indian art. Recreational facilities include tennis courts,
nearby golf, jogging trails, horseback riding and a pool. Ultra-deluxe.

Scottsdale's Fifth Avenue Inn (6935 5th Avenue; 602-994-9461), a
secluded retreat right in the heart of Scottsdale's premier shopping
district, sprawls out around a central courtyard with a large heated
swimming pool. Its 92 newly decorated guest rooms feature desert
colors, king and double-queen beds, and separate dressing areas. Rates
includes a full breakfast. Moderate.

One of the oldest homes in the area, **Hays House** (5615 Lafayette
Boulevard; 602-947-0488) is a former citrus ranch house turned into a
bed and breakfast. It offers three suites in the main house and two
adjoining apartments. All have private baths and are furnished with
Persian rugs and an assortment of antique furnishings and paintings.

"It's not quite museum status," says the English-born owner. The British background is reflected in the full sumptuous breakfasts served each morning. Two acres of orange and grapefruit trees surround the house. Moderate.

The **Thunderbird Inn** (7515 East Butherus Drive; 602-951-4000) may be a Best Western property, but don't let its chain affiliation throw you. It's a four-story, all-suite, deluxe-category hotel designed in a courtyard setting with a heated pool and spa. Each of the hotel's two-room suites is styled in desert mauve and teals with light southwestern contemporary furnishings.

The **Scottsdale Princess** (7575 East Princess Drive; 602-585-4848), an ultra-deluxe resort in the pretty-in-pink tradition of Princess hotels everywhere, has 600 rooms. It's one of the valley's largest hotels. Set on 48 elaborately landscaped acres with a central courtyard, waterfall and three swimming pools, the Princess is one of the most visually arresting of its kind. The rooms are large, decorated in Southwest furnishing, with a hint of Santa Fe.

With 423 rooms, **Marriott's Camelback Inn** (5402 East Lincoln Drive, Paradise Valley; 602-948-1700) outside Scottsdale is yet another glorious world-class retreat dramatically nestled in the foothills between the Camelback and Mummy mountains, where landscaped paths wind through gardens of cactus and desert palms. Its Southwest pueblo architecture and adobe-style casitas blend harmoniously into the stunning desert background. For the sportsminded, there are championship golf and tennis, swimming, trail rides, weekly cookouts and fitness facilities. Ultra-deluxe.

Marriott's Mountain Shadows (5641 East Lincoln Drive, Paradise Valley; 602-948-7111) offers palm trees, waterfalls, sparkling streams and lakes, and that's just the golf course. At the foot of Camelback Mountain, with over a hundred acres of land, Mountain Shadows seems designed for the sports devotee. Along with its pro 54 holes of golf, it has lighted tennis courts, putting greens, and swimming pools. The hotel's 388 guest rooms are clustered over the entire property; each room, designed in muted Southwest colors, has a private lanai. The resort has four restaurants. Ultra-deluxe.

SCOTTSDALE RESTAURANTS

The first thing seasoned travelers look for when staking out a new town is a good place to have breakfast. In Scottsdale, **Boman's N.Y. Kosher-style Restaurant & Deli** (373 North Scottsdale Road; 602-947-2934) hits the spot. Small and nondescript, it has a deli counter on one side, separated from the blue formica tables and banquets by a white picket fence. Ceiling fans, an advertisement for Dr. Brown's

Cream Soda and an indifferent waitress pretty much set the ambience. The focus is on good food at moderate prices—french toast, applejack pancakes, ham and eggs. It's also open for lunch and dinner (pastrami on rye, pickles, brisket, chicken in the pot, stuffed cabbage). A sign on the cash register says, "Shalom, Y'all."

A traditional breakfast spot (it also serves lunch) is **The Original Pancake House** (6840 East Camelback Road; 602-946-4902), in business over 40 years, serving up steaming stacks of golden flapjacks, topped with melted butter, honey, maple syrup, berries or whatever's your pleasure. The restaurant is small—11 tables and ten booths. The decor is southwestern, with light green and tan colors dominating. Large picture windows in front keep it bright and cheerful. Budget.

Don't be surprised if your waiter breaks into song after you've ordered at **Ristorante Sandolo** (7500 East Doubletree Ranch Road; 602-991-3388), a moderately priced Italian café known for their singing servers. The restaurant dishes out Venetian-style entrées and gourmet pizzas, followed by complementary sandolo (similar to gondola) rides on the waterway winding through the Hyatt Regency Scottsdale.

People flock to **Sfuzzi** (4720 North Scottsdale Road; 602-946-9777) to eat Tuscan cuisine amidst faux Roman ruins, giant pillars and halogen lights. Rock-and-roll music sets the mood, and dining on the moderately priced gourmet pizzas and pastas can be done indoors or out on the patio.

If you're expecting red-checked tablecloths, don't come to **Bice** (4343 North Scottsdale Road; 602-949-2423). Cool and sophisticated describes this upscale northern Italian eatery where white-jacketed servers lay platters of food on white tablecloths. The fare is fresh, with specialties such as herb-crusted salmon or angel hair fettucini with bay scallops. A must is the tiramisu, or lady finger cookies dipped in espresso coffee with Mascarpone cheese and cocoa. Moderate to deluxe.

Thick wormwood tables, bright blue, yellow and green colors, and tin palm trees add to the southwestern ambiance at **Z'Tejas Grill** (7014 East Camelback Road; 602-946-4171). Try the Voo Doo Tuna blackened with a spicy soy mustard and black pepper vinaigrette, followed by ancho chili fudge pie. The southwestern cuisine is also laced with flavors from Louisiana. Moderate.

For burgers, chicken and greasy appetizers in a trendy eatery, stop by **AZ88** (7353 Scottsdale Mall; 602-994-5576). Although furnishings are dark, the place becomes cheery by floor-to-ceiling windows overlooking the green Civic Center Mall and lots of climbing vines. Fresh flowers dot tabletops and light music plays in the background for a soothing meal. Budget.

In the heart of the Scottsdale shopping district is **Jacqueline's Marketplace & Café** (7303 East Indian School Road; 602-947-8777), an upscale, whimsical café/shop with lots of southwestern gifts and bright coyote paintings and cards by artist Holly Haas. For dining, choices include table service or self-service, selecting from the wide variety of pastas, salads and sandwiches. The outdoor patio with its plants, brick walls and southwestern tiles are a favorite in warm weather. Budget.

Any restaurant that combines American decor with traditional Greek flourishes (would you believe a bellydancing lounge?) has to be interesting. The food at **Andros** (8040 East McDowell Avenue; 602-945-95673) runs from chicken and burgers to rolled grape leaves, rice and olives, and there's all that great Greek music in the background. Moderate.

The **Marquesa** (7575 East Princess Drive; 602-585-4848) is one of the top restaurants in the valley. Even people who normally avoid hotel dining rooms flock to this one in the Scottsdale Princess Resort to soak up all of its Old World Spanish ambience and nibble on tapas before settling down to more serious pursuits. Roast grouse, in season, with brandy sauce and cranberries, for instance, or steaming Mediterranean-style paella for two. The Marquesa is also known for its excellent wine list. Deluxe.

Don't wear a necktie if you're going to the **Pinnacle Peak Patio** (10426 East Jomax Road; 602-967-8020) because they'll snip it off and hang it from the rafters. That's part of the appeal of this highly informal, western-style steak house where 16-ounce mesquite-broiled steaks, with all the beans and fixin's, top the menu and the walls reverberate with the sounds of live country-and-western bands nightly. Moderate.

Get out of town one evening and treat yourself to a breathtaking view of pristine desert landscape and the city lights beyond at **The Vistas at Oaxaca** (8711 East Pinnacle Peak Road; 602-998-2222). Specialties here are baby-back ribs, prime rib and seafood, along with an extensive wine list. Open only for dinner. Deluxe.

Greasewood Flats (27000 North Alama School Road; no phone) is a hot dog, chili and beer kind of place housed in an old graffiti-covered

---

A LITTLE BIT OF SPORTS HEAVEN

Whatever your game, Phoenix is sports heaven. In professional competition, Phoenix has baseball (the Triple-A Firebirds), hockey (the Roadrunners) and basketball (the Suns). Plus, the Arizona State University Sun Devils play football, basketball and baseball. Still other spectator sports include rodeos and horse racing. For the active set, there are 125 golf courses and hundreds of tennis courts, as well as bike, jogging and horse-riding trails, and opportunities for all kinds of other recreational activities.

wooden shack in what appears to be a western junk yard, with discarded school desks, wooden wagons, saddle frames, wagon wheels, milk cans and egg crates all around it. But folks line up to get in. Budget.

Malee's on Main Thai Gourmet (5641 East Lincoln Drive; 602-947-6042) is a charming little spot with a bar in one corner, tables inside and a patio, weather permitting, for dining outside. Attractive tableware is set against peach and green tablecloths. Popular with the art crowd (in Scottsdale that covers a wide swath), its extensive menu comes in various degrees of spicy intensity. Moderate.

House of Yang (14016 North Scottsdale Road; 602-443-0188) is small, only a few tables and chairs, and it appears to do a large take-out business. But whether you eat in or take out, the House of Yang is a course in Chinese cuisine, serving Szechuan, Hunan, Mandarin and Cantonese. Shrimp comes in a variety of forms: with lobster sauce or black bean sauce, or stir-fried together with onions and peppers. Try the traditionally cooked thinly sliced Mongolian beef. Moderate.

The Spanish Colonial setting is spectacular, with high *viga* ceilings, white walls, antique furnishings and sweeping views of the valley, at **La Relais** (8711 East Pinnacle Peak Road; 602-998-0921). Very French and very fine, both nouvelle and traditional French dishes fill the two-page menu—loin of lamb with garlic and basil, medallions of veal, poached stingray—all served by attentive, black-tied waiters. Ultra-deluxe.

Voltaire (8340 East McDonald Drive; 602-948-1005) is another bastion of French gastronomy, all candlelight and crystal. Boned chicken à la Normande with apples, sautéed sand dabs, rack of lamb, and sweetbreads sautéed in lemon butter and capers highlight the extensive menu. Deluxe.

Rawhide Steakhouse and Saloon (23023 North Scottsdale Road; 602-563-5600) is the place to belly up to the bar in Scottsdale's popular Old West frontier town. There's good things to eat, too—mesquite broiled steaks, prime rib, barbecued chicken, baby back ribs and even fried rattlesnake. The saloon has an antique bar, gambling tables (but no gambling), "crooked" card dealers and live country music. Prices are deluxe.

Julio's Barrio (7234 East Camelback Road; 602-423-0058), established in 1934, somehow manages to combine art deco, Santa Fe and Mexican truck-stop decor—ceiling fans, black-tile walls and framed vintage-Mexican advertisements—into a trendy contemporary look. The food is much more clearly defined—*pollo Mexicana*, beef tacos, bean tostadas, steaming bowls of rice and beans, chili con carne and tortillas. Prices are moderate, and the staff is friendly and attentive.

If you're looking for shades of the 1960s, you'll find it at **The Soapbox Coffeehouse** (6208 North Scottsdale Road; 602-998-4766), where espresso, quiche, soups, homemade muffins, desserts and exotic teas and coffees are served in that quintessential ambience of chess, backgammon, poetry readings, hot-topic discussions and live jazz, blues and folk music. Moderate.

One of the oldest, and many consider the finest, Mexican restaurants in Scottsdale is **Los Olivos Mexican Patio** (7328 East 2nd Street; 602-946-2256). The restaurant was founded in 1945, but the adobe building in which it's located was built in 1928 and is officially listed as one of Scottsdale's historic landmarks. Large and rambling, with *viga* ceilings, it has several individual dining rooms inside and patio dining outside. The Mexican cuisine served is primarily Sonoran—enchiladas, seasonal green corn tamales, chimichangas, *chile rellenos* and steak picado. The decor is festive (clay pots, flowers and piñatas) and there's live music and dancing on weekends. Aficionados rate its margaritas among the best in the state. Moderate.

If a touch of old Boston at the turn of the century strikes your fancy, stop into the **American Grill** (6113 North Scottsdale Road; 602-948-9907) and you'll think you're there. Dark-wood paneling, polished brass and glass, exposed tile, ceiling fans whooshing over comfortable tables and booths, and a busy open kitchen. Made-to-order clam, Manhattan, corn, fish and cheddar chowders, served with sourdough bread, are the house specialties. Grilled mustard shrimp, Cajun blackened rockfish, prime rib and hickory-smoked grilled chicken also get big play. This place is popular with the after-work white-collar crowd and tends to be boisterous at times. Moderate.

Shells Oyster Bar & Seafood (5641 East Lincoln Drive, Paradise Valley; 602-948-7111) is the best-known of the four restaurants located at Marriott's Mountain Shadows Resort. Live miniature fish swim in an illuminated aquarium. The decor is bright and airy, with nautical touches, polished brass, etched mirrors and natural wood finishes. Seafood entrées come in a variety of preparations—flame broiled, steamed, sautéed, pan-fried or blackened Cajun-style, accompanied by a selection of special butters and sauces. Ultra-deluxe.

SCOTTSDALE SHOPPING

Scottsdale lifts shopping malls and mall shopping to the realm of high art. The **Scottsdale Galleria** (4343 North Scottsdale Road; 602-951-1262), for instance, is a glitzy shopping complex that breaks the mold with its musical fountains and million-gallon aquarium in the atrium where a tropical rainforest has been created. Oh, yes, there are 165 shops, boutiques, bookstores, galleries and restaurants, including **Shakespeare and Beethoven** (602-945-2646) for all the latest best sellers and a full range of classical records and tapes and **L'Escale Paris** (602-488-2123) for ladies' apparel with a French flair.

After New York City and Santa Fe, Scottsdale is the busiest art center in the country, with more than 200 galleries.

The **Borgata of Scottsdale** (6166 North Scottsdale Road; 602-998-1822) may just be a harbinger of a striking new trend in shopping centers—mini-theme-park shopping malls—this one, a 14th-century-styled village with medieval courtyards. International fashions, fine jewelry, unusual gifts, a book and music store and a spate of art galleries await.

Despite the trendy intrusions, **Scottsdale Fashion Square** (7000 East Camelback Road; 602-990-7000) remains Scottsdale's most fashionable shopping complex. It features such top-quality stores as **Neiman Marcus** (602-990-2100), **Dillard's** (602-949-5869) and **Robinson's** (formerly Goldwater's) (602-941-0066). There's even a shop for the kids—**The Disney Store** (602-423-5008).

The **Fifth Avenue Shops** (6940 East 5th Avenue; 602-947-5377) comprise the landmark shopping area in the heart of downtown Scottsdale, a sprawl of specialty shops, boutiques, bookstores, galleries, jewelry stores, Indian crafts shops and restaurants, more than 70 in all by latest count. Among them: **Sewell's Indian Arts** (602-945-0962) for Native American jewelry, kachina dolls, Pueblo pottery and Navajo sandpaintings; **Lemonade Folk Art** (602-945-2219) for tole painting, howling cows and other country and Southwest folk art and gifts; **Oz Turkish & Oriental Handicrafts** (602-423-5026) for outstanding gifts and imports; **Gallery 10** (602-994-0405) for prints and posters galore, featuring contemporary, Native American and western artists; and the **Brass Pelican** (602-949-7997) for bells, scrimshaw, lamps, portholes, sextants, binoculars and other things nautical.

Arizona Sun Products (7136 East 5th Avenue; 602-941-9067) has fun gift items, but specializes in a wonderful moisturizer containing native plants such as aloe vera, jojoba, wild roses and cacti. A colorful desert scene on the front makes it a good souvenir, too.

Elsewhere, mystery lovers should seek out **The Poisoned Pen** (7100 East Main Street; 602-947-2974), a bookstore specializing in crime, detective and suspense books from American and British publishers.

For you cowpokes, **Porters** (3944 North Brown Avenue; 602-945-0868) is one of the oldest names in Scottsdale cowboy gear and features top-of-the-line name brands.

If you're interested in the local art scene, the **Scottsdale Art Association** (602-941-0900) conducts art walks every Thursday evening, October through May, from 7 p.m. until 9 p.m., visiting many of the leading galleries. At other times of the year, the Art Walks are conducted on the third Thursday of each month. Walks begin at the **Scottsdale Center for the Arts** (7383 Scottsdale Mall; 602-944-2787).

If you want to check out the art scene on your own, consider **Arizona West Galleries** (7149 Main Street; 602-994-3752), which specializes in American 19th- and 20th-century western art, including works by Frederic Remington, Charlie Russell and Maynard Dixon.

The **Biltmore Galleries** (7113 Main Street; 602-947-5975) also features 19th- and 20th-century art, including works by early New Mexico master Nicolai Fechin, Joseph Sharp and Ernest Blumenschein.

Buck Saunders Gallery (2724 North Scottsdale Road; 602-945-9376) has long been the exclusive representative of Arizona's best-known, best-loved artist, Ted De Grazia.

Specializing in abstract and Southwest representational art is **Galerie Sloan** (4151 North Marshall Way; 602-945-8512). Works by the much-in-demand Cherokee artist Bert Seabourn can be found here.

Glenn Green Galleries (6000 East Camelback Road; 602-990-9110) uses the elegant grounds of the posh Phoenician Resort (the gallery is in the hotel's retail corridor) to display the mammoth bronze and stone sculptures of famed Native American artist Alan Houser.

J. R. Fine Arts (4151 North Marshall Way; 602-945-7856) handles serigraphs, lithographs, oils and sculpture, including those by top contemporary Indian painters R. C. Gorman and Earl Biss.

To get your practical shopping done in one convenient stop, drive to **Scottsdale Pavilions** (corner of Pima and Indian Bend roads; 602-866-0900), a 1.2 million-square-foot complex that includes a discount shop, pharmacy, clothing stores, fast-food stops, a bookstore and a home improvement store.

SCOTTSDALE NIGHTLIFE

For starters, try the big-band sounds at the Royal Palm Inn's **El Mirage Lounge** (5200 East Camelback Road; 602-840-3610), live contemporary dance music at The Phoenician Resort's **Charlie Charlie's** (6000 East Camelback Road; 602-423-2445), and jazz at the Scottsdale Hyatt Regency's **Lobby Bar** (7500 East Doubletree Ranch Road; 602-991-3388) or **JD's Lounge** (7220 North Scottsdale Road; 602-948-5000) at the Scottsdale Plaza Resort.

Lulu Belle's (7212 East Main Street; 602-994-9800) is the sole survivor of Scottsdale's two original bars (the Pink Pony burned down) and a live country-and-western band keeps a mostly older crowd tapping their toes.

For beer brewed on the premises, stop by **Hops Restaurant & Brewery** (7000 East First Avenue, #A; 602-945-4677). Favorites are the award-winning unfiltered German Wheat Beer or Hops Amber.

The decor is high-tech, with glass block partitions, modern paintings and a black, gray and orange decor.

J. Chew & Company (7320 Scottsdale Mall; 602-946-2733) has live jazz music nightly in an intimate, European-style pub with french doors leading to two outdoor patios with fireplaces.

Scottsdale Center for the Arts, located in the beautifully sculptured Civic Center Mall, hosts a variety of events, including the Scottsdale Symphony, guest performing artists, concerts, lectures, classic cinema and art exhibitions. During the summer, music lovers flock to the concerts held outside on the grassy lawn at the east end of the mall. For a schedule, call 602-994-2787.

Actors Lab Theater Center (7223 East 2nd Street; 602-990-1731) is the home of Scottsdale's resident professional theater company. It has two stages offering a variety of Broadway productions.

The audience gets involved in solving crimes at **Murder Ink Productions** (4110 North Goldwater Boulevard, #107; 602-423-8669), a murder mystery dinner theater.

Tempe/Mesa Area

Immediately east of Phoenix are the communities of Tempe and Mesa. It's as though, heading east, all the big-city sheen dissolves in degrees into the West of the Old West, the pace slows down, and you can almost reach up and feel the sky in your hands.

Bordered by Scottsdale, Mesa, Phoenix and Chandler, **Tempe** was founded in 1872 by Charles Turnbell Hayden, who established the Hayden Flour Mill that year. **Old Town Tempe** (North of University Street along Mill Avenue; 602-894-8158) is the site of the original settlement, set up around the old Hayden Flour Mill. Today, many of the early homes and buildings have been renovated and serve as restaurants, shops, offices and galleries. Stop by the **Tempe Convention and Visitors Bureau** (60 East 5th Street, Tempe, AZ 85281; 602-894-8158) for maps and information.

Forming the character of Tempe is **Arizona State University**, located in the heart of the city. Home of the Fiesta Bowl, it has the largest enrollment of any school in the Southwest. With its 700-acre main campus, where strikingly modern buildings rise from a setting of palm trees and subtropical plants, Arizona State provides the chiefly residential city with its main industry. A number of outstanding museums dot the campus and are open to the general public. **Arizona State University Art Museum** (602-965-2787) has an extensive collection of American paintings, prints and crafts, as well as artworks from Africa, Latin America and the South Seas. The **Museum of Anthro-**

pology (602-965-6213) includes archaeological, physical and socio-cultural anthropology exhibits. Highlight exhibits at the **Museum of Geology** (602-965-5081) focus on rare geological specimens, seismographs and earthquake displays.

Tempe also houses the outstanding **Tempe Historical Museum** (809 East Southern Avenue; 602-350-5100; admission), which covers the history of Tempe from early Indian days to the present. Three changing galleries offer exhibits of contemporary, Native American and western artists. There are also hands-on displays for children.

For art buffs there is the **Tempe Arts Center and Sculpture Garden** (54 West 1st Street; 602-968-0888), which features eight changing gallery exhibits of contemporary arts, crafts and sculpture. Large-scale works are showcased in the adjoining Sculpture Garden, with many of the works for sale.

Just east of Tempe, you'll come to the town of **Mesa**. The town was founded by Mormons in 1883 and was long a farming community. Irrigation canals built by the Hohokam Indians were still used here until fairly recent times. For information on sights and services in the area, stop by the **Mesa Convention and Visitors Bureau** (120 North Center Street; 602-969-1307).

Mesa Southwest Museum (53 North MacDonald Street, Mesa; 602-644-2230; admission) covers the history of the Southwest from the time of the dinosaurs to the settlement of the West, with hands-on exhibits inside and a one-room schoolhouse and a gold-panning stream outside.

A find for aviation aficionados, the **Champlin Fighter Museum** (4636 Fighter Aces Drive; 602-830-4540; admission) has a collection of 30 restored fighters from World War I, World War II and the Korean and Vietnam wars. Historic weaponry is also displayed. An art gallery, video theater and pilot-memorabilia gift shop round out the bill.

Twenty minutes north of Mesa in Fountain Hills is the **Out of Africa Wildlife Park** (2 South Fort McDowell Road; 602-837-7779; admission) where lions, tigers, leopards and giant pythons do their things. There are shows, natural habitat viewing, cub-petting and a playground for the kids. There's also a gift shop and restaurant.

TEMPE/MESA AREA LODGING

Westcourt in The Buttes (2000 Westcourt Way, Tempe; 602-225-9000) is a dramatic 300-room, four-story resort built into the mountainside, with Southwest styling and art throughout. All guest rooms feature a decor of rose and earth tones, cactus and wood furnishings. There are two restaurants, a nightclub, pools, tennis and all of the modern trim and trappings associated with luxury resort living in the

The Hayden Flour Mill, founded in 1872, in Tempe is the oldest continuously operating business in Arizona.

valley, including cascading waterfalls and two romantic mountainside whirlpools. Ultra-deluxe.

Located in the heart of Old Town Tempe is the **Sheraton Tempe Mission Palms Hotel** (60 East Fifth Street; 602-894-1400), with 303 deluxe, southwestern-style rooms and a lobby splashed with copper and turquoise colors. Nice touches in the rooms include paintings of pottery on the walls, pastel bedspreads, bathrooms with marbleized sinks and a small makeup bureau. Most rooms overlook the lush, palm tree-dotted courtyard with fountains and a swimming pool. Other amenities include two restaurants, a sauna, whirlpool, exercise room and tennis courts.

Sprawling across 33 acres, the **Fiesta Inn** (2100 South Priest Drive, Tempe; 602-967-1441 or 1-800-528-6481) offers 270 deluxe, southwestern-style rooms, almost half of which are mini-suites with refrigerators. The fitness-minded will find a swimming pool, jacuzzi, a golf practice facility with a lighted driving range and putting greens, tennis courts and an exercise room. There's also a restaurant on the premises.

A little bit of Ireland located within walking distance of the ASU campus is found at the **Valley 'o the Sun Bed and Breakfast, Tempe** (P.O. Box 2214, Scottsdale, AZ 85252; 602-941-1281). It has three rooms (two with connecting bath) located in a ranch-style home with a view of the Papago Mountains. The owner is from the Old Sod, and the decor and decorations reflect a note of nostalgia. Full or continental breakfast, as desired, is included. Budget.

Cornerstone of downtown Mesa, **The Centennial Hotel** (200 North Centennial Way; 602-898-8300) has 280 rooms, contemporary furnishings, lounge, restaurant and swimming pool. Deluxe.

Buckhorn Mineral Wells (5900 East Main Street, Mesa; 602-832-1111) is a motel and natural hot water mineral springs bath house where massages and therapeutic hot soaks are offered. The motel has 14 rooms in contemporary Southwest decor. Budget.

TEMPE/MESA AREA RESTAURANTS

Mill Landing (398 South Mill Avenue; 602-966-1700) is a handsome restaurant housed in an historic building in the downtown Old Town section of Tempe offering a variety of light meals, salads, soups, sandwiches and seafood specialties. There's dining in the patio, weather permitting. Deluxe.

In a similar mold and in a similar building (the Andre, built in 1888), **Paradise** (401 South Mill Avenue, Tempe; 602-829-0606) specializes in prime rib and fresh fish. Moderate.

Casa Reynoso (3138 South Mill Avenue, Tempe; 602-966-0776) is one of the better Mexican restaurants in town, despite its modest appearance—vinyl booths and wrought iron. Try the *gollo burro* or *chile rellenos*. Moderate.

The Coffee Plantation (Mill Avenue and 6th Street, Tempe; 602-829-7878) is a Caribbean-style coffeehouse and retail store in a two-story plantation house. Beans are roasted daily in a rustic roasting shack. There's indoor and outdoor seating where espresso, cappuccino and specialty coffees are served, along with pastries and desserts, breakfast, light lunch and dinner. Budget.

A little bit of the Big Island went adrift and ended up in Tempe. **McGurk's of Hawaii** (909 East Elliott Road; 602-730-9009) is the place to go for ribs Kamehameha, Mai Mai and chicken *panido*, clams, lobster and hickory barbecued chicken, island-style—all served in an atmosphere of early Trader Vic's and Gilligan's Island. Moderate.

The decor is plain and simple, while the food is anything but, at **Char's Thai Restaurant** (927 East University Drive; 602-967-6013) where an exotic touch of the East comes to Tempe with such offerings as chicken soup with coconut milk, smoked beef salad, curried duck and seafood combinations in peanut sauce. There's also a good selection of Asian beers. Moderate.

Mother Tucker's (1457 West Southern Avenue, Mesa; 602-898-0880) is a clone of Mother Tucker's in Phoenix—informal atmosphere, Early American tables, hanging greenery, cozy booths and country-beamed ceilings. The house specialty is roast prime rib of beef. The chef slices it to order. The salad bar has over 50 items. Deluxe.

For a good solid breakfast or lunch, they don't come much better than the **Ripe Tomato Café** (745 West Baseline Road, Mesa; 892-4340) where it's always wall-to-wall people. It's a great find for breakfast, and the steak, sandwiches and Mexican specialty lunches aren't bad either. Moderate.

TEMPE/MESA AREA SHOPPING

Historic **Old Town Tempe** exudes ambiance with its old-fashioned red-brick sidewalks and planters, tree-lined streets and quaint street lamps. Walk the area and you'll find dozens of shops and restaurants. With light music floating in the background, you can scan the shelves at the **Changing Hands Bookstore** (414 South Mill Avenue; 602-966-0203), which has more than 50,000 new and used books on three floors. Specialties are spirituality, psychology, literature, women's is-

Mesa in Spanish means "tabletop," appropriate since the town of Mesa sits on a plateau.

sues, and travel. **Circus** (501 South Mill Avenue; 602-968-2610) has Arizona souvenirs, cacti, southwestern cookbooks, truffles and other gift items. For clothing, gifts and accessories from around the world, try **Mazar Bazaar** (514 South Mill Avenue; 602-966-9090).

Chief Dodge (601 South Mill Avenue, Tempe; 602-967-9365) is an Indian jewelry store with a wide variety of turquoise and silver bracelets, squash blossom necklaces, bolas and belts, all made right on the premises.

If you want to wear a souvenir home, try **The U Shop** (725 South Rural Road, Tempe; 602-829-1743), which has a large selection of Arizona State University clothing and gift items, as well as Phoenix Cardinal and Phoenix Sun merchandise.

Superstition Springs Center (intersection of Power Road and the Superstition Freeway, Mesa; 602-832-0212) is the newest mega-mall in the Phoenix area. In addition to the usual mall lineup of anchor stores and chain specialty shops, this center has a full-size carousel for the kids, a desert botanical garden with more than 100 plants, a playground with a 15-foot-tall Gila Monster slide, short hiking trails, and a stage for free concerts.

For quality Indian arts, the **Warbonnet Gallery** (1234 West Madero Avenue; 602-733-6258) in Mesa offers modern Indian paintings, Navajo rugs, kachina dolls and sandpaintings. Represented here are Marina Martinez and Joseph Lonewolf, among other Native American artists.

The Lenox Factory Outlet (2121 South Power Road, Mesa; 602-986-9986) offers selected seconds on the company's famous china and crystal products, as well as candles, silver and other tabletop accessories.

TEMPE/MESA AREA NIGHTLIFE

Grady Gammage Memorial Auditorium (602-965-3434), at the Arizona State University campus in Tempe, is a 3000-seat auditorium designed by Frank Lloyd Wright. Its entertainment features range from Broadway productions to symphony orchestra concerts and ballet. Guided tours of the center are offered on Monday and Saturday.

The Butte's swinging **Chuckwalla's** (2000 Westcourt Way; 602-259-9000), with its 24-foot video screen, karaoke bar and live entertainment, is one of hottest spots in Tempe.

Bandersnatch (1253 East 5th Street, Tempe; 602-966-4438) is big with the ASU college crowd, which means lots of beer and a house special brew that may or may not be homemade. Live jazz and, for those so inclined, live volleyball. **Chuy's** (310 South Mills Avenue, Tempe; 602-967-2489) is another college hangout where alternate live sounds can be heard: blues, rhythm-and-blues, rock and jazz.

Bobby McGee's (1320 West Southern Avenue, Mesa; 602-969-4600) has a disk jockey, great sounds and big crowds.

For live dinner theater, it's the **Landmark** (809 West Main Street; 602-962-4652) in Mesa on Wednesdays and weekends—from melodramas to suspense and comedy—and the food is good, too.

Chandler Center for the Arts (250 North Arizona Avenue, Chandler; 602-786-3954; admission) has three stages hosting musical, dance and theater performances by local and national performers. In addition, artwork is displayed in the foyer.

TEMPE/MESA AREA PARKS

McDowell Mountain Regional Park, a 21,099-acre wilderness expanse 15 miles northeast of Scottsdale, is one of the region's most scenic parks with an abundance of vegetation and majestic mountain views. Elevation ranges from 1600 feet at the southeast corner to 3000 feet along the western boundary. The area is ideal for camping, picnicking, horseback riding and hiking. Located via McDowell Mountain Road, four miles northeast of Fountain Hills.

North of Phoenix

From cactus flowers to remote mountain lakes, here is a region rich in scenic wonders. Best known for its resorts, cool forests and desert playgrounds, this recreational paradise also includes the Wild West town of Wickenberg—the Dude Ranch Capital of the World—as well as some interesting old mining towns.

Established in 1950, **Carefree** is a planned community situated in the scenic foothills of the Arizona desert. To the north and east stretches the immense Tonto National Forest. Next door, you'll find an old-time town, **Cave Creek**. Once a booming mining camp in the 1880s (gold and silver), Cave Creek wasn't incorporated until a hundred years later. Sheep and cattle were raised here, as well. Today Cave Creek leans heavily on its Old West past, with its Frontier Town recreation and annual spring rodeo. For additional information, contact **Carefree/Cave Creek Chamber of Commerce** (748 East Street, Carefree; 602-488-3381).

At the peak of the gold rush, Wickenburg had more than 80 mines, with the town growing into what was Arizona's third-largest city at the time.

Cave Creek Museum (6140 East Skyline Drive; 602-488-2764) offers a living-history exhibit of the desert foothills region, with a restored 1920s tuberculous cabin and a 1940s church, as well as displays of pioneer living, ranching, mining, guns and Indian artifacts.

To the northwest, on Route 89, you will come to the site of the richest gold strike in Arizona. Named after Henry Wickenburg, the Russian settler who struck it rich at the Vulture Mine in 1863, **Wickenburg** is known today primarily as a winter resort. Here, the flavor of the Old West still lingers: western buildings line main streets, horses aren't an uncommon sight, and numerous guest ranches sprawl across the area.

Frontier Street preserves Wickenburg's turn-of-the-century character with its old-time train depot now housing the **Wickenburg Chamber of Commerce** (602-684-5479) and a number of vintage wood and brick buildings. One, the Hassayampoa, was once the town's leading hotel. Maps for a self-guided historic walking tour are available at the chamber office. Before the town jail was built, the nearby **Jail Tree** (Tegner Street and Wickenburg Way) was used to chain criminals. Friends and relatives brought them picnic lunches. Today, the tree is on the property of the Chaparral Ice Cream Parlor, and tykes eat their ice cream cones in the shade of its branches, probably none the wiser.

Venture over to the **Desert Caballeros Western Museum** (20 North Frontier Street; 602-684-2272; admission), which covers the history of Wickenburg and surrounding area with major exhibits divided into various rooms. "Period" rooms include the Hall of History and a Street Scene representing Wickenburg at the turn of the century. Others focus on 19th- and early 20th-century lifestyles. Its art gallery features Native American art and western masters of the past and present. The Museum Park outside offers unique desert landscaping and plants.

Those interested in gold mines and ghost towns might want to visit **Vulture Mine** (Vulture Mine Road; 602-377-0803; admission). This is an historic gold mine and ghost town of sorts. The home of the town founder of Wickenburg can be seen, as well as an early assay office, blacksmith shop, stamp mill, a 3000-foot mine shaft and even a hanging tree.

One of Arizona's newer attractions is **Robson's Arizona Mining World** (Route 71, 24 miles northwest of Wickenburg; 602-684-5838; admission), a reproduction of an old mining town that supposedly has the world's largest collection of antique mining equipment. Along with seeing the thousands of pieces of equipment, you can stroll through a mineral and gemstone museum, hotel, print shop, trading post and several other buildings.

To the northeast of Phoenix lies **Payson**, district headquarters for the Tonto National Forest. Driving from Phoenix to Payson, the elevation rises and the cactus gives way to cool pine country. In fact, Payson is within the world's largest ponderosa pine forest and has some of the cleanest air in the United States. It also provides a base camp for numerous scenic attractions within the forest primeval. Founded over a century ago as a tiny mining and ranching community, it now thrives on its recreation industry. The **Payson Chamber of Commerce** (1006 South Beeline Highway; 602-474-4515) offers information on the area.

Payson Zoo (602-474-5435), six-and-a-half miles east of town, has 60 animals, many of them trained "movie stars" who have appeared in films shot in and around Payson.

A state historic monument, **Strawberry Schoolhouse** (village of Strawberry; 602-476-3547) is the oldest standing schoolhouse in Arizona. Built in 1884, its last class was held in 1916. The small mountain village at 6000 feet was named for the many wild strawberries that covered the area when pioneers first arrived.

NORTH OF PHOENIX LODGING

Located just northeast of Scottsdale, **The Boulders** (34631 North Tom Darlington Drive, Carefree; 602-488-4118) is built directly against a stunning backdrop of 12-million-year-old granite boulder formations that soar hundreds of feet against the desert sky. Situated on 1300 acres, the resort consists of a main lodge and 136 adobe-style casitas, each individually designed to fit the sculptured contours of the desert and the rocks. The hotel is designed in broad architectural sweeps and makes dramatic use of Indian and regional art and artifacts—Navajo blankets, weavings, pottery, ceramics, paintings, stone sculptures and basketry. Guest rooms feature earth-tone furnishings, hand-hewn *viga* ceilings, fireplaces, wet bars, ceiling fans and oversized windows for broad desert vistas. Ultra-deluxe.

Tumbleweed Hotel (6333 East Cave Creek Road; 602-488-3668) is a small downtown Cave Creek hotel made of white slumpstone brick, with 16 rooms in the main building and eight casita-style guest houses, all with modern western-style furnishings and decor. The hotel has a swimming pool. Moderate, dropping to budget during the summer.

Spread across 20,000 acres, the **Rancho de los Caballeros** (Vulture Mine Road, Wickenburg; 602-684-5484) resort/guest ranch has a homey feel, having been owned by the same family since it opened in

1947. Out here, boredom is impossible. There's golfing on a championship 18-hole course, horseback riding, a skeet and trap range, tennis courts, a swimming pool and programs for the kids. The 73 rooms and suites are southwestern in style, with private patios and indoor sitting areas. The ranch is on the full American plan and is closed from the end of May to early October. Ultra-deluxe.

There's not a lack of activities at **The Wickenburg Inn** (eight miles north of town on Route 89), a "tennis and guest ranch" that waits at the end of a dusty road. Choices include playing on one of 11 tennis courts, viewing displays at the Desert Nature Center, followed by hiking, sand volleyball, swimming, horseback riding, archery, painting or jewelry making at the arts and crafts center, or spending money in the gift shop. Many of the 41 casitas and six lodge rooms have kitchenettes and cozy fireplaces beneath beamed ceilings. The ultra-deluxe room price includes all meals.

Flying E Ranch (2801 West Wickenburg Way, Wickenburg; 602-684-2690) is both a working cattle ranch and guest ranch—complete with trail rides, hay rides and chuckwagon dinners on its 21,000-acre spread. There are 16 rooms, plus a heated pool, sauna and whirlpool, along with tennis and shuffleboard. Four miles west of town, it's open November to May. Deluxe.

Another top-notch dude ranch in Wickenburg (this one's listed in the National Historic Register), the **Key El Bar Ranch** (Rincon Road; 602-684-7593) has room for 20 guests in hacienda-style adobe buildings beneath huge salt cedar trees. The lobby has a stone fireplace, and outside there's a pool for soaking after those long hours in the saddle. Open October 15 to May 1. Deluxe.

The Rancho Grande Motel (293 East Wickenburg Way, Wickenburg; 602-684-5445) is a one- and two-story 80-room Best Western

KOHL'S RANCH LODGE

*A landmark around these parts for years, **Kohl's Ranch Lodge** (East Highway 260, Payson; 602-478-4211 or 800-331-5645) sits on the banks of Tonto Creek 17 miles east of Payson. Many of the 49 rooms and cabins overlook the creek and are equipped with outdoor grills and patios. Cabins have stone fireplaces, vaulted ceilings and kitchenettes, but furnishings are rather plain. Rooms in the lodge have rather tacky, but fun, carpeting that resembles a wood-plank floor. Open the sliding glass door to the patio and you'll hear the deafening sound of crickets. Amenities here include a restaurant, lounges, gift shop, pool and horseback riding. Moderate.*

*Ten miles north of Payson, **Tonto Natural Bridge** (602-476-3440) in the Tonto National Forest, is the largest natural travertine bridge in the world.*

with a pool, whirlpool and playground. Rooms are furnished in a contemporary motif. Budget to moderate.

Swiss Village Lodge (Route 87, Payson; 602-474-3241) is a handsome, two-story hotel with lots of Alpine flavor in the midst of a European-style village of shops and restaurants. Its 99 rooms are decorated in contemporary furnishings, plain and simple. Some have fireplaces. A café, bar and swimming pool are on the premises. Moderate.

NORTH OF PHOENIX RESTAURANTS

The Satisfied Frog (6245 East Cave Creek Road, Cave Creek; 602-488-3317) captures a bit of the Old West with wood tables, sawdust on the floor and weird things on the walls—animal heads, posters, old farm tools. House specialties include barbecued beef, pork and chicken. The Frog has its own micro-brewery and produces four house brands. Moderate.

Another amphibian-named eatery, **The Horny Toad** (6738 Cave Creek Road, Cave Creek; 602-997-9622) is a rustic, informal restaurant with wooden tables and booths, seating about 150 for lunch and dinner. Added touches are a small bar and lots of greenery. Moderate.

Ready for some old-time Wild West flavor? You'll find it at the **Gold Nugget** (222 East Wickenburg Way, Wickenburg; 602-684-2858), a bar and restaurant with red-flocked wallpaper, brass chandeliers and turn-of-the-century decor. Steaks, prime rib and chicken dominate the menu. Moderate.

Don't be fooled by the delicate pink tablecloths and soft country music. At **Charley's Steak House** (1089 West Wickenburg Way, Wickenburg; 602-684-2413), bring your appetite to chow down on thick steaks served with salad, baked potato, cowboy beans and desert. Prices hover in the moderate to deluxe range.

Payson offers **Aunt Alice's** (512 North Beeline Highway; 602-474-4720), green and blue on the outside, down-home on the inside. Aunt Alice serves up fish, burgers and chicken-fried steak in a country-style setting. Budget.

La Casa Pequeña (911 South Beeline Highway, Payson; 602-474-6329) features chimichangas, burritos and chicken Acapulco in a pleasant, south-of-the-border atmosphere. There's music on weekends. Prices are in the moderate range.

A western theme dominates at the **Kohl Ranch Restaurant** (East Highway 260, Payson; 602-478-4211), where painted cowboys cook over a campfire on one wall and a replica of an 1884 hotel, complete with stained-glass windows, covers another wall. Beneath the glow of a wagon-wheel chandelier, diners can enjoy barbecued ribs, chicken, steaks and seafood. Budget to moderate.

Sit on the screened porch and catch the sweet, fragrant scent of pine from the sawmill across the street at the **Heritage House Garden Tea Room** (202 West Main Street, Payson; 602-474-5501). In the background, tunes play from a replica of a 1930s era jukebox. The fare is light, such as the Heritage tarragon chicken sandwich followed by a slice of homemade pie. Budget.

On weekends, piano music spills from the bar onto the patio at **The Oaks** (302 West Main Street, Payson; 602-474-1929), where you can order fresh steaks and seafood. There's also plenty of indoor seating at this 50-odd year old renovated ranch house. Moderate.

NORTH OF PHOENIX SHOPPING

Wickenburg has several southwestern gift shops and art galleries. Sit on the porch at **Grit** (279 North Frontier Street; 602-684-2132) and drink cappuccino, or browse through the shop for southwestern gourmet food such as cactus salsa, chile vinegar and chocolate fettucini pasta. Sister store **Grit Too!** (186 North Tegner; 602-684-2119) has southwestern contemporary clothing and Birkenstock sandals.

It's hard to miss **Ben's Saddlery & Shoe Repair** (183 North Tegner, Wickenburg; 602-684-2683), with a life-sized horse on top of the building. This place has been around for about 40 years. The owner is a roper, and even if you're not in the market for authentic western gear, it's fun to breathe in the heady smell of leather and saddle soap while walking down aisles stocked with spurs, saddles, boots and ropes for lassos.

The **Gold Nugget Art Gallery** (274 East Wickenburg Way, Wickenburg; 602-684-5849) is housed in an adobe building built in 1863 that was once Old Fort Wickenburg, a U.S. Cavalry base. Inside these historic walls are original southwestern woodcarvings, pottery, designer jewelry and Native American art.

A fixture for almost 20 years is the **Wickenburg Gallery** (67 North Tegner, Wickenburg; 602-684-7047), which showcases national and regional fine art including sculpture, paintings and traditional Navajo weavings.

It's hard to decide what's more satisfying at the **Heritage House** (202 West Main Street, Payson; 602-474-5501)—shopping or porch-sitting. Some come to shop in this quaint 1925 house for furniture, handmade tablecloths, picture frames, baskets and afghans. Others just sit in the twig and wicker furniture on the porch, relaxing and watching the world go by just beyond the picket fence.

Antique lovers have several options in the Payson area, with the majority of shops located just off the Beeline Highway. A few include: **Johnson's Antiques & Stuff** (1001 South Beeline, Payson; 602–474–8988), housing dolls, furniture and primitives by a variety of dealers; **Payson Lock and Key** (410 West Main Street, #D, Payson; 602–474–0147), with its Elvis Memorabilia and oldie records; and **Glass Slipper Antiques** (603 South Beeline; 602–474–6672) with glassware, furniture, estate jewelry, books, mill spools and linens.

NORTH OF PHOENIX NIGHTLIFE

Cozy booths inside and a balcony with tables overlooking Tonto Creek outside draw people to **The Cowboy Bar** (East Highway 260, Payson; 602–478–4211) at Kohl's Ranch Lodge. The rustic log building has been around for years, as has the huge oak tree that grows through the ceiling. On weekends, bring your boots and dance to live country music.

NORTH OF PHOENIX PARKS

A green desert oasis, **Hassayampa River Preserve** (602–684–2772) is a riparian area along the Hassayampa River featuring a cottonwood-willow forest and other vital Sonoran Desert habitats that are being protected by the nonprofit Nature Conservancy. Sit by the banks of spring-fed Palm Lake, a four-acre pond and marsh habitat, and you might spot water birds such as great blue herons or snowy egrets, or see migrating waterfowl. Birdwatchers also gather here to see the more than 220 species of birds that pass through this migration corridor. Naturalists offer guided walks along paths ranging from desert areas with cacti to lusher stretches along the river. Tours start at the Visitor Center, housed in an historic adobe building. The preserve is located on Route 60, 3 miles southeast of Wickenburg near mile marker 114.

White Tank Mountain Regional Park (602-506-2930), covering 26,337 acres of desert, canyons and mountains, is the largest park in the Maricopa County Park System. Elevations range from 1402 feet at the park entrance to 4083 feet at the park's highest point. White Tank contains an excellent hiking and riding trail system, a seasonal flowing waterfall (reached by a mile-long self-guided hiker's trail) and scattered Native American petroglyphs throughout. The park is located on Dunlap Avenue, 15 miles west of Glendale.

South of Phoenix

Out beyond the metropolis, where the bright lights give way to Native American ruins, you'll find the homeland of the Pima and Maricopa people, the site of Arizona's only Civil War battlefield and cotton fields that stretch for miles. Also, mountain peaks, great fishing and, for the born-to-shop crowd, factory-outlet malls. It is an intriguing blend of old and new Arizona.

Gila River Indian Center (602-315-3411) in the Gila River Reservation has a museum, gift shop and restaurant featuring authentic Indian fry bread and southwestern food. Here, too, is **Heritage Park,** featuring about half a dozen mini Indian villages. The center is located off Route 10, via Route 93 (exit 175). The museum is free and you can also take an interpretive walking tour of Heritage Park conducted by Native American Joe Enos. Several tours are offered during the day, but it's best to call ahead to find out approximate times.

Farther south is **Casa Grande**, named for the Indian ruins northeast of town. Casa Grande is known primarily for cotton-growing, industry and for the many name-brand factory-outlet stores that have mushroomed here in recent years. For additional information, contact **Casa Grande Chamber of Commerce** (575 North Marshall Street; 602-836-2125).

Casa Grande Ruins National Monument (Route 87, about 20 miles east of Casa Grande; 602-723-3172), houses the remains of a village originally built by the Hohokam Indians in the early 1300s and abandoned by the end of that century. Four stories high, and covered recently by a large protective roof, the main structure is the only one of its size and kind in this area. (The monument grounds contain about 60 prehistoric sites.) The ruins are easily explored on well-marked self-guided tours. There's a visitor center and museum where ranger talks are presented.

For cowboy fans, the **Tom Mix Monument** (Pinal Pioneer Parkway out of the town of Florence; 602-868-9433) honors the silent-movie cowboy star near the spot where he died in an auto wreck in 1940. "In memory of Tom Mix whose spirit left his body on this spot and whose characterizations and portrayals in life served to better fix memories of the Old West in the minds of living men," reads the inscription.

SOUTH OF PHOENIX LODGING

Francisco Grande Resort and Golf Club (26000 Gila Bend Highway; 602-836-6444) is where it's all at in Casa Grande. The tallest building in Pinal County (eight stories), the hotel's tower building contains most of its 112 rooms, while other rooms are located motel-style around the patio. Furnishings are Southwest throughout, including the paintings on the guest-room walls—cowboys and western landscapes. The hotel has a restaurant, lounge (with nightly entertainment), swimming pool and golf. Deluxe.

Holiday Inn (777 North Pinal Avenue, Casa Grande; 602-426-3500), a three-story, Spanish-style stucco building, has 175 rooms in contemporary styling, an outdoor pool and spa, restaurant and lounge. Prices are moderate.

SOUTH OF PHOENIX RESTAURANTS

Gila River Arts and Crafts Restaurant (Gila River Reservation; 602-315-3411) features Indian fry bread along with burritos, tacos, hamburgers, homemade pies and coffee. Budget.

Mi Amigo Ricardo (821 East Florence Boulevard, Casa Grande; 602-836-3858) offers up hot and spicy Mexican specialties—chimichangas, enchiladas, frijoles, tamales, flautas and *posole*—with beer and wine to soothe the flames. The decor is Mexican, of course, and quite attractive. Moderate.

Bring a big appetite to the **Golden Corral** (1295 East Florence Boulevard, Casa Grande; 602-836-4630). It's a traditional western steak house where owner Vicki Carlson cuts her meat fresh daily and the salad bar has 150 items. Moderate.

Bedillon's (800 North Park Avenue, Casa Grande; 602-836-2045) is a restaurant and museum in two separate buildings. The museum features Indian artifacts and western memorabilia. The menu offers a full range of American cuisine. Moderate.

A small, downtown Casa Grande bakery and café, **The Cook E Jar** (100 West 2nd Street; 602-836-9294) serves up breakfast and lunch, as well as take-out bakery goods (even wedding cakes) and sandwiches. Budget prices.

TEA AT THE SPICERY

To the west of Phoenix, check out **The Spicery** *(7141 North 59th Avenue, Glendale; 602-937-6534) located in the Catlin Court Shops District, a downtown area where historic homes have been preserved. This moderate-priced eatery is in a charming, 1895 Victorian house. It offers tea service all day, as well as food the way mother used to make it—homemade soups, salads, chubby sandwiches, fresh-baked bread and pies.*

SOUTH OF PHOENIX SHOPPING

Gila River Indian Center (Gila River Reservation; 602-315-3411) has a shop selling traditional Native American arts and crafts, silver and turquoise jewelry, sandpaintings, kachina dolls, baskets and blankets.

Gila River Arts and Crafts (Casa Blanca Road, Sacaton; 602-963-3981) sells quality Native American items, including jewelry, baskets, kachina dolls, rugs and baskets.

Casa Grande, the main town along Route 10 between Phoenix and Tucson, is the site of the largest number of factory-owned **outlet stores** in Arizona. More than 70 are located in two sprawling commercial malls off Route 10 (take Exit 149, Florence Boulevard). More than a million shoppers a year come to Casa Grande seeking bargains from such major represented firms as **Liz Clairborne, American Tourister, Bugle Boy, Royal Doulton** and **Westpoint Pepperell**. For information, call Casa Grande Factory Stores at 602-421-0112.

The Sporting Life

Arizona's climate is ideal for recreational pursuits—most of the time. But during the summer scorchers, dry heat can be deceiving and you may think it's cooler than it actually is. So keep summer exertion to a minimum and play indoors, where there's air-conditioning, if you can.

RIVER RAFTING/TUBING

Three main rivers in central Arizona—the Verde, the Salt and the Gila, all east of Phoenix—offer a wealth of recreational activities year-round. In summer, they provide a welcome reprieve from the desert heat. A number of companies provide half-day, day and overnight rafting and tubing expeditions, with pick-ups, meals and guides included. Among them are the **Cimarron River Co.** (6925 5th Avenue, Suite E-6, Scottsdale; 602-994-1199); **Desert Voyagers Guided Rafting Tours** (P.O. Box 9053, Scottsdale, AZ 85252; 602-988-7238); and **Salt River Recreation Inc.** (Bush Highway and Usery Pass Road, Mesa; 602-984-3305).

JOGGING

The valley's extensive network of canals provides ideal, often shaded tracks. If you want to jog during the hot summers, stick to cooler early-morning hours. Phoenix's **Encanto Park**, three miles north of the Civic Plaza, is an excellent jogging trail. Scottsdale's **Indian Bend Wash Greenbelt** is a dream trail for joggers. It runs north and south for the entire length of Scottsdale, including 13 winding miles of jogging and bike paths laid out within the Greenbelt's scenic system of parks, lakes and golf courses.

SWIMMING

There are no beaches to speak of, but have no fear: So many swimming pools are found in south central Arizona that gathering rain clouds, so it's said, are often colored green from all the chlorine. Numerous public pools are available, more than 30 in Phoenix alone. To name just a few: **Cactus Pool** (3801 West Cactus Road; 602-262-6680); **Grant Pool** (701 South 3rd Avenue; 602-261-8728); **Starlight Pool** (7810 West Osborn Road; 602-495-2412); and **Washington Pool** (6655 North 23rd Avenue; 602-262-7198). For additional information and listings, call 602-258-7946.

More varied watery delights can be found at **Waterworld U.S.A.** (4243 West Pinnacle Peak Road, Phoenix; 602-266-5299; admission), which offers 20 acres of ridin', slidin', fun and sun with its Breaker Beach wave pool and six-and-a-half-story Avalanche Slide.

The Adobe Dam Recreation Area (northwest of Adobe Dam, just south of Pinnacle Peak Road between 35th and 51st avenues, Phoenix; 602-581-6691) also has a Family Water Park featuring a wave pool and waterslides.

In Tempe, **Big Surf** (1500 North Hayden Road; 602-947-7873; admission) includes 20 acres of sandy beach, a 300-foot surf slide, swimming and raft-riding in a gigantic, mechanically activated freshwater pool.

GOLF

Some of the country's finest courses can be found among south central Arizona's resorts, parks and country clubs. Two of the most spectacular are the **Wigwam Gold** (Litchfield and Indian School roads, Litchfield Park; 602-935-3808) and the **Gold Canyon Golf Club** (6100 South Kings Ranch Road, Apache Junction; 602-982-9449). The **Arizona Golf Association** (800-458-8484) can supply specifics.

Among the top public courses in Phoenix are **Encanto Park** (2705 North 15th Avenue; 602-495-0333); **Papago Golf Course** (5595 East Moreland Street; 602-495-0555); and **Palo Verde Golf Course** (6215 North 15th Avenue; 602-249-9930).

More than half of Arizona's 205 golf courses are located in south central Arizona, making Phoenix and environs the undisputed Golf Capital of the Southwest.

Scottsdale's top public courses include: **Continental Golf Course** (7920 East Osborn Road; 602-941-1585); **Coronado Golf Course** (2829 North Miller Road; 602-947-8364); **Tournament Players Club of Scottsdale** (17020 North Hayden Road; 602-585-3600); and the **Villa Monterey Golf Course** (8102 East Camelback Road; 602-990-7100).

Tempe has a number of fine courses open to the public, including **Ken McDonald Golf Course** (Western Canal and Rural roads; 602-350-5250); **Pepperwood Golf Course** (647 West Baseline Road; 602-831-9457); and **Rolling Hills Golf Course** (1415 North Mill Avenue; 602-350-5275).

TENNIS

The Valley of the Sun has even more tennis courts than it has swimming pools. Almost all of the parks in the valley's vast network have a court; for more information, call the **Parks and Recreation Department** (Phoenix, 602-262-6861; Scottsdale, 602-994-2408; or Maricopa County, 602-272-8871).

Among the Phoenix's numerous public courts are: **City Center Tennis Courts** (121 East Adams Street, atop the parking garage roof; 602-256-4120); the **Hole-in-the-Wall Racquet Club** (7677 North 16th Street, at the Pointe at Squaw Peak Resort; 602-997-2543); **Phoenix Tennis Center** (6330 North 21st Avenue; 602-249-3712); **Pointe Tapatio Cliffs Racquet Club** (11111 North 7th Street; 602-997-7237); and **Mountain View Tennis Center** (1104 East Grovers Avenue; 602-788-6088).

In Scottsdale, try **Indian School Park** (4289 North Hayden Avenue; 602-994-2740); **Chestnut Park** (4565 North Granite Reef Road; 602-994-2408); and **Mountain View Park** (8625 East Mountain View; 602-994-2584). Outstanding in Tempe is the **Kiwanis Recreation Center** (611 South All-American Way; 602-350-5201).

HORSEBACK RIDING

Dozens of stables, dude ranches and equestrian outfitters are available for saddling up and heading off into desert wilderness for a few hours or a few days under the supervision of a crusty trail boss. If there was ever a place for horsing around, it's here. For information, contact the **Arizona Equestrian Center** (1750 Notton Lane, Litchfield Park; 602-853-0011) or **Westworld** (16601 North Pima Road, Scottsdale; 602-483-8800). Or you can check out any of the following stables: **All Western Stables** (10220 South Central Avenue, Phoenix; 602-276-5862); **North Mountain Stables** (25251 North 19th Avenue, Phoenix; 602-581-0103); **Hank's Horse World Stables** (16601 North Pima Road, Scottsdale; 602-941-4756); **Old MacDonald's Farm** (26540 North Scottsdale Road, Scottsdale; 602-585-8239); and **Papago Riding Stables** (400 North Scottsdale Road, Tempe; 602-966-9793).

BALLOONING AND HANG GLIDING

Steady but manageable winds and constantly shifting updrafts and downdrafts make the valley ideally suited for ballooning. For gliding enthusiasts, the surrounding mountains provide the perfect setting to let it all hang out.

Dozens of firms will be happy to take you up, up and away, including **Aerostats Inc.** (21632 North 7th Avenue, Phoenix; 602-252-2664); **Xanadu Balloon Adventures** (3745 West Columbus Drive, Phoenix; 602-938-9324); **Hot Air Affair** (2980 North 73rd Street, Scottsdale; 602-423-8551); **Unicorn Balloon Co.** (15001 North 74th Street, Scottsdale; 602-991-3666); and **Adventures Aloft** (6716 East Malcomb Drive, Paradise Valley; 602-951-2650).

For hang gliding, try **Sky Sail School of Hang Gliding** (2237 East Karen Drive, Phoenix; 602-493-1216) or **Arizona Windsports** (1327 East Bell De Mar Drive, Tempe; 602-897-7172). Both offer instructions.

BICYCLING

A basic bikeway system was set up for Phoenix in 1987, and since then more than 100 miles of bike paths have been added. Unfortunately, there's a lot of traffic, so be ever cautious. A free Phoenix Bikeway System map is available at most bike shops, or call the Parks, Recreation and Library Department (602-262-6861); for bicycling events call 602-262-6542. Also, for special-event biking activities contact Arizona Bicycle Association (602-345-8747).

Phoenix's **South Mountain Park** (10919 South Central Avenue), **Cave Creek** and **Carefree**, 30 miles northeast of town, offer excellent biking conditions. Also popular is **Papago Loop Bicycle Path** through the rolling hills that border the canal edging Papago Park. In Scottsdale, the **Indian Bend Wash Greenbelt** has miles of excellent bike paths.

BIKE RENTALS   Bike-rental shops include the following: **Bike Den** (3450 West Dunlap Avenue, Phoenix; 602-973-3450); **Landis Cyclery** (712 West Indian School Road, Phoenix; 602-264-5681); **Try Me Bicycle Shop** (1514 West Hatcher Road, Phoenix; 602-943-1785); **Airplane and Bicycle Works of Wilbur and Orville** (4400 North Scottsdale Road, Scottsdale; 602-949-1978); **Bicycle Warehouse Co.** (4420 North Miller Road, Scottsdale; 602-949-7106); **Fun on Wheels** (7607 East McDowell Road, Scottsdale; 602-945-2881); **Tempe Bicycle** (267 East Bell Road, Tempe; 602-375-1515); and **Baseball Bicycles** (825 West Baseline Road, Tempe; 602-491-3921). **Bicycle Outfitters** (208 South Beeline, Payson; 602-474-3144) rents bicycles and rollerblades.

HIKING

With all that elbow room and knockout scenery, south central Arizona is a hiker's paradise. Visitors, in fact, have been known to park their cars on the highway and impulsively hike up the side of a mountain. Many of the parks have excellent hiking trails and there are some wonderful trails in other areas, as well.

PHOENIX AREA TRAILS   One of the best park trails in Phoenix's South Mountain Park is the **Hidden Valley Loop of the National Trail** (8 miles) that begins at the Buena Vista parking area and ends at Pima Canyon at 48th Street and Guadalupe Road. The trail passes stands of saguaro, but the highlights are The Tunnel—rock formations transformed into a water slide when it rains—and Fat Man's Pass, a tight squeeze between huge boulders where it is cool year-round.

The **Phoenix Mountain Preserve** has 200 miles of trails and nearly pristine areas virtually in the center of Phoenix. It stretches from Lincoln Drive in Paradise Valley north to Bell Road, bordered on the west by 19th Avenue and on the east by Tatum Boulevard. The Phoenix Parks, Recreation and Library Department (602-262-7901 or 602-262-7797) offers a free map of 45 marked trails within the preserve.

The preserve's most popular trail is the **Squaw Peak Summit Trail** (1 mile) that wraps its way up Squaw Peak, offering good lookout points along the way and, from its 2608-foot summit, a dramatic view of the city. (The only drawback is the number of fellow hikers you'll meet along the way.)

Be sure to take water with you when hiking in desert locations, and allow plenty of time to get there and back.

A more demanding trek, for experienced hikers only, is **Circumference Trail** (3.5 miles), beginning at the parking area at the end of Squaw Peak Drive and looping around the base of the peak in a northerly direction.

SCOTTSDALE AREA TRAILS   **Camelback Mountain** is the valley's best-known landmark, and serious hikers truly haven't hiked Arizona until they've conquered it. Part of the Echo Canyon Recreation Area (602-256-3220), Camelback offers sheer red cliffs that in some places rise 200 feet straight up its side. An interpretive ramada near the parking area offers information about the various trails.

A relatively easy climb of about four-fifths of a mile goes from the ramada to **Bobby's Rock**, a landmark formation of rocks set aside from the cliff and perfect for rock climbers. Also beginning at the ramada, the route to **Praying Monk** is more difficult. A stone formation rises at its summit high above Echo Canyon cliffs. From Praying Monk, the trail continues to the tip of Camelback Mountain, 2704 feet above sea level, 1.3 ever-upward miles. Echo Canyon is off McDonald Drive east of Tatum Boulevard.

NORTH OF PHOENIX TRAILS   A favorite at North Mountain Recreation Area is the **North Mountain National Trail** (1.6 miles) just off Seventh Street north of Peoria. The moderate to difficult paved trail climbs from 1490 feet to 2104 feet with scenic views along the way. It ends at the AK-CHIN picnic area.

The historic, 51-mile-long **Highline Trail** in the Tonto National Forest was established in the late 1800s to link various homesteads and ranches under the Mogollon Rim. In 1979, it was designated a National Recreation Trail. With 23 trailheads and spur trails, hikers can explore it in segments and loops. But a word of caution—most of the trails from the highline to the top of the rim are steep, rocky and rugged.

The main trail begins at the Pine Trailhead 15 miles north of Payson off Route 87 on Route 297, and ends at Two-Sixty Trailhead on Route 260. Shorter jaunts include **East Webber Trail** (3 miles), a difficult, little-used stretch that follows Webber Creek before ending at a spring. The most popular is **Horton Creek Trail** (4 miles), which starts at the Upper Tonto Creek Campground.

For the Highline Trails Guide, contact the Payson Chamber of Commerce (West Main Street; 602-474-4515) or the Payson Ranger Station on Route 260.

Transportation

BY CAR

Visitors driving to Phoenix by car are in for a treat. Arizona's highways are among the best in the country, gas is traditionally cheaper here and the scenery in any direction is spectacular—lofty saguaros, magnificent mountains, a cowboy here, a pickup truck there, beer signs blinking faintly in the purple glow of evening. Along the way, small western towns unfold like storybook pop-ups. **Route 10** traverses the city from the east (El Paso) and west (Los Angeles), passing through Tucson to the southeast. From the northwest, **Route 40**, once the legendary Route 66, enters Arizona near Kingman; **Route 93** continues on from there to Phoenix. **Route 17** heads north to Flagstaff and Sedona in the direction of the Grand Canyon.

BY AIR

With the recent completion of the Barry M. Goldwater Terminal 4 and a new four-gate international concourse, **Sky Harbor International Airport**, four miles from downtown Phoenix, is served by Aero California, Alaska Airlines, America West Airlines, American Airlines, Continental Airlines, Delta Airlines, Mesa Air, Northwest Airlines, Skywest Airlines, Southwest Airlines, Trans World Airlines, United Airlines and USAir.

A variety of ground transportation options are available from Sky Harbor Airport. **SuperShuttle** (602-244-9000) offers airport-to-door service 24 hours a day. **Courier Transportation** (602-244-1818) also provides transfers to and from the airport. **Arizona Shuttle Service** (602-795-6771) has service to and from Tucson. **Air Coach** (602-882-7661) provides shuttle service between Sky Harbor and Tucson. If you're heading north to red rock country, the **Sedona/Phoenix Shuttle Service** (602-282-2066) departs three times daily from Sky Harbor, making stops in Cottonwood and Sedona.

BY BUS

Greyhound Bus Lines has service to Phoenix from all around the country. The main Phoenix terminal is at 525 East Washington Street (602-248-4040). Other stations are found in Mesa (1423 South Country Club Drive; 602-834-3360) and Tempe (502 South College Avenue; 602-967-4030).

CAR RENTALS

If you arrive by air, you'll find plenty of car-rental agencies with counter space at the airport. These include **Advantage Rent A Car** (602-244-0450), **Alamo Rent A Car** (602-244-0897), **Avis Rent A Car** (602-273-3222), **Avon Rent A Car** (602-257-7777), **Budget Rent A Car** (602-267-4000), **Dollar Rent A Car** (602-275-7588), **Hertz Rent A Car** (602-267-8822), **National Interrent** (602-275-4771), **Resort Rent A Car** (602-220-0122) and **Superior Rent A Car** (602-275-5177). Agencies with pick-up service are **American International Car Rental** (602-273-6181), **Courtesy Rent A Car** (602-273-7503), **Enterprise Leasing and Rent A Car** (602-225-0588), **General Rent A Car** (602-273-0991), **Thrifty Car Rental** (602-244-0311) and **Value Rent A Car** (602-273-7425). For other agencies in south central Arizona, consult the local yellow pages.

PUBLIC TRANSPORTATION

The **Phoenix Transit Bus System** (602-253-5000) covers Phoenix and Scottsdale and provides express service to and from other districts within the valley. It also serves the Phoenix airport. Express buses access Phoenix from Mesa, Tempe and other suburbs. **The Molly Trolley** (602-941-2957) offers rubber-tire trolley service from 22 Scottsdale resorts and 12 shopping areas on day-pass basis; rides are free within the downtown shopping area. **Downtown Dash** (602-253-5000) serves the downtown Phoenix area with free shuttles that depart every ten minutes and loop the downtown area between the State Capitol, Arizona Center and the Civic Plaza weekdays.

TAXIS

Taxis are expensive in Phoenix, since the city sprawls out in all directions. Going from Point A to Point B, at times, may seem like you're crossing the entire state. Some of the major companies in the south central Arizona area are **AAA Cab** (602-253-8294), **ACE Taxi** (602-254-1999), **All American Cab** (602-252-1277), **American Cab** (602-941-0007), **ABC Cab** (602-254-8022 or 602-375-5079), **Courier Cab** (602-232-2222), **Quick Silver Taxi** (602-437-9063) and **Yellow Cab** (602-252-5252). AAA, Courier and Yellow are contracted with the airport in Phoenix.

AIR TOURS

Because Arizona is big-sky country, a great way to see it is by air. Several firms, all based out of Scottsdale's Airpark, offer tours of the Grand Canyon, Sedona, Monument Valley, Lake Powell and other scenic destinations. Among them are **Arizona Air** (602-991-8252), **Flight Quest Aviation** (602-991-5557) and **Sky Cab** (602-998-1778). **Corporate Jets** (602-948-2400) offers sunset champagne tours (none for the pilot) and Grand Canyon tours.

GLENN KIM.

NINE

Eastern Arizona

Perhaps no other region of the state is as geographically diverse as eastern Arizona. The seemingly endless urban sprawl of Phoenix, Tempe and Mesa quickly gives way to breathtaking scenery in the form of desert gardens, jagged river canyons, rolling grasslands and deep pine forests. Venture here and you'll find a wide variety of recreational opportunities, everything from fishing and hunting to hiking and skiing. There's also plenty of history—Indian ruins and old mining towns—to be discovered along the way.

The strip of eastern Arizona stretching 203 miles east of Phoenix along Routes 89, 60 and 70 to the New Mexico state line is known as The Old West Highway. Rich in frontier history, it travels a route of the notorious—from Coronado to Geronimo to Billy the Kid.

Anchored on the west by Apache Junction, a growing suburb of the Phoenix metropolitan area and a winter retreat for thousands of snowbirds, the Old West Highway is also the starting point for a scenic detour along the Apache Trail (Route 88). Today's adventurers can wend their way along the trail through the Superstition Mountains, to the reconstructed Goldfield Ghost Town, a series of lakes originating from the Salt River, colorful Tortilla Flat, the Lost Dutchman's Mine and finally Theodore Roosevelt Dam and Lake.

Continue east on the Old West Highway and you'll come to Globe, a quiet town that retains the flavor of the late 1800s. The Old West Highway flattens out east of Globe, and the countryside becomes more arid as you descend into the lower desert. The Mescal Mountains to the south escort you into the Gila River Valley, where the mesas and buttes of the San Carlos Apache Reservation stand out against the sky.

The "Apache Trail" was originally a construction road for the Theodore Roosevelt Dam, the country's first Federal Reclamation project, completed in 1911.

Route 70 branches off Route 60 east of Globe and crosses the southern tip of the 1.8-million-acre San Carlos Apache Reservation, which stretches from the White Mountains to within two miles of Globe, north to the Mogollon Rim and south to Coronado National Forest. An estimated 10,000 Apache live on the reservation, much of it wooded forests that are home to elk, mule deer, wild turkeys, black bear and mountain lions.

On the southern horizon stands Mount Graham, at 10,713 feet one of Arizona's highest peaks. In addition to being a popular fishing, camping and hiking area, the mountain is the site of the Mount Graham Observatory and Planetarium.

Route 70 continues on to the town of Safford, an important trade center for the Gila River Valley's numerous cotton farmers. From Safford, the Old West Highway cuts through the pastoral Duncan Valley, with its green alfalfa fields, grazing horses and trickling creeks at the eastern edge of Arizona. Duncan, the birthplace of Supreme Court Justice Sandra Day O'Connor, is a treasure trove of prehistoric Indian relics unearthed by builders of nearby irrigation canals. It is also a fertile source of fire agate, a relatively rare semi-precious stone, which can be picked up right off the ground in designated Bureau of Land Management areas.

North of Duncan on Route 666 is the historic mining town of Clifton, the southern anchor of the Coronado Trail, which climbs through the Apache-Sitgreaves National Forest on its 105-mile journey to Alpine, in the heart of Arizona's Alps.

The Coronado Trail, named for the Spanish explorer who sought the Seven Cities of Gold nearly 500 years ago, practically brushes the Arizona-New Mexico border. The trail runs north-south as Route 666 from St. Johns to Clifton via a winding and twisting paved highway, cutting through rugged mountains and magnificent forests—some of the most spectacular scenery in the Southwest.

The White Mountains offer high, cool country dotted with fishing lakes and blanketed in ponderosa pine, spruce, aspen and Douglas fir. At the heart of this area are Pinetop-Lakeside, Show Low and Greer. The main reason folks venture to this part of eastern Arizona is to enjoy the outdoors, whether by fishing, skiing, hiking or simply sitting on a rock with a picnic lunch, breathing in the scent of pine and watching the breeze ripple across a lake. These towns all abound with rustic lodges, inexpensive eateries and plenty of scenic beauty.

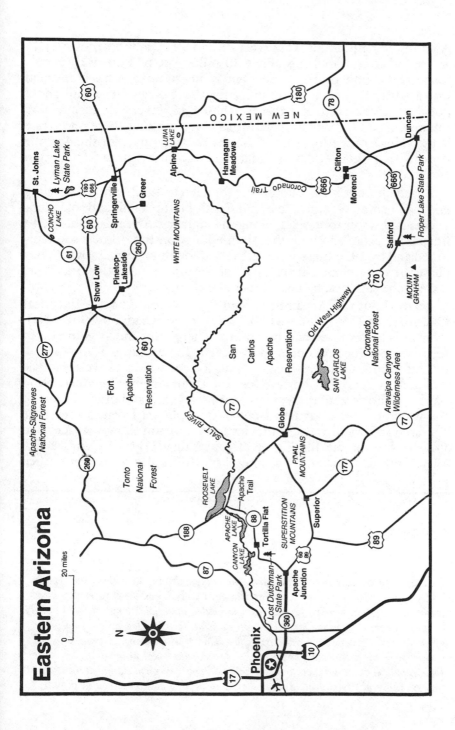

Eastern Arizona

Apache Junction Area

At the meeting point of Routes 60, 88 and 89, **Apache Junction** is in an area of rough lowlands about 30 miles east of Phoenix. Once a sunburned babble of bars, motels and filling stations, it has blossomed into a rustic bedroom community for the Valley of the Sun and a popular snowbird retreat that attracts about 35,000 people each winter, causing local dude ranch operators to complain that there's no range left to ride. Apache Junction is also the starting point for the 48-mile Apache Trail, Route 88, which slices its way through the Superstition Mountains.

Apache Junction was unofficially founded in 1922, when a traveling salesman named George Cleveland Curtis put up a tent and sold sandwiches and water to travelers along the highway. A year later he filed a homestead claim and built the Apache Junction Inn. Others soon followed and by 1950 there were enough residents to form a town. They chose the name Superstition City, but because it was an historical site, the Apache Junction name could not be changed.

Learn about the area's history and sights at the **Apache Junction Chamber of Commerce** (1001 North Idaho Road; 602-982-3141), which dispenses maps and brochures. There's not much going on in town, except for **Apacheland Western Town** (Kings Ranch Road, just off Route 60), a re-created back-lot collection of western-style buildings, wagon and horse rides, entertainment by the Apacheland cowboys, mock gunfights, songs, stories, legends and guided tours. If the structures look vaguely familiar, it might be because they have appeared in several western movies and television shows. Apacheland was the site for the filming of "Death Valley Days," "Gambler II," "The Apache Trail" and "Flaming Star." It has also been host to such

---

APACHE TRAIL

*For a truly spectacular view of the mountains, take a driving tour along the **Apache Trail**, which is Route 88 between **Tortilla Flat** and **Theodore Roosevelt Lake**. It was named after the Apache Indians who hauled materials along this road to help build Theodore Roosevelt Dam. The trail starts at Tortilla Flat, an old stagecoach stop with a café, general store and a post office. Then it winds along a narrow, unpaved road through the mountains, past Canyon and Apache lakes to the dam. En route, you can pull off at certain spots for hiking, picnicking or just plain staring at the beautiful scenery. Leave plenty of driving time; there's no turning back once you've begun.*

The triangular-shaped mountain east of the Superstitions is Weaver's Needle, which treasure hunters say is a marking point for the Lost Dutchman Mine.

---

movie stars and political figures as Ronald Reagan, Glen Ford, Audie Murphy, Elvis Presley and James Stewart.

The **Apache Trail**, Route 88 from Apache Junction to Roosevelt Lake, is less than a 100-mile drive, round-trip, but allow at least three hours for the winding journey. Once past the outskirts of Apache Junction, the trail enters the dacite cones of the **Superstition Mountains**, formed 20 million years ago when cataclysmic earthquakes and widespread volcanic eruptions pushed land masses thousands of feet into the air, and left a depression 20 miles wide. Magma from below the earth's surface flowed in and the Superstitions were formed.

With blunted peaks reaching well over 6000 feet and razor-edged canyons plunging into the pit of the earth, the Superstition Mountains now comprise an area 40 miles long and 15 miles wide—some of the roughest, rockiest, most treacherous terrain in the United States. But with the help of experienced guides, you can lash your gear to pack-horses and mount up for a three-day to seven-day—or longer—trip where you can pan for gold or search for the legendary Lost Dutchman Gold Mine, for which the mountains are most famous.

Treasure hunters may want to visit the **Superstition Mountain/ Lost Dutchman Museum** (Route 88; 602-983-4888; admission), which displays historical artifacts pertaining to the legend of the Lost Dutchman Gold Mine, along with folk art, prehistoric Indian artifacts, Spanish and Mexican crafts and documents, pottery and relics of early cowboys, prospectors and miners.

For a taste of the Old West, stop at **Goldfield Ghost Town** (four miles north of Apache Junction; 602-983-0333), which saw its heyday in the 1890s when gold was discovered at the base of the Superstitions. The weathered-wood buildings that house a restaurant, museum and antique shop look original, but they are actually re-creations, constructed in 1988. The old mining and railroad equipment scattered about are authentic, as are the museum's geology and mining exhibits and the underground mine, which you can tour.

Another mile along Route 88 is **Lost Dutchman State Park** (6109 North Apache Trail; 602-982-4485; admission), 292 acres of nature trails through saguaro, palo verde and other desert flora. Interpretive tours by park rangers are conducted from October through April.

Continuing north on Route 88 you'll find a chain of lakes originating out of the Salt River. They include Saguaro, Canyon and Apache lakes. The most accessible is **Canyon Lake**, which wends its way six-

and-a-half miles upstream through one continuous deep canyon. There are private and public boat facilities, beaches, picnic sites, a snack bar and campsites. Recreational activities include fishing (bass and walleye) and waterskiing. There's also a replica of a double-deck sternwheeler that plies the waters with its cargo of tourists and photographers.

Proceeding upstream, you'll pass geodes imbedded in sheer rock walls, deposited by eruptions millions of years ago, on your way to **Tortilla Flat** (17 miles from Apache Junction), which boasts a population of six people. One of the last remnants of the Old West, the town was once a stagecoach stop, complete with a school, general store, restaurant/saloon, hotel and post office, and was home to about 125 people. Today, only the general store, post office and restaurant remain. The restaurant/saloon, which looks like a wood-planked western movie set, is one of the most popular in the area and has hosted travelers from all over the country. Years of memorabilia hang from the natural-wood walls and ceiling, but most interesting are the thousands of dollar bills and foreign currency stuck to the walls with business cards from all over the world.

About five miles east of Tortilla Flat, the paved road surrenders to dirt and gravel and climbs to the top of Fish Creek Hill, which provides spectacular views of the canyon below. Descending the hill, the road twists through a narrow chasm along Apache Lake and finally arrives at **Theodore Roosevelt Dam** (45 miles east of Apache Junction). Completed in 1911, the 280-foot-high dam is the world's tallest. It is also the world's largest masonry dam, constructed entirely of quarry stone. Currently under construction is a concrete addition that will raise the dam's height by 77 feet and increase the reservoir's surface area by 200,000 acre-feet. A quarter-mile upstream from the dam, a

---

LOST DUTCHMAN GOLD MINE

One local legend that has endured for years is that of Dutchman Jacob Waltz, who supposedly found an old Spanish mine in the Superstition Mountains near what is now Apache Junction. He was vigilant about keeping its whereabouts secret, and died in the early 1890s without revealing its location. For a while people looked for the mine, then it was forgotten for about 30 years.

In the 1930s, Dr. Adolph Ruth came to the area claiming to have a map of the mine. One hot summer day he went into the area to search, and was never seen again. A few months later his skull was found with what looked like a bullet hole in it. Once again, interest in the mine was sparked and people continued the search. To this day, the treasure has never been found, but they're still looking.

Boyce Thompson Southwestern Arboretum claims to have the world's most extensive collection of desert plants.

1000-foot steel arch bridge spans a portion of the reservoir, Roosevelt Lake, giving tourists—and photographers—a better view of the dam.

From Roosevelt Dam you can return to Apache Junction, or continue on Route 88 (which becomes paved again) to **Tonto National Monument** (Arizona 88, Roosevelt; 602-467-2241), which contains the ruins of the apartment-style dwellings of the Salado people and is one of the state's better-preserved prehistoric Indian ruins. At the visitor center, you can see Salado crafts and tools and an audio-visual program. A highlight of the park itself is a steep, half-mile self-guiding trail that climbs 350 feet up to the 19-room Lower Ruin. With advance reservations, you can also tour the 40-room Upper Ruin.

Back on Route 60 about 25 miles east of Apache Junction near the tiny mining camp of Superior, is the **Boyce Thompson Southwestern Arboretum** (Route 60; 602-689-2811; admission). Located in the small town of Pinal, this Eden-like preserve boasts over 1500 specimens, including cacti, succulents and water-efficient trees and shrubs. Created between 1923 and 1929 as a museum of living plants, the arboretum has more than two miles of easy walking trails that wind through 35 acres of outdoor displays and historic buildings. Maintained by the University of Arizona as a desert biology research station, the arboretum also is home to 150 kinds of birds and 40 wildlife species. All the plants have tags for easy identification, including one of the long-time residents, a red gum eucalyptus that rises more than 100 feet and boasts a trunk eight feet in diameter. It was planted in 1929 as a six-foot sapling. Also of interest are the **Clevenger House**, a stone cabin built into a hillside, and the 26-room mansion, **Picket Post House**, built by copper magnate William Boyce Thompson in 1927. The arboretum's visitor center, a 1920s cut-stone house listed on the National Register of Historical Places, has an information desk and gift store selling books, cacti and various succulents.

Heading east from the Arboretum, Route 60 gradually climbs through Gonzales Pass until the desert gives way to the Tonto National Forest. The two-lane highway cautiously winds through enchanting **Devils Canyon**, an eerie though picturesque region that seems to change its mood as the day's sunlight progresses. Near sundown, when the shadows grow long, the granite rock formations take on the shape of giant trolls and gnomes, and appear to be crouching, as if to pounce on passing motorists. The canyon and highway are narrow, but there are ample pullouts to photograph or simply enjoy the scenery.

APACHE JUNCTION AREA LODGING

Equestrians will like **Meanwhile Back at the Ranch Guest Ranch** (6300 East Pioneer Street, Apache Junction; 602-982-2112), a bed and breakfast for both riders and horses set in the compound of a former working ranch. Its seven buildings accommodate 14 guests and as many horses, all of whom receive breakfast (continental for riders, feed for horses). Guest cabins are individually furnished, maintaining original western trappings, colonial rockers, bed covers with Native American and Southwest designs and paneled walls. Moderate.

The 130-room **Superstition Grande Hotel** (201 West Apache Trail, Apache Junction; 602-982-7411), at the gateway to the Superstition Mountains, is set up wagon wheel-style—a main building with a central courtyard is surrounded by eight motel-type spurs running from it. The Spanish-style main building is red-brick tile and white stucco. Rooms, brightly colored in pink and green, have modern furnishings; some have kitchenettes. The lobby is contemporary, the bar western with copper appointments. Outside, you'll find tennis and shuffleboard courts. A favorite of film crews shooting westerns in the area, the hotel has hosted John Wayne, Ronald Reagan, Richard Boone and other Hollywood stalwarts. Rooms where they stayed bear their names. Moderate in price.

The small, family-run **Palm Springs Motel** (709 East Ninth Avenue, Apache Junction; 602-982-7055) has clean, well-maintained rooms, some with refrigerators, all at budget prices.

In the Superstition foothills, the **Gold Canyon Resort** (6100 Kings Ranch Road, Apache Junction; 602-982-9090) features chalet-style guest rooms with dark-wood furniture, stone fireplaces, spa tubs, private patios and impressive views of the nearby mountain. Prices range from moderate to deluxe.

APACHE JUNCTION AREA RESTAURANTS

There's no shortage of charm at **Tortilla Flat Restaurant** (Route 88, 18 miles north of Apache Junction; 602-984-1776), whose weathered-wood exterior suggests a Wild West saloon. Inside, the natural-wood walls are covered with mining and cowboy artifacts, as well as business cards and currency from around the world. Home-cooked specials include oversized burgers, spicy hot chili and a few Mexican dishes. In the saloon section, you can belly up to the solid-wood bar, plant yourself on barstools topped with leather saddles, and pretend you're in Dodge City. Harry Connick, Jr. on the Wurlitzer jukebox will bring you back to reality.

The **Mining Camp Restaurant and Trading Post** (6100 East Mining Camp Road on the Apache Trail; 602-982-3181) is almost as famous as the Lost Dutchman Gold Mine—and it's easier to find. It's worth looking for, offering long wooden tables, planked floors, tin trays and cups, and family-style, all-you-can-eat dining—chicken, beef and barbecued ribs. Expect to be entertained by cowboy singers and slapstick western shootouts. Moderate.

Lake Shore Restaurant (14011 North Bush Highway; 602-984-5311) is a rustic, casual dining facility on Saguaro Lake with a deck where you can dine while enjoying a view of the lake. Shaded by a giant awning, this outdoor eatery is cooled by a mist system and ceiling fans. Start with a frozen strawberry daiquiri and then order from the menu featuring burgers, salads, sandwiches and fried fish (all you can eat on Friday). The upbeat tempo is enhanced by reggae, oldies and classical music. Moderate.

For a view of Canyon Lake, **Lakeside Canyon and Cantina** (Route 88; 602-380-1601) features three levels of dining and a deck built over the lake. The decor—mauves and teal—is more Californian than Arizonan. Out of the kitchen comes burgers, sandwiches, chicken and grilled rib eye steaks with mushrooms and onions. Featured is an all-you-can-eat fish fry on Fridays. Moderate.

For true western flavor, hitch your horse up at the always-crowded **Los Vaqueros** (101 West Apache Trail; 602-982-3407) and settle down to a rib-eye or T-bone, baked potato, biscuits and beans. There's foot-stomping music and occasionally a brawl at the bar. Los Vaqueros means "the cowboys," and there are plenty of them here. Moderate.

The **Sundancer Restaurant** (1535 East Highway 60; 602-982-6474) is a western-style steak house and saloon specializing in steaks, barbecued ribs, chicken, seafood and huge helpings of homemade desserts. On weekends, live country-and-western music fills the place with two-steppers. Moderate.

PINAL'S PAST

The small town of Pinal sprung up in the late 1800s after silver was discovered in the surrounding mountains. In addition to milling ore from the Silver King Mine, the town was a stopping-off place for such Old West legends as Bat Masterson, Wyatt Earp and Doc Holliday. In fact, Holliday's girlfriend, Bignose Kate, died at Pinal, and is buried there.

APACHE JUNCTION AREA SHOPPING

If you plan to track down the Lost Dutchman Gold Mine, or even if you don't, **Pro-Mack South** (940 West Apache Trail; 602-983-3484) sells prospecting supplies, gold pans, lanterns, picks, boots and just about everything but the treasure map. You'll find a few souvenirs at gift shops in the **Tortilla Flat Restaurant** (Route 88, 18 miles north of Apache Junction; 602-984-1776) and **Goldfield Ghost Town** (Route 88, four miles north of Apache Junction; 602-983-0333).

APACHE JUNCTION AREA NIGHTLIFE

A live western band stomps away every night at **Los Vaqueros** (101 West Apache Trail; 602-982-3407); that's where everybody goes.

APACHE JUNCTION AREA PARKS

Just northwest of the Superstition Mountains is the **Usery Mountain Recreation Area**, a 3324-acre wilderness area with an extensive hiking and riding trail system. The Salt River chain of lakes—Saguaro, Canyon and Apache—are developed for fishing, boating, swimming, picnicking, hiking and camping. Facilities include RV sites with hookups, picnic sites, restrooms, showers and horse staging areas. The Apache Lake Marina (Route 88; 602-467-2511) offers boat rentals, storage and gas, plus a motel and restaurant. Canyon Lake Marina (Route 88; 602-986-5546) is a full-service marina with a restaurant and campgrounds. To get there from Apache Junction, drive north on Ellsworth

---

TONTO NATIONAL FOREST

*Ranging from Sonoran Desert to sprawling forests of ponderosa pine, **Tonto National Forest's** nearly 2.9 million acres serve as an outdoor playground for visitors, who can enjoy tubing, rafting and fishing on the Salt and Verde rivers. Forest lakes— Saguaro, Apache, Canyon, Roosevelt, Barlett and Horseshoe Reservoir—serve as watersheds, wildlife habitats and recreational sites for camping, swimming, fishing and boating. Tonto Natural Bridge, the largest known travertine bridge in the world, is a popular attraction, as was Zane Grey's cabin until it burned down in 1990. (The Zane Grey Society has plans for its restoration.) The famed Apache Trail is found here as well, via Routes 60 and 89 east. The scenic drive follows the trail originally used by the Apache as a shortcut through the Superstition Mountains.*

In Apache Junction, a statue of Jacob Waltz in the center of the town honors the man believed to have discovered an elusive gold treasure, but who died with the secret of its location unspoken—the Lost Dutchman Gold Mine.

Road, which becomes Usery Pass Road at McKellips Road. Continue to the park entrance.

Fed by Tonto Creek from the north and the Salt River from the east, **Theodore Roosevelt Lake** has more than 88 miles of shoreline, and hundreds of coves that provide excellent bass and crappie fishing, as well as hideaways for campers and picnickers. On Route 88 near Theodore Roosevelt Dam, facilities at the lake include a boat launch and rentals, a grocery store, snack bar, restrooms and picnic tables. There's also a resort motel with a steak house, cocktail lounge and trailer park.

Globe

East of Devils Canyon, the Pinal Mountains rise to dominate the horizon, until the historic old copper-mining town of **Globe** wrests control of the horizon. This quiet old copper town with its many Victorian homes dotting the hillsides, retains the flavor of the late 1800s with a turn-of-the-century main street, complete with an old-fashioned F. W. Woolworth store. Here, you'll find one of the finest Native American archaeological sites in the state.

Globe began as a mining town in the 1860s after silver was discovered on the Apache reservation. It is named for a spherical silver nugget with markings that resemble the continents. After the silver mines were depleted, copper was discovered, but those mines, too, were shut down by the Great Depression. The town has been dozing in the sun ever since.

On your drive into Globe (if arriving from the west), you'll notice massive man-made hills of bleached-out dirt, a by-product of the copper mining operations here. The white mesas, which stretch for a couple of miles, are what's left after the ore has been bleached, crushed and smelted. Attempts to grow vegetation in the miniature moonscape have been all but futile, so the mountains of residue remain, perhaps to be recycled as new mining techniques allow extraction of more copper from them.

Also on the west side of town along Route 60 are five mines that you can visit on a "drive-by" tour. Among them are the Pinto Valley Mine, which produces six pounds of copper from each ton of rock; the Blue Bird Mine, which boasts the first solvent extraction electro-winning operation in the world; and the Sleeping Beauty Mine, which produced copper until 1974, when it was converted to a turquoise operation. For a map of the driving tour, as well as other information, stop at the **Greater Globe–Miami Chamber of Commerce** (1360 North Broad Street, Globe; 602-425-4495). Be sure to ask for the walking tour of downtown Globe, and directions to the archaeological ruins.

Set among modern homes and paved streets, **Besh–Ba–Gowah Archaeological Park** (one mile southwest of town on Jess Hayes Road near the Globe Community Center; 602-425-0320; admission) is a prehistoric pueblo village built from rounded river cobblestone and mud walls, which surround rooms and plazas. Here, you can climb a rough wooden ladder and examine rooms with pottery and utensils that were used 600 years ago. There's also a weaver's loom, a pot over a firepit, manos and metates. A nearby museum displays artwork and utensils of the Salado, an advanced band of hunters and gatherers who lived here from 1100 to 1400 A.D. The Salado built a pueblo of more than 200 rooms (146 on the ground floor and 61 second-story rooms) around three central plazas, which housed an estimated 1400 people during its peak. During their stay, they farmed along the banks of Pinal Creek, growing crops of corn, beans, squash and possibly cotton. The community was also a trade center: Archaeologists have found evidence of trade in the form of copper bells and feathers from Meso America; shells from either the coast of present-day California or the Gulf of Mexico; and pottery from various regions.

The Salado made pottery of their own, which is on display: black-and-white designs on red clay. They also wove baskets, sandals and mats of sotol and yucca fibers, as well as fine cotton cloth. Bracelets, rings and necklaces were made from the shells they received in trade. A great drought during the 15th century is believed to have driven the Salado from the region. In addition to the partially restored pueblo,

---

ARIZONA'S RENAISSANCE FESTIVAL

*Just 12 miles east of Apache Junction on Route 60, you'll see a flat piece of grassland called Queen's Valley, which undergoes an interesting transformation each February and March when the **Renaissance Festival Arizona** takes place. Hundreds of costumed performers recreate the atmosphere of an Elizabethan Market Faire with jousting tournaments, strolling musicians and jugglers, medieval games and festive ceremonies. The event is staged over six weekends and draws more than 100,000 visitors. For information, contact Renaissance Festival Arizona (12601 East Highway 60; 602-463-2600).*

Globe, at the eastern end of the Apache Trail, was originally named "Besh-Ba-Gowah" by the Apache, meaning "place of metal" or "metal camp."

there's a museum/visitors center that displays artifacts found during early excavations.

After leaving the archaeological park, you can get an eagle's eye view of the Globe-Miami area by making a right turn on Jess Hayes Road, then driving to Ice House Canyon Road and Kellner Canyon, where you will circle up through the beautiful Pinal Mountains for 15 miles. At the 7850-foot level you'll pass through ponderosa pine, ferns and thick foliage. Pull out anywhere and the overlooks will give you sweeping views of Globe-Miami below.

In town, the area's frontier past is recorded in the **Gila County Historical Museum** (1330 North Broad Street, Globe; 602-425-7385), a 1914 Spanish-style bungalow with an arched entry and red-tile roof, which once served as the Dominion Mine rescue station. Inside, there's a mint-condition Seagrave fire engine, completely furnished miner's shack, tack room with cowboy gear, an early bedroom with frontier clothing, a wet plate camera and other artifacts.

The **Old Dominion Mine**, across from the museum on Broad Street, is what's left of what was once the world's richest copper mine. In the 1930s, the depressed price of copper, coupled with increasing water seepage into the mine shafts, forced the closure of the mine. Today the mine belongs to Magma Copper Company and is a valuable source of water, which is vital to the company's other operations in the area.

Drive about a mile south on Broad Street until you reach downtown Globe, where a stroll is a walk into history. Standing tall at the end of the block is the former **Gila County Courthouse** (100 North Broad Street) built in 1906. This stately sandstone-brick structure, which was named to the National Register of Historic Places in 1975, now houses the Cobre Valley Center for the Arts. Climb the 26 stone steps (wheelchair entrance is on Oak Street) and enter the carved wooden doors to find finished hardwood floors, arched passways, grand rooms with high ceilings and tall windows, and a staircase accented with copper banisters and overhead skylight. Notice that in nearly every room there's a vault. When the building served as a courthouse, various documents were stored in the building; the vaults were added for their protection. The entire first floor is currently a gallery for the Arts Guild. The second floor is home to the Copper Cities Community Players, who have converted the large rooms into studios and a small theater.

Also worth visiting are the **Globe Elks Lodge** (155 West Mesquite Avenue), the country's tallest three-story building, built in 1910; the

old **Gila County Jail** (behind the Gila County Courthouse), constructed of reinforced concrete in 1909, with cell blocks transported
from the Yuma Territorial Prison; and the **Gila Valley Bank and
Trust Building** (corner of Mesquite Avenue and Broad Street), with
its white terra-cotta facade, an unusual example of the Beaux-Arts
neoclassical style of 1909. The building was the pioneer branch of
what is now Valley National Bank.

The **Country Corner Antique Store** (383 South Hill Street) was
the town's grocery and mercantile when built in 1920. If the shape of
the building seems odd it's because the structure was designed in the
shape of the state of Arizona. The **F. W. Woolworth** (127 North Broad
Street) is part of the Sultan Building, originally built as a two-story
brick structure in 1909. Next door, the art deco-style **Globe Theater**
(141 North Broad Street) was built in 1918 and features copper-covered
pillars under the marquee. A block west of Brush Street in Oak Street
Park you'll find old **Engine No. 1774**, one of only seven remaining
steam locomotives in existence. Originally, 355 were built between
1899 and 1901. Cowboy star Gene Autry owns one of the other seven.

If you want more history, the city sponsors an **Historic Home and
Building Tour and Antique Show** in February. Many of the structures were built by the same stonemasons who worked on nearby Roosevelt Dam. The tour usually consists of six to eight buildings. A recent
one included a 1911 home built from dacite stones, a material quarried
locally; a church that was hand-built by Episcopalian priests between
1900 and 1908; and a plantation-style mansion built in the late 1800s,
complete with upper and lower verandas.

GLOBE LODGING

Despite the town's careful attention to preserving historic buildings,
Globe's accommodations are strictly standard highway motels, nearly
two dozen of them. But they provide reliable service at budget to
moderate prices. Recommended are the **Copper Manor Motel** (637

THE SAN CARLOS APACHE RESERVATION

Globe is the commercial gateway to the **San Carlos Apache Reservation***, the two-
million-acre expanse that's home to nearly 10,000 Apache. Rambling and remote,
lush and rustic, the land is a natural habitat for javelina, elk, bear, waterfowl, grouse,
quail, rabbits and a variety of fresh-water fish. Camping, hunting and fishing are permitted, with licenses. Contact the Recreation and Wildlife Department, 602-475-2343.*

As you leave the San Carlos Apache Reservation, notice the telephone poles sunk into the ground near Calva Crossing. They control rain run-off and were planted there after the flood in 1983.

East Ash Street; 602-425-7151), which has 62 modern guest rooms, an outdoor pool and all-night restaurant. Budget.

One of the nicer motels is the **Cloud Nine Motel** (1699 East Street; 602-425-5741), which offers ultra-clean guest rooms decorated in cool pastels with refrigerators and spa tubs. Moderate.

A perfect lakeside retreat for water sports enthusiasts is the **Roosevelt Lake Marina Motel** (Route 88; 602-467-2245) with 21 rooms overlooking the lake. It's rustic (no television or telephone), but the staff couldn't be more folksy. Budget.

GLOBE RESTAURANTS

Most locals agree some of the best food in town is at **Jerry's Restaurant** (699 East Ash Street; 602-425-5282), a fast-paced, coffee-shop style eatery that dishes up hearty portions of steaks, chops, meatloaf, fish and other American stand-bys. Moderate.

Don't let the decor at **La Luz Del Dia** (304 North Broad Street; 602-425-8400) fool you. Despite the old-fashioned counter, mushroom stools and vinyl booths, this isn't a 1950s burger joint; it's a Mexican bakery and coffee shop with a tasty selection of Mexican sweet rolls, buns and churros, as well as quesadilla and tortillas. Budget.

For a more varied Mexican menu, try **El Rey Café** (Route 60-70; 602-425-6601), which might be small in size but is big in flavor. House specials include enchiladas, chile rellenos, green-corn tamales, tacos and chimichangas. Moderate.

The **Blue Ribbon Café** (474 North Broad Street; 602-425-4423) in Globe's historic downtown district is a popular breakfast spot because of the homemade biscuits and gravy. It's also busy at lunchtime serving sandwiches, salads, burgers, pasta and pasties—beef, potatoes and onions wrapped in pastry. Don't leave without trying a wedge of homemade pie. Moderate.

If you prefer oriental cuisine, the **Jasmine Tea House** (1097 North Broad Street; 602-425-2503) serves Mandarin and Szechuan dishes of pork, beef, duck, chicken and seafood. Moderate.

GLOBE SHOPPING

If you enjoy leisurely browsing, come to the **Rose House Gallery** (306 Cotton Street; 602-425-3461), a converted two-story brick home with a pillared porch built in 1906. Inside, it has an open staircase, sliding pocket doors, ornate carved woodwork and a tiled fireplace. For sale and on display are arts and crafts by local artists in oils, acrylic, pastels, pen and ink, quilting and woodwork.

For more art and culture, it's the **Cobre Valley Center for the Arts** (100 North Broad Street; 602-425-0884), in the historic Gila County Courthouse. Here you'll find arts and crafts produced by local members of the Cobre Valley Fine Arts Guild (cobre is Spanish for copper). Media represented include stain glass, ceramics, painting (oil, acrylic, watercolors), sculpture (stone, metal, wood, plastic), photography, jewelry (silver, stone, beaded) and mixed media. There are also prints, batik silk scarfs and gift items such as southwestern-designed soap and stationary, books and painted furniture. Climb a flight of stairs and you'll find studios of the Copper Cities Community Players. The huge room on your right is the Players' theater, but was once the old county courtroom. If you're lucky, you may happen onto a rehearsal for an upcoming play or dance recital.

The flavor of the Old West Highway is found at **The Diggin's** (254 North Broad Street; 602-425-0355), which has a fine selection of bronze western sculpture, antiques and collectibles, ceramics, original paintings by DeGrazia and Rockwell, wood crafts, pewter figures, tin toys and porcelain dolls.

Don't be surprised to run across genuine cowboys at **Bacon's Boots and Saddles** (290 North Broad Street; 602-425-2681) the home of the last of the great saddle makers. Owner Ed Bacon has been hand-crafting saddles for more than 40 years. His shop also features a full range of western wear, leather goods and hand-crafted silver belt buckles.

Antique shops are always fun and **Around the Globe Antiques** (286 North Broad Street) is no exception with its interesting selection of old radios, appliances, glassware and other collectibles.

THE REAL GERONIMO

The San Carlos Apache Reservation was where Geronimo and his Chiricahua followers were vanquished with other Apache tribes. But twice he left the reservation to resume his war with the U.S. Army. Born near Clifton, Geronimo gained notoriety in the 1870s when he and his braves terrorized southern Arizona and northern Mexico. Although there is little dispute that Geronimo participated in several massacres, recent historians are defending him as a protector of his homeland and a victim of wild stories spread by frightened settlers. Geronimo surrendered three times to the U.S. Army—the last time in 1886—before ending his personal war, and spent his final years raising watermelons and vegetables at Fort Sill, Oklahoma, where he died of pneumonia.

In Globe, Woolworth has occupied the same building since 1916, making it the oldest continuously operating Woolworth west of the Mississippi.

West of Globe on Route 60, **Pastime Antiques** (1068 Adonis Street, Miami; 602-473-3791) is filled with antique furniture, paintings, western memorabilia, historic photos, old magazines, postcards, posters and other relics and remnants of the past. Even the building is a treasure. It used to be the town library.

GLOBE NIGHTLIFE

Not much happens after dark, but you can see current movies at the **Globe Theater** (141 North Broad Street; 602-425-5581), or have a drink at **Under the Palms Cocktails** (230 North Broad Street; 602-425-2823).

GLOBE PARKS

San Carlos Lake was created by the construction of the Coolidge Dam, is about 30 miles east of Globe. When full, the lake has 158 miles of shoreline. Anglers will be challenged by catfish, bass and crappie. For information about camping and hiking on tribal lands and fishing in San Carlos Lake, stop at the tribal administration office in San Carlos.

Safford Area

Lying low in the fertile Gila River Valley is **Safford**, a trade center for the valley's numerous cotton farmers, and jumping-off point for outdoor recreation in the Coronado National Forest. Just west of town are the adjoining communities of Thatcher and Pima. Named to commemorate a Christmas visit by Mormon apostle Moses Thatcher, the town is home to Eastern Arizona College; nearby Pima is the site of the Eastern Arizona Museum.

Safford's main highway is lined with modern shopping centers, but the downtown district, with its wood-frame and mason buildings, suggests a Midwestern burrough. Despite the arid climate, the valley is irrigated by the Gila River and cotton is king here. The **Safford Valley Cotton Growers** (120 East 9th Street; 602-428-0714) has one of a handful of gins in the area that you can tour in season, typically September through January. Call ahead for reservations.

Underground hot springs are another natural resource in Safford. To take a dip, stop by **Kachina Mineral Springs Spa** (Cactus Road just off Route 666; 602-428-7212; charge for services) where you can soak in springs funnelled into tiled, Roman-styled tubs. Other amenities include massages, sweat wraps and reflexology (therapeutic foot massage). Although it's a tacky, run-down place, the baths are wonderful and the tubs are clean.

A good first stop is the **Safford-Graham County Chamber of Commerce** (1111 Thatcher Boulevard; 602-428-2511) for brochures and maps. One of the town's main landmarks is the **Safford Courthouse** (8th Avenue at Main Street), a neo-colonial brick building with white pillars built in 1916. Across the intersection is the 1898-vintage **city hall** (717 Main Street), which was the town's original schoolhouse.

Just outside of town, the quiet residential neighborhoods are dotted with elegant old homes. One of them is the **Olney House** (1104 Central Avenue), built in 1890 by George Olney, a former sheriff of Graham County. The two-story home features a plantation-style upper and lower front veranda. It is currently used as a bed-and-breakfast inn (see "Safford Area Lodging" below for more information).

For a glimpse at the area's past, visit the **Graham County Historical Society Museum** (808 Eighth Avenue; 602-428-1531), which contains a photo gallery of Graham County along with western and Native American artifacts.

The **Eastern Arizona Museum** (Highway 70 at Main Street, Pima; 602-485-2288) is small, but has an interesting collection of pioneer and Indian relics in a turn-of-the-century building.

Archaeology buffs can check out the **Museum of Anthropology** (Eastern Arizona College, 400 College Avenue, Thatcher; 602-428-1133). Exhibits include pottery and jewelry, a stratigraphic depiction

---

THE LEGACY OF BILLY THE KID

Although William Bonney—alias "Billy the Kid"—established his legend in New Mexico, local historians say he killed his first victim in Bonita, about 35 miles south of Safford on Route 266. The town's two-story general store, which was originally built in the 1870s as George Atkins' Saloon, remains a gathering place for local ranchers and farmers, who will point out bullet holes in the store's ceiling; outside, they'll show you the spot that Billy the Kid shot and killed Francis P. "Windy" Cahill on August 17, 1877.

of Gila Valley prehistory, and a diorama of late Ice Age Arizona. Indian artifacts on display include arrowheads, pottery and jewelry, plus a hands-on area for children, who can try chiseling their own arrowheads or rubbing sticks together to create fire.

Nearby 10,717-foot **Mount Graham** makes for good scenic drives, and its unique ecosphere provides a succession of climate zones, each with its own ecology. The main access road to the mountain is Swift Trail, which at first passes through stands of prickly pear, mesquite, creosote and ocotillo in the lower foothills. As you rise in elevation, the dominant trees are various types of oak, alligator juniper and piñon pine. At the highest elevation (8000 feet) you'll find a profusion of ponderosa pine, Douglas fir, aspen and white fir, some of them dating to 1200 A.D. Botanists say the Douglas firs have survived because the rocky cliffs of the mountains have protected them from the harsh environment. On the drive up the mountain you'll notice an apple orchard maintained under a special use permit from the U.S. Forest Service. During the late summer and early fall you can purchase fruit at roadside stands. The first 28 miles of Swift Trail are paved, the last seven are gravel.

The **Mount Graham International Observatory** (602-621-6524) on Emerald Peak features a 12-meter binocular telescope—the world's largest of its type—as well as a 1.8-meter Lennon Telescope and a Submillimeter telescope. Expansion of the facility will add three other telescopes including an eight-meter class infrared/optical telescope. Check with the University of Arizona's Department of Astronomy (602-621-6524) for progress on the expansion projects.

SAFFORD AREA LODGING

The nicest accommodations are at the **Olney House Bed and Breakfast** (1104 Central Avenue, Safford; 602-428-5118), a western Colonial Revival home with three guest rooms, all with original oak fireplaces and antiques. Scattered throughout are Asian decorations from the owners' travels, and in the dining room is a mural painted by a Native American artist. Guests start the morning with a western breakfast. Before leaving, be sure to see the pecan tree, which they claim is the tallest in Arizona. Moderate.

The rest of Safford's lodgings are mostly chain motels. You won't be disappointed with the **Budget Host Sandia Motel** (520 East Highway 70; 602-428-5000 or 800-578-2151), which features moderately priced rooms with refrigerators and microwaves, a pool, hot tub and even an outdoor basketball court.

The **Country Manor Motel** (420 East Highway 70, Safford; 602-428-2451) also features modest, well-kept rooms with refrigerators and barbecue facilities. Moderate.

SAFFORD AREA RESTAURANTS

The best restaurant in town is **El Coronado** (409 Main Street; 602-428-7755), a friendly place with blue-vinyl booths, ceiling fans and a deep narrow dining room. The tasty Mexican specialties include green chile chimichangas and quesadillas stuffed with green chili, meat, chicken, chorizo and chopped green chile. American dishes include chicken fried steak, shrimp and sandwiches. Budget.

    El Charro (628 Main Street; 602-428-4134) is a homey little café with wood-paneled walls and Native American accents. The specialty here is spicy green chili chimichangas, chicken tacos, enchiladas and fajitas. You can also order tasty fried shrimp or cod fillet dinners. On Wednesday nights, the Old Time Fiddlers keep the place hopping.

    For a late-night meal, the **Country Manor House** (420 East Route 70; 602-428-2451), adjacent to the Country Manor Motel, is open 24 hours a day. Old farm implements hang on the walls and you're likely to see a table of old-timers shooting the breeze and eating home-cooked meals such as chicken-fried steak, liver and onions and meatloaf. Budget.

    The Branding Iron Restaurant (north on Eighth Avenue and left on River Road; 602-428-6252) is a ranch-style building flanked by large trees. They serve western broiled steaks, chicken, seafood, barbecued ribs in a dining room that overlooks the Gila Valley. Moderate.

SAFFORD AREA SHOPPING

Rockhounds will love **Arizona Gems and Crystals** (414 5th Street; 602-428-5164), which has a wide variety of minerals, jewelry, beads, southwestern art and crafts, and lapidary supplies. It's also one of the largest retailers of green peridot—80 percent of it is mined from the local Apache reservation.

    If you haven't yet found the right gift to take home, try **Brown's Turquoise Shop** (2248 First Avenue; 602-428-6433), which offers a variety of southwestern jewelry and crafts such as hand-crafted sterling silver, kachinas, Mana pottery and black gold. Also of interest is the rough and cut natural Morenci turquoise.

    You can't miss **Pollock's Western Outfitters** (610 Fifth Street; 602-428-0093) with its distressed-wood exterior and horse statue on the roof. Inside, there's the latest western fashions, accessories and tack. Suppliers include Levi, Rocky Mountain, Justin, Tony Lama, Stetson and Resistol. You'll also find Murphy leather goods and King ropes.

    The small shops on downtown's Main Street are fun to explore. In addition to T-shirt and thrift shops, jewelry stores and western-wear boutiques, you'll find **Toys 'n Tools** (419 Main Street; no phone), a funky little shop where you can buy a stuffed animal, Barbie doll or a torque wrench. The **Safford Book Center** (430 Main Street; 602-428-1529) has an interesting selection of southwestern books, maps and cards, plus Native American pottery and other crafts. At the **Gila Music Company** (406 Main Street; 602-428-0340), you can buy a new guitar pick or pick up a pinball machine or arcade game for your rumpus room.

SAFFORD AREA NIGHTLIFE

Locals converge on **Smokey Bob's** (503 Main Street; 602-428-2727) for country music and line dancing every weekend. **The Saddleman Steakhouse and Lounge** (400 East Route 70; 602-428-2694) also offers country music (what else?) on weekends along with free dance lessons.

SAFFORD AREA PARKS

Roper Lake State Park, six miles south of Safford off Route 666, offers swimming in a 30-acre lake with a beach, or you can soak outside in a rock tub filled with hot springs bubbling up from the ground. The 240-acre park also includes a refuge for endangered fish in two ponds. For meals, sit out on the peninsula's grassy picnic area under a grove of shade trees.

Mount Graham in the Pinaleno Mountains is a favorite with hikers, campers and anglers, who find fighting trout in 11-acre Riggs Lake near its summit. There are several picnic areas and national campgrounds along the drive to the peak. Noon Creek Picnic area (5800 feet) has tables, grills for cooking and bear-proof trash cans. Overnight camping is allowed at Arcadia Campground (6700 feet), offering campsites, water and restrooms. Beware of poison ivy in this area. Ten miles farther up the road is Shannon Campground (9100 feet) with water, restrooms, campsites and a creek that meanders through the meadow. At the end of the road is Riggs Flat, which adjoins the man-made lake stocked with trout. Facilities include campsites, water, restrooms and picnic areas. Overall, there are seven developed campgrounds (fee for overnight camping) and free primitive camping allowed anywhere in the area. To get there, drive south from Safford for seven miles on Route 666 and turn west at the Mount Graham sign.

Six miles farther south on Route 666 is **Dankworth Pond**, which features two developed areas, each flanking a small man-made lake. Along the west side of the lake are picnic ramadas and restrooms, with camping available. Facilities include a boat ramp, swimming beach and nature trails. You'll also find some mineral hot springs here.

Aravaipa Creek flows through the 11-mile-long **Aravaipa Canyon Wilderness**, bordered by spectacular cliffs. Lining the creek are large sycamore, ash, cottonwood and willow trees, making it a colorful stop in the fall. You may spot javelina, coyotes, mountain lions and desert bighorn sheep, as well as nearly every type of desert songbird and more than 200 other bird species. To get to the East Trailhead, drive on Route 70 about 15 miles northwest of Safford, then turn off on Klondyke Road. Or follow Route 666 19 miles south of Safford and turn on the Fort Grant Road, then follow the signs.

Cluff Ranch Wildlife Area (602-485-9430), about nine miles northwest of Safford, contains 1300 acres of wildlife sanctuary and recreational areas. Streams from Mount Graham feed four ponds that provide year-round fishing for trout, catfish, largemouth bass and bluegill. Birding is also excellent here.

St. Johns Area

If you're coming from the north, the **Coronado Trail** (Route 180/666), named after the Spanish explorer who first sojourned here, begins innocently enough in the high desert area near St. Johns, a region of juniper-dotted hillsides, alfalfa pastures, grazing cattle and a few sandy-topped buttes about 44 miles southeast of Petrified Forest National Park. The trail meanders south through Apache-Sitgreaves National Forest to Clifton.

Built along the banks of the Little Colorado River, **St. Johns**, with a population of about 4000, serves as the Apache County seat. The town has few sights, except for the **St. Johns Equestrian Center** (adjacent to St. Johns Airport; 602-337-4517), which is rapidly becoming one of the premier equestrian facilities in the Southwest, attracting horses and riders from New Mexico, Colorado and Utah, as well as throughout Arizona. Surrounded by rolling hills and juniper-studded deserts, amenities include an 80-acre cross-country course, rodeo arena, show and dressage rings, six-furlong race track, stables and RV sites. In the spring and summer, the center hosts local and regional events, both western and English, rodeos and other horse competitions.

You can find out about the area's history at the **Apache County Historical Society Museum** (180 West Cleveland Avenue; 602-337-4737; donation), which houses displays that include a set of prehistoric woolly mammoth tusks and a camel's leg bone, both estimated to be about 24,000 years old.

As the Coronado Trail climbs on its journey south, chaparral gives way to pine and aspen, and you pass **Nelson Reservoir**, a 60-acre lake stocked with rainbow, brown and brook trout. If you're ready for a break, there are picnic grounds, restrooms, a boat ramp, but no overnight camping.

South of the reservoir are the rolling **Escudilla Mountains**, a 5000-acre wilderness area with forests of spruce, fir, pine and aspen, and nature trails where hikers are often rewarded with raspberries, elderberries and gooseberries, and glimpses of elk and deer in their natural habitat.

ST. JOHNS AREA LODGING

St. Johns' lodging scene is unexceptional, but you'll find well-maintained budget-priced rooms at **Trail Riders Inn** (125 East Commercial Street; 602-337-4422), a trailer-court type of motel with old-fashioned casement windows and adobe-like walls. The always-dependable **Whiting Brothers Motor Hotel** (75 East Commercial Avenue; 602-337-2990) offers all the standard amenities including outdoor pool, phones, in-room coffee and cable color television at budget rates.

ST. JOHNS AREA RESTAURANTS

A popular local hangout and city landmark is **Katie's Kountry Kitchen** (106 West Cleveland Street; 602-337-2129), which features a stagecoach and wagon wheels at the entrance. Inside, the western atmosphere is punctuated by dark-wood paneling, open-beam ceilings and cast-iron utensils on the walls. Seating is of the early dinette variety, but the unpretentious American fare is plentiful. Specialties include chicken-fried steak, roast beef and rib-eye steaks. Budget to moderate.

For a more varied menu, try the **Rhino's Horn** (855 West Cleveland Street; 602-337-2223), which orchestrates a good rendition of several Italian dishes including lasagna, cioppino and pasta with a delicious marinara sauce. You can also feast on frisbee-sized burgers, a slab of barbecue ribs or fresh catfish. Budget to moderate.

ST. JOHNS AREA PARKS

Framed by rocky hillsides and jagged canyons, **Lyman Lake State Park** (602-337-4441) has a boat dock, boat rentals and excellent year-around lake fishing. There's also waterskiing, windsurfing and swimming beaches. The hiking trails lead to petroglyphs and a herd of buffalo roaming across 100 protected acres. Facilities include full RV hook-ups and campsites with showers and restrooms. To get there, drive 12 miles south on Route 180.

A peaceful spot to drop a line is **Concho Lake** (602-337-4695), which is stocked with rainbow and brook trout. Next door is a nine-hole golf course and restaurant. The mini-resort is about 16 miles west of St. Johns on Route 61.

Pinetop-Lakeside Area

Where Route 60 intersects with Route 666 and the Coronado Trail, you'll come to the town of Springerville, where you can make a detour and head west to the recreation and ski area of **Pinetop-Lakeside**, a winter resort popular with Phoenix residents.

In the Springerville area, there are two places of interest worth stopping for. Situated on a rim of volcanic rock overlooking the Little Colorado River's Round Valley is **Casa Malpais Pueblo** (318 Main Street, Springerville; 602-333-5375; admission). Tours originate at the museum in Springerville. Here, you'll learn that the Mogollon people abandoned the pueblo in 1400 A.D., and now the archeological dig is open to the public. For the best pueblo views, take the guided tour up a steep basalt staircase to the top of the mesa. A tour highlight is the Great Kiva made of volcanic rock.

Follow a dusty, bumpy road for several miles and the unlikely reward is the **Little House Museum** (X Diamond Ranch, South Fork Road, Springerville; 602-333-2286; admission) on the X Diamond Ranch. Inside the two-story building are exhibits relating to the area's history, including ranching and horse show memorabilia. Beside it are two restored cabins more than 100 years old. One contains antique musical instruments ranging from a player piano to a Wurlitzer circus organ. The museum is three and two-tenths miles south of Highway 260 off South Fork Road. Advance reservations are suggested.

Climbing the steep incline of the Mogollon Rim leads to **Show Low**, **Pinetop** and **Lakeside**, forested hamlets of cabins, motels, resorts and campgrounds in a pine woods setting. Most of the commercial activity takes place in Show Low along Route 60. The population of Show Low swells from about 5500 year-round residents to more than 13,000 during the summer, when the big attractions are excellent

---

SHOW LOW

There are some fascinating stories behind how towns are named, and Show Low has one of them. Government scout Croydon E. Cooley and partner Marion Clark had a ranch here in the 1870s, but decided that it wasn't big enough for both of them. So they played a card game of Seven-Up to decide who would move. On the last hand, Cooley only needed one point to win. Clark said, "If you can show low, you win." Cooley threw down his hand and said "Show low it is," and pulled out an unbeatable deuce of clubs. He took the ranch, and it has been called Show Low ever since. In fact, the main street through town is called Deuce of Clubs after the winning hand.

trout fishing and big game hunting in the Mogollon Rim country and White Mountains. Also popular are hiking, horseback riding, golf and scenic drives. Many Arizonans also keep summer homes at the 6400-foot-elevation town to escape the blistering summer temperatures in Phoenix and other "flatlander" communities. During winter, the Sunrise ski resort on the White Mountain Apache Reservation is famous for its downhill runs and cross-country trails.

Southeast of Show Low lie the mountain resort twins of Pinetop and Lakeside, and beyond, the Indian towns of Whiteriver and Fort Apache. Lakeside is a starting point for hiking, fishing, camping and backpacking in and near the three resort communities, which are connected by a highway lined with motels, restaurants, gas stations and small businesses.

PINETOP-LAKESIDE AREA LODGING

Built in 1916, **Lakeview Lodge** (2251 White Mountain Boulevard, Pinetop-Lakeside; 602-368-5253) is one of the oldest lodges in Arizona. The rustic lounge has a fireplace, high-beamed ceilings and Indian rugs hanging from the second-story railing. The nine rooms and cabins are simply furnished and come with a complementary bottle of wine. Fishermen can use the private pond, then grill their catch on the premises. Moderate.

One step short of camping out is staying at the **Lake of the Woods Resort** (2244 West White Mountain Boulevard, Pinetop-Lakeside; 602-368-5353). Twenty-four moderately priced log cabins are scattered amidst pine trees beside a private lake. All cabins have fireplaces, televisions, kitchen and dining areas and outdoor barbecues. Although some cabins are geared toward honeymooners, most are more family oriented. Amenities include shuffleboard, horseshoes, spas, a sauna, playground, ping-pong and pool tables.

A beautiful setting amidst pine trees, rather than luxurious accommodations, are what you pay for at **Hawley Lake Resort** (Route 473; 16 miles east of McNary; 602-335-7511). The resort is remote—12 long, winding miles off Highway 260—and situated on a lake in one of the highest points in the White Mountains. Open from May through November, the resort offers twelve motel rooms and eight cabins overlooking the lake. If you get lucky fishing, grills are available outside and cabins have kitchenettes. This moderately priced resort is located on the White Mountain Apache Reservation. Amenities include a café, boat rentals, gas and a store.

Pastoral is the only word for the setting at **Greer Lodge** (Route 373, Greer; 602-735-7515), located on the Little Colorado River with a view of meadows and mountains. To many, it is the place to stay. Built by hand as a church retreat 45 years ago out of ponderosa pine and aspen, it now is a charming getaway with ten rooms in the main lodge and eight cabins. The lounge/restaurant area has comfy couches, a huge fireplace, vaulted ceilings and almost floor-to-ceiling windows where guests can look out at the snow falling in winter. Country furnishings warm up the rooms, along with cozy rocking chairs and quilts on the beds. Upon arrival, guests receive a wine and fruit basket; at night, homemade cookies. Deluxe.

Molly Butler Lodge (Route 373, Greer; 602-735-7226) is the oldest lodge in Arizona, built in 1910. Rooms are tiny and a bit run-down, but prices are budget. A nice touch are the plaques on each door with the name and information about a local pioneer. The restaurant on premises serves dinner only.

The lounge at the **Bear Pond Inn** (sign off Route 373; Greer; 602-735-7576) beckons with its polished wood floors, vaulted ceilings, huge Mexican wrought-iron chandeliers and stacks of puzzles. Sit out on the porch and you'll see Bear Pond (yes, bears do sometimes drink here) stocked with trout, or soak in the indoor hot tub with a view of the forest. The four rooms are wood-paneled with shutters on the windows and have fairly plain furnishings, while the three cabins have two bedrooms, a loft, kitchenette and a stone fireplace in the sitting area. Moderate.

Located on Sunrise Lake near the ski resort four miles south of Route 260 is **Sunrise Park Resort** (Route 273, McNary; 602-735-7676 or 800-554-6835), owned and operated by the White Mountain Apache Tribe. Guests come to fish in summer and ski in winter, staying at one of the 91 modern, nicely furnished hotel rooms. Amenities include an indoor pool, spa and restaurant. Moderate.

PINETOP-LAKESIDE AREA RESTAURANTS

If you like pigs, you'll like **Piggin's Eatery** (2251 Highway 260, Pinetop-Lakeside; 602-368-5253). Pigs adorn tablecloths, shelves and handmade quilts. And if you still want to eat after looking at all these pigs, the well-lit, cheerful restaurant has salads, sandwiches and hamburgers in the budget range.

Charlie Clark's Steak House (1701 East White Mountain Boulevard, Pinetop-Lakeside; 602-367-4900) has been around since 1938. A western theme predominates, with stuffed buffalo and deer, a glass-topped, wagon-wheel coffee table, and wildlife paintings throughout the restaurant. There's even a silver saddle once used by movie stars and politicians. Steak and seafood in the moderate range are the primary offerings, followed by offtrack betting in the back bar.

Catch your own rainbow trout in Fred's Lake, just outside the door at **Farmer Dunn's Vittles** (2152 East Fir; Pinetop-Lakeside; 602-367-3866), and they'll cook it for you! An adjoining concession rents fishing equipment. Fridays are fish fry nights; otherwise, the fare is burgers, sandwiches and chicken. Inside the cheery, barn-like building, farm implements hang on the walls. A cow-colored clawfoot bathtub holds the salad bar, while soup warms on a wood-burning stove. Budget.

For gourmet dining, try the **Bear Pond Inn** (sign off Route 373, Greer; 602-735-7576). Cuisine includes Moroccan lamb with couscous, salmon poached in wine and a proper English trifle. Classical music plays in the background and brass candlesticks adorn tables in the restaurant's two intimate rooms. Moderate.

PINETOP-LAKESIDE AREA SHOPPING

Antiquing is popular in this area. Choices include The **Orchard Antiques** (1664 West White Mountain Boulevard, Pinetop-Lakeside: 602-368-6563) with jewelry, Nippon china, vintage clothing and primitives in an old house. **My Favorite Things** (476 West White Mountain Boulevard, Pinetop-Lakeside; 602-367-5184) has silver estate jewelry, depression ware, china and furniture, and **Billings Country Pine Antiques and General Store** (103 West Yaeger Street, Pinetop-Lakeside; 602-367-1709) sells primitives, pine and oak furniture, quilts, gifts and gourmet coffee beans.

PINETOP-LAKESIDE AREA NIGHTLIFE

Watch "cliffhanging sagas of lecherous villains and helpless maidens" at **Theatre Mountain** (Rainbow Lake Drive, Pinetop-Lakeside; 602-368-8888; admission). Located in an old movie house, patrons boo and cheer the melodramatic characters while slurping down ice-cream sundaes and snacks.

SALT RIVER CANYON

*Nicknamed the miniature Grand Canyon, the **Salt River Canyon** is a spectacular sight that you can drive right through on Route 60 about 50 miles south of Show Low. There's a bridge where Route 60 crosses the Salt River, which carved the canyon millions of years ago. Seven miles downstream from the bridge via a paved road are fascinating salt banks sacred to the Apache and colored with green, red and orange minerals and algae.*

PINETOP-LAKESIDE AREA PARKS

Woodland Lake Park, a small but scenic park in the middle of Pinetop-Lakeside, offers hiking, equestrian and mountain biking trails, volleyball courts, softball fields, boating and playgrounds. Tall, thin pine trees surround the lake where people fish for trout from the shore and pier. A one-and-a-quarter-mile paved loop trail circles the lake. The park is also connected with the White Mountain Trail System (see "Hiking" at the end of the chapter). For further information, contact the Pinetop-Lakeside Parks and Recreation Department (1360 North Niels Hansen Lane; 602-368-6700). The park is located a quarter-mile south of Route 260 off Woodland Lake Road.

A small herd of buffalo greets visitors at the entrance to **Lyman Lake State Park** (602-337-4441). Farther on, a 1500-acre lake lures both fishing and boating enthusiasts. Trout, bass, catfish and bluegill are plentiful in the lake, which was formed by damming the Little Colorado River and is fed by snowmelt from the slopes of Mount Baldy and Escudilla Mountain. Other attractions include hiking the three trails, which range from a half a mile to one mile in length, and are dotted with Indian petroglyphs. This 1180-acre park was the first recreational state park in Arizona and sits at an elevation of 6000 feet. The park is ten miles south of St. Johns off Route 666.

Alpine Area

Back on the Coronado Trail (Route 666), the forest deepens as it continues its slow ascent, and you enter the mountain village of **Alpine**, in the heart of Apache-Sitgreaves National Forest, or the "Arizona Alps," as it is called locally. The town was founded in 1879 by Mormon settlers who originally named it Frisco, after the San Francisco River. The name was later changed to Alpine because residents thought the area resembled the Alps. The Arizona Alps don't attract the large number of tourists who flock to the Grand Canyon, the Colorado River or other state attractions, but nature buffs will love the area's abundance of outdoor activities—hiking, camping, hunting, fishing and cross-country skiing.

Alpine has no traffic lights, video stores or neon signs, just a handful of year-round residents and even fewer commercial attractions. Actually it's nothing more than an intersection of Routes 666 and 180, but there are dependable services and lodging. More important, within a 30-mile radius there are 200 miles of trout streams, 11 lakes, numerous campgrounds, plus a country club and golf course.

In the winter, Alpine doesn't hibernate with the black bear, but keeps busy offering visitors cross-country skiing, snowmobiling, sledding and ice fishing opportunities.

The region is also a favorite with hunters because it is home to nine of Arizona's ten big game species, including mule deer, elk, black bear, bighorn sheep and mountain lion. Small-game hunters stalk blue grouse, Gambel's quail and a host of waterfowl. The forest is also habitat for a wide variety of rare and endangered birds, including the Mexican spotted owl, bald eagle and peregrine falcon.

From Alpine, you can strike out in any direction and discover unspoiled forests of tall pines, shimmering aspens, trickling streams, wildflower meadows and clear blue lakes. For detailed maps and descriptions of the area, stop at the **U.S. Forest Service** (42634 Route 180; 602-339-4384), where rangers can also advise on current road conditions.

Twenty-two miles south of town along Route 666 is **Hannagan Meadow**, a grassy clearing framed by stately ponderosa pine and blue spruce forests. In addition to excellent hiking trails, there's a rustic mountain lodge, and, in winter, cross-country skiing and snowmobiling.

Another picturesque spot is **Williams Valley**, an unspoiled wilderness area seven miles northwest of Alpine via Route 666 and Forest Road 249. Here, you can explore 15 miles of hiking trails through wooded forests, or drop a line in tiny Lake Sierra Blanca, which is stocked with rainbow and brook trout.

A nice scenic drive from Alpine is the **Blue River-Red Hill Loop**. Drive east three miles from Alpine on Route 180 to Forest Road 281 (the Blue Road turnoff). To the north is the western tip of **Luna Lake**, 80 acres of crystal-clear waters surrounded by green meadows and pine forests. Facilities include a boat dock and small store.

From Route 180, Blue Road winds south through ten miles of rugged hills until it descends past a few horse ranches into Box Canyon, where the road follows the **Blue River**. Continue downstream past jagged Maness Peak nine miles to the junction with Forest Route 567 (Red Hill Road). Along the way, you'll find tributaries, such as Centerfire Creek, which are home to small schools of rainbow and brook trout. Drive north on Red Hill Road, which twists and climbs out of the valley, often following ridges with panoramic vistas back to Route 666, about 14 miles south of Alpine.

ALPINE AREA LODGING

The peak-roofed, cedar-paneled **Talwiwi Lodge** (Route 666, four miles north of Alpine; 602-339-4319) brings the pine forest closer to guests with its tall windows and upstairs veranda. The modern rooms feature contemporary furnishings, some with Swedish fireplaces and spa tubs. The restaurant serves breakfast and dinner. Moderate.

If you came to the mountains seeking a cozy retreat, try the **Alpine Cabins** (42650 Route 180; 602-339-4378), which feature fireplaces, kitchenettes and four-poster beds. Budget. About a mile north of town, **Judd's Ranch** (42576 Route 180; 602-339-4326) rents small wood-frame cabins that feature creaky hardwood floors, knotty-pine walls and small kitchens. You can drop a line in the fishing lake or horseback ride along 15 miles of forested trails. Closed from November to mid April; budget. Surrounded by pine forests, the **Coronado Trail Cabins** (25303 Route 666; 602-339-4772) offers a few farm-house-style cabins with fireplaces, outdoor verandas, hardwood floors and quilted bed covers. Budget.

A pair of Alpine motels offer clean, well-maintained rooms—some with kitchenettes—at budget prices. They are the **Mountain Hi Lodge** (42698 Route 180; 602-339-4311) and **Sportsman Motel** (Route 666; 602-339-4576).

About 22 miles south of Alpine, **Hannagan Meadow Lodge** (Route 666 at Hannagan Meadow; 602-339-4370) rents rustic cabins with fireplaces and antique furnishings, and has a dining room that stays open year-round. One of the oldest inns in the state, the lodge also has a few curio shops, general store and gasoline pump. Moderate.

ALPINE AREA RESTAURANTS

The **Sundowner** (Route 180, a half-mile east of Route 666; 602-339-4451) is a log-cabin-style restaurant with paneled walls, dark-wood tables and a chatty local clientele. The house special is a charbroiled, 16-ounce rib-eye steak, but you can also feast on moderately priced pork chops, catfish, shrimp, stir-fry chicken or a delicious boneless chicken breast in teriyaki sauce. Among the budget-priced Mexican dishes, the green chili and chicken burrito and chicken chimichangas are the best.

You'll find more home cooking at the **M&J Corral Restaurant** (42650 Route 180; 602-339-4378), a converted house that exudes a casual, friendly atmosphere. Traditional favorites include roast brisket of beef, chicken pot pie, homemade bread and muffins. Moderate.

ALPINE AREA SHOPPING

One-stop shopping is the specialty at the **Tackle Shop and Alpine Garage** (25373 Route 666; 602-339-4338), where you can fill your tank, restring your cross-bow, buy a canoe, eat lunch or rent a movie on video. If you need to stock up on groceries (other than tortilla

---

Founded by Mormons in 1879, Alpine is at the highest elevation of any Arizona town, 8046 feet.

---

chips and bean dip), head to **Alpine Market** (42651 Route 180; 602-339-4914) for a standard selection of meat, produce and canned goods, as well as the latest gossip circulating the mountain village.

ALPINE AREA NIGHTLIFE

The most popular gathering spot is the **Sundowner** (Route 180, half a mile east of Route 666; 602-339-4451), which features a brick fireplace, solid oak bar, juke box, pool table and mounted deer heads on the wall. During the summer, there's foot-stomping country music and dancing. In winter, locals watch reruns of "Wheel of Fortune" on the television set above the bar.

Morenci-Clifton Area

When traveling south from Alpine, make sure you have enough fuel and provisions before leaving town. The 105-mile stretch to Clifton has no towns or services. Also be aware that the same roads are subject to closure during winter snow storms. (If the road is closed by winter snow or mudslides, you can drive to Clifton via Routes 180 and 78 through western New Mexico. The detour adds only 20 miles to the trip.)

About halfway to Clifton, you can stop at **Rose Peak**, which offers panoramic vistas of the Escudilla Mountains. For even better views, you can hike to the forest lookout tower, about a half-mile off the highway.

Continuing south past the Juan Miller and Granville campgrounds, the highway descends a series of switchbacks into a high desert climate zone, with juniper trees seemingly growing from the red rock formations. As the highway flattens, you'll find **Morenci**, a town owned and built by Phelps Dodge Corporation, which operates the open-pit copper mine here. The copper mine is the second-largest in North America and open to public tours.

The **Morenci Open Pit Mine** (602-865-4521) is an awesome sight from the overlooks along Route 666, but you can get a closer look into the depths of the mine through tours offered by Phelps Dodge. Most impressive are the earth moving equipment with tires so huge they dwarf a man, the scoop shovels that can unearth 35 cubic tons of ore with one bite, and the futuristic dump trucks with wedge-shaped bays that haul 190 tons of ore. The tour also includes the mine's crushers, concentrators and electrochemical extraction operation, which processes the copper ore into three-foot-square sheets, each weighing about 200 pounds. The tours, which last about three-and-a-half hours, are conducted by retired miners who explain the state-of-the-art electro-winning process, which has replaced outdated smelting and refining.

Today's Morenci was built by Phelps Dodge in 1969. It consists of a motel/restaurant, a school, library, two shopping centers, bowling alley and the Phelps Dodge Mercantile, a combination supermarket and discount department store.

Route 666 follows the San Francisco River, much the way Francisco de Coronado and his conquistadores did, around the bend and into the historic little mining town of **Clifton**, built along the banks of the river.

All around Clifton, the red sandstone cliffs paint a brilliant contrast to the grays and tans of the shale and the tin-and-brick buildings which are reminiscent of the town's golden days at the turn of the century, when copper was king.

The town was founded around 1865, but didn't prosper until copper deposits were discovered in 1872. At first, copper ore had to be shipped to Swansea, Wales, for smelting. Then miners built their own crude adobe smelters along Chase Creek Street, and set up a narrow-gauge railroad to transport the ore from the mines on the surrounding hillsides.

Many of the remnants of early mining operations remain, along with dozens of old buildings—47 are on the National Register of Historical Places—in turn-of-the-century architecture. You'll find most of them along **Chase Creek Street**, which was once the town's main thoroughfare, lined on both sides with stores, saloons, brothels, churches and even an opera house. Today, the four-block-long street, plus a few narrow alleys, parallels Coronado Boulevard (Route 666), separated by a rudimentary brick wall. But you can still walk among the buildings, many of which have been damaged by time and natural disasters. Most, however, retain their architectural splendor.

For instance, the **Catholic Church**, which was rebuilt in 1917 after being destroyed by flood and fire, features leaded and stained-glass windows, a marble altar and porcelain figures imported from Italy. Down the street is Clifton's first **Town Jail**, which is carved into the side of a granite cliff. Next door is the **Copper Head**, a 19th-century locomotive that once carried ore to the smelters. Across the river, the

Carmichael House is now headquarters for mine officials. It was built in 1913 for mine president James Carmichael, who once had to flee through the home's storm sewer system to escape a mob of angry strikers.

The **Greenlee County Chamber of Commerce** (251 Chase Creek Street; 602-865-3313), which has its offices in what was once the town barber shop, dispenses maps and information about the sights and history of the area. Be sure to ask for the walking-tour map of historic Chase Creek. If you have any questions about the history of the area, ask Charles Spezia, who put together the tour.

You'll notice a few caves in the mountain above the south side of Chase Creek. These were built by merchants to store valuables such as whiskey, meat and vegetables. They often had rugged steel doors and sometimes were vented with a vertical shaft.

The renovated **Greenlee County Historical Museum** (317 Chase Creek; 602-865-3115) on the west end of Chase Creek, has assembled an impressive collection of early Clifton memorabilia, including recollections of Geronimo's birth near the Gila River about four miles from downtown. Also on display are a photo gallery of the region's history, old bank cabinets and a PBX switchboard, a frontier wedding dress and paintings by Ted DeGrazia, one of Arizona's most famous artists and a native of Morenci.

Phelps Dodge Corporation became a major player in Clifton's development in the 1880s, when it took over most of the local mining operations, about four miles north of town. At the time, the mining camp was called Joy's Camp, but was later renamed Morenci, after a town in Michigan. Over the next 50 years, Phelps Dodge, or "PD" as the locals call it (often confused with "Petey"), became one of the largest producers of copper in the world.

MORENCI-CLIFTON AREA LODGING

The more modern **Morenci Motel** (Route 666, Morenci; 602-865-4111) sits on a hill overlooking Clifton and features an adobe brick

---

THE TOWN THAT WAS SWALLOWED

Ore testing in the 1930s revealed that Morenci sat on vast copper deposits, so a new community was formed (the site of present-day Morenci) and the original town was swallowed up by the new open pit mine. There's no trace of old Morenci left, only a gigantic hole in the ground measuring two miles across, nine miles around and more than 1800 feet deep.

exterior, wrought-iron fixtures and a tiled lobby. The large modern rooms are decorated with dark-wood, Mediterranean-style furnishings and light pastel colors. Budget.

Each town has its own motel. Clifton's **Rode Inn Motel** (186 South Coronado Boulevard; 602-865-4536) is a somewhat rickety place with a weather-beaten exterior, but the budget-priced rooms are well-kept and offer in-room coffee and color cable television.

MORENCI-CLIFTON AREA RESTAURANTS

The best place to eat is the **Copperoom Restaurant** (Morenci Motel; 602-865-4111), a somewhat plain but cavernous dining room with ceiling fans, wooden tables, captain chairs and a seldom-used brick fireplace. The house specialties include steaks, prime rib, chicken, liver and onions, halibut and several Mexican dishes. Besides delicious dishes in massive portions, the two sisters who manage the motel are so accommodating that they'll cook dinner for late-arriving guests after the dining room has closed. (The chicken fajitas were delicious!) Budget to moderate.

In Clifton, **PJ's Restaurant** (307 Coronado Boulevard; 602-865-3328), a storefront hole-in-the-wall near the old section of town, is popular with locals who feast on chimichanga, chili cheese crisps and red or green chili plates. Seating is at the counter or formica dinettes, but the food is tasty and plentiful. Budget.

MORENCI-CLIFTON AREA SHOPPING

Not much here, but if you run out of toothpaste try **Phelps Dodge Mercantile** (Morenic Plant Site shopping center; 602-865-4121), a combination grocery and discount department store. On your tour of Clifton's historic Chase Creek, stop at **Kit N Kaboodle**, a quaint arts-and-craft shop that sells handmade quilts, tea cozies, dried-flower arrangements and other gift items.

MORENCI-CLIFTON AREA NIGHTLIFE

For contemporary surroundings, try the **Copperoom Lounge** (Morenci Motel, Morenci; 602-865-4111), a small but surprisingly active bar with a handful of wooden tables, copper memorabilia hanging from the ceiling and a jukebox blasting away in the corner.

On historic Chase Creek in Clifton, you can bar-hop while imagining the strains of a reverberating player piano and the heavy aroma of Pabst Blue Ribbon beer. Find the building with a balcony overhanging the sidewalk and head into **Zorrilla's Meat Market** (259 Chase Creek;

602–865–3702), circle the meat counter and walk into the back room, sit on a 1928 Manila Soda Works crate, order a Budweiser and visit with Jesus and Lolo Zorrilla, proprietors since 1927. Although the brothers opened the shop as a meat market, it's now a bar and liquor store. Down the street, you can imbibe at the **El Rey Bar** (287 Chase Creek; 602–865–2022), part of the stately Cascarelli Building built in 1914. Little of the architecture has changed: the brick facade has a wrought-iron balcony and leaded-glass windows, all topped by a pressed-tin dome parapet. Inside, you're greeted by a black-and-white tiled entry and a solid oak, mahogany-stained bar.

Sporting Life

FISHING

Anglers will find plenty of challenge—and game fish—along the Old West Highway. In the Apache Junction area, **Saguaro, Canyon, Apache** and **Roosevelt lakes** are popular year-round fishing meccas, as are **San Carlos Lake** near Globe and **Roper Lake** in Safford.

For a fishing license, tackle or bait, try **Griffith Tire and Radiator** (3 East Center Street, Pima; 602–485–9636).

In the St. Johns area, 1500-acre **Lyman Lake** is a good spot for catfish, largemouth bass, walleye, crappie and northern pike. Or try 60-acre **Concho Lake** for rainbow and brook trout (shore fishing only). For fishing and camping supplies or a license, check with **Western Drug** (105 East Main Street, Springerville; 602–333–4321).

In the Alpine area, **Bear Wallow Creek**, a tributary of the Black River, is famous for Arizona Native trout. Also on the **Black River** at different stops you can try for rainbow trout, while trout and catfish can be found in **Eagle Creek**. East of Alpine and dropping off into the Blue Primitive Area, rainbow trout can be found in **Luna Lake** and the ruggedly remote **Blue River**. North of Alpine you'll find rainbow, brown and brook trout in **Nelson Reservoir**. More casual anglers can seek catfish in the **San Francisco River** near Clifton. You can buy bait and a license or rent tackle at the **Alpine Tackle Shop** (25373 Route 666; 602–339–4338) and **Alpine Hardware and Building Supply** (42653 Route 180; 602–339–4711).

Eastern Arizona is a fisherman's paradise with lakes dotting the region around Pinetop-Lakeside and Greer. To fish at the lakes on the White Mountain Apache Reservation, which are stocked with rainbow and brown trout, contact the **Game and Fish Department** (Route 73, Whiteriver; 602–338–4385). For general fishing information in the White Mountains, stop by the **Arizona Game and Fish Depart-**

Swimming is ideal at Canyon, Apache and Roosevelt lakes.

ment (2870 East White Mountain Boulevard, Pinetop-Lakeside; 602-367-4281).

There are quality waters with rainbow, brown and Apache trout at **Hawley Lake** (McNary; 602-335-7511). For private fly-fishing, catch and release, try **X Diamond Ranch** (X Diamond Ranch, Springerville; 602-735-7515). **Lyman Lake State Park** (Route 666, St. Johns; 602-337-4441) has a lake stocked with trout, bass, catfish and bluegill.

GOLF

In Apache Junction, try **Gold Canyon Golf Club** (6100 South Kings Ranch Road; 602-982-9090). **Cobre Valley Country Club** (Route 88 north of Globe; 602-473-2542) has a nine-hole course.

In the Safford area, the **Mount Graham Golf Course** (two miles south of Safford at Daley Estates; 602-428-1260) offers an 18-hole course for year-round play, a pro shop, cart rentals and cocktail lounge.

You can tee off at the **Alpine Country Club** (58 North County Road 2122; 602-339-4944), which features a nine-hole course, restaurant and lounge.

Pinetop-Lakeside offers **Silver Creek Golf Club** (White Mountain Lake Road; 602-537-2744); **Pinetop Lakes Golf & Country Club** (602-369-4184); **Show Low Country Club** (Show Low; 602-537-4564); and **Alpine Country Club** (58 North County Road; 602-339-4944).

HIKING

APACHE JUNCTION AREA TRAILS **Usery Mountain Recreation Area** offers the well-maintained **Wind Cave Trail** (1 mile), which is moderately challenging and popular with local climbers. **Pass Mountain Trail** (7 miles) takes about four hours to complete.

SAFFORD AREA TRAILS **Arcadia Trail** (5.1 miles) on Mount Graham passes through a forest of Douglas fir, aspen and pine trees, along with wild raspberry vines. As the highest range in southern Arizona, hikers will see a panoramic view of the area.

ST. JOHNS AREA TRAILS There's excellent hiking in the Escudilla Wilderness Area, an alpine forest with peaks over 10,000 feet, ten miles north of Alpine. The **Escudilla National Recreation Trail** (3.3 miles) from Terry Flat takes you to the summit of Escudilla Mountain through pine forests and grassy meadows. The trailhead is along Forest Route 56, four-and-a-half miles east of Route 666. Rangers at the **U.S. Forest Service** (42634 Route 180; 602-339-4384) will provide detailed trail maps and advice on current conditions.

PINETOP-LAKESIDE AREA TRAILS   The **White Mountains Trail-system** contains about 180 miles of interconnecting loop trails from Vernon in the east to Pinedale in the west. For a map of trails, stop by the Pinetop-Lakeside Chamber of Commerce (592 West White Mountain Boulevard; 602-367-4290). When the Trailsystem is completed, there will be about 20 to 25 loop trails. Some highlights are **Blue Ridge Trail** (9.5 miles) in Pinetop-Lakeside, which is easy to moderate. It passes Billy Creek and climbs through tall pines to the top of Blue Ridge with vistas along the way. The **Ghost-of-the-Coyote Trail** (14 mile loop) begins near Pinedale. The fairly flat trail winds through oak and pine forests.

The **Mogollon Rim Overlook** (1 mile) is an easy hike with interpretive placards along the way and beautiful views of the valley below the Mogollon Rim. It's two miles north of Pinetop-Lakeside off Route 260.

ALPINE AREA TRAILS   In the Alpine area, the 450,000-acre Apache-Sitgreaves National Forest is a hiker's paradise, with terrain ranging from piñon and juniper woodlands to high-elevation forests of spruce and fir, meadows and alpine lakes.

An easy hike is to **Jackson Springs** (3 miles), about five miles southeast of Alpine. Drive three miles east on Route 180 and turn right on County Route 2266, then continue south to Route 2210, where you will turn left. Go about a half-mile and turn right on Forest Route 572, then continue to the top of the hill and park. Hike down the hill past the site of the old Civilian Conservation Corps (CCC) camp and along the spring. The hand-hewn log trough nearby was made by CCC volunteers, and the ruins in the clearing were once a doctor's office.

About 14 miles south of Alpine, heartier hikers can explore the **Red Hill Trail No. 56** (10 miles), a trek along a dirt road that leads into the Blue Range Primitive Area. From the upper trailhead at the Right Fork of Foote Creek, just off Forest Route 567 a mile east of Route 666, the trail traces the ridges of the Red Hill mountains, then descends along Bush Creek on its way to the Blue River. The lower trailhead is at Blue Camp, an old CCC camp that's now a school, just off Forest Route 281. (If you like to do your hiking by horseback, corrals have recently been built at the upper trailhead.)

In the **Blue Range Primitive Area**, you'll find spectacular rock formations with steep escarpments, along with thick forests of spruce, fir and ponderosa pine. Keep a sharp watch for black bear, Rocky Mountain elk, javelina, mule deer, mountain lion and other wildlife.

The area is excellent for birdwatching; keep your binoculars trained for such birds as the Arizona woodpecker, spotted owl, aplomado falcon, American peregrine falcon and southern bald eagle.

West of the Coronado Trail (Route 666), the **Bear Wallow Wilderness** contains 11,000 acres including one of the largest stands of virgin ponderosa pine in the Southwest. **Bear Wallow Trail No. 63** (7.6 miles) traces Bear Wallow Creek downstream from the K. P. Cienega Campground (off Route 666, about 30 miles south of Alpine) through jagged canyons of juniper west to the San Carlos Apache Reservation's eastern boundary. Two shorter trails connect with the main trail and creek from the north: **Reno Trail No. 62** (1.9 miles) and **Gobbler Point Trail No. 59** (2.7 miles). Guides and outfitters in the Alpine area include **Alpine Adventures** (P.O. Box 349, Alpine, AZ 85920; 602-339-4915); **Larry Garberg** (P.O. Box 335, Alpine, AZ 85920); and the **Tackle Shop and Alpine Garage** (P.O. Box 124, Alpine, AZ 85920; 602-339-4839).

HORSEBACK RIDING

Try **Don Donnelly Stables at Gold Canyon** (6010 North Kings Ranch Road, Apache Junction; 602-982-7822); and **Superstition Mountain Guide Service** (Apache Junction; 602-982-4040). You can ride wilderness trails, camp, cook, bathe in icy streams and sleep out under the stars in the Superstition Mountains on guided three- to seven-day pack trips. For information, contact **Peralta Riding Stables and Pack Trips** (Meridian Road; 602-982-5488); **Superstition Stables** (North Meridian Drive; 602-982-6353); or the **Superstition Mountain Guide Service** (602-982-4949), all in Apache Junction.

In Greer, try **Lee Valley Outfitters** (602-735-7454). In Pinetop-Lakeside, there's **Pinetop Lakes Riding Stables** (Buck Springs Road; 602-369-1000).

HUNTING

Hunters love the forests surrounding Alpine because of the abundance of both big and small game—such as mule deer, whitetail deer, elk, javelina, black bear, mountain lion, Merriam's turkey, bighorn sheep, pronghorn antelope, blue grouse, Albert's squirrels, cottontail rabbits, mourning doves, Gambel's quail and a host of waterfowl. You can buy a license and supplies at the **Alpine Tackle Shop** (25373 Route 666; 602-339-4338) and **Alpine Hardware and Building Supply** (42653 Route 180; 602-339-4711). For maps and information about the area, check at the **U.S. Forest Service Office** (42634 Route 180, Alpine; 602-339-4634).

WINTER SPORTS

Cross-country skiing, sledding and snowmobiling are popular at **Hannagan Meadow**, 22 miles south of Alpine on Route 666, where there are over 11 miles of machine-packed trails, which are serviced after each storm. The snowmobiles in the area are prohibited from designated ski trails. Another good spot for cross-country skiers is **Williams Valley**, which features nine miles of groomed ski trails, plus an additional five-and-a-half miles of marked trails. From Alpine, drive one-and-a-half miles north on Route 666 to the Williams Valley turnoff, Forest Road 249, and continue for five miles.

You can rent a snowmobile at **High Image Snowmobile** (Hannagan Meadow Lodge; 602-339-4370), which maintains trails at Bear Creek, Lost Cienega and Hannagan Meadow, and conducts night tours.

SKIING

Sunrise Park Resort (McNary; 602-735-7669 or 800-772-7669) has 800 acres of skiable area on three mountains and 11 lifts.

Transportation

BY CAR

The western anchor of the Old West Highway, Apache Junction, is about 30 miles east of Phoenix via **Route 60**. On its eastern end you can join the Highway at Safford via **Routes 666** from Clifton, or **Route 70**, which crosses to Lordsburg, New Mexico. **Route 180/666** links the Coronado Trail towns of St. Johns, Alpine and Clifton. You can get to the Pinetop-Lakeside area from the west via Route 60, turning onto **Route 260** at Show Low. From the east, Route 260 connects to Route 180 at Springerville.

BY BUS

The closest **Greyhound Bus Lines** terminal to Coronado Trail towns is in Safford, about 30 miles southwest of Clifton.

CAR RENTALS

Along the Old West Highway, you can rent a car or van at **Cobre Valley Motors** (Route 60, Globe; 602-425-4487) and **Hatch Brothers Auto Center** (1623 Thatcher Boulevard, Safford; 602-428-6000).

TEN

Southern Arizona

Southern Arizona is a vast region of grasslands and desert punctuated by some of the state's most beautiful mountains. Four ranges have peaks higher than 9000 feet—the Santa Catalinas, Santa Ritas, Huachucas and Chiricahuas. At the heart of the region is Tucson, an urban metropolis rising out of the Sonoran Desert. A rich cultural tradition ranging from the Pima tribe to the Jesuits reflects this community's close ties to neighboring Mexico.

Scattered east of Tucson are portions of the Coronado National Forest. To the southeast, the rolling grasslands and woodland hills around Patagonia are some of the state's best cattle and horse ranchland, while the Elgin area has acres of green vineyards where local wines are produced. Farther east is Sierra Vista, whose claim to fame is Fort Huachuca, an historic military base whose troops defeated Apache leader Geronimo. Some 11,400 soldiers and civilians are still based here. Nearby Tombstone and Bisbee are old mining towns. Tombstone, the town "too tough to die," survives by selling its history. There are museums and exhibits on every corner—each, of course, charging for the pleasure of your company. Visitors flock here to relive the rowdy life of the Old West, from the shootout at O.K. Corral to the gambling at Birdcage Theater. Bisbee has become a quiet artists' colony with a more bohemian flavor. Here, visitors can shop in historic buildings along Main Street, tour old mines and walk along the narrow, hilly streets dotted with Victorian architecture. Up around Willcox are orchards teeming with fruit and vegetables. In autumn, you can pick your own or stop at one of the many roadside stands.

Tucson has more sunshine than any other city in the United States—about 350 days each year.

South of Tucson is the most populated portion of southern Arizona. Off Route 19 is Tubac, an artists' community with about 50 studios and galleries. Farther south is the border town of Nogales, where you can bargain for Mexican crafts and sample authentic cuisine. Southwest of Tucson is a large, scarcely populated area containing the Papago Reservation, Cabeza Prieta National Wildlife Refuge and Organ Pipe Cactus National Monument. In the westernmost corner of the state is Yuma, an historic town on the Colorado River that attracts residents with its lush, subtropical climate, farmlands fertile with vegetables, citrus trees and groves of date palms.

Although Tucson and southern Arizona abound with history, the real reason people visit is for the natural beauty—for the meditative solitude of a desert that seemingly rolls on endlessly, creating vast spaces for the imagination.

Tucson

The ultimate insult to a Tucson resident is to say his town is just like Phoenix. Like bickering siblings, the two cities have never gotten along well and each is proud of its unique personality. While Phoenix is a vast, sprawling city that welcomes booming development, Tucson would just as soon stay the same size and keep developers out—especially those who would alter the environment. Phoenix thrives on a fast pace; Tucson is informal, easygoing and in no great rush to get anywhere.

Surrounded by five mountain ranges and sitting in a cactus-roughened desert, Tucson is an arid, starkly beautiful place with wide-open skies and night silences broken only by the howling of coyotes. The highest mountains are powdered with snow in winter; the desert is ablaze with cactus blooms in spring.

Most of Tucson's 11.4 inches of annual precipitation arrives during the late summer monsoon season when afternoon thunderstorms roll through the desert with high winds and dramatic lightning shows. During summer, the average high temperature hovers around 98. In winter, average highs are about 65, making the city a popular spot for winter visitors, who come to golf and relax in the balmy weather.

Basically, Tucson is an affable, unpretentious town that feels comfortable with itself. There's no need to impress anyone here with high fashion—blue jeans are good enough for most places. Nor do wealth

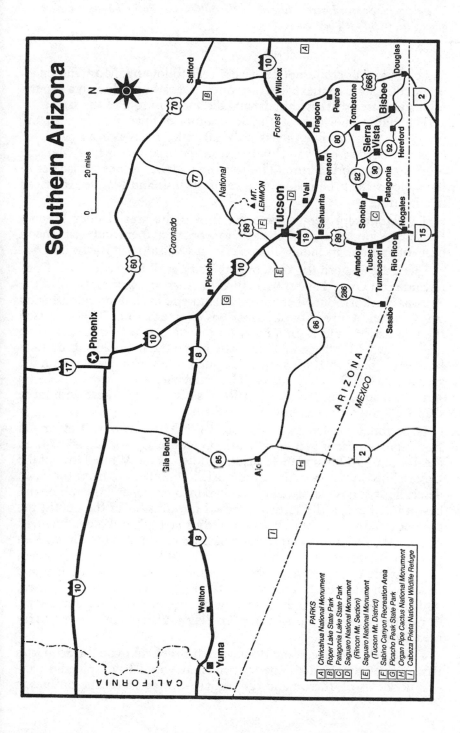

Southern Arizona

N

20 miles

PARKS
A Chiricahua National Monument
B Roper Lake State Park
C Patagonia Lake State Park
D Saguaro National Monument
   (Rincon Mt. Section)
E Saguaro National Monument
   (Tucson Mt. District)
F Sabino Canyon Recreation Area
G Picacho Peak State Park
H Organ Pipe Cactus National Monument
I Cabeza Prieta National Wildlife Refuge

The Arizona-Sonora Desert Museum on the outskirts of Tucson has been ranked among the world's ten best zoos.

and conspicuous consumption have a large following. Most Tucsonans don't come here to make lots of money, but rather to live in a beautiful, natural area that's within driving distance of more of the same.

The cultural heritage of Tucson is a mix of Spanish, Mexican and Native American. The city is only 60 miles from Nogales and the Mexican border, but you don't have to go that far to find Mexican food, artwork and culture. The red-tiled adobe homes spread across the valley reflect the residents' love of Spanish and Native American architecture.

The Hohokam people were the first in the area. Father Eusebio Francisco Kino, a Jesuit priest, came to work with them and established a chain of missions, including Tucson's famous Mission San Xavier del Bac.

Later, the Spanish flag flew over the city, as did the Mexican, Confederate and United States flags. In 1867, Tucson was the capital of the Arizona Territory. But when the capital moved north, disgruntled Tucson was given the University of Arizona as compensation. This increased the population, and it jumped again just before World War II when nearby Davis–Monthan Air Force Base began training pilots to fly B-17 bombers. Today 700,000 people call Tucson home and live within the metro area's 500 square miles. The university has grown to 35,000 students, and Davis–Monthan is still an active military base with more than 7500 military personnel and civilians.

Nine miles southwest of Tucson is the **Mission San Xavier del Bac** (signs appear as you drive south on Route 19; 602–294–2624) on the Tohono O'Odham Reservation. Known as the White Dove of the Desert, this stunning white adobe brick church rises from the open desert floor and is picturesquely framed by blue sky and the mountains beyond. Although the Jesuits founded the mission in the 1600s, the present building was built between 1783 and 1797. It is a combination of Spanish, Byzantine and Moorish architecture. Visitors can walk in through weathered mesquite doors, sit on the worn wooden pews, and feast their eyes on the ornate statues, carvings, painted designs and frescoes. In addition to touring the facility, you can attend daily mass, which is open to the public, or visit during one of the celebrations. Across the square in the **San Xavier Plaza**, Native Americans sell fry bread, arts and crafts.

Drive north to Speedway Boulevard, turn left and you'll reach Gates Pass, where the road begins to twist and you'll have splendid panoramic views of Tucson and the saguaro-dotted landscape of Tucson

Mountain Park. This is where you'll find **Old Tucson Studios** (201 South Kinney Road; 602-883-0100; admission), a re-creation of an old western frontier town. Columbia Pictures created Old Tucson Studios in 1939 as a movie location for the film *Arizona*, and since then more than 200 films and television episodes have been shot here including *Rio Bravo, Gunfight at the O.K. Corral* and *El Dorado*. If a film crew is in town, you can watch them shoot. Otherwise, ride the narrow-gauge railroad, watch shootouts on the wide dirt streets, enter the adobe and slatboard buildings and listen to dance-hall music, or indulge in shopping.

Just a few minutes down Kinney Road, **The Arizona-Sonora Desert Museum** (2021 North Kinney Road; 602-883-2702; admission; all exhibits wheelchair-accessible) is a cross between a zoo and botanical garden with more than 200 different animals and 400 plant species

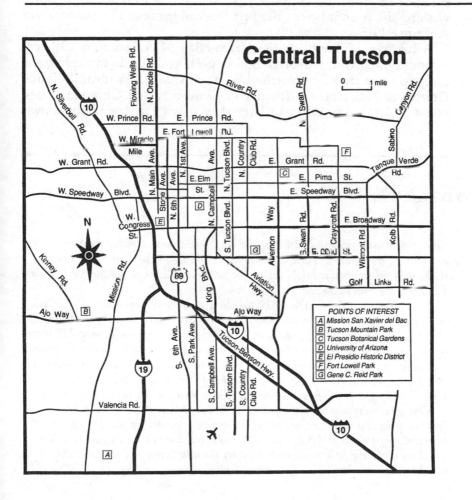

indigenous to the Sonoran Desert. Visitors can inspect the aquatic exhibits and the animals in their desert habitats, or walk inside an aviary and a re-created limestone cave. Definitely worth a visit.

Another place to find plants indigenous to the area is the **Tucson Botanical Gardens** (2150 North Alvernon Way; 602-326-9255; admission), which contains a small field of Native American crops, a cactus and succulent garden, tropical greenhouse, and a xeriscape (arid landscaping) demonstration garden. Perhaps most unusual is the historic garden—lush foliage and flowers that surround and reflect the era of the 1920s Porter House.

For a panoramic view of Tucson from 3100 feet, drive to the top of **A Mountain** (take Congress Street exit west off Route 10 to Cuesta Street, then go south onto Sentinel Peak Road). In territorial days, settlers used it as a lookout for Apache raiders. The latest raiders here are students from the University of Arizona, who have been whitewashing the A on it before the first football game of the season every year since 1915.

A big part of Tucson is the **University of Arizona**, a 298-acre campus dotted with red-brick buildings. If you decide to explore the campus, there are a few worthwhile stops. One is **Flandrau Science Center & Planetarium** (corner of University and Cherry avenues; 602-621-7827; admission to laser shows) with its laser light shows,

---

TED DE GRAZIA

One of Arizona's greatest artists was Ted De Grazia, who depicted the Southwest in paintings, prints, bronzes and collector's plates. His distinctive, impressionistic-style works with their signature bright colors and featureless faces hang in the De Grazia Gallery of the Sun in Tucson.

Born in Morenci, Arizona in 1909, the son of an Italian copper miner, De Grazia spent his life traveling throughout Mexico and the Southwest, learning the lore of the Apache, Navajo, Yaqui and Papago tribes and collecting three art degrees. His work can be found on anything from refrigerator magnets to a number of books and magazines because he believed an artist's work should be shared, not hidden away in museums. While alive, he was often found working in his gallery, wearing jeans and a hat, his rugged-looking face brown from the sun and covered by a salt-and-pepper colored beard.

One of his most surprising and publicized moves came in 1976. To protest the severe taxes on heirs of artists, he went to the Superstition Mountains and burned 150 of his painting—valued at 1.5 million dollars. He was irate that his wife would have to sell most of these paintings in order to pay the inheritance tax on their value whenever he died. In 1982, De Grazia died of cancer.

Student volunteers take visitors on free tours of the sprawling University of Arizona campus once or twice a day. For tour schedules, call 602-621-3641.

---

science store, public observatory with a 16-inch telescope available for public use and science exhibits such as a walk-through model asteroid and night skies exhibit. The **Center for Creative Photography** (1030 North Olive Street; 602-621-7968) has a collection of more than 50,000 photographs, along with galleries, a library and research facilities. Photography exhibitions from the permanent collection and traveling exhibitions are displayed in the galleries. The **University of Arizona Museum of Art** (Olive Street near Speedway Boulevard; 602-621-7567) has Renaissance and later European and American art, including works by Rembrandt, Picasso, Rothko and O'Keeffe. The collection includes more than 3000 paintings, sculptures, drawings and prints.

El Presidio Historic District (Church Avenue to Alameda Street) was once the Presidio of San Augustin del Tucson, which the Spanish army enclosed with a 12-foot-high adobe wall in 1783. Today, the main attraction in El Presidio is the **Tucson Museum of Art** (140 North Main Avenue; 602-624-2333; admission), a complex specializing in pre-Columbian, modern American and Southwest art, along with several historic houses and the Plaza of the Pioneers—a showplace for the museum's sculpture collection.

Fort Lowell Museum (2900 North Craycroft Road; 602-885-3832) is a reconstructed commanding officers' quarters from the days when it was a key military post during the Apache Indian wars of the 1870s and 1880s. Life on a military post in frontier Arizona is revealed through furnishings, artifacts and displays of military equipment.

The late Ted De Grazia gained fame painting impressionist-style portrayals of the Southwest and its people. Today, his home and galleries, the **De Grazia Gallery in the Sun** (6300 North Swan Road; 602-299-9191; admission), are open to the public. Skylights in the adobe structures bathe his paintings in light. Walking through, you pass beneath brick archways and through the landscaped courtyards that he so lovingly tended when he lived here. The unusual architecture, including an iron gate inspired by the historic Yuma Prison, is worth a visit in itself.

Arizona's oldest historical museum, the **Arizona Historical Society Museum** (949 East Second Street, Tucson; 602-628-5774) has everything from a full-scale reproduction of an underground mine tunnel to a history-of-transportation exhibit.

Pima Air Museum (6000 East Valencia Road; 602-574-0462; admission) contains one of the largest collections of historic aircraft in the world. Among the 160 aircraft on display here are the Boeing B-29 Superfortress, the type of plane that dropped the first atomic bomb on Japan, and the first jet fighter to exceed the speed of sound in level flight.

For a truly unusual experience, stop by **Biosphere 2** (Route 77 Mile Marker 96.5, Oracle; 602-825-6200; admission), a controversial three-acre enclosed miniature replica of the earth, complete with a tropical rainforest, savannah, marine marsh and desert. The airtight structure has been home to a research team of eight men and women who first entered the biosphere in the fall of 1991. They grow their own food, raise animals and are totally self-sufficient. Although you can't go inside the structure, you can check out the outside of this high-tech, space-age, glass-and-steel monolith, look through its glass walls and stop by the visitor center.

TUCSON LODGING

Built in the 1930s, the **Arizona Inn** (2200 East Elm Street; 602-325-1541) is an historic gem. Although it's in the middle of town, it feels like a lush oasis with 14 acres of lawns and gardens thick with orange trees, native cypress and date palms. No two of the resort's 80 rooms are alike, but all are decorated to the 1930s period and some have antiques. This deluxe-priced inn also has a pool, tennis courts, a restaurant and a cocktail lounge decorated with 19th-century Audubons.

Looking for a little pampering? Then check out the **Tucson National Golf and Conference Resort** (2727 West Club Drive; 602-297-2271 or 800-528-4856) where you can relax in the European spa with a massage, facial, herbal wrap and other treatments. Located on the northern edge of town, away from the city's hustle and bustle, the resort offers quiet and mountain views. The 119 ultra-deluxe-priced rooms have wet bars and refrigerators, and most have private patios overlooking the championship 27-hole golf course. Other amenities include a gift shop, restaurant, beauty salon, pool, tennis and basketball.

Spread on 80 acres in the foothills of the Catalina Mountains, **Westward Look Resort** (245 East Ina Road; 602-297-1151 or 800-722-2500) is a scenic getaway. The 244 moderate-to-deluxe-priced rooms here are actually worth spending time in with their beamed ceilings, couches, refrigerator and wet bar, skylights, balconies and Mexican tile trim on the extra-long bathroom sinks. If you ever leave the room, check out the tennis courts, fitness center, pools, spas, restaurant or lounge.

For an all-suite hotel in the deluxe range, stop by **Hotel Park Tucson** (5151 East Grant Road, Tucson; 602-323-6262 or 800-257-7275). The small lobby has a mural of Mexican village life and waterfalls. The newly renovated rooms are southwestern in style, but lean toward darker shades rather than pastels. All feature a couch, table, wet bar, coffee

---

*In May and June, if rainfall has been sufficient, saguaro cacti by the thousands burst
forth with their creamy blossoms, which are the state flower of Arizona.*

---

maker, fridge, a television in an armoire, and a tiny balcony just outside the sliding glass door. Amenities include a swimming pool, restaurant, jacuzzi, exercise room, sauna and steam room.

Hotel Congress (311 East Congress Street; 602-622-8848) is a
piece of Tucson's history. The block-long classical brick-and-marble
structure was built in 1919 to serve Southern Pacific railroad passengers, and members of John Dillinger's gang were among its guests.
Geometric Indian designs add character to the lobby, which also provides seating for the tiny Cup Café and overflow from the nightclubs.
The renovated hotel rooms are decorated with black-and-white tile
bathrooms, black headboards and salmon-colored walls. The hotel's
40 rooms are budget-priced, and seven are hostels with bunk or single
beds and private baths. None of the rooms have televisions, but they *do*
have a rarity nowadays—windows that open.

Bed and breakfasts are proliferating in Tucson. Built in 1905, the
Peppertrees Bed and Breakfast (724 East University Boulevard;
602-622-7167) is a Territorial home dominated by two large California pepper trees. There are two southwestern-style guest houses, and
two main rooms furnished with period pieces from England. French
doors lead outside to a beautifully landscaped patio. Moderate.

La Posada del Valle (1640 North Campbell Avenue; 602-795-
3840) is a stucco-and-adobe inn built in 1929. A novelty is afternoon
tea, served in a living room furnished with art deco antiques from the
1920s and 1930s. The 1920s' theme carries over to the five guest rooms,
and each is named after famous women of that era. Zelda's Room is a
favorite, with a 1920s' inlaid queen-size bedroom set. Moderate.

Centrally located, **North Campbell Suites Hotel** (2925 North
Campbell Avenue; 602-323-7378) offers four-room suites with kitchens at budget prices. The 11 rooms aren't fancy, but are homey and
functional with adequate furnishings and a hide-a-bed in the living
room for extra sleeping space. A swimming pool and trees help soften
the look of the motor court.

Tanque Verde Inn (7007 East Tanque Verde Road; 602-298-2300) is
an 89-room, hacienda-style inn with rooms overlooking a lush courtyard
dotted with Mexican fountains. Rooms are clean and comfortable;
some are kitchenettes. Breakfast is complimentary at this moderately
priced inn that also boasts a pool and local health club privileges.

For an assortment of budget motels, drive down Miracle Mile, once
the main thoroughfare through the city. The area is a bit seedy with

several strip joints, but there are a few decent places. One is the **Best Western Ghost Ranch Lodge** (801 West Miracle Mile; 602-791-7565). The lodge sits on what was once a working cattle ranch. Today, the property has 81 rooms housed in brick buildings surrounded by grassy lawns, palm trees and cactus gardens. The theme is western, with a cow skull over the lobby fireplace and western memorabilia throughout. There's also a restaurant, pool and whirlpool.

The Lodge on the Desert (306 North Alvernon Way; 602-325-3366) is a garden resort hotel with 40 adobe-colored villas grouped around patios that open to lawns and gardens. Rooms have beamed ceilings, hand-painted Mexican tile accents, Monterey furniture, and many have mesquite-burning beehive fireplaces. Other amenities include a restaurant and pool with mountain views. Moderate.

A bit north of Tucson on Mount Lemmon is the **Alpine Inn** (12925 East Sabino Canyon Road, Summerhaven; 602-576-1500). It's part pub, part country store, part six-room bed and breakfast. Rooms are plainly furnished with light-brown carpet, a card table with chairs, a dresser and shower/bathroom. Moderate.

The resorts are expensive during winter high season, but most slash prices during the hot summer months. Among the best resorts is the **Westin La Paloma** (3800 East Sunrise Drive; 602-742-6000). The 487 southwestern-style rooms have private balconies or patios, a sitting area, oversized closet and a stocked fridge. Many of the suites have woodburning fireplaces and sunken spa tubs. For recreation, there's a large swimming pool with swim-up bar, Jack Nicklaus golf course, tennis and racquetball courts, a health center and, for tired parents, day care for the small fry! Ultra-deluxe.

Located in the foothills of the Santa Catalina Mountains, **Loews Ventana Canyon** (7000 North Resort Drive; 602-299-2020) is another 93-acre, ultra-deluxe-priced resort. Highlights are an 80-foot waterfall cascading down into a lake and secluded paths lined with mesquite, squawbush and blue palo verde. Many of the 398 southwestern-style rooms have original artwork, burnished-pine furnishings, private balconies and bathrooms with marble floors. Amenities include five restaurants and lounges, tennis, golf, fitness trails, pools, a health club and shops.

One of the most luxurious getaways is **Tanque Verde Ranch** (14301 East Speedway Boulevard; 602-296-6275). It comes complete with indoor and outdoor swimming pools, tennis courts, an exercise room and, of course, horseback riding. Guests stay in one of 60 casitas and patio lodges, some with beehive fireplaces, antiques and Indian bedspreads. Sliding glass doors offer stunning desert views. To relax, cozy up in the lounge with a good western novel by the stone fireplace. The ultra-deluxe ranch has been around since the 1880s.

White Stallion Ranch (9251 West Twin Peaks Road; 602-297-0252) sprawls across 3000 acres—grazing land for their herd of Longhorn. Guests take breakfast rides, watch rodeos every Saturday afternoon, and pet deer, sheep and pygmy goats at the on-site zoo. Rooms at this deluxe-priced ranch are rustic with western decor.

Don't look for televisions or telephones inside the 20-room **Lazy K Bar Ranch** (8401 North Scenic Drive; 602-744-3050), because here you're meant to leave the outside world behind. Ranch-style meals are served in a dining room, and Saturday night is set aside for steak cookouts beside a ten-foot waterfall. Afterwards, you can relax in the comfortable library with wood paneling and beams, bookshelves, a fireplace and card table. Rooms are rustic. Deluxe.

North of town is **The Triangle L Ranch** (2805 Triangle L Ranch Road, Oracle; 602-623-6732), an 1880s' homestead on an 80-acre ranch. The four private cottages include an ivy-covered adobe cottage with a clawfoot tub in the bathroom and screened sleeping porch, and one with a stone fireplace, rose arbor entry and private patio. A wood-burning stove warms the kitchen for breakfast, which consists of eggs from the owner's chickens and other homemade treats. Moderate.

Picacho Motel (6698 Eisenhower Street, Picacho; 602-466-7500) has been around since the 1930s. Waitresses in the lobby restaurant often double as receptionists to check guests into this casual, budget-priced motel. Just outside the 17 rooms are palm and fruit trees, while inside is somewhat worn wood paneling hung with country pictures, along with bureaus and desks.

TUCSON RESTAURANTS

There is an eclectic mix of cuisine in Tucson, but Southwest and Sonoran-style Mexican fare are the specialties. For southwestern food, try **Café Terra Cotta** (4310 North Campbell Avenue; 602-577-8100). The outdoor patio is lit by miniature white lights at night, while the indoor section is decorated in turquoise and terra cotta colors. Entrées include large prawns stuffed with herbed goat cheese and southwestern tomato coulis, stuffed red and green chilies, and innovative pizzas that are cooked in the woodburning oven and topped with ingredients such as chorizo, herbed mozzarella, lime and cilantro. Moderate.

Although Key lime pie is on the menu, most of the other dishes at the **Presidio Grill** (3352 East Speedway Boulevard; 602-327-4667) are southwestern in flavor. Try an appetizer of Anaheim chili stuffed with chorizo, fresh corn, cilantro and havarti, followed by innovative pizzas, pastas and grilled meats. Decor here is postmodern with an unusual color scheme of black, green, orange and yellow. And for those booth aficionados among us, it's nice to find a place with more booths than tables. Priced in the moderate range.

You can't beat **Janos** (150 North Main Avenue; 602-884-9426) for American nouvelle cuisine with a southwestern twist. The adobe house shares a courtyard with the Tucson Museum of Art, and inside displays of original art hang below ocotillo ceilings on 20-foot-high walls. Menus change with the seasons, but typical entrées are lobster with papaya and champagne, or a meal of hickory smoked duck, chestnut mousse and cranberry butter. Ultra-deluxe.

It's hard to beat dining at **Anthony's in the Catalinas** (6440 North Campell Avenue; 602-299-1771) with its top-notch views and ambiance. The almost floor-to-ceiling windows look out over the city lights in this hacienda-style building. Dinner is served on Villeroy & Boch china with pale pink linens, fresh flowers and classical music playing in the background. Chandeliers hang from the vaulted, beamed ceiling and a large fireplace warms the room in winter. The continental specialties include veal Catalina with artichokes, mushrooms and green onions, lamb Wellington and chicken Cordon Bleu. Wash it down with a bottle from their extensive selection of about 1300 wines. Deluxe

Drive about a half-mile off Tanque Verde Road into a landscape full of cactus and mesquite and you'll find **The Tack Room** (2800 North Sabino Canyon Road; 602-722-2800), a truly western dining experience. Inside the Italianate villa, the feel is rustic with horse saddles, a deer head above the fireplace, rough-hewn beamed ceilings and a stone fireplace. But instead of western wear, waiters sport tuxedos and the ultra-deluxe-priced food with a twist of Southwest flavor is anything but casual. Try the rack of lamb with mesquite honey, which comes with chile-cheese corn muffin, the Norwegian salmon with cilantro butter, or other steak and seafood entrées.

Café Magritte (254 East Congress Street; 602-884-8004) is an intimate, artsy café located in the heart of the arts district. The two-story eatery has wood floors and brick walls hung with local artwork. The food is eclectic, but has a hint of the Southwest. Specialties include brie melted over crabmeat tortilla rolls, and chicken simmered in garlic, mixed with cheese, corn, green chilies and red peppers. Budget.

Just down the road is **Bentley's House of Coffee & Tea** (121 East Congress Street; 602-798-1715). Here, you choose the ambience. One dining room is sophisticated, with black tables and chairs and modern artwork, while the other room is cozier and contains shelves lined with books. Food is typical café fare—soups, sandwiches, quiches— while beverages include espresso, gourmet coffee and a wide range of Italian cream sodas. Budget.

Tucsonans love Mexican food, and there are no lack of choices. Rosita Sinbres presides over **El Arte de Rosita** (1944 East Prince

Road; 602-881-5380), cooking all of their tasty Mexican food. On the walls hang photographs of Rosita with the late artist and friend Ted De Grazia, along with some of his prints. Handmade crocheted curtains cover the windows, while outside Christmas lights line the porch year-round and plants take root in clawfoot tubs. Eclectic homestyle best describes the atmosphere, while the prices are budget.

Mi Nidito Café (1813 South 4th Avenue; 602-622-5081) is a tiny, tacky, crowded Mexican joint with great food, from enchiladas to menudo. Portions are generous and there are always plenty of locals lining up to fatten their waistlines. Walls are covered with murals of palm trees and lighted plastic flowers. Budget.

Micha's (2908 South 4th Avenue; 602-623-5307) is a larger restaurant owned by the Mariscal family for many years and whose portrait is just inside the door. On weekends, mariachi bands stroll through the restaurant. You won't leave here hungry—even the flour tortillas are about a foot in length. Don't miss the chimichangas, topopo salad or grilled shrimp fantasia. Budget.

Walk into **Café Poca Cosa** (88 East Broadway Boulevard; 602-622-6400) and you're surrounded by festive colors. Green paint covers the ceilings, red chili peppers dot the walls, lights hang on indoor trees, and purple, green and red tiles cover the tables. The menu changes two or three times daily, and is written on a blackboard that's brought to the table. Dishes are homestyle Mexican. Specialties include chicken breast in mango sauce, *pollo en chitotle* (chili) sauce and pork marinated in beer. Breakfast is also served. Budget to moderate.

Located in the warehouse district, **Tooley's** (299 South Park Avenue; 602-798-3331) is little more than a glorified taco stand with good food. Customers order food at an outdoor window, then sit at one of the handful of tables on the sidewalk or perch on the curb. The menu boasts that Tooley's is home of the turkey taco, and turkey is used instead of chicken on all their entrées. If you're watching your wallet, you can't beat the super budget prices here.

If you'd rather stay away from high-calorie Mexican food, try **The Good Earth** (6366 East Broadway Boulevard; 602-745-6600), the local choice for health foods. The extensive menu has salads, hot and cold sandwiches, pasta, seafood, chicken, vegetarian dishes and breakfast items that are served all day long. Although spacious, the atmosphere is nevertheless cozy with earth-toned decor, solid wood tables, lots of hanging plants, and a cactus garden to add a touch of the Southwest. Budget.

Tork's Café (1701 North Country Club Road; 602-325-3737) is a tiny, family-run place with only a handful of tables and delicious Middle Eastern food. The *shawerma* plate with beef, chicken or lamb contains strips of meat cooked with onions and bell peppers. Other choices are the vegetarian falafel plate, hummus dip, tabuli and kabobs. Prices are in the budget category.

Buddy's Grill (4821 East Grant Road; 602-795-2226) is a white-collar hangout. The narrow, blue-and-white room consists mainly of booths. Here, you'll find fajita salads, sandwiches, burgers cooked on a mesquite-wood grill and delicious baked French onion soup. You might also take a peek at the exhibition kitchen. Budget.

Classical music, fresh flowers and candles—all help set a romantic mood at **Le Rendezvous** (3844 East Fort Lowell Road; 602-323-7373), a French restaurant where the specials change daily depending on the market. Try the Grand Marnier soufflé, which takes 45 minutes to make, the duck à l'orange, or veal medallions with apple and calvados. Moderate to deluxe.

As the name suggests, diners at **Van Gogh's Ristorante Italiano** (7895 East Broadway Boulevard; 602-722-5518) can eat Italian food amid reproductions of Van Gogh's artwork. Along with traditional, moderately priced fare, you'll find more imaginative specials such as roast duck stuffed with smoked oysters and pine nuts, served with a Grand Marnier sauce. In addition, diners can hear live jazz music on the enclosed patio.

Don't let the shopping center location stop you from visiting **Boccata** (5605 East River Road; 602-577-9309), whose main draws are city views and good Northern Italian/Southern French food. The ambiance is simple and sophisticated, with plum and yellow walls dotted with contemporary art. Among the moderately priced choices are the Penne Ciao Bella with grilled chicken, roasted peppers, artichoke hearts and pine nuts in white wine sauce, or the Veal Ravioli in a goat cheese cream sauce.

For the innovative in pizza, try **Magpies Pizza** (605 North 4th Avenue; 602-628-1661). Pizzas you may want to try include "The Greek," with spinach, basil, garlic, piñon nuts, feta cheese, cheese and sundried tomatoes, and "Cathy's," with garlic, stewed tomatoes, mushrooms, artichokes, roasted red peppers and Romano cheese. Located in a small strip center, Magpies has a contemporary look with its black-and-white tile floor, red chairs and modern art on the walls. Prices range from budget to moderate.

In the next block is **Delectables** (533 North 4th Avenue; 602-884-9289), where waiters with ponytails often hover over tables. Inside are wood-beamed ceilings and curving windows that look out onto 4th Avenue, while outside are somewhat rundown green metal tables with matching chairs. Moderately priced salads and sandwiches, such as turkey breast with havarti and avocado, are the choices here.

Walk through antique, hacienda-style doors and you're inside **Tohono Chul Tearoom** (7633 North Paseo Del Norte; 602-797-1711),

The two boulevards boasting the largest concentration of restaurants in town are Broadway and Speedway.

located in a rustic, 50-year-old house in the midst of Tohono Chul Park. Unless the weather is bad, opt for outdoor dining on a patio that sits amid palo verde trees and cactus, and offers free entertainment from the birds and other critters that come to nibble. For lunch, innovative sandwiches are served on croissants or sourdough bread. Other choices are breakfast, Sunday brunch and afternoon tea complete with finger sandwiches, scones and pastries. Budget.

The **Olympic Flame** (7970 East Broadway Boulevard; 602-296-3399) offers something rare in a Greek restaurant—white tablecloths and fresh flowers. They serve flaming *saganaki* at the table amid a chorus of opas, as well as pastitsio, moussaka, gyro, steaks and Greek-style salads. Moderate.

Jamaica Bay Café (6330 East Speedway Boulevard; 602-296-6111) has, as one would expect, a tropical setting with high ceilings, plants and colorful carpeting. Specialties of this moderately priced Caribbean restaurant include tomato-based Jamaican stew with sirloin and potatoes, Jamaican black bean soup and, for dessert, *tembleque* (Jamaican coconut custard pudding).

Farther down the road is **Szechuan Omei Restaurant** (2601 East Speedway Boulevard; 602-325-7204), a Chinese restaurant where you can choose from more than 130 entrées, including lunch specials. Decor is nothing fancy, just red tablecloths and chairs and the usual Chinese lanterns and paintings. Budget.

Meat lovers may want to pull up a chair at **The Ranchers Club** (5151 East Grant Road; 602-797-2624), where you can order aged prime beef and seafood grilled over your choice of mesquite, hickory, wild cherry or sassafras wood. There is also a variety of sauces, butters and condiments, including wild-mushroom sauce, onion marmalade and Cajun rémoulade. A harpist plays while diners are seated at tables set with pink tablecloths and candles, but this elegant setting has a western twist, with decorative touches such as cow horns and other western paraphernalia. Deluxe.

Webb's Old Spanish Trail Steak House (5400 South Old Spanish Trail; 602-885-7782) specializes in delicious barbecue ribs and chicken, as well as steaks. The moderately priced restaurant is casual with a few picnic tables thrown into the seating plan. At night, settle down by the picture window and you're likely to see javelinas stop by to feed.

At the **Arizona Inn** (2200 East Elm Street; 602-325-1541), you choose the ambience: formal dining room, casual patio or courtyard ablaze with tiny lights in the trees. The fare includes Continental, Southwest, nouvelle and traditional selections. One treat is the fresh steamed fish, enhanced with ginger and leeks, and served at your table from a bamboo steamer. Or how about trying those buffalo burgers? Moderate prices.

The **Gold Room** (245 East Ina Road; 602-297-1151) is at the Westward Look Resort. Dine with a stellar view of the city. Meats and seafood are prepared with a French twist, such as veal Oscar with crab meat, roast rack of lamb and châteaubriand. A few entrées are Mexican in style, such as a broiled New York steak sandwich served on toast with green chilies, cheese and red onions. Deluxe.

At the **Blue Willow Restaurant** (2616 North Campbell Avenue; 602-795-8736), you can either dine inside the house with its light blue walls and artsy posters, or opt for the brick, vine-covered courtyard. Either choice is a winner. Although they serve sandwiches and salads at lunch and dinner, breakfast is the most popular meal here with 24 omelettes, including one with spinach, tomatoes and onions, or one with avocado, jack cheese and green chilies. Prices fall in the budget category.

The **Alpine Inn** (12925 East Sabino Canyon Road, Summerhaven; 602-576-1500) offers Eastern European cuisine such as beef stroganoff and an alpine Bavarian grill that includes grilled knockwurst, smoked wurst, German-style potato salad and cabbage. To really get decadent, top it off with Swiss white-chocolate fondue laced with frangelica and piñons. Moderate.

Although it's in the lobby of the Picacho Motel, the **Picacho Restaurant** (6698 Eisenhower Street, Picacho; 602-466-7500) is a cozy affair with dark-wood ceilings and booths and a southwestern flavor with cow skulls and Indian rugs on the wall. People come mainly for the over-sized hamburgers, although sandwiches, steaks and Mexican food are also served. Budget.

TUCSON SHOPPING

For shopping mixed with entertainment, head for the **Tucson Arts District** (located downtown roughly between Congress and Cushing streets, and Main and 4th avenues; 602-624-9977) on the first and third Saturday of the month. Stores and restaurants stay open late, musicians perform in the streets, and the area becomes a hot night spot for entertainment seekers and shopaholics. There are 28 galleries, in addition to antique, novelty and specialty shops.

B&B Trading Co. (300 East Congress Street; 602-798-3906) carries southwestern antiques and collectibles, including cowboy saddles and spurs. **Berta Wright Gallery** (260 East Congress Street; 602-

882-7043) has a wide range of high-quality Mexican imports. For the tykes, there's **Yikes!** (278 East Congress Street; 602-792-9505), a toy store with unusual gifts, small toys and books. **Periwinkles** (266 East Congress Street; 602-624-9941) specializes in children's footwear—one whole wall is devoted to unusual socks!

Nearby is **4th Avenue** with about 70 shops and restaurants. Shops in this older neighborhood contain vintage clothing, unique fashions, jewelry, books and art. Don't be surprised to find some distinctive touches, such as incense burning in the shops.

Antigone Books (600 North 4th Avenue; 602-792-3715) specializes in books for and about women. **The Jewel Thief** (557 North 4th Avenue; 602-623-7554) offers a huge selection of earrings, with most hanging on large boards around the shop and priced under $10. For clothing, try **Jasmine** (423 North 4th Avenue; 602-629-0706) with its natural-fiber clothing, some handwoven in Morocco, or **Del Sol** (435 North 4th Avenue; 602-628-8765) with its southwestern-style clothes, scarves and jewelry, and a huge selection of Indian rugs.

In the El Presidio Historic District downtown is **Old Town Artisans** (186 North Meyer Avenue; 602-623-6024), an 1850s restored adobe structure with surrounding shops that fill an entire city block. In the outdoor courtyard hang chili peppers and handmade hummingbird feeders, along with Mexican fireplaces. Inside the 13-room marketplace is southwestern folk art made by Arizona artisans, Native American tribal art and imports from Latin America. Another worthwhile stop in this area is the **Tucson Museum of Art gift shop** (140 North Main Street; 602-624-2333), which offers contemporary pottery and other artistic gifts.

Many Hands Courtyard of Artisans (3054 North 1st Avenue) is styled after a Mexican village and sells handmade works by local artists. Shops here include **The Artist's Threads** (602-798-3454) with handwoven clothing and accessories, **Anni's Ears Galleria** (602-299-0523) with southwestern furniture, turquoise jewelry and oxidized copper jewelry, and **This and That Crafts** (602-623-3260) with kachina dolls, paintings, stitchery and wooden crafts.

For Mexican imports, check out what is unofficially called the Lost Warehouse District—a group of shops located in old, red-brick warehouses. **Rustica** (200 South Park Avenue; 602-623-4435) sells southwestern and Mexican furnishings and accessories at wholesale prices, while **Magellan Trading** (228 South Park Avenue; 602-622-4968) has great buys on Mexican glassware and handcrafted imports from Mexico and the Pacific Rim that include antique furniture, wood carvings and folk art.

St. Philips Plaza (corner of River Street and Campbell Avenue) is a cluster of southwestern-style shops with red-tile roofs that include

B&B Cactus Farm (11550 East Speedway Boulevard, Tucson; 602-721-4687) has more than 600 varieties of cacti and succulents from around the world.

art galleries, clothing stores and restaurants. **Bahti Indian Arts** (602-577-0290) offers Native American crafts such as drums, jewelry, rugs and kachina dolls, while **Mercado de las Americas Gallery** (602-577-0640) has imports from Mexico, Peru, Chile and Ecuador, including pottery, masks and folk art. Check out the bridge and pond in the back of the store. For pricey Italian shoes, stop by **Espada Footwear** (602-299-6650).

Drive farther down River Road and you'll see **River Center** (corner of River Street and Craycroft Road) a southwestern-style shopping plaza. The stores surround a brick courtyard with a fountain and waterway. **Totally Southwest** (602-577-2295) has southwestern gifts while **Gift Alternatives Inc.** (602-299-8121) has unusual items for gift baskets from prickly pear erasers to chocolate caramel-covered tortillas. **The West** (602-299-1044) has cookbooks, cards, kids' gifts and needlework supplies, with proceeds going to local charities.

Built in 1932, **Broadway Village** (corner of Broadway Boulevard and Country Club Road) was one of the first shopping centers in Arizona. It houses a variety of shops in whitewashed red brick buildings. Among the more unusual is a tiny mystery bookshop called **The Footprints of a Gigantic Hound** (16 Broadway Village; 602-326-8533), where a huge Irish wolfhound is often found sprawling across most of the floor. There are also two expensive, fashionable children's boutiques called **Boomers** (602-323-2441) and **Angel Threads** (602-326-1170), and a fun, unusual children's toy store called **Mrs. Tiggy-Winkle's** (602-326-0188).

For antiques outside the downtown area, browse through **Unique Antique** (5000 East Speedway Boulevard; 602-323-0319), a 75-dealer antique mall that owners claim is the largest in southern Arizona, or **Sandy's Antiques** (4500 East Speedway Boulevard, Suite 78; 602-327-0772), which specializes in gold and silver jewelry from the Navajo and Zuni, as well as furniture, collectibles, clocks and dolls.

Casas Adobes Shopping Center (7051 North Oracle Road) is yet *another* southwestern-style shopping plaza with a variety of specialty shops. A favorite is **Antigua de Mexico** (602-742-7114), a Latin American import store with Mexican Colonial and southwestern furniture, folk art, pottery, glassware, tinware, sterling silver and jewelry from Taxco.

North Campbell Avenue has a number of shopping venues. One of the most popular, judging by the ever-crowded parking lot, is **Book-**

man's (1930 East Grant Road; 602-325-5767)—*the* place for biblio-philes to browse. The owner claims the largest selection of used books and new magazines in the Southwest. Bookman's also has a rare book room and sells used magazines, records, tapes and CDs. As an added bonus, classical guitarists or jazz pianists perform live every day. There's also **African Arts Ltd.** (3025 North Campbell Avenue, Suite 151; 602-795-1997) with traditional and contemporary African items, from beer pot covers to baskets made of banana leaves.

Upscale shopping in a beautiful setting describes **Foothills Mall** (602-742-7191). Painted clouds cover the ceiling between skylights, and a waterfall tumbles down steps from ceiling to floor. For culture, stroll through the toy train museum or The Old Pueblo Museum with changing displays, then stop by the specialty shops. Jazz music plays in the background at **Suttons** (602-297-1308), where shoppers find clothes by national designers such as Calvin Klein. More expensive clothing is displayed at **Cele Peterson's** (602-297-1035). Department stores are **Dillard's** (602-742-2171) and **Foley's** (602-742-8151). With only about 40 specialty stores and restaurants, shopping here tends to be more relaxed than at the megamalls in town.

TUCSON NIGHTLIFE

THE BEST BARS   **Bum Steer** (1910 North Stone Avenue; 602-884-7377) is a casual place in a large, barnlike building containing a restaurant, several bars, a video arcade, volleyball court and small dance-floor. Inside, everything from cannons to airplanes hang from the vaulted roof. The campus crowd flocks to the place.

Even if you don't plan to eat or drink, the **Solarium Restaurant and Lounge** (6444 East Tanque Verde Road; 602-886-8186) is worth a visit just to see the architecture. The best description defies description, but the three-story wood structure is a cross between a ship and a greenhouse. Enter through large floral iron doors, and inside are lots of windows, plants and wood planks. An acoustical guitarist performs Tuesday through Saturday.

The Chicago Bar (5954 East Speedway Boulevard; 602-748-8169) offers a heady mix of music. There's rock-and-roll on Monday and Tuesday, reggae on Wednesday and Thursday, blues on Friday and Saturday, and Motown on Sunday. Chicago memorabilia covers the walls, from White Sox parking signs to hometown banners. Cover.

Berkey's Bar (5769 East Speedway Boulevard; 602-296-1981) is another good place to hear the blues with live music all week long. An older crowd hangs out here, ordering drinks from the glass block bar, dancing and shooting pool.

Gentle Ben's Brewing Co. (841 North Tyndall Avenue; 602-624-4177) is a microbrewery near campus with delicious European-style ales, the most popular being Red Cat Amber and Tucson Blonde. If you're there at the right time of month, you can actually see workers doing the brewing. Inside, the wooden floors and tables have obviously been much worn by the campus crowd, and outside is a big patio to see and be seen. There's live reggae and rock on Friday and Saturday.

Laffs Comedy Nightclub (2900 East Broadway Boulevard; 602-323-8669) hosts everything from national to local acts. Tuesday is open mike night, Wednesday is ladies night and Thursday is college and military I.D. night.

The smell of money is thick in **The Board Room** (5350 East Broadway Boulevard; 602-750-7555), where lawyers and other professionals meet. Pictures of courtrooms adorn the place, along with lots of oak and brass. While you're there, don't forget to try Dave's Electric Beer brewed in Bisbee, Arizona.

Follow the cowboy hats and neon lights and you'll end up at **Cactus Moon** (5470 East Broadway Boulevard; 602-748-0049), a huge place specializing in country music. Western artwork hangs on the walls and rodeos roll on movie screens. A glittering, colored light shines on the dancefloor, which is big enough for two-steppers not to be toe-steppers. Cover on weekends.

Cactus Moon is tiny compared to **Wild Wild West** (4385 West Ina Road; 602-744-7744), a music hangout that sprawls over an entire acre. Inside are both a country and a rock-and-roll bar, each with its own dancefloor. Around the perimeter of the Wild Wild West are stores selling items from cowboy hats to photographs, and in the middle is Tucson's only racetrack dancefloor. There's no live music; weekend cover.

A green neon sign announces the **Green Dolphin** (95 North Park Avenue; 602-622-6099), a college hangout with green walls, graffiti on the ceilings, lots of beer posters, beer mirrors and assorted other clutter. Although there's live music occasionally, people mainly come here to drink and shoot pool.

For salsa and traditional jazz music, stop by **Café Sweetwater** (340 East 6th Street; 602-622-6464), a narrow bar squeezed next door to the restaurant.

Graffiti on the tables and walls is the decor at **Bob Dobbs' Bar & Grill** (2501 East 6th Street; 602-325-3767), a local hangout for the college and older crowd. A bright, noisy place, it has indoor and outdoor seating and plenty of televisions for catching the latest sports coverage.

For alternative music—and alternative crowds—peek into **Club Congress** (311 East Congress Street; 602-622-8849) adjoining the Hotel Congress. Tucson's unconventional set mixes with the college crowd at this cavern-like place with a red-and-brown-tile floor and dark walls. Cover.

Once a blacksmith shop, store and nightclub in the 1930s, today **Cushing Street Bar and Restaurant** (343 South Meyer Avenue; 602-622-7984) is a popular bar featuring live blues, jazz, rock and reggae. Patrons here enjoy drinks in turn-of-the-century tables and chairs amid antiques such as a floor-to-ceiling, 1880s legal bookcase and a circa-1850 cut-glass globe above the bar. There's also an outdoor patio. Cover.

Tucson McGraws (4110 South Houghton Road; 602-885-3088) is a Mexican cantina with a bar and dining room. Step outside, walk down the steps and you'll land on the terrace ramada that looks toward the Santa Rita Mountains and Tucson's beautiful sunsets. An outdoor fireplace warms customers on cold evenings, and a guitarist entertains on weekends.

If you're a beer lover, don't miss **The Shanty** (401 East 9th Street; 602-622-7107) with more than 100 different beers from around the world, including Peru and Tahiti. Push a heavy copper door and you'll enter a room with a copper-topped bar and tables. Outside diners enjoy drinks on a brick-paved patio surrounded by vine-covered wrought-iron walls. The place has been around since 1937, but it's in a somewhat seedy area of town so watch your step.

THEATER   **Arizona Theater Company** (330 South Scott Avenue; 602-884-4875) has been unofficially called the State Theater of Arizona and performs six varied productions in Phoenix and Tucson from October to June. Plays by the Arizona Theater Company and other groups are performed in the restored Spanish Colonial Revival **Temple of Music and Art**, built in 1927.

Gaslight Theatre (7000 East Tanque Verde Road; 602-886-9428) offers corny musical melodramas. Patrons eat free popcorn while hissing at the villains and cheering for the hero or heroines. Many of the comedies are original, written especially for the theatre.

Invisible Theatre (1400 North 1st Avenue; 602-882-9721) has classics, musicals and Off Broadway plays by Arizona playwrights and contemporary dramatists. During the lunch hour, they offer brown-bag play festivals.

OPERA, SYMPHONY AND DANCE   **Ballet Arizona** (602-882-5022) is the state's professional ballet company that performs in both Tucson and Phoenix. They perform a repertoire of classical and contemporary works, including world and national premieres.

Southern Arizona Light Opera Company (908 North Swan Road; 602-323-7888) performs four Broadway musicals a year at the Tucson Convention Center Music Hall.

For the romantically inclined, the Sabino Canyon shuttle has moonlight rides during full moons from April to June and September to December.

Arizona Opera (3501 North Mountain Avenue; 602-293-4336) serves both Tucson and Phoenix and produces Grand Opera. The Tucson season runs from October through March, and productions have included *Don Giovanni*, *Otello* and *Madame Butterfly*.

For classical, pops and chamber concerts, there is the **Tucson Symphony Orchestra** (443 South Stone Avenue; 602-792-9155).

Centennial Hall (University of Arizona, Building 29; 602-621-3341) hosts a full lineup on an international scale, from Chinese acrobatics to African dances. Past performers include Itzhak Perlman, Prague Symphony Orchestra and George Winston.

A professional modern dance company, **Tenth Street Danceworks** (738 North 5th Avenue; 602-628-8880) performs about four times a year and specializes in mixed media videography, projecting video images on a screen or on the dancers.

TUCSON PARKS

Gene C. Reid Park (602-791-4560) is a lush oasis in the desert with grassy expanses dotted with mature trees. There are a wide variety of recreational facilities here, including two golf courses, a swimming pool, pond, tennis and racquetball courts and Hi-Corbett field, where major league baseball teams come for Spring Training. Other attractions are Reid Park Zoo and a rose garden with more than 2000 plants. The park is between Broadway Boulevard and 22nd Street, Country Club Road and Alvernon Way.

Winding, hilly roads take you through **Tucson Mountain Park**, an 18,000-acre, high-desert area located about ten miles west of the city limits brimming with ocotillo, palo verde, mesquite and saguaros, and punctuated by mountains with rugged volcanic peaks. A popular spot is the Gates Pass overlook just past Speedway, where you can pull off the road and get a panoramic view of Tucson, Avra Valley and Kitt Peak. It's also a good place to watch Arizona's renowned sunsets. The park also includes the Arizona-Sonora Desert Museum and Old Tucson.

Fort Lowell Park (2900 North Craycroft Road), with its blend of history and recreation, is an ideal family getaway. Fort Lowell was once a major military post and supply depot. Stroll between the trees on Cottonwood Lane, and you'll see a number of ruins, including that of the adobe post hospital built in 1875. There's a museum in the reconstructed officers' quarters. The 59-acre park also has a pond with a fountain and plenty of hungry ducks around the perimeter, tennis and racquetball courts, and a trail with marked exercise stops along the way.

Established in 1933 to protect the saguaro cactus (found mainly in Arizona), **Saguaro National Monument** is divided into two segments on opposite sides of Tucson. The most popular is the 66,336-acre Rincon Mountain Unit east of town. Begin your tour at the visitor center, which offers dioramas and other exhibits of the geological and botanical history of the monument. Then drive along Cactus Forest Drive, a scenic eight-mile loop showing off tall saguaro cacti with their splayed arms.

The 20,738-acre Tucson Mountain District to the west features the six-mile-long Bajada Loop Drive that passes dense saguaro forests and Indian petroglyphs. Overall, the monument has more than 100 miles of hiking trails. Drive east on Old Spanish Trail about three miles beyond Tucson's city limits to get to the Rincon Mountain Unit; the Tucson Mountain District is two miles beyond the Arizona-Sonora Desert Museum off Kinney Road. For information, call 602-296-8576.

Sabino Canyon, one of the most scenic spots in the region, is a route that cuts through the Santa Catalina Mountains in the Coronado National Forest. You can either hike or take the shuttle on a seven-and-a-half-mile round trip that climbs a road lined with cottonwoods, sycamores, ash and willow trees. Along the route flows Sabino Creek with its pools and waterfalls that tumble underneath arched stone bridges. The shuttle makes nine stops along the way, so you can jump on or off as you go. The shuttle will also take you on the two-and-a-half-mile trip to Bear Canyon Trail, where you then hike two more miles to Seven Falls, which cascade almost 500 feet down the side of a hill. (For general information: 602-749-3223; shuttle information: 602-749-2861.)

In the hour's drive from Tucson to the top of **Mount Lemmon**, you travel from a lower Sonoran Desert zone to a Canadian zone for-

---

SURVIVAL OF THE SAGUARO

In order to live in the desert, the saguaro cactus has had to be very inventive. The green weight in a mature saguaro is from 75 to 95 percent water. When the weather is so dry that the roots can no longer get water from the soil, there is enough water in the saguaro tissue to stay alive. During dry months, the saguaro's diameters shrink and fold in like an accordion and their ribs become more angled. Even with an 80 percent water loss from their stems, a young saguaro can live. (A human can't live with even a 12 percent water deficit.) The saguaro's roots are shallow—usually not more than three feet below the surface, but extend as much as 100 feet laterally from the plant to eke every bit of moisture from the earth.

est, from cactus to pine forest. For this reason, Tucsonans flock here in summer to escape the heat, and in winter to ski at Mount Lemmon Ski Valley, the southernmost ski area in the United States. If you take Catalina Highway to the top, the steep and winding mountain road will pass Rose Canyon Lake stocked with trout, and the town of Summerhaven, with its handful of shops and restaurants. Once on Mount Lemmon, you can hike on your choice of some 150 miles of trails.

Few tourists seem to know about **Tohono Chul Park**, a treasure hidden in northwest Tucson. But walk down the winding paths of the 35-acre park and you'll discover about 400 species of arid-climate plants, many of which are labeled, along with water fountains, grotto pond areas and a greenhouse with plants for sale. In addition, you'll find an art gallery, two gift shops and a tea room. The park is located off Route 89 at 7366 North Paseo del Norte, about six miles north of the Tucson city limits.

Catalina State Park (602-628-5798) is a 5500-acre preserve set in the foothills of the Santa Catalina Mountains. Highlights include Romero Canyon, a beautiful area with clear pools shaded by sycamore and oak trees, and adjacent Pusch Ridge Wilderness, home to desert bighorn sheep. The Hohokam once farmed the area, and as you walk through the park, you'll see some of the pit houses and ball court ruins.

The most dramatic part of **Picacho Peak State Park** is Picacho Peak, a landmark formation that rises 1500 feet above the desert floor and can be seen for miles around. The peak is believed to be 22 million years old and was used as a landmark by early explorers. It was also the site of the battle of Picacho Pass during the Civil War. The 3400-acre park is located 40 miles north of Tucson just off Route 10 and offers hiking trails that wind past saguaro cacti.

East of Tucson

The Wild West comes to life in this area of Arizona where murder and lynching were once considered leisure activities, poker was more popular than Sunday church services and whiskey was king. While this region is best known for infamous spots like Boot Hill and the O.K. Corral, it's also the home of historic mining towns like Bisbee, mineral spas and a cowboy hall of fame.

Get on Route 10 heading east and one of the first attractions you'll pass is **Colossal Cave** (off Old Spanish Trail in Vail; 602-791-7677; admission), one of the largest dry caverns in the world. Set in the Rincon Mountains, it was once home for Indians and outlaws. During 50-minute tours, hidden lights illuminate formations such as the Frozen Waterfall and Kingdom of the Elves.

Farther east on Route 10 is Benson, where the **Arts & Historical Museum** (180 South San Pedro Street; 602-586-3070) tells the story of how Benson grew along with the arrival of the railroad. Inside are antiques, artifacts and a huge mural running down one wall depicting the Pony Express from Dragoon to Benson. A gift shop offers local arts and crafts.

On your way to the Old West towns of Bisbee and Tombstone, take a detour toward Elgin. You will enter what at first seems an oxymoron—Arizona **wine country**. But there are several wineries out here, and it's a pretty drive through the vineyards. In the town of Elgin, you'll find **The Chapel of Santa Maria**, a small chapel set amid grasslands, vineyards and cottonwood trees that is open for contemplation and administered by the Monks of the Vine, a Wine Brotherhood of area vintners.

Head south on Route 90 and you can't miss **Fort Huachuca** (Sierra Vista; 602-538-7111), a National Historic Landmark founded in 1877 to protect settlers from Apache raiders. The Fort Huachuca soldiers eventually tracked down and defeated Apache leader Geronimo. Today, 11,400 people are garrisoned or working at this 73,000-acre installation. One highlight is the Fort Huachuca Museum, located in a turn-of-the-century building first used as a bachelor officers' quarters. Inside are military artifacts, dioramas and the history of the fort. For a panoramic view of the fort and town, drive up Reservoir Hill Road. If you'd prefer picnicking, there are plenty of scenic spots amid large, old trees on base. For a map, stop at the visitor center at the entrance.

Take Route 92 south and you'll find a place known to birders worldwide. **Ramsey Canyon Preserve** (Route 92, five miles south of Sierra Vista; 602-378-2785) is home to 14 species of hummingbirds (more than anywhere else in the United States) and 200 species of other birds. The Nature Conservancy owns this 280-acre wooded gorge filled with hiking trails set in the Huachuca Mountains.

Hop on Route 90 again for the quick trip to **Bisbee** near the Mexican border. An old mining town and now an artists' enclave, the town is full of Victorian architecture perched on hillsides, along with funky shops and restaurants. For the full history of the town, start at the **Bisbee Mining & Historical Museum** (5 Copper Queen Plaza; 602-432-7071; admission) located in the former General Office Building of the Copper Queen Consolidated Mining Co. On the front lawn is old mining equipment, while inside the 1897 red-brick building are photo murals, artifacts and walk-in displays that highlight Bisbee's history.

For a firsthand view of mining history, put on a slicker, hard hat and battery-pack light and hop on the underground train at the **Queen Mine Underground Tour** (118 Arizona Street; 602-432-2071; admission). An ex-miner narrates as he takes you through the Copper

Queen Mine, which prospered for more than 60 years before it closed in 1943. The journey is a cool one, so bring a jacket. From here, you can also take the **Lavender Open Pit Mine Tour**, a narrated, 13-mile bus tour around a 300-acre hole where more than 380 million tons of ore and waste have been removed.

Continue your time travel to the Old West at **Slaughter Ranch** (Geronimo Trail; 602-558-2474; admission), located near the Mexican border in the small town of Douglas. Now a National Historic Landmark, it was once the home of John Slaughter, a former Texas Ranger, sheriff of Cochise County and one of the founders of Douglas. He bought the fertile grassland in 1884 and developed it into a cattle ranch. Slaughter's house and half a dozen other buildings furnished to reflect the era are still on the 140-acre site.

Northwest of Douglas is **Tombstone**, the town "too tough to die." Prospector Ed Shieffelin staked a silver claim here in 1877 and the place developed into a wild Wild West town. Today, unfortunately, the town is extremely touristy and every attraction is out to make a buck, but there are a few worthwhile stops. The **Tombstone Courthouse** (219 Toughnut Street; 602-457-3311; admission) has a restored courtroom and two floors of historic exhibits that reflect the ups and downs of this once-rowdy town. Now part of the Arizona State Park system, the red-brick building was the town's courthouse from 1882 until 1931.

Allen Street is the heart of Tombstone. At one end is the **Bird Cage Theatre** (6th and Allen streets; 602-457-3421; admission), a famous night spot in the late 1800s. Overlooking the gambling casino and dance hall are birdcage-like compartments where prostitutes plied their trade. Never a dull place, the theater was the site of 16 gunfights. If you bother to count, you'll find 140 bullet holes riddling the walls and ceilings. Also, the longest poker game in the history of the West reputedly unfolded here . . . it lasted more than eight years. Is this an ace attraction or what?

DOC GOODFELLOW

In the early 1880s, Tombstone was full of colorful characters, one of whom was Doc Goodfellow—a man much needed during those rowdy, dangerous frontier days. Nicknamed the "gunshot physician," he had an office over the Crystal Palace Saloon. Some of his exploits included commandeering and driving a steam locomotive in order to expedite getting a gunshot victim to a Tucson hospital, crawling into a mine shaft filled with smoke to save some miners, and riding his horse to a remote region in the mountains to doctor a cattle rustler sick with lead poisoning.

The time to travel out to the Willcox area is fall, when farms and roadside stands are selling their produce.

The most famous of Tombstone's numerous gunfights occurred in 1881 at the **O.K. Corral** (Allen Street; 602-457-3456; admission) just down the street from the Bird Cage Theatre. Lifesize figures stand in the corral as a narrator describes the shootout. An adjacent building showcases old Tombstone photographs and other historic items.

The losers of the shootout and other gunslingers lay buried at **Boot Hill Graveyard** (Route 80 West; 602-457-3348). Enter the graveyard through the gift shop to see rows of graves—little more than piles of rocks with white metal crosses to mark them—as well as a spectacular view of the area.

A huge rose bush that spreads across 7000 feet of supports is the main attraction at the **Rose Tree Inn Museum** (4th and Toughnut streets; 602-457-3326; admission). Planted in 1885, the bush is an especially awesome sight if you come in spring when it's covered with white blossoms. You can also tour the historic adobe home with local artifacts and period rooms.

After looping off Route 10 to see Sierra Vista, Bisbee and Tombstone, get back on Route 10 and go east to Dragoon, home of the **Amerind Foundation** (Triangle T Road; 602-586-3666; admission) and little else. This is a real treasure tucked away amidst the rock formations of Texas Canyon. The research facility and museum have been devoted to Native American culture and history since they opened in 1937. Visitors walk through the Spanish Colonial Revival-style buildings to see Native American pieces, such as beadwork, costumes, ritual masks and weapons, as well as western artwork, including works by Frederic Remington and William Leigh.

More western history is on display farther east on Route 10 in Willcox at the **Museum of the Southwest and Cowboy Hall of Fame** (1500 North Circle I Road; 602-384-2272) adjoining the Cochise Information Center. Highlights include portraits by cowboy artist Carl Clapp and photographs of the cowboys who pioneered the area. There's also a bust of Chief Cochise, Indian artifacts, a horse-drawn carriage and a mineral and rock collection.

The most famous cowboy of the area was Rex Allen, born in Willcox in 1920. **The Rex Allen Arizona Cowboy Museum** (155 North Railroad Avenue; 602-384-4583; admission) features mementos of Rex Allen's life, from his homesteading and ranch life in Willcox to his movies and television shows. Another section features the pioneer settlers and ranchers of the West.

EAST OF TUCSON LODGING

You won't find any ritzy accommodations in Benson, but some of the budget-priced motels aren't too bad. The **Oasis Court** (363 West 4th Street; 602-586-9784) is a family-run motor court that has been around since the 1920s. All five units are kitchenettes, and each has covered parking. Rooms are clean and comfortable.

Most accommodations in Sierra Vista are located along Fry Boulevard—the main commercial thoroughfare through town—and on South Route 92. **Sierra Suites** (391 East Fry Boulevard; 602-459-4221) is a two-story, red-brick hotel that lures guests with complimentary breakfast and cocktails. The 100 rooms face courtyards, and inside are mirrored sliding glass closet doors, small glass tables and a chest of drawers. Most even have refrigerators. The moderate price includes use of the pool and whirlpool.

Thunder Mountain Inn (1631 South Route 92, Sierra Vista; 602-458-7900) is a two-story, beige-colored brick building with 102 rooms, a dining room and lounge. Lower-level rooms facing the pool have sliding-glass doors. Most accommodations have double beds and a desk. Budget prices.

For a really secluded getaway, venture out to **Ramsey Canyon Inn** (31 Ramsey Canyon, Hereford; 602-378-3010), located in the Huachuca Mountains along a winding mountain stream and adjacent to the Nature Conservancy's Mile Hi/Ramsey Canyon Preserve and the Coronado National Forest. Accommodations consist of three cabins and six rooms furnished with country antiques. Moderate.

Built in 1917, **The Bisbee Inn** (45 OK Street, Bisbee; 602-432-5131) overlooks Brewery Gulch, once one of the Southwest's wildest streets. Each of the 18 rooms has handmade quilts on the beds, antique dressers with mirrors and its own sink. Guests share bathrooms in the hall. This red-brick inn offers an all-you-can-eat breakfast. Budget.

Petra Bed & Breakfast (818 Tombstone Canyon, Bisbee; 602-432-2996) is a large, restored, 1917 red-brick schoolhouse just above Garfield Playground. The ten rooms are fairly large and each has a private bath with a large tub. A southwestern breakfast is served family-style in the dining room. Budget to moderate.

The Copper Queen Mining Company built the **Copper Queen Hotel** (11 Howell Avenue, Bisbee; 602-432-2216) just after the turn of the century when it was a gathering place for politicians, mining officials and travelers, including the young Teddy Roosevelt. A plaque on one door marks the room where John Wayne stayed. The hotel is in the midst of an ongoing restoration, so ask for the restored rooms when you go. These are decorated Victorian-style with floral wallpaper and tile bathrooms. The four-story building contains 45 budget-to-moderate-priced rooms, along with the Copper Queen Saloon and Dining Room.

The Bisbee Grand Hotel (61 Main Street, Bisbee; 602-432-5900) is ideally located in the main shopping area in town. The original hotel was built in 1906, and the 11 rooms reflect the era with red carpeting, floral wallpaper, brass beds and antiques. They also have sinks and ceiling fans. The rooms are upstairs, while downstairs is the old saloon, Victorian Ladies Parlor and a theater for melodramas. Moderate.

The Gadsden Hotel (1046 G Avenue, Douglas; 602-364-4481) is a National Historic Monument that opened in 1907 as a hotel for cattlemen, miners and ranchers. Although the 160 rooms are plain, the lobby is magnificent. It contains a solid white Italian-marble staircase, four marble columns with capitals decorated in 14K gold leaf, and vaulted stained-glass skylights that run the length of the lobby. Several Hollywood movies have been filmed here. Other amenities include the Saddle and Spur Lounge, El Conquistador Dining Room and The Cattleman's Coffee Shop. Budget.

Price Canyon Ranch (Route 80 to 400-mile marker, go left at cattle guard into dirt road and drive seven miles, Douglas; 602-558-2383) in the Chiricahua Mountains is a working cattle ranch with one- and two-room bunk houses with baths. Meals are served in the 100-year-old main ranch house. Visitors can ride on short trips or go on longer overnight pack trips for two to ten nights. Accommodations are moderately priced, with meals and horseback riding included.

If you're a John Wayne fan, ask for room #4 at the **Hacienda Huachuca Motel** (320 Bruce Street, Tombstone; 602-457-2201). It's where the Duke himself stayed when he shot one of his movies in town. The seven kitchenettes face a small pool, and all have a rustic feel with wood-beam ceilings and overstuffed chairs. All the rooms have a small patio area, and some have mountain views. Be sure to say hello to Scooter, the talking cockateel, when you check in. Budget.

GADSDEN HOTEL

Built in 1907, with no expenses spared, the Gadsden Hotel in Douglas was the social and financial center for cattlemen and rich miners. Cattlemen would frequent the hotel's Saddle and Spur Saloon where, for a fee, they could have their ranch brands painted on walls. And a favorite gathering place for Douglas residents during the Mexican Revolution was, of all places, the hotel roof! This gave them ringside views of General Francisco "Pancho" Villa's army battling the Federales at Agua Prieta. The only drawback—stray bullets sometimes sent the spectators running for cover.

Early residents of Tombstone included Wyatt Earp, Doc Holliday and Bat Masterson.

The seven-room **Tombstone Boarding House** (108 North 4th Street, Tombstone; 602-457-3716) is housed in an adobe building constructed around 1879. Rooms are tastefully decorated in pastel colors with lacy curtains and Victorian-era furnishings. A full breakfast is served in the parlor, and guests who know how to play the piano are welcome to entertain. Budget to moderate.

Grapevine Canyon Ranch (Highland Road, Pearce; 602-826-3185) offers deluxe-priced accommodations in rooms with country-ranch furnishings and Native American touches. Visitors also lounge in the sitting room, a cozy place with a wood-beamed ceiling, Indian blankets and steer horns over the fireplace. At this working cattle ranch, horseback riding is the main attraction.

EAST OF TUCSON RESTAURANTS

Horseshoe Restaurant & Lounge (154 East 4th Street, Benson; 602-586-3303) is a family-owned restaurant that has been around for more than 50 years. On the walls are western murals by artist Vern Parker, and the posts in the café display cattle brands of southern Arizona. A neon horseshoe on the ceiling helps light the room. Entrées include chili, sandwiches, omelets, burgers, steaks and Mexican specialties. Budget.

Peking Chinese Cuisine (1481 East Fry Boulevard, Sierra Vista; 602-459-0404) is located in a small strip center with neon signs in the windows. The best deal here is an all-you-can-eat lunch buffet. The place is casual with red booths and tables, and Chinese-type lanterns and fans hanging from the ceiling. Budget.

Speaking in relative terms, the **Thunder Mountain Inn Restaurant** (1631 South Route 92, Sierra Vista; 602-458-7900) is one of the more expensive places in town. Diners can enjoy moderately priced prime rib and seafood in a setting of pink tablecloths and booths divided by etched glass.

Fine continental cuisine is the last thing you'd expect to find out here, but **Karen's** (4907 South Route 92 near Sierra Vista; 602-378-2355) fits the bill. The ultra-deluxe-priced menu changes weekly, but a typical entrée is grilled chicken breast stuffed with mozzarella and herbs, then covered with sun-dried tomato sauce.

Bisbee has a number of small eateries that almost defy description. One is **18 Steps** (41½ Main Street; 602-432-3447). Just as the name implies, you must climb 18 steps to get to this tiny, budget-priced restaurant. Three tables are in one room, while in another room is a table and a small sitting area with a couch and bookshelves. If you'd prefer to eat on the couch, it's perfectly okay with the owners. The menu is on a blackboard and features delicious homemade specialties such as brie crêpe with raspberry sauce and tomato cheese pie.

Just below 18 Steps is **The Wine Gallery Bistro** (41 Main Street, Bisbee; 602-432-3447) with seating in the sunny, open street-level room or the more intimate basement. Victuals here include gulf shrimp with roasted garlic, sundried tomatoes and almond pasta, and orange roughy with macadamia nuts. Moderate.

The **Renaissance Café** (10 A Lyric Plaza, Bisbee; 602-432-4020) is a tiny, no-frills place where the locals hang out. Local artists' works hang on the walls, bulletins paper the front window, and a radio station plays in the background. There are a few tables inside, and a few out on the sidewalk. Offerings include sandwiches, hot bagel melts, quiche, pizza, salads and desserts, as well as espresso and herbal teas. Budget.

At **Golden China** (15 Brewery Gulch, Bisbee; 602-432-5888), the bargain is the big lunch buffet. Some favorite menu items are beef with scallops on a sizzling platter and lobster Szechuan-style. Along with the standard Chinese decor is a splashing rock fountain in the back of the restaurant. Budget.

The **Nellie Cashman Restaurant** (121 South 5th Street, Tombstone; 602-457-2212) is housed in an 1882 building with decor to reflect the era, including a stone fireplace, high wood ceilings and photos of bygone years. Although they serve sandwiches and burgers, they're best known for their homemade berry pies. Budget.

Known for its ribs, **The Lucky Cuss Restaurant** (414 East Allen Street, Tombstone; 602-457-3561) serves meat after smoking it for 14 hours on a mesquite-wood fire. The walls of this moderately priced place are falsefronts of historic Tombstone buildings, such as the Bird Cage Theatre and *Tombstone Epitaph* newspaper.

If you're in the mood for the biggest hot dog in Cochise County, weighing in at a half-pound and measuring a foot long, then saunter over to the **Longhorn Restaurant** (501 East Allen Street, Tombstone; 602-457-3405) and order a Longhorn Dog. If that's not what you crave, they offer a wide selection of Italian, Mexican and American food. The decor is strictly western, with longhorns hanging over the door and yellowing wanted posters of characters such as Billy the Kid laminated on the tables. Budget.

EAST OF TUCSON SHOPPING

Singing Wind Bookshop (Ocotillo Road, two-and-a-quarter miles north of Route 10, Benson; 602-586-2425) isn't easy to find. No signs announce it, only the name on a mailbox. Don't let the chained green cattle gate stop you—just open it and drive on in and down to the ranch house. Here, there are two huge rooms full of new books about the Southwest, western Americana and other categories. If you're friendly, the owner just may give you some coffee or food, or spin a yarn or two.

In downtown Benson, **Zearings Mercantile Store** (305 East 4th Street; 602-586-3196) is a narrow, high-ceilinged place that has been around as long as anyone can remember. Inside, you'll find guns, gifts, relics and every imaginable kind of knickknack. For trendier items, stop in **Kiva Gifts** (363 West 4th Street, Benson; 602-586-9706) next to the Chamber of Commerce where they sell southwestern, Native American and Mexican arts, crafts and clothing.

Head south to Sierra Vista and you'll discover **Misty's Gift Gallery** (228 West Fry Boulevard; 602-458-7208), one of the largest collectors' galleries in the Southwest, with names that include Goebel, Hummel, Lladro, Gorham, De Grazia and Perillo. There is also a gallery with original artwork, lithographs and bronzes.

Bisbee is a real shopping mecca, especially for art lovers. Pick up a map at the Chamber of Commerce to aid in navigating the spending trail. The majority of shops are on Main Street, including **The One Book Bookstore** (38 Main Street; 602-432-5512). You can literally buy only one book here (you don't expect us to give away the title, do you?) But here's a hint: Author Walter Swan sits in the bookstore window wearing overalls and a black cowboy hat, ready to spin tales and talk about the book that describes his childhood in Cochise County. Next door is **The Other Book Bookstore** which, you guessed it, houses his other books.

Across the street is the **Johnson Gallery** (69 Main Street, Bisbee; 602-432-2126), a huge place with a variety of imports including Native American serigraphs and etchings, Mexican and Indian masks, Tarahumara artifacts, Native American arts and Quezada family pottery.

Curves (55 Main Street, Bisbee; 602-432-4694) is a fine art gallery and eclectic shop featuring what they claim are handmade clothing and art from everywhere in the world except Antarctica. For local stuff, jump **Into the Fire** (45 Main Street, Bisbee; 602-432-4690) with its contemporary pottery and porcelain. Or stop by **The Gold Shop** (9 Howell Avenue, Bisbee; 602-432-4557), which features innovative, contemporary jewelry created by about a dozen craftspeople from Bisbee and elsewhere in the Southwest.

Jack a Lope (9 Naco Road, Bisbee; 602-432-7833) has used, rare and out-of-print books, as well as records, cassettes and CDs.

Allen Street is the heart of shopping in Tombstone, where you'll find lots of souvenir shops mixed in with higher-quality jewelry and clothing stores. **Arlene's Southwest Silver & Gold** (404 Allen Street; 602-457-3344) is a large place with Native American jewelry and artwork including pottery, baskets, kachina dolls and rugs. **Gabe's Dolls & Museum** (312 Allen Street; 602-457-3419) is one of the oldest shops in Tombstone. The place is crammed full of dolls, dollhouse pieces, Victorian cards, collectibles and more than 150 paper dolls. In the back of the shop is a museum with dolls dating back to the 1830s.

Looking for antique African clam shell discs, camel bone beads or yak bone beads handcarved in Pakistan? Even if you aren't, the **Bovis Bead Co.** (220 East Fremont Street, Tombstone; 602-457-3359) has them, and one of the largest selections of beads in the country. They import from all over the world, and also make their own beads.

Eagle's Nest Leathers (509 Allen Street, Tombstone; 602-457-3805) has leathers and western wear, including handmade belts, moccasins, hats, buckles and knives.

In Willcox, the Chamber of Commerce has a brochure listing 27 orchards and mills where you can stop. One is **Stout's Cider Mill** (1510 North Circle I Road; 602-384-3696) where, in season, you can pick your own produce or buy apples, cider, dried fruit, nuts, peaches, apple pies, chili peppers and Arizona desert preserves.

EAST OF TUCSON NIGHTLIFE

Arena Bar & Rodeo Grounds (250 North Prickly Pear Street, Benson; 602-586-9983) overlooks the rodeo grounds—a plus when there's something to watch, but that's not too often. Inside, a western theme dominates. A lasso hangs on the door, cow skulls decorate walls, and

---

HOW TOMBSTONE GOT ITS NAME

When prospector Ed Schieffelin headed to what is now Tombstone in hopes of staking a silver claim, he was warned by friends that all he'd find was his own tombstone. Instead, he got rich and named the town after their warning—Tombstone. When he discovered silver, Ed's brother Al commented, "You're a lucky cuss," and the profitable mine was named "Lucky Cuss." Names for other Tombstone area mines were equally colorful, including Goodenough (which is open for tours), Tough Nut and Contention, named after a claims dispute between several men.

Tombstone reputedly at one time had saloons and gambling halls making up two of every three buildings.

---

you can warm yourself by the big rock fireplace. There are also a pool table and dancefloor, along with outdoor picnic benches.

Established in 1902, **St. Elmo Bar and Grill** (15 Brewery Avenue, Bisbee; 602-432-2775) in historic Brewery Gulch is a tradition around here. Memorabilia such as old maps hang on the walls, and seating is mainly stools at the counter. On weekends, there's live music and dancing. Entertainment during the week is supplied by change in the jukebox or pinball machines.

Adjoining the Copper Queen Hotel, the **Copper Queen Saloon** (11 Howell Avenue, Bisbee; 602-432-2216) is a small, dark, intimate place with some turn-of-the-century furnishings and live music on weekends.

At the **Stock Exchange Bar** (15 Brewery Avenue, Bisbee; 602-432-2775), almost one whole wall is covered with an original board from the New York stock exchange. This historic building has a pressed-tin roof, worn wooden floors and copper-topped tables.

Walk through swinging doors of **Big Nose Kate's Saloon** (417 East Allen Street, Tombstone; 602-457-3134) and you step back into the Old West. Waitresses dressed as saloon gals serve drinks in the same place where Lily Langtry and Wyatt Earp once tipped their glasses. Lighted, stained-glass panels depict Tombstone's characters, and old photos hang on the walls. On weekends, you'll find live country music and skits of western brawls.

The Crystal Palace (420 East Allen Street, Tombstone; 602-457-3611) has been restored to look like it did when it was built in the 1880s. The long, narrow room has old wood tables and red drapes underneath a pressed-tin ceiling. Live music is performed Wednesday through Sunday.

Johnny Ringo's Saloon (404 Allen Street, Tombstone; 602-457-3101) is an historic, intimate bar where the main attraction is the collection of more than 600 military patches on the walls.

EAST OF TUCSON PARKS

The Chiricahua Apaches called the **Chiricahua National Monument** area the Land of the Standing-Up Rocks because throughout the park are huge rock spires, stone columns and massive balanced rocks perched on small pedestals. Geologists believe that these formations were created as a result of explosive volcanic eruptions. For an overview of the park, drive up the winding, eight-mile-long Bonita Canyon Drive. You'll pass pine and oak-juniper forests before reaching Massai Point at the top of the Chiricahua Mountains, where you can see the park, valleys and the peaks of Sugarloaf Mountain and Cochise Head. You can also explore the park on foot via about 20 miles of trails. Other attractions include historic Faraway Ranch and Stafford Cabin. To get there, take Routes 10 and 666 south from Tucson, then go east on Route 181.

South/West of Tucson

Far off the beaten track, southwestern Arizona is home to the world's leading astronomical center, remote ghost towns, wildlife preserves and a sanctuary dedicated to the unusual Organ Pipe Cactus. This is also where civilization disappears and the desert blooms.

Heading south on Route 19, you will pass the retirement community of Green Valley and arrive at the **Titan Missile Museum** (1580 Duval Mine Road; 602-791-2929; admission). Here, you'll be taken to the bowels of the earth, experience a countdown launch of a Titan missile (actually a movie soundtrack) and view a silo. It's an eerie excursion.

To get away from the high-tech missiles and delve deeper into the area's history, continue farther south on Route 19 to Tubac. The Spanish founded a presidio here in 1752 to protect settlers from the Indians. At **Tubac Presidio State Historic Park** (602-398-2252; admission), visitors can see the remains of the original presidio foundation and wall, an 1885 schoolhouse and a museum detailing Tubac's history.

A few more minutes down Route 19 are the adobe ruins of a Spanish frontier mission church at the **Tumacacori National Monument** (Route 19 at exit 29, Tumacacori; 602-398-2341). Along with the museum, visitors can walk through the baroque church, completed in 1822, and the nearby ruins, such as a circular mortuary chapel and graveyard. Since little has been built in the vicinity, walking across the grounds feels like a walk back in time.

Continuing south, Route 19 hits the Mexican border. **Nogales, Mexico,** is a border town offering bargain shopping, restaurants and some sightseeing. On the other side is Nogales, Arizona. Photographs and artifacts detail the town's history at the **Pimeria Alta Historical Society Museum** (223 Grand Avenue; 602-287-4621), a 1914 mission-style building that once housed the city hall, police and fire departments.

Just off of Route 82, you'll pass by some **ghost towns**, including Harshaw and Duquesne. Duquesne was a mining center established around the turn of the century with a peak population of 1000 residents, including Westinghouse of Westinghouse Electric. Harshaw was settled around 1875 and operated about 100 mines. Today, all that's left are ruins and graveyards. Some of the roads en route are extremely rugged and bumpy, so be prepared.

One of the most famous of Arizona's many astronomical observatories is the **Kitt Peak National Observatory** (50 miles southwest of Tucson off Route 386; 602-325-9200; admission). Drive up a mountain road and you'll come across the observatory's gleaming white domes and its 21 telescopes. During tours, you can step inside some of the telescopes, including the 19-story-high Robert R. McMath solar telescope. There's also a Visitor Center with exhibits on the observatory. If you're planning on staying awhile, bring food—it's a long haul up the mountain and there's nothing to nibble on at the top.

Continue to the west about 100 miles on Route 86 and you'll come to **Ajo**, a small scenic town whose center is a green plaza surrounded by Spanish Colonial-style buildings. It is also an old copper mining town and as such shows its scars. The **New Cornelia Copper Mine** (La Mina Road; 602-387-5631) is one of the largest open-pit copper mines in the world, stretching a full mile in diameter. Although operations ceased in 1984, you can go to the pit lookout and learn about mining operations at the adjacent Mine Lookout Visitor Center.

From the mine, you can see the **Ajo Historical Society Museum** (160 Mission Street; 602-387-7105) located in St. Catherine's Indian Mission, a stucco church built in the 1940s. Inside, there are artifacts from Ajo's history, including a blacksmith shop, dentist's office, printing shop and Native American artifacts such as old saddles found on graves.

From Ajo, drive north on Route 85 until you reach Route 8; proceed west and you'll eventually hit Wellton. Don't blink, or you'll miss the **McElhaney Cattle Company Museum** (Avenue 34; 602-785-3384) with its amusing collection of antiquities, including buggies, carriages, a popcorn wagon, an old hearse, several stage coaches, a fire wagon and antique cars.

Much farther west, near the California border, is **Yuma**. Once a steamboat stop and major crossing on the Colorado River, today it is a bustling city that supports farming and basks in a subtropical climate. The first major construction here was the **Yuma Territorial Prison** (209 North Penitentiary Avenue; 602-783-4771; admission), a penitentiary between 1876 and 1909, and now a state historic park. Known as the Hell-hole of Arizona, life inside the walls were rough, and prisoners who escaped faced hostile deserts and the currents of the Colorado River. Today, visitors can walk through the gloomy cells and climb the guard tower, from which you can view the river and surrounding area.

Just across the river from the prison is **The Quechan Indian Museum** (Indian Hill Road, Yuma; 619-572-0661; admission), one of

The Titan Missile Museum is the only intercontinental ballistic missile complex in the world that's open to the public.

the oldest military posts in the area. Currently, it is headquarters for the Quechan Indian Tribe and houses their artifacts.

The military supply hub for the Arizona Territory was the **Yuma Quartermaster Depot** (North 2nd Avenue, Yuma; 602-329-0471; admission), which served the Southwest until it closed in 1883. Several of the original buildings remain, including the commanding officer's quarters and Office of the Quartermaster Depot. Costumed interpreters provide tours of the complex.

More of Yuma's history comes to light in the **Arizona Historical Society Century House Museum** (240 South Madison Avenue; 602-782-1841). Once the home of pioneer merchant E. F. Sanguinetti, it now has artifacts, photographs and furnishings from Arizona's territorial period. Just outside are colorful gardens and aviaries with exotic birds.

The **Yuma Art Center** (281 Gila Street; 602-783-2314; admission) is in the restored Southern Pacific Railroad Depot and features changing exhibits by contemporary and traditional artists.

SOUTH/WEST OF TUCSON LODGING

Located in Madera Canyon, **Santa Rita Lodge Nature Resort** (Sahuarita; 602-625-8746) is a perfect birders getaway. Just outside the large windows in each of the 12 rooms are feeders that attract a number of bird species. Inside the rooms, charts hang with pictures of different types of hummingbirds. The lodge also offers nature programs in the patio area, and staff birders will take guests on birding walks. Moderate.

Bing Crosby founded the **Tubac Golf Resort** (1 Otero Road, Tubac; 602-398-2211) back in 1959. The 32 rooms and suites have wood-burning fireplaces, Mexican furniture, tiled bathrooms and patios facing the mountains. The resort has a golf course, tennis court, pool and spa, hiking trails and a full-service restaurant and bar. Moderate.

Rancho Santa Cruz Guest Ranch (off the Route 19 frontage road, Tumacacori; 602-281-8383) is a 112-acre working ranch that opened in the 1920s. The eight adobe-and-stucco rooms are modest, but comfortable, and the three suites have fireplaces. A grassy courtyard with chairs beckons visitors to relax, as does the outdoor pool. Budget to moderate.

Rio Rico Resort & Country Club (1069 Camino Caralampi, Rio Rico; 602-281-1901) is a beautiful resort in the Cayetano Mountain range. Many of the rooms have wood-beamed ceilings, sliding glass doors overlooking the pool or mountains, and contemporary southwestern decor in pastel colors. Amenities include a golf course, horse stables, jacuzzi, exercise room, restaurant and lounge. Moderate.

Sitting in the foothills of Baboquivari Peak near the Mexican border, **Rancho De La Osa** (28201 West La Osa Ranch Road, Sasabe; 602-823-4257) is a 200-year-old Territorial-style ranch. Made of handmade adobe block, rooms have fireplaces and Indian and Spanish furnishings. Activities here include riding pure-bred quarterhorses and swimming, or sampling cocktails in the Cantina, an old Spanish/Indian mission. Moderate.

The Stage Stop Inn (303 McKeown Avenue, Patagonia; 602-394-2211) is a 43-room hotel with a restaurant and clean, comfortable rooms facing the pool in the middle. Movie casts and crew often stay here while filming in the area. The western lobby showcases a moose skull above the fireplace, cattle brands on the tile floor and western paintings on the walls. Budget.

A tiny treasure, **The Little House** (341 Sonoita Avenue, Patagonia; 602-394-2493) is an adobe home with two rooms. Each has a sitting area with corner fireplace, a private bath and patio, and contemporary southwestern furnishings. Guests are invited for complimentary continental or full breakfasts with eggs, sausage, fruit and breads. Prices are in the moderate category.

Circle Z Ranch (Patagonia; 602-287-2091) in the foothills of the Santa Rita Mountains is a colorful, unpretentious place built in the early 1920s. Teddy Roosevelt was just one of the many famous visitors here. The deluxe-priced ranch accommodates no more than 45 people at a time. The ranch's adobe cottages are decorated with brightly painted wicker furniture and Mexican crafts, but don't have televisions or telephones. Instead, evening recreation centers around the lodge with its massive stone fireplace and bookshelves filled with classics, including Zane Grey titles.

Looking like a miniature dollhouse, **The Guest House Inn** (3 Guest House Road, Ajo; 602-387-6133) is a charming, white house with blue trim and a long front porch dotted with white wicker furniture for lazing away the hours. Phelps Dodge built it in 1925 to entertain dignitaries, and breakfast is now served on the 20-foot-long walnut dining table where these guests once ate. Inside, the setup is unusual, with a living room in the middle and guest rooms lining either side of the house. Each of the four bedrooms has a private bath and its own decorating scheme, such as Santa Fe or Victorian. Moderate.

Located atop the highest hill in Ajo, **The Mine Manager's House Inn** (1 Greenway Drive; 602-387-6508) was built in 1919 for the mine manager's family. You can see the mine from the house, while inside

---

Tucson and the surrounding area—with more astronomical observatories than any-where else on earth—is known as the Astronomy Capital of the World.

---

old photos of the mine hang in the cozy living room. Instead of reflecting the house's history, room furnishings are modern. But breakfast is served at the huge pecan table original to the house. During free time, stop in the reading room or soak in the outdoor hot tub. Moderate.

A number of Gila Bend's motels were built in the 1960s and their decor reflects that era. For instance, the **American Western Inn** (1046 East Pima Street; 602-683-2248) is a throwback from the 1960s, with its orange-and-yellow exterior and red doors. The 60 rooms have full-length windows, white-brick walls and odd furniture. Amenities include a pool, restaurant and lounge. Budget.

Built during the space race with the Russians, the theme at the **Best Western Space Age Lodge** (401 East Pima Street, Gila Bend; 602-683-2273) is obvious. Sputniks are perched on the roof, and rooms have pictures of rockets blasting off into space. The rooms contain whitewashed wood furniture, pastel colors and large, well-lighted mirrors above the counter. There's also a pool and coffee shop. Moderate.

La Fuente Travelodge (1513 East 16th Street, Yuma; 602-329-1814) has 96 Southwest-style rooms decorated in pastels. Some rooms face the grassy interior courtyard and pool. Prices include a complimentary continental breakfast, happy hour and use of the fitness room. Moderate.

Shilo Inn Hotel (1530 South Castle Dome Avenue, Yuma; 602-782-9518) offers 133 deluxe rooms decorated in pastel colors with couches, patios and tile bathrooms. Suites with kitchenettes are also available. A three-story-high lobby with marble floors and mirrored columns welcomes guests. Amenities include a swimming pool, whirlpool bath, exercise rooms, sauna and steam room.

SOUTH/WEST OF TUCSON RESTAURANTS

Even though there's not much in Amado, it's worth a stop to eat at **The Cow Palace** (28802 South Nogales Road; 602-398-2201), a local landmark that has been around since the 1920s. While in town to shoot movies, western stars have frequented the place and their photos hang on the walls. Decor is rustic western, with a wagon wheel for a chandelier and red tablecloths, carpet and curtains. Entrées carry on the theme with names such as The Trail Boss porterhouse steak and Chuck Wagon burger. Budget.

If you've never dined in a 150-year-old horse stable, stop in at **The Montura** (1 Otero Road, Tubac; 602-398-2211) restaurant at The

Tubac Golf Resort. Actually, the place is quite nice. Inside, are arched windows, cobblestone floors and pottery made by Mexicans and Native Americans. Look closely and you might find Apache arrowheads embedded in the restaurant's adobe walls. Dinner focuses on steak, pasta, seafood and Mexican specialties with a southwestern twist. Prices are moderate.

Finding a good German restaurant in Tubac was quite a surprise, but **Johanna's Café International** (192 Tubac Road; 602-398-9336) fits the bill. It's homey and airy with lots of windows covered by lace curtains and German music playing in the background. The owner, Édith Bobbitt, once owned a famous Munich restaurant. Entrées include *Schweine Kotelett*, or a pork chop prepared like a schnitzel (dipped in egg, breaded and pan-fried), potato pancakes, bratwurst and German-style bread. Moderate.

Sergeant Grijalva's Restaurante y Cantina (257 Camino Otero, Tubac; 602-398-2263) adjoins and partially merges with the Misty Mountain Gallery, lending a feel of sophistication to this otherwise typical Mexican restaurant. You can also dine in the covered, outdoor patio. Budget.

Opened in the 1940s as a coffee shop in someone's home, **Wisdom's Café** (Route 19 service road, Tumacacori; 602-398-2397) is now a restaurant crammed with old photographs, farming tools, velvet paintings, patchwork rugs and other odds and ends. You can spot it on the road by the two gigantic imitation chickens in front. If you can get by the chickens, try some of their Mexican food. Budget.

La Cima (1069 Camino Caralampi, Rio Rico; 602-281-1901) in the Rio Rico Resort & Country Club offers American and Mexican cuisine, as well as a Sunday champagne brunch. Two walls have floor-to-ceiling windows with panoramic views of the mountains. The interior is rustic with wood beams, lanterns and wicker chairs. Moderate.

Home Plate (277 McKeown Avenue, Patagonia; 602-394-2344) is a greasy spoon where the locals meet to chow down on burgers and hot and cold sandwiches. Civic-club banners circle the room and partially cover the brick walls. Budget.

The Stage Stop Inn (303 McKeown Avenue, Patagonia; 602-394-2211) carries the hotel's western theme with cattle brands on the floors, a chuckwagon containing a salad bar, and a Cowboy Steak Sandwich. Other offerings here are hot and cold sandwiches, burgers, Mexican food and homemade desserts. Budget.

The name is fancier than the place, because basically the **Territorial House Restaurant & Deli** (100 Estrella, Ajo; 602-387-7322) is a budget-priced deli with counter service. There's ample seating, inside and out, at plastic-covered tables underneath hanging plastic plants. The sandwiches are decent, as are the side orders.

Although the exterior of **Dago Joe's** (2055-A North Route 85, Ajo; 602-387-6904) is rather plain, the owners have livened up the interior with contemporary decor—framed posters, plants, and a peach-accent wall with matching tablecloths. The menu is varied, but they're known for moderately priced steaks.

A Yuma tradition for more than a decade, **Hensley's Beef Beans and Beer** (2855 South 4th Avenue; 602-344-1345) is the place for prime rib, lobster, seafood and hamburgers. Moderately priced dishes are served amid walls covered with cowboy pictures, cow horns and Indian blankets.

For budget-priced burgers, try **Lutes Casino** (221 Main Street, Yuma; 602-782-2192). The history adds ambiance, as this large, dark pool hall, domino parlor and restaurant was a casino back in 1920s.

A ladies luncheon kind of place, **Garden Café** (250 Madison Avenue, Yuma; 602-783-1491) in back of the Century House Museum offers sandwiches, salads and quiche. The setting is charming amidst gardens and aviaries full of birds. An added perk is outdoor misters that help keep diners cool on hot days. The Garden Café serves breakfast and lunch only; budget.

SOUTH/WEST OF TUCSON SHOPPING

About 50 shops and restaurants make up **Tubac**. Although it's geared to tourists, they've managed to avoid the rubber-tomahawk syndrome and you'll find high-quality artwork. All of the shops here are within walking distance, but the bulk are along Tubac Road, which is off to the right as you enter from the frontage road beside Route 19.

Highlights along this road include **Tortuga Books** (190 Tubac Road; 602-398-2807) known throughout the Southwest and specializing in philosophy, psychology, children's books, greeting cards and southwestern literature. **The Pot Shop Gallery** (166 Tubac Road; 602-398-2898) features R. C. Gorman signed lithographs, prints, pottery and clay artwork created by Arizona artisans. **Chile Pepper** and **Chile Pepper, Too** (201 Tubac Road; 602-398-2921) offer Southwest gourmet foods, chili food products, chili wreaths, coffees and teas. Victorian **Tubac House** (602-398-9243) has southwestern art by more than 50 Arizona artists. For handcrafted Native American jewelry, kachinas, sandpaintings, baskets and pottery, stop in at **Old Presidio Traders** (27 Tubac Road; 602-398-9333).

To shop in the older, more historic section of town, go to Calle Iglesia. In this area, you'll find **Hugh Cabot Studios & Gallery** (Calle Iglesia, Tubac; 602-398-2721) housed in a 250-year-old adobe building that used to be a hostelry for Spanish soldiers. This nationally known artist creates western and general-interest works in several mediums and makes his home in Tubac. At **VIDA de la TIERRA** (Calle Iglesia; 602-398-2936), you can sometimes catch artisans Penny and John Duncklee at work creating pottery and mesquite wood furniture. For authentic Navajo, Santo Domingo and Hopi art crafted by old-timers, stop next door at the **Peck Gallery El Nido** (Plaza de Anza; 602-398-2683).

Also in town you'll find **Tubac Ironworks** (217 Plaza Road, Tubac; 602-398-2736) with its metal arts including copper bird feeders and fountains, metal bells and wind chimes by southwestern artisans.

A handful of shops line Patagonia's main street, including **J. Nickerson Gold & Silver Smith** (602-394-2690). His specialty is silver jewelry, including earrings somehow made out of snowflakes using silver as a medium. He also designs jewelry with local materials such as turquoise, malachite, azurite and Patagonia red jasper.

If you drive through Sonoita, stop by **La Pradera** (Route 82; 602-455-5612). The owner of the racehorse Secretariat built it to look like his barn, and the original Triple Crown trophy awarded to Secretariat is displayed in the hall. Inside are five shops, including the **Turquoise Tortoise Gallery** (602-455-5853) with paintings, jewelry, pottery and sculptures by Native Americans.

Housed in a long, narrow, 1916 building on the plaza, **Kliban's Variety Store Inc.** (29 Plaza, Ajo; 602-387-6421) offers an eclectic mix of hardware, clothing, baby stuff and old knickknacks. Another Ajo stop is the **Ajo Art Gallery** (671 North 2nd Avenue; 602-387-7525) with a mixture of contemporary paintings by California and Arizona artists.

SOUTH/WEST OF TUCSON NIGHTLIFE

Scenic mountain views from picture windows draw people to **La Cantina** (1069 Camino Caralampi, Rio Rico; 602-281-1901) at the Rio Rico Resort & Country Club. The contemporary, Spanish-style bar has live Top-40, jazz and dance music on weekends.

Luts Casino (221 Main Street, Yuma; 602-782-2192) is one of the oldest continually owned and operated pool and domino parlors in the state. Open since 1920, the place is crammed full of farm implements, paintings and historic memorabilia.

SOUTH/WEST OF TUCSON PARKS

Patagonia Lake State Park is where you'll find the largest recreational lake (275 acres) in southern Arizona. Patagonia Lake, nestled amid rolling hills, was created by the damming of Sonoita Creek in 1968. A small, sandy beach lures swimmers. Because of its elevation of

Birdwatchers from all over the world come to Patagonia Sonoita Creek Sanctuary to catch a glimpse of more than 200 species of birds that have been spotted here.

3750 feet, the 600-acre park offers moderate temperatures throughout the year. You can find it off Route 82 about 12 miles north of Nogales. Follow the signs to the park.

Nine miles north of Patagonia Lake State Park is the 312-acre **Patagonia Sonoita Creek Sanctuary,** set in a narrow flood plain between the Santa Rita and Patagonia mountains. It encompasses a one-and-a-half-mile stretch of Sonoita Creek lined with large stands of cottonwoods—some a hundred feet tall—as well as Arizona walnut, velvet ash, willows and Texas mulberry. Known for it's diverse bird population, the park is also home to white-tailed deer, bobcat, javelina, coyotes and the most endangered fish in the Southwest, the Gila Topminnow. To get there from Patagonia, turn northwest off Route 82 onto 4th Avenue, then go left on Pennsylvania Avenue. When the pavement ends you'll cross a creek, and then you're in the sanctuary. An information board is inside the gate.

Coronado National Forest has 1.7 million acres of public land in 12 sky islands, or mountain ranges, that jut above the surrounding desert. Following are three of the highlights:

Madera Canyon is a great place for birdwatching, with more than 200 species, including several varieties of woodpeckers, hawks, wrens and vultures. Driving up through the canyon, the desert changes from grassland to forest. Trees on the lower slopes of the Santa Rita Mountains are mesquite, and farther up are live oaks, alligator junipers, cottonwoods and sycamores along Madera Creek. There are over 70 miles of trails. Located 35 miles south of Tucson; take Route 19 south from Tucson to Green Valley's Continental Road, then go southeast 13 miles.

Pena Blanca Lake is a 57-acre lake surrounded by oak, cottonwood and mesquite trees and light-colored bluffs. The lake is at 4000 feet—making it higher and somewhat cooler than Tucson. A trail leads around it. For information, call 602-281-2296. Pena Blanca Lake Resort (602-281-2800) has a lodge, restaurant, fishing supplies and boat rentals. The lake is located five miles north of the Mexican border; take Route 19 south from Tucson to Ruby Road, then go west for about nine miles.

Parker Canyon Lake is an 80-acre fishing lake east of the Huachuca Mountains and surrounded by grassy, rolling hills. From Sonoita, take Route 83 south for 30 miles until it runs into the park.

Organ Pipe Cactus National Monument (602-387-6849) is a 330,000-acre refuge that became a national monument in 1937 to protect the Sonoran Desert's plants and animals, especially the unique Organ Pipe Cactus. Start at the visitor center 17 miles south of the northern entrance. Here, you can see exhibits and pick up a self-guided tour pamphlet. A good tour is the **Puerto Blanco Scenic Drive**, a 53-mile graded dirt loop with numbered stops described on the tour. The only paved road through the park is Route 85. While exploring the monument, you'll pass mountains, plains, canyons, dry washes and a pond surrounded by cottonwood trees. You can also camp. The monument is 35 miles south of Ajo; the visitor center is at the 75-mile marker on Route 85.

    Cabeza Prieta National Wildlife Refuge was established in 1939 to protect the desert bighorn sheep. The 860,000-acre refuge is an arid wilderness rife with cactus and mountains. Passing through the park is the 250-mile El Camino del Diablo (Highway of the Devil) that was pioneered by Spanish Conquistador Captain de Anza in 1774—and stretches from Mexico to California. Along the way, you pass Cabeza Prieta Mountain with its lava-topped granite peak, and Mohawk Valley with sand dunes and lava flows. Since roads here are rugged and unimproved, four-wheel-drive vehicles are required. Also, beware of the six species of rattlesnakes. The refuge is sometimes closed for military use; call ahead to see if it is open. You can't enter without a valid Refuge Entry Permit, so stop by the refuge office in Ajo (1611 North 2nd Avenue; 602-387-6483). You'll need explicit directions, which you can get when you pick up the entry permit in Ajo.

The Sporting Life

BOATING, CANOEING, WATERSKIING

Although water isn't plentiful in southern Arizona, there are a few lakes. Boat rentals are available at **Patagonia Lake State Park** (Patagonia; 602-287-6965), **Parker Canyon Lake** (off Route 83 near Sierra Vista; 602-670-6483) and **Pena Blanca Lake** (off Route 289, Nogales; 602-281-2800). You can rent paddle boats at **Gene C. Reid Park** (between Broadway Boulevard and 22nd Street, Country Club and Alvernon Way, Tucson; 602-791-4560).

SWIMMING

For a retreat from the heat, take a plunge! Tucson public pools include **Fort Lowell Park** (2900 North Craycroft Road; 602-791-2585); **Himmel Park** (1000 North Tucson Boulevard; 602-791-4157); **Morris K. Udall Park** (7200 East Tanque Verde Road; 602-791-4004); **North-**

Yuma River Tours (1920 Arizona Avenue, Yuma; 602-783-4400; admission) offers jetboat rides past petroglyphs, steamboat landings, mining camps and other landmarks on the Colorado River.

west District (1400 North Silverbell Road; 602-791-4752); and **Jacobs Park** (1010 West Lind; 602-791-4358.)

East of Tucson, try **Safford City Government** (Firth Park, Safford; 602-428-6666).

HORSEBACK RIDING

A western town like Tucson wouldn't be the same without opportunities to go horseback riding. Dudes and dudettes can saddle up at **Desert-High Country Stables Inc.** (6501 West Ina Road; 602-744-3789); **El Conquistador Stables** (10000 North Oracle Road; 602-742-4200); **Pusch Ridge Stables** (11220 North Oracle Road; 602-297-6908); **Tucson Trailrides DBA Pantano Stables** (4450 South Houghton Road; 602-298-9076); and **Wild House Ranch Resort** (6801 North Camino Verde; 602-744-1012).

Elsewhere, you can ride at **Rio Rico Stables** (320 Stable Lane, Rio Rico; 602-281-7550) and **Equi-Sands Training Center** (5706 South Kino Road, Sierra Vista; 602-378-1540).

BALLOONING

There's nothing like floating above it all. To see Tucson from on high, contact any of the following companies in Tucson: **A Balloon Experience** (602-747-3866); **A Southern Arizona Balloon Excursion** (602-624-3599); **Desert Breezes Balloon Adventures** (602-299-6308); and **Balloon America** (602-299-7744).

SKIING

There's only one place to ski in these parts—the **Mount Lemmon Ski Valley** (Mount Lemmon; 602-576-1400). The southernmost ski area in North America, Mount Lemmon Ski Valley offers 15 runs, equipment rental, a ski school and a restaurant.

GOLF

Mild winters make most of southern Arizona ideal for golfers, and aficionados can choose between a wide range of private and public courses.

In the Tucson area, these include **Tucson National Golf Club** (2727 West Club Drive; 602-575-7540); **Tournament Players Club At Star Pass** (3645 West 22nd Street; 602-622-6060); **Sun City Tucson** (1495 East Rancho Vistoso Boulevard, Catalina; 602-825-3110); **Randolph Golf Course** (600 South Alvernon Way; 602-791-4161); **El Conquistador Country Club–Sunrise Course** (10555 North La Canada Drive; 602-742-7300); **Dorado Golf Course** (6601 East Speedway Boulevard; 602-885-6751); **Arthur Pack Desert Golf Course** (9101 North Thornydale Road; 602-744-3322); **Ventana Canyon Golf & Racquet Club** (6200 North Club House Lane; 602-577-1400); **Cliff Valley Golf Course** (5910 North Oracle Road; 602-648-1880); **El Rio Golf Course** (1400 West Speedway Boulevard; 602-791-4229); **Fred Enke** (8215 East Irvington Road; 602-296-8607); and the **Silverbell Golf Course** (3600 North Silverbell Road; 602-791-5235).

Other prime golfing spots in the area include **Coyote Hills** (800 East Country Club Road, Benson; 602-586-2323); **Fort Huachuca** (Fort Huachuca, Sierra Vista; 602-538-7160); **Turquoise Valley** (Naco Highway, Bisbee; 602-432-3091); **Douglas Municipal Golf Course** (on Leslie Canyon Road, Douglas; 602-364-3722); **Rio Rico Golf Course** (1410 Rio Rico Drive, Rio Rico; 602-281-8567); **Tubac Valley Country Club** (Tubac; 602-398-2211); **Mount Graham Golf Course** (Golf Course Road, Safford; 602-428-1260); and **Mesa Del Sol Golf & Tennis Club** (10583 Camino Del Sol Avenue, Yuma; 602-342-1817).

TENNIS

When it's not too hot to serve, try the public tennis courts in Tucson. Call **Fort Lowell Park** (2900 North Craycroft Road; 602-791-2584); **Himmel Park** (1000 North Tucson Boulevard; 602-791-3276); **Jesse Owens Park** (400 South Sarnoff Drive; 602-791-4821); **Randolph Tennis Center** (100 South Randolph Way; 602-791-4896); and **Pima Community College** (2202 West Anklam Road; 602-884-6005).

In Yuma, play at the **Mesa Del Sol Golf & Tennis Club Ltd.** (10583 Camino Del Sol Avenue; 602-342-1817).

BICYCLING

Tucson is a very popular area for bicycling. Some favorite routes include riding on **Oracle Road** north of Ina Road, where cyclists find wide shoulders and beautiful mountain views. Ride about 15 miles to Catalina, where the road narrows and is best left to experienced riders. On the way back, turn into Sun City Vistoso, a large retirement community where the roads are wide and the scenery pretty.

Another popular ride is parallel to the Santa Catalina Mountain foothills along Sunrise Drive to **Sabino Canyon**, where you can climb up a challenging, four-mile road through the mountains. Because of the trolley, Sabino Canyon is only open to bicyclists before 9 a.m. and after 5 p.m.

Starting on North Campbell Avenue and running along the banks of the dry **Rillito River** is a hike-and-bike trail. Currently, it's about three miles long, although it's still under construction and more trails are added annually.

The **Saguaro National Monument**, both east and west, also offers a number of good trails, both for mountain and road bikes, as does the hilly **Tucson Mountain Park**. Both are in scenic areas studded with cactus. Another enjoyable route is along the **Old Spanish Trail** from Broadway Boulevard to Colossal Cave.

For more information and maps on bicycling in the area, contact the **City of Tucson bicycling coordinator** at 602-791-4372.

Good areas for bicycling can also be found elsewhere. Take **Route 83** from Colossal Cave, past Sonoita and Patagonia to Nogales. This road has little traffic and wide shoulders. Other bikeable roads are **Route 90**, which you can take to Sierra Vista and then on to Bisbee, and **Route 80** through Tombstone.

BIKE RENTALS   There are a handful of places in Tucson where you can rent bicycles, including **The Bike Shack** (835 North Park Avenue; 602-624-3663); **Broadway Bicycles** (140 South Sarnoff Drive; 602-296-7819); **Desert Pedals** (2131 East 5th Street; 602-884-8838); and **Southwest Cycle & Sport** (818 East University Boulevard; 602-791-0818).

HIKING

TUCSON TRAILS   In the Rincon Mountain District in **Saguaro National Monument** you'll find the **Freeman Homestead Nature Trail** (1 mile), a loop that starts off the spur road to the Javelina picnic area and descends from a saguaro forest to a small wash filled with mesquite trees. Along the way you pass the ruins of an adobe house built in the 1920s.

An innocent-looking cactus can fool you. If you get stuck, use tweezers or two sticks to remove the thorn.

The **Cactus Forest Trail** (2.5 miles) takes you though a saguaro forest between Broadway Boulevard and Old Spanish Trail. You also pass the remains of the first ranger station built in the monument, and two kilns used around the turn of the century to manufacture lime.

For a trek on **Mount Lemmon,** follow the **Wilderness of Rocks Trail** (5.2 miles). It starts at the Marshall Gulch Picnic Area. On the way are pools along Lemmon Creek and thousands of eroded and balanced rocks.

Pima Canyon Trail (7.1 miles) in the Santa Catalina Mountains is a difficult trail that climbs from 2900 to 7255 feet through a bighorn-sheep management area. Along the way you'll pass Pima Canyon Spring and good views of Tucson and A Mountain. To get there, follow Christie Drive north until it dead-ends at Magee Road. Go right and park.

In the **Tucson Mountain District**, the **King Canyon Trail** (3.5 miles) begins off Kinney Road across from the Arizona-Sonora Desert Museum, then climbs up to a picnic area and beyond to the top of Wasson Peak (elevation 4687), the highest point in the area.

The short **Signal Hill Petroglyphs Trail** (.25 mile) goes up a winding path along a small hill off Golden Gate Road. At the top are rocks with ancient Indian petroglyphs on them.

The **Valley View Overlook Trail** (.75 mile) on the Bajada Loop Drive descends into two washes and ends on a scenic ridge overlooking most of Avra Valley.

Hunter Trail (2 miles) in **Picacho Peak State Park** offers scenic lookouts as it climbs from 2000 to 3374 feet in height. It was named for Captain Sherod Hunter, a Confederate officer who placed lookouts at Picacho Pass and was involved in the battle that occurred here in 1862.

EAST OF TUCSON TRAILS   To find **Lutz Canyon Trail** (2.9 miles), drive 12 miles south of Sierra Vista on Route 92 to Ash Canyon Road. Hikers walk past old mine workings in a narrow, deep canyon with oak, juniper and Douglas fir.

Crest Trail (10.6 miles) in the **Coronado National Memorial** runs along the crest of the Huachuca Mountains, and affords a great view of northern Mexico on clear days.

Within the **Chiricahua National Monument** you'll find **Massai Point Nature Trail** (.5 mile), which starts at the geology exhibit at Massai Point and takes you past a large balanced rock, a board with a description of the park's geological story and views across Rhyolite Canyon.

Natural Bridge Trail (2.5 miles) begins at the Bonita Canyon scenic drive, then passes a natural rock bridge and climbs through oak and juniper woodlands to a pine forest.

Heart of Rocks Trail (3.5 miles) winds through pine and fir forests and some of the park's most impressive rock formations, including Big Balanced Rock, Punch and Judy and Totem Pole.

Built as a supply artery for fire fighters stationed in the high Chiricahuas, **Greenhouse Trail** (3.75 miles) ascends 3000 feet. Along the way you'll pass Cima Cabin, the fire fighters' headquarters, and Winn Falls, which flows at a peak during the summer. To get there, go north off Cave Creek Spur Road onto Greenhouse Road and drive half a mile.

The **Coronado National Forest** offers the **South Fork Trail** (7.25 miles). Beginning off Cave Creek Road at the road end in South Fork Forest Camp 3.5 miles above Portal, Arizona, it passes South Fork Cave Creek, one of the most famous birdwatching canyons in the Chiricahua Mountains, and a 70-foot-tall finger of red rhyolite called Pinnacle Rock. It starts in a forest of sycamores, maples and black walnut trees and leads to huge Douglas fir trees and the small bluffs above the South Fork Cave Creek.

SOUTH/WEST OF TUCSON TRAILS   **Kent Springs-Bog Springs Trail Loop** (5.7 miles) within the Santa Rita Mountains climbs from 4820 feet to 6620 feet. Along the way are three springs, which create an unusually lush area with large sycamore and walnut trees. Exit off Route 19 at Madera Canyon and park near Bog Springs campground.

Transportation

BY CAR

From Tucson, **Route 10** runs north toward Phoenix, then crosses **Route 8**, which heads west toward Gila Bend and Yuma. **Route 85** from Gila Bend goes south, turns into **Route 86**, cuts through the Papago Reservation and goes to Tucson. South of Tucson is **Route 19** to Nogales, while the main thoroughfare east from Tucson is Route 10 toward New Mexico. Jutting south off Route 10 are **Route 83** to Sonoita, **Route 90** to Sierra Vista, **Route 666** to Douglas and **Route 186** to Chiricahua National Monument.

BY AIR

Tucson International Airport is served by America West Airlines, American Airlines, Delta Air Lines, Northwest Airlines, Trans World Airlines and USAir.

Yuma International Airport is served by America West and Skywest, and **Sierra Vista Municipal Airport** by Mesa Airlines.

BY TRAIN

Amtrak (800-872-7245) has train service to the area on both the "Texas Eagle" and the "Sunset Limited." Train depots are found in Tucson (400 East Toole Avenue), Benson (4th and San Pedro streets) and Yuma (281 Gila Street).

BY BUS

Greyhound Bus Lines services Tucson from around the country. The downtown terminal is at 2 South 4th Avenue (602-792-3475). Other stations in southern Arizona include Nogales (35 North Terrace Avenue; 602-287-5628) and Yuma (170 East 17th Place; 602-783-4403). There are also terminals in Benson, Sierra Vista, Bisbee, Douglas, Willcox and Safford.

CAR RENTALS

At Tucson International Airport are **Avis Rent A Car** (602-294-1494); **Dollar Rent A Car** (602-573-1100); **Hertz Rent A Car** (602-294-7616); and **National Interrent** (602-573-8050).

Agencies at the Yuma International Airport are **Avis Rent A Car** (602-344-5772); **Budget Rent A Car** (602-344-1822); **Hertz Rent A Car** (602-726-5160); **National Interrent** (602-726-0611); and **Sears Rent A Car** (602-344-1824).

Enterprise Rent A Car (602-458-2425) and **Rent A Ride** (602-459-1296) serve the Sierra Vista Municipal Airport.

PUBLIC TRANSPORTATION

For extensive bus service throughout Tucson, call **Sun Tran** (602-792-9222). Local bus service in Nogales is **Dabdoub Bus Service** (602-287-7810).

TAXIS

Leading cab companies in Tucson include **ABC Cab Co.** (602-623-7979), **Allstate Cab Co.** (602-888-2999), **Checker Cab Co.** (602-623-1133) and **Yellow Cab Co.** (602-624-6611). In Sierra Vista, try **Call A Cab** (602-458-5867) or **Cochise Cab Co.** (602-458-3860).

Note from the Publishers

An alert, adventurous reader is as important as a travel writer in keeping a guidebook up-to-date and accurate. So if you happen upon a great restaurant, discover an intriguing locale or (heaven forbid) find an error in the text, we'd appreciate hearing from you. Just write to:

Ulysses Press
3286 Adeline Street, Suite 1
Berkeley, CA 94703

It is our desire as publishers to create guidebooks that are responsible as well as informative. We hope that our guidebooks treat the people, country and land we visit with respect. We ask that our readers do the same.

Index

Also Available From Ulysses Press

HIDDEN GUIDES

Adventure travel or a relaxing vacation?—"Hidden" guidebooks are the only travel books in the business to provide detailed information on both. Aimed at environmentally aware travelers, our motto is "Adventure Travel Plus." These books combine details on unique hotels, restaurants and sight-seeing with information on camping, sports and hiking for the outdoor enthusiast.

HIDDEN BOSTON AND CAPE COD *228 pages. $7.95*
HIDDEN COAST OF CALIFORNIA *480 pages. $14.95*
HIDDEN FLORIDA *492 pages. $14.95*
HIDDEN FLORIDA KEYS & EVERGLADES *156 pages. $7.95*
HIDDEN HAWAII *468 pages. $14.95*
HIDDEN MEXICO *444 pages. $13.95*
HIDDEN NEW ENGLAND *564 pages. $14.95*
HIDDEN PACIFIC NORTHWEST *528 pages. $14.95*
HIDDEN SAN FRANCISCO
   AND NORTHERN CALIFORNIA *444 pages. $14.95*
HIDDEN SOUTHERN CALIFORNIA *516 pages. $14.95*
HIDDEN SOUTHWEST *504 pages. $14.95*

ULTIMATE GUIDES

These innovative guides present the best and most unique features of a destination. Quality is the keynote. They are as likely to cover a mom 'n pop café as a gourmet restaurant, a quaint bed and breakfast as a five-star tennis resort. In addition to thoroughly covering each destination, they feature short articles and one-line "teasers" that are both fun and informative.

ULTIMATE CALIFORNIA *516 pages. $14.95*
ULTIMATE WASHINGTON *300 pages. $11.95*
DISNEY WORLD AND BEYOND:
   The Ultimate Family Guidebook *300 pages. $9.95*
DISNEY WORLD AND BEYOND:
   Family Fun Cards *90 cards. $7.95*
DISNEYLAND AND BEYOND:
   The Ultimate Family Guidebook *240 pages. $9.95*
FLORIDA'S GOLD COAST:
   The Ultimate Guidebook *192 pages. $8.95*
LAS VEGAS: The Ultimate Guidebook *240 pages. $9.95*
THE MAYA ROUTE: The Ultimate Guidebook *432 pages. $14.95*

VIRAGO WOMAN'S TRAVEL GUIDES

Written through a woman's eye and steeped in the grand tradition of travel literature, these guides speak directly to the special interests of solo female travelers, businesswomen and women traveling with children. Each title offers a fascinating blend of practical information and cultural insights. History, art and contemporary society are examined from a woman's point of view with fascinating results.

NEW YORK *350 pages. $13.95*

PARIS *350 pages. $13.95*

ROME *350 pages. $13.95*

OTHER ULYSSES PRESS TRAVEL TITLES

Critically acclaimed as the best resource to Costa Rica in print, *The New Key to Costa Rica* has captured the imagination of travelers everywhere. This edition is completely updated with hundreds of details on tropical rainforests, endangered species and awesome volcanoes.

THE NEW KEY TO COSTA RICA *312 pages. $13.95*

FOR A FREE CATALOG OR TO ORDER DIRECT   For each book send an additional $2 postage and handling (California residents include 8% sales tax) to Ulysses Press, 3286 Adeline Street, Suite 1, Berkeley, CA 94703. Or call **800-377-2542** or 510-601-8301 and charge your order.

About the Authors

David Stratton, author of Ulysses Press' *Las Vegas and Beyond: The Ultimate Guidebook,* has worked as a newspaper reporter and editor for eight years. A resident of Las Vegas, he is currently staff writer, editor and graphic designer for a publisher of gaming books and a monthly game room magazine.

Richard Harris has written many guidebooks, including Ulysses Press' *Hidden Southwest* and *The Maya Route: The Ultimate Guidebook.* While working his way through college and law school as a tour guide, Harris' interest in travel writing grew. Since then he has edited more than 60 travel books. He lives in Santa Fe, New Mexico.

Carolyn Scarborough is an award-winning freelance writer living in Phoenix. A former travel editor of *Southern Living* magazine and member of the Society of American Travel Writers, her writing credits include more than 300 published articles in magazines and newspapers across the country.

Mary Ann Reese was associate travel editor at *Sunset* magazine for 17 years, covering Arizona and New Mexico. She also wrote wilderness and urban stories about the West and foreign countries. Earlier, she was London Bureau Chief for the *Stars and Stripes* newspaper.

About the Illustrator

Glenn Kim is a freelance illustrator residing in San Francisco. His work appears in numerous Ulysses Press titles, including *Hidden Southwest* and *Disneyland and Beyond: The Ultimate Family Guidebook.* He has also done illustrations for the National Forest Service, a variety of magazines, book covers and greeting cards.